EMPIRE AND REVOLUTION

Empire and Revolution

THE UNITED STATES
AND THE THIRD WORLD
SINCE 1945

Edited by
Peter L. Hahn
Mary Ann Heiss

OHIO STATE UNIVERSITY PRESS
COLUMBUS

Library of Congress Cataloging-in-Publication Data

Empire and revolution : the United States and the Third World
    since 1945 / edited by Peter L. Hahn, Mary Ann Heiss.
        p. cm.
    Includes bibliographical references and index.
    ISBN 0-8142-0856-8 (alk. paper) —
ISBN 0-8142-5060-2 (pbk. : alk. paper)
        1. Developing countries—Foreign relations—United States.
    2. United States—Foreign relations—Developing countries.
    3. United States—Foreign relations—1945–1989.   4. United
    States—Foreign relations—1989-   .   5. Imperialism—United
    States—History—20th century.   6. Revolutions—Developing
    countries—History—20th century.   I. Hahn, Peter L.   II. Heiss,
    Mary Ann, 1961–
    D888.U6E46 2000
    327.730172'4—dc21   00-009085

Text and cover design by Paula Newcomb.
Type set in Adobe San Serif by Keystone Typesetting, Inc.
Printed by McNaughton & Gunn.

9 8 7 6 5 4 3 2 1

CONTENTS

CULTURE

ECONOMIC DEVELOPMENT

ACKNOWLEDGMENTS

We owe a debt of thanks to a number of individuals who helped to facilitate the publication of this volume. Barbara Hanrahan, Malcolm Litchfield, Emily Rogers, and Ruth Melville of the Ohio State University Press supported and encouraged us as we prepared the manuscript. Robert J. McMahon was gracious enough to write the volume's excellent general introduction. And the authors whose work is included here not only allowed us to publish or republish their essays but also delivered them before our publication deadline. We are also grateful to *Diplomatic History* and *The Journal of American History* for permission to reprint essays that originally appeared in their pages. We also wish to thank Robert Buzzanco, Nick Cullather, Douglas Little, Stephen G. Rabe, and Andrew Rotter for agreeing to designate the customary republication fees as royalties to the Lawrence Gelfand–Armin Rappaport Fund of the Society for Historians of American Foreign Relations (SHAFR). The Gelfand-Rappaport Fund, which supports the publication of *Diplomatic History,* will also receive the royalties derived from the sale of this book. We naturally encourage other scholars to support SHAFR's outstanding journal by making their own contributions to the Gelfand-Rappaport Fund.

We are pleased and honored to dedicate this volume to Michael J. Hogan and Melvyn P. Leffler, our advisers in graduate school and two of the world's finest diplomatic historians. Both continue to serve as inspirations, models, and supporters, for which we are immeasurably grateful.

Introduction: The Challenge of the Third World

ROBERT J. MCMAHON

The rise of the Third World stands unquestionably as one of the key defining features of modern international history. The newly emerging areas of Asia, Africa, the Middle East, and Latin America threw off the shackles of colonialism and neocolonialism in the half century that followed World War II, boldly articulated their own national aspirations, strove to achieve economic as well as political independence, and became increasingly influential actors on the world stage. In the broadest world-historical sense, the rise of the Third World posed a fundamental challenge to Western global dominance—the most sweeping such challenge of the modern era. "We propose to stand on our own legs," proclaimed India's Jawaharlal Nehru in March 1947. "We do not intend to be the playthings of others."[1]

The emergence of the Third World, together with the bloody, conflict-ridden process of decolonization that brought it forth, not only coincided temporally with the Cold War but was inextricably shaped by that same Cold War—as each of the essays in this volume powerfully demonstrates. Indeed, it was the all-encompassing struggle between the United States, the Soviet Union, and their respective allies for global power, influence, and ideological supremacy that gave birth to the very term *Third World*. A convenient political catchphrase that rather loosely lumped together the predominantly poor and uncommitted areas of the planet, *Third World* originally connoted an arena of contestation between West and East, the so-called First World and Second World. It was an arena, in the view of many pundits, academics, and geopoliticians, whose ultimate political orientation might well determine the outcome of the Cold War.

The United States and the Soviet Union each identified vital national interests in Third World territories. For Washington, as for Moscow, the developing areas appeared critical to the achievement of basic strategic, economic, political, and ideological goals. Significantly, most of the major East-West crises of the Cold War era erupted in the Third World, including nearly all that threatened to escalate into direct U.S.-Soviet confrontations. The only wars involving U.S. military forces during this period also took place in the Third World. In fact, the vast bulk of the armed conflicts that have broken out since the end of the Second World War have been fought there. It is particularly telling that all but two hundred thousand of the estimated twenty million people who died in wars fought between 1945 and 1990 were felled during conflicts that raged across various parts of the Third World.[2]

The United States's interest in and involvement with the Third World is not, of course, exclusively a post-1945 phenomenon. The United States itself became a Third World power—though the term itself had not yet been coined—when it seized possession of several Pacific and Caribbean territories following the Spanish-American War of 1898. Its extensive trade links with the non-Western world, of course, long predated the imperial surge of the 1890s. During the administrations of Theodore Roosevelt and Woodrow Wilson, the United States substantially deepened its diplomatic, military, and commercial involvement with non-Western areas. Roosevelt and Wilson went a long way toward converting the Caribbean into a U.S. lake; they helped establish, in the process, the commercial and military preeminence of the United States throughout Latin America. Each of those activist presidents also regularly inserted the United States into East Asian affairs, viewing that corner of the globe, too, as a necessary preoccupation for a burgeoning industrial power with rapidly expanding commercial and geopolitical interests. Even if other parts of the Third World—Africa, the Middle East, Southeast Asia—commanded considerably less attention from U.S. leaders at this time, the U.S. fixation with the Third World during the post–World War II era clearly had strong historical antecedents.

But U.S. concern about, and involvement with, the Third World assumed dramatically increased proportions during the post–World War II period. That concern derived from an interrelated set of economic, geostrategic, political, ideological, and psychological factors—many of which predated the Cold War and all of which were further magnified by U.S.-Soviet antagonism. The lessons U.S. planners took from the Second World War had elevated the importance of Third World territories well before the onset of the U.S.-Soviet struggle. Determined to build a more peaceful, stable, and prosperous world order out of the ashes of humanity's most horrendous conflict, and realizing that technology and trade had shrunken the globe, Roosevelt and Truman administration planners were convinced that the United States needed to assume a more activist role in the Third World. To actualize their vision of an open, orderly, and peaceful world—and hence a more secure and prosperous United States—U.S. strategists believed it essential to integrate the developing regions more fully into the global economy, spur freer trade, ensure equal access to all of the planet's resources and markets, and establish a reliable, worldwide network of U.S. military bases. Those strategists also considered it imperative that the nationalist aspirations of dependent peoples be accommodated so as to defuse more revolutionary tendencies. Sumner Welles, Roosevelt's undersecretary of state, cautioned that failing to plan for the transfer of power to "peoples clamoring for freedom from the colonial powers" would "be like failing to install a safety valve and then waiting for the boiler to blow up."[3] The Cold War reinforced and strengthened each of those already established priorities; it did not by itself create them.

Long-standing U.S. interests in the raw materials and markets of the developing world deepened appreciably as a result of World War II. U.S. planners were keenly aware of how important Third World resources had been in the German-Japanese drive for world hegemony. Control over such resources had strengthened the Axis powers militarily and economically, bolstering significantly their ability to wage global war. U.S. industry's dependence on the tin and rubber of Southeast Asia was painfully driven home when the Japanese occupation of key tin- and rubber-producing areas caused major production bottlenecks for the United States. And perhaps no lesson of World War II proved more basic to Western strategists than that concerning the crucial importance of oil to modern warfare. Much of the world's oil, of course, was located beneath the soil and seas of Third World territories, a fact that would have spurred much closer U.S. attention to those areas after the war even if no Soviet Union had existed. The close economic links between the industrialized nations and the primary producing areas of the Third World also drew U.S. interest and involvement; world economic recovery, one of the top postwar policy goals of the United States, was in large part dependent upon the rapid reestablishment of such links.[4]

The enhanced strategic value of the Third World for the United States also derived in significant measure from the lessons of World War II. As technology, and especially air power, seemed to contract the globe, U.S. generals and admirals grew convinced that their nation's security demanded a defense that began well beyond the home shores. The concept of defense in depth, widely accepted by military planners of the Roosevelt and Truman administrations, necessitated the development of an integrated network of air and naval bases, along with widespread military air transit rights, so that the

United States could project its power more easily into trouble spots while providing an extra measure of protection against prospective enemies. In 1946, the State Department formulated an expansive list of "essential" or "required" base sites that included, among others, Burma, the Fiji Islands, New Zealand, Cuba, Ecuador, French Morocco, Senegal, Liberia, Panama, and Peru. That same year, the Joint Chiefs of Staff approved a list of twenty locales where the United States desired military air transit rights; they included Algiers, Cairo, Dhahran, Karachi, Saigon, Acapulco, San Jose, and the Cook Islands.[5] From the very inception of the postwar era, then, the United States was identifying vital economic and security interests across the Third World.

The Cold War made those interests ever more vital. U.S. policy makers feared that some of the resources and markets of the Third World, already deemed indispensable to the health of the world economy, the economic recoveries of Western Europe and Japan, and the United States's own commercial and military requirements might fall under Soviet control. The Soviet Union could, as a result, realize an appreciable gain in its military and economic capabilities, much as Germany and Japan had during the Second World War; the West would then be correspondingly weakened. Furthermore, if the Cold War ever turned hot, U.S. war plans called for the use of Middle Eastern base sites for air and atomic attacks against the Soviet heartland. Those expansive economic and strategic priorities were woven into the seamless web of U.S. national security requirements.[6] The containment of the Soviet Union and the construction of "a healthy international environment" were, as National Security Council Paper 68 (NSC-68) pointed out in April 1950, the two most basic policy goals of the United States—distinct, but overlapping.[7] The Third World clearly was crucial to the achievement of each.

Other factors also contributed to the U.S. Cold War fixation with the Third World. For one, the political exigencies of the nation's two-party system made the "loss" of any additional territory to communism, from the Truman administration onward, a political liability of potentially catastrophic proportions. The vilification of Harry S. Truman by Republican opponents following the successful Chinese communist revolution of 1949 served as a powerful object lesson to all future White House occupants. Referring specifically to Vietnam, for example, President John F. Kennedy confessed to a journalist early in his presidency: "I can't give up a piece of territory like that to the Communists and get the American people to reelect me."[8] Similarly, President Lyndon B. Johnson worried, according to political adviser Jack Valenti, that Republicans and conservative Democrats together would have "torn him in pieces" had he failed to hold the line against communism in Southeast Asia.[9]

The psychological underpinnings of power, best captured by the frequently invoked concept of U.S. credibility, further elevated the stakes at play for the United States in the Third World. By the late 1940s, U.S. analysts were convinced that the belief that historical momentum lay with the communist powers and not with the West had taken hold, especially in the developing areas. They feared that such a perception, whether rooted in fact or fantasy, might take on a life of its own, producing a bandwagon effect that would pull nations inexorably out of the "Free World" pantheon and into the "communist bloc." NSC-68 warned pointedly that the Soviet Union sought "to demonstrate that force and the will to use it are on the side of the Kremlin [and] that those who lack it are decadent and doomed."[10] If the United States appeared incapable of stemming this tide, or so U.S. officials fretted, its enemies would grow more aggressive and its allies would come to doubt its power and distrust its resolve.

Given that mind-set, Washington policy makers reflexively viewed any Soviet intervention, threatened intervention, aid offer, or diplomatic initiative anywhere in the Third World as a test from which other states, large and small, would derive important lessons about the power and resolve of the respective superpowers. After 1949, U.S. officials viewed Beijing's expansive inclinations with nearly as wary an eye as Moscow's and worried that they posed just as dangerous a test. The United States, consequently, vested enormous significance in each and every Third World challenge or hot spot—from South Korea, Vietnam, Laos, and Indonesia to Egypt, the Congo, Angola, and Nicaragua—regardless of the intrinsic strategic or economic value of the territory in question. A State Department white paper on Laos of 1959, for example, insisted that that landlocked country of three million people actually constituted "a front line of the free world."[11] Similarly, President Ronald Reagan, in his various appeals for additional aid to the Nicaraguan contras, emphasized that the security and welfare of the United States were at stake in Central America. "If we cannot defend ourselves there," he warned in one speech, "we cannot expect to prevail elsewhere. Our credibility would collapse, our alliances would crumble, and the safety of our homeland would be put in jeopardy."[12]

The abiding need of the United States to demonstrate, to allies and adversaries alike, its strength, resolution, determination, and dependability thus led to a blurring of distinctions between vital and peripheral interests. By the 1950s and 1960s, U.S. officials were viewing all corners of the Third World as potentially vital to the geostrategic and politico-psychological balance of power between East and West—and to the credibility of the United States.[13] The essays in this volume by Douglas Little and Robert Buzzanco help illuminate the extent to which the United States's fixation with its credibility critically shaped the decisions to intervene in Lebanon and Vietnam, respectively, as it did in so many other areas.

The Third World posed a monumental conceptual and policy challenge for U.S. officials throughout the postwar epoch. How could the United States best use its military and economic clout, political influence, and whatever cultural or ideological appeal it might have in the quest to "win" the Third World for the West? What mix of aid offers, security commitments, diplomatic backing, multilateral or bilateral treaties, or just plain sympathy and understanding would work most effectively as it sought to convert the newly emerging areas into stable, productive nation-states firmly committed to the West? How could the United States most efficiently inoculate the diverse populations of the Third World against the communist virus? How could it most effectively harness Third World resources and markets for the cause of global capitalist resurgence—and for the benefit of U.S. industry and commerce? What means, in short, were most appropriate to the ends that the United States sought?

Those daunting instrumental challenges were further complicated by the painful legacy of colonialism. The United States's closest and most important Cold War allies were, of course, the very European powers whose heavy-handed colonial rule had triggered the wave of nationalist, anticolonial revolts that swept Asia, Africa, and the Middle East in the aftermath of World War II. The United States endeavored throughout the early Cold War period to balance its desire for friendly, cooperative relationships with the emerging postcolonial states with its need to maintain harmony within the Western alliance. It proved an impossible balancing act. Whenever Washington tilted too far toward one side, it risked alienating the other. The Truman and Eisenhower administrations' inclination to defer to the European colonial powers in Southeast Asia and the Middle East (Suez excepted) gradually gave way to the Kennedy administration's activist campaign to woo Third World states—even if European feathers got ruffled in the process. But the essential problem lingered, defying simple solutions, as Piero Gleijeses's essay on the Congo crisis of 1964–65 so expertly demonstrates.

Deep-seated rivalries among Third World states compounded the United States's policy dilemmas. If the United States forged an alliance with countries that it considered valuable strategic assets—as the Eisenhower administration did with Pakistan and Iraq, to take two prominent examples—it virtually ensured the enmity of those nations' enemies: India, in the first case, Egypt in the second. If the United States then tried to rebalance the scales by supplying economic or military assistance to nations left outside its alliance system, as the Kennedy administration was wont to do, it almost guaranteed that Third World allies would protest vigorously. How could nonalignment be seen as offering greater dividends than alignment? That dilemma, too, often proved insuperable.

The positive appeal that the Soviet Union, China, and communist ideology more broadly held for Third World states posed an equally insuperable problem. Deeply held resentments against the exploitative policies and racism of the West, joined with an abiding desire for rapid economic development, made Third World areas highly susceptible to Soviet, and Chinese, overtures. Many Third World leaders and intellectuals both admired and sought to emulate the Soviet developmental model. In little more than a generation, after all, Lenin, Stalin, and their compatriots had transformed a backward, underdeveloped country into a military-industrial powerhouse. How could the architects of Third World development help but take notice? In November 1955, the Eisenhower administration debated this issue at length during several National Security Council meetings. Allen W. Dulles, director of Central Intelligence, conceded that many Third World leaders were impressed with the Soviet Union's economic progress under a statist, command-style economy. They had come to believe, he lamented, that the Soviet system "might have more to offer in the way of quick results than the U.S. system."[14] U.S. analysts were convinced that they needed to demonstrate the efficacy of the capitalist road to economic development and prove, by any means possible, its superiority over the communist/socialist route. That task proved difficult in the extreme.

The Soviet Union held other advantages, especially during the early Cold War years. It remained unimpeachable on the all-important colonial question, whereas this issue was a crippling vulnerability for the Western powers. Moscow also appeared relatively free from the racism and the culturally superior attitudes that Third World leaders found so grating among many Westerners. Nor did the persistent efforts of U.S. diplomats to highlight the tyranny and brutality of Soviet communism meet with much success among peoples who considered the exercise of European imperial and neocolonial authority to be far more tyrannical and brutal.

The Third World has featured very prominently in the scholarly literatures on modern U.S. foreign relations and on the history of the Cold War. In view of the centrality of the Third World's place in both, that is entirely fitting. Few questions remain as central to our comprehension of the international politics of the postwar epoch than the following: How and why did the Cold War move from Europe to the Third World? Why did the developing areas become focal points for Cold War tension? What specific interests and forces led to the intensification of U.S. and Soviet interests in Third

World areas? To what degree did Third World nations themselves affect that process? And what impact has the Cold War had on the course of political and economic developments within Third World states? Given the importance and complexity of such questions, scholars have, not surprisingly, offered widely divergent answers to them. In many respects, the conflicts among scholars seeking to explicate the U.S.–Third World encounter replicate the wider interpretive battles waged by scholars over the international politics of the Cold War era writ large.

Traditional scholarship viewed the early Cold War largely through a Eurocentric lens. Historians, political scientists, and former government officials writing in that vein considered the clash between the Soviet Union and the United States of the mid- and late 1940s as essentially a struggle over the fate of Europe. Consequently, they tended to slight, or even ignore, the non-Western world. Those traditionalists, and the so-called realists that they closely resembled, interpreted the movement of the Cold War to the peripheral areas as a direct result of the Soviet- and Chinese-directed aggression that brought war to the Korean peninsula in June 1950. The Korean War, according to this framework, triggered a defensive, and wholly appropriate, Western response to the threat of unbridled communist adventurism.[15]

As with so many other issue areas, the first wave of revisionist scholars of the 1960s and 1970s proposed a radically different interpretive framework for understanding U.S. policy in the Third World. Many of the revisionists insisted from the first on the centrality of the Third World to the purported U.S. drive for global hegemony. The determination of the United States to exploit the resources and dominate the markets of the developing nations, according to historians such as Joyce and Gabriel Kolko, stood as a prime causal factor in the onset of the Cold War.[16] For the revisionists, it was the desire of the United States to dominate and exploit the Third World for the benefit of U.S. capital—and to help underwrite the United States's larger mission of global hegemony—that lay behind the rapid expansion of U.S. interests and commitments into the periphery.

Recent scholarship has offered a variety of middle grounds. Some historians, often labeled by the vague and imprecise tag of "postrevisionists," have emphasized the centrality of strategic variables in the United States's Third World policies. Melvyn P. Leffler, for example, has highlighted the critical importance of the Third World in U.S. global planning and strategy, insisting that the geopolitical dimension of U.S. interests significantly outweighed the economic dimension. He argues that the Truman administration valued Southeast Asia and the Middle East primarily for the commercial links that both regions maintained with core states in Western Europe and Japan, states whose quick recoveries were essential to the U.S. blueprint for maintaining a preponderance of global power. With Peter Hahn and others, Leffler likewise underscores the salience that Truman and Eisenhower administration planners attached to the valuable military base sites located in the Middle East; they loomed as indispensable in all U.S. war-fighting scenarios.[17]

Still other experts, in addressing some of the aforementioned questions, have attempted to move beyond the long-standing debate between those who stress the primacy of geopolitics and those who stress the primacy of political economy. A growing number of historians of U.S.-Third World relations have called needed attention to the rich tableau of culture, exploring the manifold ways in which cultural biases and predispositions among Westerners and non-Westerners alike shaped and colored all interactions between societies with markedly different histories, traditions, values, and needs. They have also begun to examine the impact that the United States exerted on the cultural systems and values of Third World societies, a particularly compelling issue in an age in which the symbols of U.S. popular culture—from music, movies, and television programs to fast food franchises, consumer products, and styles of clothing—have become ubiquitous in virtually every corner of the globe. Other scholars have concentrated more on developments *within* Third World societies, analyzing how various Third World statesmen tried to manipulate Cold War tensions for their own purposes or exploring the Cold War's effect on struggles for power inside Third World countries.

Still others have focused on the differential impact that foreign aid, domestic development priorities, and macroeconomic growth strategies have had on the economic performances of Third World states. And some U.S.-Third World scholars have scrutinized the manifold contributions made by various nonstate actors, ranging from businessmen and investors to labor unionists, missionaries, philanthropists, and lobbyists of every imaginable stripe.

Finally, an important trend spurred by the recent opening of long-closed archival sources in Russia and China has been the careful examination of the "other side." Much of the important and innovative work that has used sources from former "enemy" archives in the search for a more fully rounded history of the Cold War has been set in the Third World—including seminal books and articles on the Korean War, the Cuban missile crisis, and the Vietnam imbroglio.

For all those wide variations in interpretation, focus, and approach, and perhaps in part *because* of those differences, scholarship on the United States and the Third World has ranked among the more vigorous and pioneering subfields within twentieth-century diplomatic history.[18] The essays in this book provide ample testimony of the strengths as well as the diversity of that literature. No overarching synthesis is presented here; nor should one be expected. The theories, methods, and sources used by the individual authors represented in this volume differ nearly as markedly as do the geographical targets of their respective scholarly investigations. The interested reader should expect no comforting consensus, no new master narrative. Instead, this volume offers a multihued, panoramic portrait of the Cold War in the Third World. It contains a provocatively wide-ranging collection of ten state-of-the-art surveys of ten singular diplomatic episodes. Although each essay is self-contained, each also illuminates the critical intersection between postwar U.S. power, the Cold War, and an increasingly assertive, nationalistic Third World. Taken together, these ten essays help us appreciate the manifold ways in which that intersection shaped the modern world.

Douglas Little, Stephen G. Rabe, and Piero Gleijeses all emphasize the national security dynamic in U.S. policy making. A connective thread runs through all three contributions. The U.S. dispatch of troops to Lebanon in 1958, U.S. enlistment of Venezuela in various initiatives aimed at overthrowing both the Dominican Republic's right-wing autocrat Rafael Trujillo and Cuba's left-wing autocrat Fidel Castro, Washington's encouragement of and support for the white mercenaries who helped suppress a secessionist insurgency in the Congo in 1964–65—all were prompted by Cold War fears. Those fears, according to Little, Rabe, and Gleijeses, derived from the heightened sense of vulnerability that led U.S. strategists in the Eisenhower, Kennedy, and Johnson administrations to exaggerate the potential dangers posed to U.S. interests by instability, communist inspired or not, anywhere in the Third World. Each of those essays also thoughtfully probes the tangled consequences and troubled legacy of intervention—for the United States as well as for the nations that became targets of covert or overt U.S. meddling. Although the United States always professed that it stood foursquare for freedom, democracy, human rights, and self-determination and held that those principles lay behind its Cold War struggle with the Soviet Union, each of these episodes provides powerful evidence of how the U.S. drive for security and stability often came to trump more idealistic values.

Of course, idealism never disappeared entirely from U.S. Cold War policy making, as Elizabeth Cobbs Hoffman reminds us in her examination of the genesis of John F. Kennedy's Peace Corps. Cobbs Hoffman demonstrates how a genuine commitment to the alleviation of Third World poverty could coexist and merge seamlessly with a nakedly self-interested determination to win Third World hearts and minds for the United States's Cold War purposes. Her contribution also underscores the multiple diplomatic and domestic contexts that brought forth a voluntarist initiative not just in the United States but throughout other "First World" countries as well. Cobbs Hoffman's internationalist perspective shows, as many of the more accomplished studies of the U.S.–Third World encounter have, that a wider angle of vision can open fresh interpretive vistas.

In their contributions, Nick Cullather and Darlene Rivas direct their vision in other directions. Cullather's analysis of Taiwan's industrial surge of the 1950s and 1960s proves that it was in every sense a collaborative U.S.-Taiwanese project. The Taipei officials who forged a statist growth strategy did so with the active support and encouragement of U.S. development specialists, individuals who displayed a surprising degree of flexibility in their approach to development issues. In the long run, U.S. dollars and expertise wound up underwriting an industrial growth strategy that actually represented a fundamental departure from the liberal, free-market gospel so ritualistically identified by the U.S. government as the one true path to economic success. For her part, Rivas focuses on the role that private businessman Nelson Rockefeller played in Venezuela's early postwar development efforts. Rockefeller's influence flowed not just from the enormous capital that he and his firms commanded but also from the congruence between his own vision for Venezuelan economic progress and that held by the postwar *Acción Democrática* (AD) government. Those parallel strategies ultimately failed, however, in the face of staunch resistance from opposing commercial-political interests within Venezuela.

Although Cold War–derived priorities often prompted U.S. economic initiatives, governmental and private, both the Cullather and Rivas essays make clear that the fate of such initiatives was determined in the end by the shifting currents of Third World political and economic nationalism. Those currents formed a critical part of the larger pattern of conflicting institutional and individual agendas within host societies, a subject fully as complex as that of the competing institutional and individual agendas within the U.S. policy-making community.

Like Rivas, Peter Hahn also focuses centrally on nonstate actors: in his case, the labor union leaders in the United States and Israel who together sought to forge a stronger U.S.-Israeli relationship. To be sure, the precise impact of the numerous lobbying efforts so expertly detailed in Hahn's essay elude precise measurement. But his innovative study certainly demonstrates how extensive such efforts were, while calling attention to the probable influence that appeals from prominent laborites exerted on Washington policy makers. The corporatist structure of the U.S. state, in which close cooperation among governmental authorities, union spokesmen, and business people often proved the norm, makes approaches such as Hahn's especially valuable to students of U.S. foreign relations.

The new cultural history has of late also inspired an expansion in the traditional scholarly boundaries of U.S.–Third World studies. Culturalist approaches are well represented in the present volume with the unusually provocative contributions of Mary Ann Heiss and Andrew Rotter. Each author imaginatively exposes the deep cultural biases that conditioned U.S. attitudes toward non-Western societies and leaders—attitudes that abounded with dismissive stereotypes regarding the presumably effete, emotional, unstable, and, above all, inferior nature of Third World peoples. Such deepseated attitudes could, and did, influence policy decisions, even if the direct relationship between generalized attitudes and specific policies remains hard to pin down. Heiss and Rotter, both closely attuned to the symbolic importance of language, show how traditional narratives about conflicts in the economic and geopolitical realms can be deepened, if not transformed, through an examination of the fundamental cultural chasm between Western and non-Western societies that undergirded virtually all such conflicts.

Robert Buzzanco's essay reflects other important scholarly trends in U.S.–Third World studies. He correctly depicts the Vietnam War as a critical episode in the international history of the modern world, weaving together the distinct but intersecting stories of U.S. fear and ambition, revolutionary nationalism within Vietnam, and the Sino-Soviet struggle for leadership of the Communist bloc. Buzzanco thus aligns himself firmly with those scholars—Cobbs Hoffman, Rivas, and Hahn among them—who seek to decenter the United States in their studies of the diplomacy of the Cold War era. The recent availability of Chinese and Soviet archival sources relating to Vietnam allows Buzzanco to paint on an impressively wide canvas. At the same time, he aligns himself interpretively with revisionist scholars who emphasize the primacy of internal, material forces in propelling the United States's expanding global commitments in Southeast Asia and elsewhere. Indeed, Washington's role as leader of the world capitalist system serves for Buzzanco as the most compelling explanation both for its decision to intervene in Vietnam in the mid-1960s *and* for its decision to disengage from Vietnam in the late 1960s.

All of the essays in the present volume engage long-standing debates among scholars about the nature and impact of the U.S.–Third World encounter. Yet taken together they also succeed in pushing those debates in exciting new directions. The rich diversity of *Empire and Revolution,* accordingly, provides students and specialists alike with a superb introduction to a topic of commanding importance. Understanding the complex relationship between the United States, the Third World, and the Cold War remains, quite simply, essential for all who seek to understand the second half of the twentieth century.

Notes

1. Quoted in Dennis Merrill, *Bread and the Ballot: The United States and India's Economic Development, 1947–1963* (Chapel Hill, NC, 1990), 15.

2. David S. Painter, "Explaining U.S. Relations with the Third World," *Diplomatic History* 19 (Summer 1995): 525.

3. Quoted in Thomas G. Paterson, *On Every Front: The Making and Unmaking of the Cold War* (New York, 1992), 32–33.

4. See, e.g., Aaron David Miller, *Search for Security: Saudi Arabian Oil and American Foreign Policy, 1939–1949* (Chapel Hill, NC, 1980); and Daniel Yergin, *The Prize: The Epic Quest for Oil, Money, and Power* (New York, 1991).

5. Paterson, *On Every Front*, 107–8; Michael S. Sherry, *Preparing for the Next War: American Plans for Postwar Defense, 1941–45* (New Haven, CT, 1977); Melvyn P. Leffler, "The American Conception of National Security and the Beginnings of the Cold War, 1945–1948," *American Historical Review* 89 (April 1984): 346-81.

6. See especially Melvyn P. Leffler, *A Preponderance of Power: National Security, the Truman Administration, and the Cold War* (Stanford, CA, 1992).

7. National Security Council, "NSC-68," in *American Cold War Strategy: Interpreting NSC 68,* ed. Ernest R. May (New York, 1993), 40–41.

8. Quoted in Thomas G. Paterson, "Introduction: John F. Kennedy's Quest for Victory and Global Crisis," in *Kennedy's Quest for Victory: American Foreign Policy, 1961–1963,* ed. Thomas G. Paterson (New York, 1989), 10.

9. Quoted in Ted Gittinger, ed., *The Johnson Years: A Vietnam Roundtable* (Austin, TX, 1993), 101.

10. National Security Council, "NSC-68," 53.

11. U.S. Department of State, *The Situation in Laos* (Washington, DC, 1959), i.

12. Ronald Reagan, address before a Joint Session of the Congress on Latin America, 27 April 1983, *Public Papers of the Presidents: Ronald Reagan,* vol. 1 (Washington, DC, 1984), 604–5.

13. Robert J. McMahon, "Credibility and World Power: Exploring the Psychological Dimension of Postwar American Foreign Policy," *Diplomatic History* 15 (Fall 1991): 455-71.

14. Memorandum of discussion at National Security Council meeting, 15 November 1955, U.S. Department of State, *Foreign Relations of the United States, 1955–1957* (Washington, DC, 1987), 8:275–76. For the wider context, see also Robert J. McMahon, "The Illusion of Vulnerability: American Reassessments of the Soviet Threat, 1955–1956," *International History Review* 18 (August 1996): 591–619.

15. Representative works include John W. Spanier, *American Foreign Policy since World War II* (New York, 1960); and Norman A. Graebner, *Cold War Diplomacy: American Foreign Policy, 1945–1960* (Princeton, NJ, 1962).

16. See especially Joyce and Gabriel Kolko, *The Limits of Power: The World and United States Foreign Policy, 1945–1954* (New York, 1972). For an important restatement and modification of the thesis presented in that book, see Gabriel Kolko, *Confronting the Third World: United States Foreign Policy, 1945–1980* (New York, 1988).

17. Leffler, *A Preponderance of Power;* Peter Hahn, *The United States, Great Britain, and Egypt, 1945–1956: Strategy and Diplomacy in the Early Cold War* (Chapel Hill, NC, 1991).

18. For historiographical reviews that assess much of this rich and diverse literature, see the essays by Gary R. Hess, Mark T. Gilderhus, Douglas Little, and Robert J. McMahon in *America in the World: The Historiography of American Foreign Relations since 1941,* ed. Michael J. Hogan (New York, 1995), 358–94, 424–61, 462-500, 501–30. For a recent effort to apply neotraditionalist interpretive categories to the Cold War in the Third World, see Peter W. Rodman, *More Precious Than Peace: The Cold War and the Struggle for the Third World* (New York, 1994); and John Lewis Gaddis, *We Now Know: Rethinking Cold War History* (New York, 1997).

National Security
and Counter-Revolution

His Finest Hour? Eisenhower, Lebanon, and the 1958 Middle East Crisis

DOUGLAS LITTLE

Whenever "Lebanon," "civil war," and "marines" are mentioned in the same sentence, most U.S. citizens probably recall that awful Sunday morning in October 1983 when a truckload of bombs leveled the U.S. military head-quarters at the Beirut International Airport and killed 241 of the few and the proud. But the United States had actually started down the road to its bloodiest setback in the Middle East twenty-five years earlier in the summer of 1958, when President Dwight Eisenhower sent a battalion of U.S. Marines ashore at Beirut, where they were greeted by friendly crowds of late afternoon beachgoers and throngs of peddlers hawking everything from hummus to Coca Cola. Much to the relief of Ike and his top advisers halfway around the world in Washington, Operation Blue Bat—the largest U.S. amphibious maneuver since Inchon eight years earlier—ran like clockwork on 15 July 1958. Before the week was out, fourteen thousand Marines stood guard at Beirut, symbols of the U.S. commitment to friends like Lebanon's president Camille Chamoun, who had appealed for U.S. troops after a bloody Bastille Day coup in Baghdad had toppled the pro-Western government of Iraq. Meanwhile, the U.S. Air Force was ferrying tons of food and fuel to the thirty-seven hundred British Tommies that Whitehall had airlifted into Amman on 17 July after Jordan's King Hussein followed Chamoun's lead and urgently requested Western military help. By the end of the month, warships of the U.S. Seventh Fleet, having steamed full speed from their base at Okinawa, lurked just outside the Straits of Hormuz with orders to defend the Persian Gulf oil fields.

For many contemporary observers and for some diplomatic historians, President Eisenhower's handling of the 1958 crisis in the Middle East constituted his finest hour. Pro-Western regimes in Beirut and Amman were shored up, the U.S. special relationship with Britain was consolidated, and oil continued to flow from the Persian Gulf without interruption. Equally important, not a shot was fired in anger, not a single U.S. soldier died in combat. Ike even saw to it that the troops were home by Christmas.[1] Having relied on a small group of tough-minded national security managers and his own legendary tactical instincts, Eisenhower himself became convinced that "the operation in Lebanon demonstrated the ability of the United States to react swiftly with conventional armed forces to meet small-scale, or 'brush fire' situations" in the Third World.[2]

Ike might claim in his memoirs that Operation Blue Bat had achieved important objectives while remaining quick, clean, and cheap, but a more careful look at his gunboat diplomacy in Lebanon suggests that both the short-term risks and the long-term costs were far higher than he was willing to acknowledge.[3] Personal connections and Cold War convictions, for example, drew Eisenhower and other high-ranking U.S. officials inexorably into the Lebanese political labyrinth, where they would offer pro-Western leaders military commitments that proved almost impossible to repudiate. Complicating matters still further, Ike and his advisers tried to mislead both Congress and the U.S. people by publicly attributing Lebanon's political instability to communist subversion while privately acknowledging that the real cause was Arab nationalism. And once Eisenhower made the decision to send troops to Beirut, he faced the frightening possibility of having to make even more fateful decisions about U.S. intervention in Jordan, Iraq, or Kuwait. Moreover, Ike's actions during July 1958 also held critical implications for U.S. foreign policy far beyond the Middle East. By emphasizing the importance of the United States's credibility as a guarantor, by misrepresenting Third World nationalism as Soviet inspired, and by waging what amounted to a limited but undeclared presidential war, Dwight Eisenhower set some dangerous precedents in Lebanon that his successors would utilize far less successfully in Vietnam.

For the millions of U.S. readers who thumbed through the forty-page pictorial on Lebanon in the April 1958 issue of *National Geographic Magazine,* the tiny Arab republic probably seemed like a political and cultural oxymoron, as familiar as Miami Beach and yet as exotic as Shangri-La.[4] A mountainous enclave, half Christian and half Muslim, wrested from unsteady Ottoman hands during World War I by French empire builders seeking a beachhead in the Middle East, Lebanon had by 1939 become a commercial center and transport hub whose thriving capital, Beirut, boasted a culture as cosmopolitan and a climate as clement as anything found on the Riviera. Before Paris could consolidate its grip on the Levant, however, World War II unleashed forces that brought humiliating defeat to France and exhilarating independence to Lebanon. With an assist from the British, who expelled the Vichy French in 1941, and also from the Americans, who helped keep the Free French at bay two years later, in November 1943 Lebanese nationalists proclaimed a republic. Its cornerstone was to be a carefully engineered political mechanism designed to preserve the delicate confessional balance reflected in the most recent census, which showed that Lebanese Christians outnumbered Lebanese Muslims by a ratio of six to five. Under the terms of the so-called National Pact of 1943, the president of Lebanon must be a Christian, the prime minister must be a Sunni Muslim, the speaker of the parliament must be a Shi'ite Muslim, and all three must work together to ensure sectarian peace at home and a nonaligned policy abroad.[5]

Lebanese leaders and U.S. diplomats agreed that a set of common principles—democracy, free enterprise, and Christianity—seemed likely to ensure friendly relations between their two nations. Bishara Khoury, the Christian strongman who served as independent Lebanon's first president, was quick to express his "heartfelt thanks for American support" in the wake of his November 1943 showdown with France. "Even when things looked blackest," he told U.S. ambassador George Wadsworth, "we never lost faith that democratic principles would prevail."[6] Eighteen months later, Wadsworth touted Khoury's Lebanon as the centerpiece of postwar U.S. policy in the region. "This little country can, as living standards rise in Arab lands," he prophesied on 11 July 1945, "become not simply the Adirondacks of the Near East but also, as American cultural and material investment increases, as it seems bound to do, a vital focus of American influence."[7] Khoury's eagerness to cooperate fully with Arabian-American Oil Company (ARAMCO) plans to build a refinery and pipeline terminus in Lebanon won praise from Wadsworth's successor, Lowell Pinkerton, who called the Lebanese "survivors of a race who really practice capitalism and mean to continue."[8] And although Lebanon, like its Arab brethren, voted against the U.S.-backed UN plan to partition Palestine in November 1947, Lebanese Christian leaders struck a more conciliatory note in their dealings with U.S. officials than the Muslim diplomats who represented Syria and Saudi Arabia.[9]

If Lebanon's relative moderation on Palestine was welcome news in Washington on the eve of the 1948 Arab-Israeli war, its strident anticommunism was more welcome still as the United States's Cold War with the Soviet Union spilled over into the Middle East later that year. Worried by "irresponsible" talk among Lebanese Muslims about "overtures to Russia," the Khoury regime imposed "severe measures" against Lebanon's tiny Communist Party in early 1948, closing its offices and disrupting its gatherings.[10] Terming Lebanon "one of the most progressive countries in the Near East," the State-War-Navy Coordinating Committee (SWNCC), the precursor to the National Security Council (NSC), recommended stepping up Washington's $5 million economic aid program in Beirut to help counteract "the emergent interest of the Soviet Union" in the Arab states. The mountainous Arab republic, SWNCC pointed out on 6 June, was "the sole country in the Near East having a Christian majority, a feature which has characterized Lebanon as a sort of occidental bridgehead in the Moslem world."[11] A year later the CIA described the Lebanese as "far more cosmopolitan and far less xenophobic" than other Arabs, and also as far more anticommunist. Because "Lebanon's basic alignment is toward the West," the CIA explained, it "has an active distrust of the USSR and keeps a close watch over Soviet-sponsored activities in the Levant."[12] After war erupted in Korea in 1950, Ambassador Pinkerton confirmed that Lebanon's attitude toward communism had "hardened" still further and that the Khoury regime had begun "to track down and arrest Party members."[13]

Bishara Khoury, however, was proving far more popular in the Cold War United States than in his fractured homeland. During its first decade of independence, Khoury's Lebanon more closely resembled an unstable confederation of fifteenth-century city-states divided by clan and cult than a twentieth-century nation-state united by abstract concepts like democracy and national identity. The Lebanese Shi'ites who farmed the lush Bekaa Valley along the Syrian frontier, for example, had long felt closer to Damascus than to Beirut. The Druze, a mysterious sect on the fringes of Islam led by Kamal Jumblatt, a "feudal socialist" who preached a blend of French Marxism and Indian pacifism, fiercely defended their autonomy in the snow-capped Shouf mountains that towered over the capital. Dismissing both the Shi'ites and the Druze as hopelessly provincial, the Sunnis along the Mediterranean coast and the Christians from Mount Lebanon continued to joust with each other, as they had for centuries, over who would control the seat of power in Beirut.[14]

The one matter that could bring these warring clans together by the early 1950s was the conviction that Bishara Khoury must go. His rank nepotism, his reputation for rigging elections, and his penchant for martial law alienated not only all the Muslim groups but also fellow Christians like the Chamouns and the Frangiehs. All seemed to agree that Khoury's autocratic style, symbolized by the constitutional amendment he had extracted from parliament in 1948 in order to secure an unprecedented second term as president, was undermining the fragile compromise set forth by the National Pact. Worried that their country was drifting toward sectarian strife, Muslim and Christian moderates, supported by high-ranking Lebanese army officers, forced Khoury to step down in a "bloodless coup" on 17 September 1952.[15]

Although State Department officials were surprised by the sudden demise of Bishara Khoury, whose "pro-western and anti-Soviet orientation" had made him a popular figure in Washington, they were delighted to learn that his successor would be Camille Chamoun.[16] The U.S. embassy in Beirut regarded Lebanon's new president as "definitely our friend" and as someone likely to "undertake significant reforms."[17] As early as February 1947, a Foggy Bottom biographical profile had pointed out that Chamoun had "a reputation for honesty," that he was "quite openly anti-Communist," and that he advocated closer ties between Lebanon and the United States.[18] A year later, while serving as Lebanon's representative at the United Nations, Chamoun impressed U.S. negotiators as someone "willing to suggest possible solutions to the Palestine Question which . . . go further than any previous position taken by the Arab states."[19] Like most other Lebanese, Chamoun had become quite frustrated by what he regarded as the excessively pro-Israel Middle Eastern policies adopted by the Truman administration. But in the wake of Dwight Eisenhower's landslide victory in the November 1952 elections, State Department Middle East experts reported that the Lebanese leader "shares the Arab hope for a 'New Deal' from the new administration in Washington."[20]

John Foster Dulles, the new administration's secretary of state, got a first-hand glimpse of rising Arab frustrations and expectations during a two-week visit to the Middle East in May 1953 that included a meeting with Camille Chamoun in Beirut. Noting that "democratic government has a broader base in Lebanon than elsewhere in the Arab world," State Department briefers had reminded Dulles that there were few Middle Eastern leaders more favorably disposed toward U.S. plans for a regional defense organization than President Chamoun. "If it ever came to war with the Soviets," Chamoun had told U.S. diplomats shortly after taking office, "Lebanon would be 100 per cent on the side of the West, our harbors would be open to your ships, our airfields to your planes."[21] Chamoun did not disappoint. "People here are well aware of the communist danger," he assured Dulles on 16 May, and they were "entirely in accord with the idea of a defense pact" designed to shield Lebanon and its neighbors from possible Soviet aggression. But there was also "a feeling of bitter disappointment as a result of Palestine," something that Chamoun hoped that the Eisenhower administration could reverse.[22]

Chamoun's views coincided with those of Charles Malik, Lebanon's long-time ambassador to the United States, whom Dulles had come to know and respect while serving as U.S. diplomatic troubleshooter during the Truman years. A Lebanese Christian with a Ph.D. in philosophy from Harvard University, Malik was a vehement anticommunist whose pragmatic negotiating style had helped the future secretary of state win Arab support for the UN Palestine Conciliation Commission in 1948 and for the Japanese Peace Treaty three years later. Six days after Dulles took over at Foggy Bottom, Malik assured his old friend that Lebanon would remain "a most important asset . . . to Western stability in the area," provided that the Eisenhower administration followed through on its plans to distance itself from Israel. Dulles replied that Ike had no intention of repeating Truman's mistakes. By early April, Malik was telling Dulles that the Middle East was " 'psychologically ready' for leadership from the United States" and that the Chamoun regime was eager to serve as "a cultural and political bridge between the East and the West."[23] But when Dulles arrived in Beirut in mid-May, Lebanese Muslim leaders rejected his personal assurances that the United States intended to pursue a more balanced policy toward the Arab-Israeli conflict as mere window dressing. An angry Dulles retorted that they were playing into the Kremlin's hands and suggested that they pay closer attention to Ambassador Malik, "who has a very profound understanding of Soviet Doctrine."[24]

Dulles and Eisenhower certainly paid a great deal of attention to both Malik and Chamoun during the next five years. Hoping to dispel the widespread belief that the United States's Middle East policy was reflexively pro-Israel, the Eisenhower administration periodically punished the Jewish state by withholding U.S. economic aid while quietly rewarding Lebanon and other moderate Arab governments with modest amounts of technical and financial assistance. Eager to foster an anti-Soviet strategic consensus in the region, top U.S. officials worked closely during the mid-1950s with the Chamoun regime, which proved far more cooperative than Egypt's Gamal Abdel Nasser, whose neutralist rhetoric and Russian connections were already undermining U.S. objectives and whose pan-Arab agenda seemed likely to undermine Lebanese independence. By late 1955, the Eisenhower administration was pouring almost $25 million into Lebanese infrastructural projects like the expansion of the Beirut airport while assuring Chamoun that the "US has come to have great confidence in his judgment, and believes that his conception of [the] best interests of Lebanon and [the] Near East coincides with ours."[25]

Further evidence of U.S. faith in Lebanon would come in early 1956. In the wake of Nasser's $100 million arms deal with the Soviet bloc and in the midst of a fresh round of Israel's retaliatory raids against its Arab neighbors, the Lebanese asked Washington for twenty-five 106 mm recoilless rifles and ammunition in April. Determined to avoid sparking a regional arms race, the Pentagon nevertheless concluded that "Lebanon has a valid requirement for the weapons requested to provide for her self-defense."[26] Not only would the proposed arms sale demonstrate U.S. willingness "to assist nations in the Near East which are oriented to the West," Admiral Arthur Radford, chairman of the Joint Chiefs of Staff (JCS), explained on 23 May, but it would also "improve US-Lebanese relations and facilitate the acquisition by the United States of base rights in Lebanon."[27] The State Department agreed, and two days later Chamoun was informed that Lebanon could purchase the recoilless rifles on a priority basis.[28] This small arms sale helped Washington reap big dividends before the year was out. During the Suez crisis of late 1956, Lebanon, unlike its radical Arab neighbors, refused to sever relations with Great Britain and France. And when pro-Nasser cabinet members blasted Chamoun as a traitor to the Arab cause, he replaced them with "pro-West" appointees, including Charles Malik, who took over the foreign ministry on 18 November. Impressed by the new cabinet's tough stand against anti-Western radicals, U.S. ambassador Donald Heath termed it the "strongest Lebanese Government in years."[29]

The new year would bring even bigger Lebanese dividends. Scrambling to shore up sagging Western interests in the Middle East in the aftermath of the Suez debacle, the White House unveiled plans for an "Eisenhower Doctrine" in January 1957. Claiming that U.S. inaction would open the door to further Soviet gains in the region, Ike won congressional authorization in early March to spend up to $200 million in economic aid and, if necessary, to send U.S. troops to defend any Middle Eastern nation threatened by aggression, whether direct or indirect, "from any country controlled by international communism."[30] Most Arabs privately regarded the Eisenhower Doctrine as a transparent ploy to promote Western influence in the Middle East by restraining Nasser's brand of nationalism, and some, like the Syrians, publicly denounced the initiative as an insidious example of U.S. "imperialism."[31] The only Arab state openly to endorse Ike's new policy without reservation was Lebanon, where, as early as 13 January, President Chamoun had told Ambassador Heath that "he supported [the] 'Eisenhower plan one hundred percent.'"[32]

With parliamentary elections scheduled for late June, however, more and more Lebanese were making it clear that they did not support the Eisenhower plan or Camille Chamoun at all. From the Bekaa Valley to the Basta, Beirut's Casbah, most Muslims idolized Nasser and applauded the increasingly anti-U.S. broadsides that he broadcast over Radio Cairo. Furthermore,

Druze chieftain Kamal Jumblatt and Sunni overlord Rashid Karame charged that Chamoun's endorsement of the Eisenhower Doctrine violated the 1943 National Pact, which had prescribed strict neutrality for Lebanon in foreign affairs. When James Richards, Ike's new roving ambassador to the Middle East, arrived in Beirut in mid-March to discuss U.S. economic assistance for Lebanon, Chamoun and Malik presented a distorted picture of their critics as crypto-communists and Nasserite stooges. "Real fear evident," Richards cabled Foggy Bottom, "over growing intensity [of] subversive activities in country by Communists supported by Syria and Egypt." Chamoun "feared Communist infiltration" and "was interested in building up forces for internal security," as was Malik, who emphasized the need "to nip Communist designs in the bud." Pointing out that the "pro-Western policies of present government will be very much on the block" during the upcoming election campaign, Richards secured Washington's swift approval for a $12.7 million military and financial aid package so that the Chamoun regime would be "in position to show tangible results from cooperation with the West."[33]

As election day approached, the Eisenhower administration evidently provided other more intangible signs of its support for the Chamoun regime as well. Sometime in early 1957, David Atlee Phillips, a CIA political action specialist who had helped overthrow Jacobo Arbenz in Guatemala three years earlier, had arrived in Beirut, where he "felt like James Bond at the barricades."[34] Phillips and other CIA operatives like Miles Copeland and Wilbur Eveland were soon distributing "campaign contributions" to pro-Western Lebanese politicians to help defeat anti-U.S. candidates backed by Nasser.[35] "News from Lebanon is very encouraging," CIA director Allen Dulles informed the National Security Council on 11 April, "with the Egyptians apparently giving up hope of exercising much influence over the forthcoming Lebanese elections."[36] But the atmosphere turned ugly in late May after troops loyal to Chamoun fired on pro-Nasser protesters in Beirut, killing seven and wounding seventy-three. By early June, Chamoun's foes charged that he had bought so many votes and gerrymandered so many districts that the balloting would be meaningless. Lest opposition leaders somehow derail U.S. plans for "a 99.9 percent-pure pro-US parliament," however, Wilbur Eveland began to make frequent late-night visits to the presidential palace, where he handed Chamoun briefcases full of cash earmarked for candidates friendly to the West.[37] Although Lebanon's new parliament may not have been as pure as U.S. officials had hoped, fifty-three of the sixty-six deputies elected at the end of June were staunch supporters of Camille Chamoun.[38]

Having swept to victory with a little help from their friends in the CIA, Chamoun and Malik redoubled their efforts to persuade the Eisenhower administration that Lebanon was a lonely pro-Western island in a sea of Arab nationalism and Soviet subversion. Eisenhower's Operations Coordinating Board (OCB), an interagency group that monitored policy in the Middle East, needed little persuading. Praising the Chamoun regime for its anticommunism and for its opposition to "irresponsible and emotional ideas emanating from within the Arab world," on 31 July the OCB recommended showcasing Lebanon as "an example of U.S.-Arab cooperation" in order to "stimulate more favorable attitudes toward the U.S." throughout the region.[39] When the Syrians and the Soviets announced a major arms deal in early August, jittery Lebanese officials urged U.S. covert action across the mountains in Damascus. "Unless the U.S. took some decisive action and means were found to overthrow the present regime in Syria," Charles Malik told a *New York Times* reporter, "the Lebanese regime could not last a year."[40] After a CIA plot to topple the left-leaning regime in Damascus backfired late that summer, top U.S. officials expected some serious fallout in Beirut, where "Syrian, Soviet, and Egyptian agents will increase their subversive activities against the pro-western Lebanese Government."[41] Hoping to boost Lebanese morale, Washington dispatched an additional $2 million worth of military hardware "on a crash basis" in mid-September to help the Chamoun regime maintain internal security.[42]

Many Lebanese and U.S. observers suspected, however, that Lebanon's internal security problems stemmed less from Syrian or Soviet subversion than from domestic opposition to Chamoun's increasingly autocratic rule. Outraged by what they regarded as massive fraud during the June elections, Chamoun's critics charged that he had packed parliament with his cronies in order to amend the constitution so that he could serve a second term as president. Rashid Karame and other Muslim leaders insisted that new elections were required to preserve Lebanon's fragile National Pact. Kamal Jumblatt, who lost the parliamentary seat he had held for more than a decade, blamed the United States, which, he claimed, intended to employ Chamoun as a pawn of "American imperialism" for the foreseeable future.[43]

The Chamoun regime responded by tarring its opponents with the brush of communism. Neutralists like Jumblatt, Foreign Minister Malik warned John Foster Dulles in mid-October, were insisting that Lebanon "alter its adherence to the Eisenhower Doctrine," a sure sign that they were playing the Kremlin's game.[44] But a State Department staff study completed later that month minimized the red threat and suggested instead that the tide of anti-U.S. sentiment surging through Lebanon "may well arise from a desire to prevent Chamoun from obtaining a further term of office." Although Foggy Bottom Middle East experts still favored modest amounts of economic and military aid to consolidate "Lebanon's position as a 'show case' of close relations with the West," they were also becoming wary of being manipulated by the Lebanese.[45] "The Arabs do not take to the idea of being taught to do things for themselves," one U.S. official stationed in southern Lebanon remarked privately in late November. "They want the Americans to do things for them."[46]

Among the most important things that Camille Chamoun wanted the United States to do in 1958 was to support his bid for another term in the presidential palace over the objections of pro-Nasser Lebanese Muslims. The new year began with the ominous news that Egypt and Syria would merge to create a single United Arab Republic (UAR). The State Department worried that Nasser would use the UAR "to threaten Lebanon" and other pro-Western regimes in the Arab world and "perhaps engulf them one by one."[47] So did Chamoun and Malik, both of whom believed that "the peril of subversion in Lebanon was immediate" and hinted that "it would be comforting if some elements of the Sixth Fleet might be moved to [the] eastern Mediterranean."[48] Robert McClintock, an unflappable and acid-tongued Cold Warrior who had served in Saigon during and after the Dien Bien Phu crisis before replacing Donald Heath as U.S. ambassador in Beirut in early 1958, wondered whether the Lebanese might be overreacting. Indeed, when Foreign Minister Malik repeatedly raised the specter of Syrian, Egyptian, and Soviet subversion in Lebanon and "reiterated his complaint [that the] US had no policy in [the] Middle East," an apoplectic McClintock cabled Washington that "if these Pirandello characters are in search of a policy we should give them one." Far from having done too little for its friends in Beirut, the new ambassador thought that the United States might already have done too much. With this in mind, McClintock recommended telling Lebanese leaders that "the Lord helps those who help themselves."[49]

Nevertheless, as the situation in Beirut deteriorated, U.S. officials realized that in the absence of divine intervention, they would probably have to help Chamoun achieve a happy ending to a story that seemed drawn straight from the theater of the political absurd. By late winter, few U.S. officials doubted that Chamoun was angling for a second term, and fewer still doubted that such action would trigger civil strife in Lebanon, where pressure was mounting for political reform among many Muslims who believed that recent demographic shifts had reversed the narrow six-to-five Christian majority enshrined in the National Pact fifteen years earlier. The "chances are great," McClintock warned on 21 February, "that an anti-Chamoun campaign would turn into a fanatic anti-Chamoun-cum-anti-US drive on [the] part of certain elements of [the] Moslem population." Yet the Christian most likely to succeed Chamoun as president was Army Chief of Staff Fuad Chehab, whose sporadic anti-Western diatribes prompted McClintock to dismiss him as "a neutral legume who would require careful pruning to grow in the right direction."[50] As Chehab's star waned in Washington, Chamoun and Malik depicted themselves as indispensable men and wrapped themselves ever more tightly in the cloak of the Eisenhower Doctrine, confident that "they could whistle up [the] Sixth Fleet any time they found themselves in trouble."[51] The Chamoun regime seemed hellbent, McClintock complained in late March, on converting Lebanon into "a sort of Christian Israel beleaguered by its neighbors and incapable of sustaining itself except under guns of foreign warships."[52]

Some at Foggy Bottom shared McClintock's mounting frustration. Official U.S. policy was to remain "aloof" from Chamoun's ill-advised bid for a second term and to "avoid any indication for [the] present that we are prepared [to] support him."[53] To do otherwise, Hugh Cumming, chief of the State Department's Bureau of Intelligence and Research, cautioned John Foster Dulles on 15 April, might "pull the keystone completely out of the delicate structure which has enabled Lebanon's Christians and Moslems to live peacefully together."[54] But after the CIA confirmed that Nasser was beaming violent anti-Chamoun radio diatribes into Lebanon and after Chamoun hinted that he might have to repudiate the Eisenhower Doctrine to placate pro-Nasser Lebanese Muslims, the focus of U.S. concern began to shift rapidly.[55] Once anti-Chamoun militants heeded Nasser's call and took to the streets of Beirut in early May, Dulles and Eisenhower agreed that "we should not look too closely into the local disaster" but should concentrate instead on the regional and global implications.[56] These implications were certainly not lost on Camille Chamoun, who believed that growing unrest in Lebanon actually strengthened his bid for a second term. Indeed, Chamoun smugly informed McClintock on 4 May that "once he has announced his intentions Western failure to support him will have repercussions among all [the] most moderate and responsible friends and allies of [the] West in [the] ME area."[57]

The Lebanese crisis escalated four days later when pro-Chamoun gunmen assassinated a leading anti-Chamoun journalist. Bloody street fighting erupted in Beirut, where a mob of angry Muslims stormed the U.S. Information Service library and burned it to the ground. According to U.S. missionaries, the situation thirty miles up the coast in the Sunni stronghold of Tripoli was also "very, very bad," so bad, in fact, that McClintock feared that foreign nationals living there might soon have to be evacuated. And to the east in the Bekaa Valley, anti-Chamoun Shi'ite militiamen began to receive crates of guns and ammunition from Syrian officials working for Nasser's new UAR. By early May, even Lebanese Christians like Fuad Chehab were telling U.S. officials that the "sole cause of [the] present revolutionary crisis in Lebanon is Chamoun's selfish determination to succeed himself in office." But true to form, Chamoun and Malik trotted out the shopworn communist shibboleth, insisting that "both [the] Soviet and UAR embassies were working on a 24-hour basis to destroy [the] integrity of Lebanon" and urging U.S. policy makers to begin "forward planning" for military intervention.[58] "Have no doubt whatever," McClintock cabled Washington on 12 May, that Chamoun "has fullest intention of requesting landing of Marines by direct message to President Eisenhower" in the near future. The principal problem, the ambassador hastened to add, was that the Eisenhower Doctrine "probably does not apply in view of [the] absence of overt Communist aggression."[59]

When Chamoun asked McClintock the next day whether the United States would in fact honor a request to send U.S. troops to Lebanon, the Eisenhower administration was forced to sort through a rapidly shrinking set of options. Neither Ike nor the top aides he invited to the Oval Office on 13 May were eager to intervene in what they regarded as a Lebanese sectarian dispute, particularly when, as Secretary of State Dulles reminded them, strictly speaking, the Eisenhower Doctrine might not be applicable. Resorting to a "gun boat policy" in the Middle East like the one that the United States had long employed in Latin America, Dulles added, "no longer represented an acceptable practice" and would unleash "a wave of feeling against us throughout the Arab world." Although Eisenhower acknowledged that "there are difficulties and dangers in taking action," he insisted that "we also had to take into account the apparently much larger problems which would arise if the Lebanese needed our intervention and we did not respond." Well aware that, from Venezuela to Indonesia, "the Communists" were "stirring up trouble in area after area," Dulles had to agree that if the United States ignored Chamoun's request for help, "we would have to accept heavy losses not only in Lebanon but elsewhere."[60] With this in mind, the Eisenhower administration informed Chamoun later that same day that it was prepared to honor his request for U.S. troops under three conditions: that he accept UN help in resolving the crisis, that he obtain support from at least one other Arab state, and that he renounce his own candidacy for a second term.[61]

Having issued Chamoun what he regarded as an ironclad pledge on 13 May, U.S. policy makers worked hard during the following two months to avoid having to fulfill it. U.S. diplomats were instructed to remind Chamoun "that he does not have a blank check re [the] sending of Western forces" and to press him to accept a political compromise whereby he would support the election of his Christian rival, General Chehab, in exchange for Nasser's pledge "to use his influence to try to end dissidence within Lebanon."[62] Moreover, although the documentary record is still extremely sketchy, the CIA seems once again to have been channeling funds into Lebanon, this time to ensure that, one way or the other, Chamoun would leave the presidential palace as scheduled later that summer. "We were progressing well on the covert side," Assistant Secretary of State for Near Eastern Affairs William Rountree told Eisenhower and Dulles on 9 June, "where greater flexibility is required in the use of money."[63] Ten days later, Lebanese junior officers contacted the U.S. embassy in Beirut to ask: "Will there or will there not be intervention if their coup against President Chamoun takes place, and/or if it succeeds?"[64] Meanwhile, UN secretary general Dag Hammarskjöld, with behind-the-scenes U.S. help, established a UN Observers Group in Lebanon (UNOGIL) in late June to curb the flow of arms across the Syro-Lebanese frontier and then pressured Chamoun to commence truce talks with his Muslim opponents.[65]

But the cagey Chamoun had been working hard since mid-May to meet the letter, if not the spirit, of the three conditions Ike and Dulles had laid out for U.S. intervention. He was grudgingly cooperating with UNOGIL and was talking with Hammarskjöld, he had persuaded two other Arab states—Iraq and Jordan—to corroborate his charges of UAR subversion, and he had privately assured U.S. diplomats that he would step down as president on schedule in late September, provided there was a suitable successor. None of this, however, was terribly reassuring either to Lebanese Muslims, who redoubled their efforts in mid-June to unseat the Christian strongman, or to U.S. policy makers like John Foster Dulles, who growled that "there is a pretty fair chance that Chamoun may call on us to come in there, perhaps not because his own forces cannot hold the situation, but because they are not willing to try adequately."[66]

Eisenhower convened an emergency meeting at the White House on Sunday, 15 June, to review the crisis in Lebanon. Everyone agreed that "the long-term prospects remained gloomy" and placed much of the blame on Chamoun, who seemed determined to retain power even at the point of U.S. bayonets. "How can you save a country from its own leaders?" Eisenhower fumed as he contemplated the prospect of sending U.S. troops to Beirut. "We would be intervening to save a nation; and yet the nation is the people, and the people don't want our intervention." Worse still, the absence of "external aggression" in Lebanon would make it hard to sell U.S. intervention on Capitol Hill and Main Street. Yet nonintervention could prove even more costly. "If Chamoun calls on us and we do not respond," John Foster Dulles prophesied, "that will be the end of every pro-Western government in the area." Eisenhower agreed. "In such circumstances," he observed, "we would have to fulfill our commitments," even if it meant, as William Rountree predicted it would, "in all probability a pro-Western dictatorship, since there is not sufficient popular support in Lebanon for Western intervention."[67]

Throughout late June and into early July, the Eisenhower administration held out some hope that the United Nations might broker a last-minute settlement in the Lebanese civil war that would avert U.S. intervention. Dulles, for example, instructed McClintock to remind Chamoun that "it is almost a sine qua non that Lebanon have . . . full recourse to [the] orderly processes of [the] UN before finally requesting and receiving friendly assistance."[68] Eisenhower likewise believed that "unless the United Nations can be effective in the matter," the United States would soon face a Hobson's choice in Lebanon. "Under certain circumstances, to avoid intervention might be fatal," he explained to a friend on 23 June. "On the other hand, to intervene would increase, in the Arab world, antagonism toward the West."[69] When Senate leaders called on Dulles later that same day to voice their concerns about Lebanon, the secretary of state replied: "We are hoping that a combined United Nations effort on the borders and the government effort within the country can bring the situation under control."[70]

But Dulles was far from confident that UN mediators could secure a settlement before Chamoun requested U.S. troops. "In effect," he informed his visitors, "President Chamoun has a check on his desk which was given to him about 5 weeks ago, and this check is that any time he wants to call on help from the United States . . . , he would be able to do that," provided he went to the United Nations first. Having sought UN help, Chamoun now seemed certain to turn once again to the United States. And Dulles believed that "if we did not supply troops if Chamoun tries to cash the check, it would raise throughout the world the question of whether the United States was willing to perform on its promises when the chips were down." To be sure, U.S. intervention might well spark an anti-U.S. backlash throughout the Arab world. But "Iran, Turkey, Pakistan, Thailand, Viet-Nam, and the Republic of China," Dulles insisted, "would all view our failure to act as an indication of lack of willingness to support our friends when they are in trouble." In short, should UN efforts to end the Lebanese civil war fail, the Eisenhower administration would probably soon be compelled to intervene in order to preserve U.S. credibility.[71]

For a brief moment in early July, it seemed that Dag Hammarskjöld had achieved an eleventh-hour breakthrough. After shuttling between Beirut and Cairo for a week, the UN secretary general flew to Washington, where he met with John Foster Dulles on 7 July to report that both Chamoun and his pro-Nasser opponents had agreed to "a cooling off period during which a compromise might be prepared." The meeting evidently went quite well, for Hammarskjöld remarked privately shortly afterward that "Dulles has swung around, and American policy has become almost parallel" to that of the United Nations.[72] By 10 July, the word from UN and U.S. officials stationed in Beirut was that Chamoun was finally prepared to step down and was willing to turn power over to General Fuad Chehab at the end of the month.[73]

Four days later, however, left-wing officers overthrew the pro-Western regime in Iraq, sending shock waves from Baghdad to Beirut, where Camille Chamoun decided that the moment had finally arrived to cash his check. Just before noon on 14 July, Chamoun summoned Ambassador McClintock and his British colleague, George Middleton, to the presidential palace. "I explained to them that the Lebanese government had until this date refrained from requesting intervention by their respective countries in the hope that it could reestablish order and security without their military assistance," Chamoun recalled in his memoirs. "But the revolution in Iraq, endorsed by the communists and Nasserites, constituted a new development of exceptional gravity that endangered not only Lebanon but the entire Middle East." Pointing to the guarantees embodied in the Eisenhower Doctrine, Chamoun "called for an affirmative response within forty-eight hours, not by words but by positive actions."[74]

The president of Lebanon would have his affirmative response in just half that time. Word of Chamoun's melodramatic appeal for U.S. and U.K. troops and of his vow "to go down fighting" had arrived in Washington at daybreak on 14 July. Although Ambassador McClintock insisted that "so far as Lebanon alone is concerned, we cannot . . . discern need for so portentous a step," he realized that the Eisenhower administration must weigh broader "political and strategic considerations affecting the entire Middle East."[75] Indeed, Ike and Dulles were already very well aware that the political upheavals in Baghdad and Beirut threatened Western interests throughout the region. Badly shaken by the Iraqi revolution, Turkey, Iran, and Pakistan were pressing hard for U.S. military intervention to contain the tide of radical nationalism sweeping the Arab world. So were the Saudis, who warned that if Britain and the United States failed to respond, "they are finished as powers in the Middle East."[76] With pro-Western leaders nervously marking time from Riyadh to Karachi, Eisenhower convened key aides later that morning to decide whether to send troops into Lebanon. Before heading for the White House, top State Department, Pentagon, and CIA officials met briefly and concluded that unless Ike honored Chamoun's request, the United States would "lose influence not only in the Arab states of the Middle East but in the area more generally." As a result, "the dependability of United States commitments for assistance in the event of need would be brought into question throughout the world."[77]

As his advisers quietly filed into the Oval Office, Dwight Eisenhower could not have agreed more. Sitting "sprawled back in the chair behind his desk," Ike struck one participant as "the most relaxed man in the room," as someone who "knew exactly what he was going to do."[78] After listening to CIA director Allen Dulles catalog a daunting list of troubles almost certain to erupt from Saudi Arabia and Kuwait to Jordan and Morocco should the United States ignore Chamoun's plea for help, "the President said that the situation is clear to him—to lose this area by inaction would be far worse than the loss of China, because of the strategic position and resources of the Middle East." Although Secretary of State Dulles expected "a very bad reaction through most of the Arab states," he agreed that "the losses of doing nothing would be worse than the losses from action—and that consequently we should send our troops into Lebanon."[79] Convinced that "we couldn't sit around and see the Near East lost," Eisenhower worried that "if there were any delay there probably wouldn't be any Lebanon to go into." Noting that "his mind had been made up long ago," he snapped that "we had to act or get out of the Middle East" and ordered General Nathan Twining, chairman of the Joint Chiefs of Staff, to prepare the U.S. Sixth Fleet for action in the eastern Mediterranean.[80]

In an effort to limit the damage on Capitol Hill, Ike went through the motions of consulting Congress a few hours later. Insisting that "this is not a matter of a decision already taken," the president asked John Foster Dulles to lay out the rationale for U.S. intervention in Lebanon to the thirty senators and congressmen who had gathered in the Cabinet Room. Insisting that Lebanon's woes were the result of Soviet-inspired UAR subversion, Dulles described the present crisis as a symbolic test of U.S. credibility, not merely in the Middle East but throughout the Third World. "Turkey, Iran and Pakistan would feel—if we do not act—that our inaction is because we are afraid of the Soviet Union," he explained. "Elsewhere, the impact of not going in—from Morocco to Indo-China—would be very harmful to us."

Unmoved by Dulles's arguments, several senators feared that, as Montana's Mike Mansfield put it, "we would be getting into a civil war." Was the crisis in the Middle East really "Soviet- or Communist-inspired," J. William Fulbright, the Arkansas Democrat who would soon chair the Foreign Relations Committee, wondered. Or was Nasser perhaps "playing his own game?" Bridling at Fulbright's suggestion that, strictly speaking, the Eisenhower Doctrine might not be applicable in Lebanon, John Foster Dulles retorted that "if we were to adopt the doctrine that Nasser can whip up a civil war without our intervention, our friends will go down to defeat." Echoing his secretary of state, Eisenhower insisted that in cases like Lebanon, "the crucial question is what the victims believe." And Chamoun, he pointed out, "believes it is Soviet Communism that is causing him his trouble."[81]

Camille Chamoun was not the only foreign leader whose beliefs were crucial in Eisenhower's decision to intervene in Lebanon. Just a little over an hour after Fulbright and his friends filed back to Capitol Hill, Ike was on the telephone with British Prime Minister Harold Macmillan, who believed that the grave crisis in the Middle East required far broader action than U.S. policy makers were contemplating. Eight months earlier, Macmillan and Eisenhower had agreed to begin contingency planning "for possible combined U.S.-U.K. military intervention in the event of an imminent or actual coup d'etat in Jordan and/or Lebanon."[82] After Lebanon's chronic political unrest flared into full-blown civil war during the spring of 1958, Whitehall and the White House had decided to convene an Anglo-American "working group" in Washington in mid-May to put the finishing touches on "Operation Blue Bat," which called for U.K. troops to be airlifted from Cyprus to assist U.S. Marines in securing the Beirut area.[83] The working group met again in London in early June, where both sides agreed that once there was a decision to intervene, "U.S.-British operations will continue until stability within Lebanon is established under a viable pro-Western government."[84]

The sudden overthrow of the pro-British regime in Baghdad on 14 July, however, prompted some second thoughts in London. Convinced that the Arab backlash against Operation Blue Bat would "destroy the oil fields and the pipelines and all the rest of it," Prime Minister Macmillan telephoned the White House to propose "a much larger operation" ranging far beyond what he termed "this 1/2 d. [half-penny] place" in Lebanon. In short, he told Ike, Britain and the United States must be ready to "carry this thing on to the Persian Gulf." Stressing that any Anglo-American agreement to mount "a big operation running all the way through Syria and Iraq" would require "decisions which are far far beyond anything which I have the power to do constitutionally," Eisenhower insisted that U.S. intervention must be limited to Lebanon. Meanwhile, British troops would be held in reserve on Cyprus for possible deployment to Beirut or to other Middle Eastern hot spots. Even these steps, Ike admitted, meant that "we are opening Pandora's box" without really knowing "what's at the bottom of it." Macmillan quite agreed.

After all, he pointed out, the Jordanians had already asked whether White-hall was willing to send paratroopers to Amman in an emergency. "The old box," Macmillan warned Ike as the two men said their goodbyes, "may do us a lot of harm."[85]

Although U.S. soldiers and diplomats were able, for the most part, to hold Pandora's mischief to a minimum in the weeks that followed, the success of Eisenhower's experiment with "limited war" in Lebanon owed as much to good luck as to wise crisis management. Even before their boots were dry, the U.S. Marines had very nearly stumbled into a D-Day shootout with Chamoun's opponents. By 15 July, Ike's principal worry was that U.S. troops might encounter hostile fire from pro-Nasser and anti-Chamoun mobs in Beirut. "The trouble is that we have a campaign of hatred against us, not by the governments but by the people," he confided to Vice President Richard Nixon that morning, and "the people are on Nasser's side."[86] In the event, however, the real danger came not from the Lebanese people, who made no move whatsoever to oppose Operation Blue Bat, but rather from Lebanon's armed forces, which, according to Ambassador McClintock, were threatening to "disintegrate on confessional lines." As the clock ticked down toward H-Hour, General Fuad Chehab warned U.S. officials that Muslim contingents of the Lebanese army might actually attack U.S. forces. With the United States and Lebanon teetering "on the brink of catastrophe," McClintock tried desperately to persuade Washington to delay the landings at the last minute.[87] Failing that, he raced to the beaches in the embassy's Cadillac, where he conferred with U.S. and Lebanese commanders, smoothed ruffled feathers on both sides, and narrowly averted bloodshed.[88]

Having had the good fortune to avoid an ugly incident at Beirut, U.S. policy makers worried that their luck was about to run out 150 miles to the southeast in Amman, where Jordan's King Hussein was pressing hard for British and U.S. military intervention. Since ascending the Hashemite throne at the age of eighteen in 1953, Hussein had faced a daunting array of problems. Nearly half of his two million subjects were Palestinians, who had fled their homeland during the 1948 Arab-Israeli war to brood in the bleak makeshift refugee camps that dotted the West Bank and ringed Amman. Devoid of the oil wealth that enriched its Arab neighbors to the east, Jordan was utterly dependent on British and U.S. financial largesse to make ends meet. Bombarded constantly by threats from Palestinian firebrands at home and from Arab rivals abroad, Hussein held power thanks mainly to the Arab Legion, a crack battalion of fiercely loyal British-trained Bedouins, assisted by an occasional show of force by the U.S. Sixth Fleet over the horizon in the eastern Mediterranean. With U.S. blessing, in March 1958 Hussein agreed to join his cousin, King Feisal of Iraq, in forming an anti-Nasser "Arab Union," a loose confederation with close ties to the West designed more to boost Hashemite morale than to enhance Iraqi and Jordanian military preparedness. The revolution that rocked Iraq four months later not only destroyed the Arab Union but also raised fresh fears in Washington, London, and Tel Aviv that a similar fate lay in store for Jordan.[89]

Upon learning of the bloody coup in Baghdad, King Hussein's first instinct had been to lead the Arab Legion into Iraq to avenge his cousin's murder. Realizing that this would require Western help, Hussein summoned U.S. and U.K. diplomats to the royal palace on 15 July and demanded to know whether the United States and Britain were willing to intervene in Jordan or Iraq, as they had done in Lebanon. Officials in Washington and London must understand that "if Iraq went, the whole Middle East would go, including Jordan and the Persian Gulf," Hussein thundered. "What were we going to do about it?"[90] Within twenty-four hours, the king forced the issue by formally requesting U.S. and U.K. military intervention in Jordan.[91]

Eager to prevent events from spiraling out of control, Eisenhower and Macmillan agreed that Foreign Secretary Selwyn Lloyd should fly to Washington on 16 July to confer with top U.S. officials. "I was determined to do all I could to help Hussein, . . . but I first had to know what the Americans proposed doing," Macmillan recalled long afterward. "We had burnt our fingers over Suez and I had no intention of doing so for a second time."[92] Lloyd reported that U.S. policy makers were deeply worried about Jordan, not least because they knew that Israel was poised to seize the West Bank, a move that would almost certainly trigger a general Middle East war. Yet according to John Foster Dulles, "at the moment the United States was inhibited" from honoring Hussein's appeal for help, in part because U.S. troops were already overextended in Beirut, in part because Ike had assured Congress "only 2 days ago that there were no plans for sending American forces other than to Lebanon." The best that the United States could offer, Dulles explained, was "logistical assistance" for a British airlift into Amman and diplomatic help in securing permission from Tel Aviv for U.K. transports to overfly Israeli territory on their way from Cyprus to Jordan.[93] Doubtless still rather uneasy over this lukewarm U.S. show of support, Macmillan nevertheless dispatched thirty-seven hundred British paratroopers to Amman, where they landed without incident just before noon on 17 July and proceeded to help the jittery young king stabilize the confused situation in Jordan.[94]

Lloyd and Dulles met later that afternoon to compare notes. They agreed that British intervention in Jordan and U.S. intervention in Lebanon had shored up Western interests in the Eastern Mediterranean and averted an

Arab-Israeli war. But what about the equally unstable situation in the Persian Gulf, where oil-rich sheikdoms like Kuwait seemed especially vulnerable to Iraqi aggression or Nasserite subversion? "If a coup could be carried out in Baghdad," Lloyd pointed out, "there was an equal danger of one in Kuwait." Dulles agreed, adding that Britain and the United States must be prepared to use force, if necessary, to retain access to Persian Gulf petroleum. "Were Nasser and his friends to get hold of the Saudi and Kuwait oil fields," Dulles feared that "they would demand terms for the supply of oil so stiff as to create the greatest dangers for the economies of the United Kingdom and Europe." So important was the oil of the Persian Gulf, he concluded, "that we should not exclude the possibility of early military action to secure Kuwait, even if the Kuwaiti authorities were not at this stage willing to invite us in."[95]

Such a scenario did not seem at all far-fetched during the summer of 1958. Britain had, of course, exercised a protectorate over Kuwait since 1922, when U.K. officials carved up the eastern fringes of the defunct Ottoman Empire with an eye to ensuring British control over the oil rumored to lie beneath the desolate sands that stretched south from the Shatt al-Arab. Relations between Whitehall and the Sabah clan, which had ruled Kuwait for nearly two centuries, remained fairly cordial until the mid-1950s, when disputes over how to put the sheikdom's enormous oil wealth to best use produced considerable friction. Nor did it help matters that Kuwait's "ruler," Sheik Abdullah al-Salim al-Sabah, came under increasing fire from Palestinian oil workers, who charged that he was little more than a British puppet. Nevertheless, down through early 1958 the British continued to work steadfastly to ensure the "preservation of the present Sabah family position" in the face of "pressures from indigenous nationalist sentiment, stimulated by Egyptian propaganda."[96] By June, however, some U.K. officials feared that "the Ruler might feel, in some future crisis, that the threat of Nasserism or the pull of Arab solidarity was so strong that he must place restrictions on our free access to Kuwait oil." And this, in turn, might necessitate a British decision "to intervene without the Ruler's consent."[97]

That future crisis seemed close at hand before the summer was out. Well aware that trouble was brewing in Kuwait, Eisenhower cabled Macmillan on 18 July that "we must, I think, not only try to bolster up both . . . Lebanon and Jordan, we must also, and this seems to me even more important, see that the Persian Gulf area stays within the Western orbit."[98] Macmillan agreed and instructed Lloyd to raise the possibility of joint Anglo-American intervention in Kuwait. "Five British battalions were converging on the Persian Gulf," Lloyd told John Foster Dulles on 19 July. "A decision had to be made within two or three days as to whether these forces should be put into Kuwait against the opposition of the Ruling family." Would the United States support such a British operation? Yes, Dulles replied, because if Arab radicals were to gain control over Kuwaiti oil, "the West would be held to ransom." To signal Washington's growing concern, Ike was moving elements of the U.S. Seventh Fleet from Okinawa to the Indian Ocean with orders to ensure that the Persian Gulf oil fields "did not fall into Nasser's hands."[99]

Although Dulles hoped it would be possible to avoid intervening in the Persian Gulf, he was far from confident. "The British were concerned over Kuwait, the brightest star in the U.K. oil galaxy," he told Eisenhower on 24 July. "Perhaps Kuwait could be held by force in the event of trouble, but it was not clear what the workers in the oil fields would do."[100] By early August, however, it was clear that the trouble had passed and that the Sabah clan would be "able [to] survive [the] latest ME upheaval for [an] indefinite period" without the help of U.S. or U.K. troops.[101] His resolve stiffened by the quiet show of force by the Royal Navy and the Seventh Fleet, Sheik Abdullah unleashed his ruthless secret police against his critics at home, distanced himself from Arab radicals abroad, and kept Kuwaiti oil flowing to Western Europe without interruption.[102]

The Eisenhower administration was lucky to have avoided U.S. intervention in Kuwait and Jordan and to have avoided bloodshed in Lebanon because grave doubts were growing on Capitol Hill about the wisdom and the legality of Ike's recent actions. Oregon's Wayne Morse had set the tone during an executive session of the Senate Foreign Relations Committee on 15 July, thundering that he was "not going to support the mixing of American blood with Arabian oil in the Middle East today" and demanding "to know what the legal basis for this intervention is." As he would six years later when he cast a lonely vote against Lyndon Johnson's Tonkin Gulf Resolution, Morse warned that "we are wrong every time we get mixed up in another country's civil war." Morse's colleagues echoed his concerns in less apocalyptic language. Massachusetts Democrat John F. Kennedy, for example, wondered whether the Eisenhower Doctrine was really applicable in the Lebanese crisis, as did Minnesota's Hubert Humphrey, who termed intervention in Lebanon "a sad mistake" that would be "bitterly resented for years to come" throughout the Arab world.[103]

The most articulate Senate critic of Eisenhower's handling of the 1958 crisis in the Middle East, however, was J. William Fulbright. Throughout the spring, the Arkansas Democrat had insisted that the disorder and instability plaguing the region resulted from Arab nationalism, not from Soviet subversion, a point he had hammered home when he and other congressional leaders met with Ike on the afternoon of 14 July. "This is a curious outgrowth of the Eisenhower Doctrine," Fulbright told his fellow senators once the Marines were ashore at Beirut. Sixteen months earlier, he reminded everyone, Congress had taken pains to authorize military intervention in the Middle East only to repel an "armed attack by any country dominated by international communism," a situation that simply "does not apply" in Lebanon. This being so, Fulbright predicted that the White House would probably try to justify its questionable actions by invoking the so-called "Mansfield Amendment," a clause in the March 1957 congressional resolution affirming that "the independence and integrity of the nations of the Middle East" were "vital to the national interests" of the United States. While the Montana Democrat who had authored the clause sat and fumed, Wayne Morse rose to suggest that Ike would be well advised to think twice, since "Senator [Mike] Mansfield himself has on the floor of the Senate on three different occasions in advance rebutted that twisting of his amendment."[104]

When Undersecretary of State Christian Herter tried to use the Mansfield Amendment to rationalize U.S. intervention in Lebanon during a closed-door hearing the next day, he was challenged by angry Senate Democrats. Pointing out that Camille Chamoun's Muslim rivals bitterly opposed Ike's action, Hubert Humphrey wondered "whether or not there was really overt Communist aggression" behind the crisis. Terming Operation Blue Bat "a tragic historic mistake," Wayne Morse insisted that "the principle of self-determination ought to prevail in Lebanon," even if this meant accepting an anti-Western regime in Beirut. And William Fulbright questioned whether the Eisenhower administration really understood "what is going on in the Middle East." Was the president, Fulbright asked Herter, responding to a "Russian-directed move both in Lebanon and Iraq or in either?" Or was he responding instead to "indigenous Arab nationalism which is seeking to bring about the unity of the Arabs regardless of what Russia may want?" In short, did the Eisenhower administration regard the present crisis as "primarily inspired by the Russians" or not? "I just wouldn't know," Herter replied softly.[105]

Actually, of course, Herter knew very well, as did his superiors, that Lebanon's woes, like the wider turmoil then sweeping the Middle East, stemmed from Arab nationalism, not from international communism. A National Intelligence Estimate dated 22 July, for example, confirmed that pro-Nasser pan-Arab radicals, not pro-Soviet subversives, were behind most of the United States's problems in the Muslim world. "The part played by local Communist parties in the area," CIA experts concluded, "is slight."[106] Ike himself admitted as much later that same day, confessing privately that "the basic reason for our Mid East troubles is Nasser's capture of Arab loyalty and enthusiasm throughout the region."[107] For Herter to have admitted this publicly during his 16 July confrontation with the Senate Foreign Relations Committee, however, would have raised awkward questions about Eisenhower's use of presidential power. It was far simpler, Ike and his advisers believed, to exaggerate the communist threat in Lebanon and stretch the logic of the Eisenhower Doctrine to the breaking point than to risk defeat on Capitol Hill by seeking congressional approval for the use of U.S. troops to combat anti-Western Arab nationalists.

As it was, Senate Democrats suggested that the president's recent actions in the Middle East went well beyond what Congress had authorized under the Eisenhower Doctrine in March 1957. Congressional leaders, John Kennedy pointed out, expected to be consulted about possible intervention in advance, not merely informed about it after the fact. "We had one other consultation on Indochina" at the time of the Dien Bien Phu crisis, Kennedy recalled, when "the Congressional leadership was given a very clear opportunity to say what they thought, and they said they were opposed to it, and I think that that turned it off." Mike Mansfield raised an even more fundamental issue. In the absence of communist-inspired aggression in Lebanon, the Montana Democrat asked Herter, was not Ike really relying upon his "residual powers as Commander in Chief," and not upon the congressional authorization whose strict terms were spelled out in the Eisenhower Doctrine, to send U.S. troops to Beirut? Herter tried to hedge, but the disquieting answer to Mansfield's question clearly seemed to be "yes."[108]

Fortunately for Dwight Eisenhower, the U.S. Marines would fare far better in Beirut during the summer of 1958 than they would seven years later after Lyndon Johnson sent them ashore on the South Vietnamese coast at Danang. By late July, U.S. troops were policing an uneasy truce between Lebanese Christians and Muslims, while special presidential emissary Robert Murphy was working behind the scenes to broker a political compromise between Camille Chamoun and his opponents. With Washington's blessing, on 31 July the Lebanese parliament voted that Chamoun should be succeeded as president by General Fuad Chehab, who promised to appoint several of his predecessor's leading critics to posts in the new cabinet. Although lame-duck foreign minister Charles Malik warned his old friend John Foster Dulles in mid-August that U.S. forces might have to remain in Beirut indefinitely to maintain law and order, the last Marines would leave Lebanon without fanfare on 25 October 1958, just one month after Chehab replaced Chamoun in the presidential palace.[109] A week later King Hussein bid a reluctant farewell to the last British Tommies, who were flown from Jordan back to their base in Cyprus by the U.S. Air Force. And by the end of the year, the Seventh Fleet had departed from a relatively tranquil Persian Gulf in order to patrol the increasingly troubled waters of the Formosa Straits.[110] "It had been the kind of intervention," Ike told Harold Macmillan with a smile during a March 1959 postmortem on Operation Blue Bat, "which had not left a nasty aftertaste."[111]

Yet what had seemed at the time to be a stunning U.S. success in the Middle East now appears to have been more risky in the short run and more costly in the long run than the Eisenhower administration realized. The entire crisis might actually have been avoided had not key officials at the White House, the State Department, and the CIA developed such close personal ties with pro-Western Lebanese leaders like Camille Chamoun and Charles Malik. Having meddled in the politics of Lebanon for almost five years, the Eisenhower administration really had little choice but to honor Chamoun's request for U.S. troops in 1958. Furthermore, despite the Pentagon's meticulous military planning, events had nearly spiraled out of control, both in Beirut, where U.S. Marines almost blundered into a shooting match with Lebanese militiamen, and in the wider arena as well, where U.K. officials lobbied for Anglo-American armed intervention in the Persian Gulf that foreshadowed Operation Desert Storm a generation later.

If U.S. intervention in Lebanon proved more risky than it had looked, it would also prove more costly. Although Eisenhower had couched his actions in the rhetoric of anticommunism and the ritual of collective security, privately he admitted in July 1958 that revolutionary nationalism was the real threat to U.S. interests in the Middle East. In so doing he helped place the United States on a collision course with Egypt's Gamal Abdel Nasser and other Arab radicals during the following quarter-century. Moreover, because the absence of communist subversion in Lebanon prevented him from acting under the auspices of the Eisenhower Doctrine, Ike had to resort instead to his powers as commander-in-chief, a maneuver that some on Capitol Hill regarded as a dangerous step down the road toward what would later be called the imperial presidency.

Why had Eisenhower insisted upon flexing presidential muscle to combat Arab nationalism in 1958? He did so for the same reason that Lyndon Johnson would plunge into the Vietnamese quagmire after 1964: credibility. Like LBJ, Ike believed that failure to support such pro-Western leaders as Camille Chamoun or Ngo Dinh Diem would erode U.S. credibility as a guarantor and invite Soviet adventurism in the Third World. For Eisenhower in the Middle East as for Johnson in Southeast Asia, the U.S. economic and strategic interests at stake seemed at times to loom larger than those in China, where during the late 1940s Harry Truman's rejection of military intervention had produced political and diplomatic catastrophe. Although Ike's cautious instincts and tactical virtuosity helped ensure that the outcome in Lebanon in 1958 was radically different from that in Vietnam in 1968, the Cold War convictions and strategic assumptions that guided Dwight Eisenhower during his finest hour in the Middle East clearly helped start the clock ticking toward the United States's darkest hour in Southeast Asia a decade later. Moreover, by meddling in Lebanon's internal political problems, Ike helped ensure that a country regarded by many during the 1950s as the Switzerland of the Middle East would by the early 1980s become the Bosnia of the eastern Mediterranean, where much blood—most of it Lebanese but some of it American—would be shed.

Notes

A previous version of this essay was published in *Diplomatic History* 20 (Winter 1996): 27–54.

1. See, e.g., Robert Stookey, *America and the Arab States: An Uneasy Encounter* (New York, 1975), 156–57; William Quandt, "Lebanon, 1958, and Jordan, 1970," in *Force without War: U.S. Armed Forces as a Political Instrument,* ed. Barry M. Blechman and Stephen S. Kaplan (Washington, DC, 1978), 225–57; William Bragg Ewald, Jr., *Eisenhower the President: Crucial Days 1951–1960* (Englewood Cliffs, NJ, 1981), 241–42; Robert A. Divine, *Eisenhower and the Cold War* (New York, 1981), 101–4; Stephen E. Ambrose, *The President,* Vol. 2 of *Eisenhower* (New York, 1984), 470–73; H. W. Brands, *Cold Warriors: Eisenhower's Generation and American Foreign Policy* (New York, 1988), 100–113; and H. W. Brands, *The Specter of Neutralism: The United States and the Emergence of the Third World, 1947–1960* (New York, 1990), 293–96.

2. Dwight D. Eisenhower, *Waging Peace, 1956–1961* (Garden City, NY, 1965), 290. For a sympathetic appraisal of Ike's decision making and an examination of the "operational code" employed by his national security advisers, see Alan Dowty, *Middle East Crisis: U.S. Decision-Making in 1958, 1970, and 1973* (Berkeley, CA, 1984), 23–108.

3. For accounts critical of various aspects of Ike's handling of the Lebanese crisis, see especially Richard J. Barnet, *Intervention and Revolution: The United States in the Third World* (New York, 1968), 140–51; Malcolm Kerr, "The Lebanese Civil War," in *International Regulation of Civil Wars,* ed. Evan Luard (New York, 1972), 65–90; D. Cameron Watt, *Succeeding John Bull: America in Britain's Place, 1900–1975* (New York, 1984), 134–35; Piers Brendon, *Ike: His Life and Times* (New York, 1986), 356–60; Robert J. McMahon, "Eisenhower and Third World Nationalism: A Critique of the Revisionists," *Political Science Quarterly* 101 (October 1986): 465–66; Thomas G. Paterson, *Meeting the Communist Threat: Truman to Reagan* (New York, 1988), 186–90; Michael Bishku, "The 1958 American Intervention in Lebanon: A Historical Assessment," *American-Arab Affairs* 31 (Winter 1989/1990): 106–19; Erika Alin, *The United States and the 1958 Lebanon Crisis: American Intervention in the Middle East* (Lanham, MD, 1994); and especially Irene Gendzier, *Notes from the Minefield: United States Intervention in Lebanon and the Middle East, 1945–1958* (New York, 1997), 264–337.

4. Thomas J. Abercrombie, "Young-Old Lebanon Lives by Trade," *National Geographic Magazine* 113 (April 1958): 479–523.

5. Fahim I. Qubain, *Crisis in Lebanon* (Washington, DC, 1961), 16–22; Leila M. T. Meo, *Lebanon, Improbable Nation: A Study in Political Development* (Bloomington, IN, 1965), 82–85; Kamal Salibi, *A House of Many Mansions: The History of Lebanon Reconsidered* (Berkeley, CA, 1988), 182–87.

6. Wadsworth telegram to State Department, 24 November 1943, U.S. Department of State, *Foreign Relations of the United States, 1943* (Washington, DC, 1964), 4:1046–47 (hereafter *FRUS*, with year and volume number).

7. Wadsworth to Loy Henderson (Bureau of Near Eastern, South Asian, and African Affairs [NEA]), 11 July 1945, General Records of the Department of State, Record Group 59, file 890E.00/7–1145, National Archives II, College Park, MD (hereafter RG 59 with file number).

8. On ARAMCO in Lebanon, see Douglas Little, "Pipeline Politics: America, TAPLINE, and the Arabs," *Business History Review* 64 (Summer 1990): 267–68. Pinkerton is quoted in Irene Gendzier, "No Forum for the Lebanese People: US Perceptions from Lebanon, 1945–1947," *Middle East Report* 20 (Jan./Feb. 1990): 35.

9. See, e.g., Warren Austin (U.S. mission to United Nations) telegram to State Department, 1 December 1947, in *FRUS, 1947,* 5:1293–94, and Pinkerton to State Department, 12 December 1947, RG 59, 890E.00/12–1247.

10. Pinkerton telegram to State Department, 12 January and 3 March 1948, RG 59, 890E.00B/1–1248 and 890E.00/3–348.

11. State-War-Navy Coordinating Committee, "Long-Range Assistance to Lebanon," 6 June 1948, RG 59, 890E.00/6–848.

12. Central Intelligence Agency, SR-13, "Arab States," 27 September 1949, CIA Office of Information and Privacy Coordination, Washington, DC.

13. Pinkerton to State Department, 11 October 1950, RG 59, 611.83A/10–1150.

14. Michael C. Hudson, *The Precarious Republic: Political Modernization in Lebanon* (New York, 1968), 105–8, 135–53.

15. Eyal Zisser, "The Downfall of the Khuri Administration: A Dubious Revolution," *Middle Eastern Studies* 30 (July 1994): 486–511.

16. State Department, "Policy Statement: Lebanon," 29 January 1951, RG 59, 611.83A/1–2951.

17. Chargé James Lobenstine (Beirut) telegram to State Department, 23 September 1952, *FRUS, 1952–1954,* 9:1008–9.

18. State Department, "Biographies of the Lebanese Cabinet," OIR Report #4308, 5 February 1947, *OSS/State Department Intelligence and Research Reports, Part 7: The Middle East,* microfilm edition (Frederick, MD, 1977), reel 2, item 14.

19. Samuel Kopper (USUN) to Austin, 14 March 1948, *FRUS, 1948,* 5:723–24.

20. Assistant Secretary of State for Near Eastern and African Affairs Henry Byroade to John Foster Dulles, 26 January 1953, RG 59, 611.83A/1–2653.

21. Department of State (DOS) briefing paper, "Lebanon," 5 May 1953, *FRUS, 1952–1954,* 9:1211–13.

22. State Department memorandum of conversation, 16 May 1953, *FRUS, 1952–1954,* 9:64–67.

23. State Department, "Malik-Dulles Conversations," 3 April 1953, *FRUS, 1952–1954, Microfiche Supplement, Memoranda of the Conversations of the Secretary of State,* item 98.

24. State Department memorandum of conversation, 17 May 1953, *FRUS, 1952–1954,* 9:77.

25. Chargé John Emmerson (Beirut) telegram to State Department, 11 October 1955, and State Department telegram to Emmerson, 28 October 1955, *FRUS, 1955–1957,* 13:177–78.

26. JCS 2099/261, "Request from the Government of London for the Sale of Military Equipment and Services," 8 May 1956, *FRUS, 1955–1957,* 13:188–91.

27. Radford to Secretary of Defense Charles Wilson, 23 May 1956, *FRUS, 1955–1957,* 13:191, note 8.

28. State Department telegram to Ambassador Donald Heath (Beirut), 25 May 1956, *FRUS, 1955–1957,* 13:191–92.

29. Heath telegram to State Department, 20 November 1956, quoted in editorial note 129, *FRUS, 1955–1957,* 13:192.

30. On the origins of the Eisenhower Doctrine, see Paterson, *Meeting the Communist Threat,* 177–83, and Brands, *Specter of Neutralism,* 282–89.

31. For the Syrian reaction, see Ambassador James Moose telegram to State Department, 11 January 1957, *FRUS, 1955–1957,* 13:609–10.

32. Heath telegram to State Department, 13 January 1957, *FRUS, 1955–1957,* 13:196–97.

33. Richards telegrams to State Department, 15 and 16 March 1957, *FRUS, 1955–1957,* 13:208–11.

34. David Atlee Phillips, *The Night Watch: 25 Years of Peculiar Service* (New York, 1977), 73.

35. Miles Copeland, *The Game of Nations: The Amorality of Power Politics* (New York, 1969), 226–27; Wilbur Crane Eveland, *Ropes of Sand: America's Failure in the Middle East* (New York, 1980), 248. See also William Blum, *The CIA, a Forgotten History: US Global Interventions since World War 2* (London, 1986), 103–7.

36. Minutes of the 319th National Security Council Meeting, 11 April 1957, *FRUS, 1955–1957,* 13:212.

37. Eveland, *Ropes of Sand,* 250.

38. *Middle East Journal* 11 (Summer 1957): 300. Richard Parker, who manned the State Department's operations center during the July 1958 crisis in Lebanon, confirmed long afterward that the CIA had helped precipitate the political upheaval in Beirut by encouraging Chamoun to "rig the election the previous year [i.e., 1957] in a scandalous way." Richard Parker Oral History Interview, Foreign Service Oral History Project, Georgetown University, Washington, DC.

39. OCB, "Operations Plan for the Lebanon," 31 July 1957, *FRUS, 1955–1957,* 13:213–16.

40. Sam Pope Brewer Diary, 31 August 1957, Sam Pope Brewer Papers, box 24, Wisconsin State Historical Society, Madison, WI.

41. William Rountree (NEA) to Dulles, 12 September 1957, *FRUS, 1955–1957,* 13:216–17.

42. State Department to Heath, 13 September 1957, *FRUS, 1955–1957,* 13:217–18; White House Staff Note #195, 19 September 1957, "Sept. 1957 Toner Notes," Ann Whitman Files, Dwight D. Eisenhower Diary Series, box 27, Dwight D. Eisenhower Library, Abilene, KS.

43. Hudson, *Precarious Republic,* 156–57; Helena Cobban, *The Making of Modern Lebanon* (Boulder, CO, 1985), 87; Alin, *Lebanon Crisis,* 57–59. Chamoun, on the other

hand, termed his critics "sore losers" who "cried scandal" and "dismissed the success of the government by pretending that the 1957 elections had been stolen," when in reality the "secret of the government's success" had been a Lebanese backlash against "Nasserite acts of terrorism." Camille Chamoun, *Crise au Moyen-Orient* (Paris, 1963), 383–85 (my translation).

44. State Department memorandum of conversation, 17 October 1957, *FRUS, 1955–1957,* 13:219–20.

45. State Department Staff Study, "United States Objectives and Policies with Respect to the Near East," 31 October 1957, *FRUS, 1955–1957,* 12:640–41.

46. Stephen Dorsey, U.S. coordinator for the Litani River irrigation project, quoted in Sam Pope Brewer Diary, 23 November 1957, Brewer Papers.

47. State Department, "Staff Study on NSC 5801," 16 January 1958, "NSC Policy Papers," Office of the Special Assistant for National Security Affairs (hereafter OSANSA), Eisenhower Library.

48. Ambassador Robert McClintock (Beirut) telegram to State Department, 30 January 1958, *FRUS, 1958–1960,* 11:8–9.

49. McClintock telegram to State Department, 9 January 1958, RG 59, 611.80/1-958; McClintock telegram to State Department, 16 January 1958, *FRUS, 1958–1960,* 11:3–5.

50. Edward Waggoner (NEA) to Stuart Rockwell (NEA), 17 January 1958; McClintock telegram to Department of State, 21 February 1958, *FRUS, 1958–1960,* 11:5–7, 10–13.

51. McClintock telegram to State Department, 5 March 1958, *FRUS, 1958–1960,* 11:14–16.

52. McClintock telegram to State Department, 20 March 1958, *FRUS, 1958–1960,* 11:18–19.

53. State Department telegram to McClintock, 18 March 1958, *FRUS, 1958–1960,* 11:17.

54. Cumming to Dulles, 15 April 1958, *FRUS, 1958–1960, Microfiche Supplement,* 11: item 11.

55. CIA, "Assessment of the Political Situation in Lebanon," 4 April 1958, quoted in Alin, *Lebanon Crisis,* 73–74; McClintock telegram to State Department, 25 April 1958, *FRUS, 1958–1960, Microfiche Supplement,* 11: item 19.

56. Dulles memorandum of conversation, 2 May 1958, *FRUS, 1958–1960,* 11:27–28.

57. McClintock telegram to State Department, 4 May 1958, *FRUS, 1958–1960,* 11:28–30.

58. McClintock telegrams to State Department, 11 May 1958, *FRUS, 1958–1960,* 11:35–38.

59. McClintock telegram to State Department, 12 May 1958, *FRUS, 1958–1960,* 11:40–41.

60. State Department memorandum of conversation, "Lebanese Crisis," 13 May 1958, *FRUS, 1958–1960,* 11:45–48; Andrew Goodpaster memorandum of conversation, 15 May 1958, Whitman File, Eisenhower Diary Series, box 33, "Staff Notes (2)—May 1958."

61. State Department telegram to McClintock, 13 May 1958, *FRUS, 1958–1960,* 11:49–50.

62. State Department telegram to McClintock, 10 June 1958, Whitman File, International Series, "Lebanon (2)"; State Department telegram to McClintock, 15 June 1958, *FRUS, 1958–1960*, 11:128–29.

63. Rountree quoted in State Department memorandum of conversation, "Situation in Lebanon," 9 June 1958, *FRUS, 1958–1960*, 11:104–6.

64. U.S. Embassy Beirut to State Department, 20 June 1958, *FRUS, 1958–1960*, 11:163, note 4.

65. Meo, *Lebanon, Improbable Nation,* 179–80; editorial note 66, *FRUS, 1958–1960*, 11:107–8.

66. Dulles phone call to Deputy Secretary of Defense Donald Quarles, 14 June 1958, *FRUS, 1958–1960*, 11:116–17.

67. State Department memorandum of conversation, "Lebanon," 15 June 1958, *FRUS, 1958–1960*, 11:133–37.

68. Dulles telegram to McClintock, 16 June 1958, *FRUS, 1958–1960*, 11:142.

69. Eisenhower to Paul Hoffman, 23 June 1958, Whitman File, Eisenhower Diary Series, box 33, "Staff Notes (2)—June 1958."

70. State Department memorandum of conversation, "The Situation in Lebanon," 23 June 1958, *FRUS, 1958–1960*, 11:171–75.

71. Dulles's remarks of 23 June, as quoted by Carl Marcy, chief counsel of the Senate Foreign Relations Committee, on 26 June 1958, in U.S. Senate, *Executive Sessions of the Senate Foreign Relations Committee (Historical Series)* (Washington, DC, 1975–1993), 10:475–78.

72. Dulles memorandum of conversation, 7 July 1958, *FRUS, 1958–1960*, 11:200–201; diary entry for 9 July 1958, in Cyrus R. Sulzberger, *The Last of the Giants* (New York, 1970), 492.

73. McClintock telegram to State Department, 10 July 1958, *FRUS, 1958–1960*, 11:204–5.

74. Chamoun, *Crise au Moyen-Orient,* 423–24, my translation.

75. McClintock telegrams to State Department, 14 July 1958, *FRUS, 1958–1960*, 11:207–8, 215–16.

76. Allen W. Dulles, "Briefing Notes," 14 July 1958, *CIA Research Reports: The Middle East 1946–1976,* microfilm edition, ed. Paul Kesaris (Frederick, MD, 1981), reel 1. Ironically, most of the Saudi warning has been excised from the version of this document published in 1993. See *FRUS, 1958–1960*, 12:308–11.

77. "Meeting re Iraq," 9:30 A.M., 14 July 1958, *FRUS, 1958–1960*, 11:209–11.

78. Robert Cutler, *No Time for Rest* (Boston, 1966), 362–63. Cutler served as Eisenower's special assistant for national security affairs during the 1958 crisis.

79. Goodpaster memorandum of conversation, 10:50 A.M., 14 July 1958, *FRUS, 1958–1960*, 11:211–15.

80. State Department memorandum of conversation, "United States Military Intervention in Lebanon," 14 July 1958, RG 59, 783A.00/7–1458.

81. Goodpaster memorandum of conversation, 2:35 P.M., 14 July 1958, *FRUS, 1958–1960*, 11:218–26.

82. Assistant Secretary of Defense John Irwin to Deputy Undersecretary of State Robert Murphy, 6 February 1958, *FRUS, 1958–1960*, 11:9–10.

83. E. M. Rose (Eastern Department), "Lebanon," 9 May 1958, Foreign Office General Political Correspondence, Record Class FO 371, 134156, Public Record Office,

Kew, England (hereafter FO 371 with filing informat:∘n); JCS 2293/1, "Review of Actions Related to U.S. Military Intervention in Lebanon (U)," 23 October 1958, *Declassified Documents Reference Service 1983,* 2324.

84. Rountree to Dulles, 17 June 1958, *FRUS, 1958–1960,* 11:150–52.

85. "Conversation between the President and Prime Minister," 10:30 P.M., 14 July 1958, FO 371, 134159. For the White House version of the conversation, which also contains the reference to Pandora's box, see *FRUS, 1958–1960,* 11:231–34.

86. Goodpaster memorandum of conversation, 9:00 A.M., 15 July 1958, *FRUS, 1958–1960,* 11:244–45.

87. McClintock telegram to State Department, 15 July 1958, and McClintock telegram to CINCNELM, 15 July 1958, *FRUS, 1958–1960,* 11:247–49.

88. Charles W. Thayer, *Diplomat* (New York, 1959), 31–34; Robert McClintock, *The Meaning of Limited War* (New York, 1967), 108–10.

89. For the background to the 1958 crisis in Jordan, see Uriel Dann, *King Hussein and the Challenge of Arab Radicalism, 1955–1967* (New York, 1989), 78–95; Michael B. Oren, "The Test of Suez: Israel and the Middle East Crisis of 1958," *Studies in Zionism* 12, no. 1 (1991): 55–83; and Ritchie Ovendale, "Great Britain and the Anglo-American Invasion of Jordan and Lebanon in 1958," *International History Review* 16 (May 1994): 285–90.

90. Chargé Paul Mason (Amman) telegram to Foreign Office, 15 July 1958, Record Class PREM 11, folder 2380, Records of the Prime Minister's Office, PRO (hereafter PREM 11 with folder number); Chargé Thomas Wright (Amman) telegram to State Department, 15 July 1958, *FRUS, 1958–1960,* 11:302–3.

91. Chargé Thomas Wright (Amman) telegram to State Department, 16 July 1958, *FRUS, 1958–1960,* 11:312–14.

92. Macmillan quoted in James Lunt, *Hussein of Jordan: Searching for a Just and Lasting Peace* (New York, 1989), 50–51.

93. Lloyd telegram to Macmillan, 16 July 1958, PREM 11, folder 2380; Dulles-Macmillan telephone conversation, 16 July 1958, and State Department memorandum of conversation, 17 July 1958, *FRUS, 1958–1960,* 11:316, 317–18.

94. Ovendale, "Britain and the Anglo-American Invasion of Jordan," 292–98.

95. Lloyd telegram to Macmillan, 17 July 1958, PREM 11, folder 2380; State Department memorandum of conversation, 17 July 1958, *FRUS, 1958–1960* (Washington, DC, 1993), 12:776–78.

96. Foreign Office Levant Department, "Review of Middle East Problems Bearing upon the Supply of Oil to the Free World," 10 May 1957, FO 371, 127757.

97. Minute by Donald Riches (Levant Department), 5 June 1958, FO 371, 133789.

98. Eisenhower telegram to Macmillan, 18 July 1958, *FRUS, 1958–1960,* 11:330–31.

99. Lloyd memorandum of conversation, 19 July 1958, FO 371, 133823.

100. Minutes of the 373rd NSC Meeting, 24 July 1958, Whitman File, NSC Series.

101. Chargé Talcott Seelye (Kuwait) telegram to State Department, 3 August 1958, *FRUS, 1958–1960,* 12:778–80.

102. Selwyn Lloyd, "Kuwait: International Relations," 4 November 1958, Cabinet Papers, Record Class CAB 129/95, PRO.

103. The Morse, Kennedy, and Humphrey remarks are in "Situation in the Middle East," 15 July 1958, in U.S. Senate, *Executive Sessions,* 10:506–7.

104. Fulbright's and Morse's comments are in "The Situation in the Middle East," 15 July 1958, in U.S. Senate, *Executive Sessions,* 10:510–11.

105. Remarks of Humphrey, Morse, Fulbright, and Herter of 16 July 1958 are all in U.S. Senate, *Executive Sessions,* 10:527, 532–34, 539, 543.

106. SNIE 30-2-58, "The Middle East Crisis," 22 July 1958, *FRUS, 1958–1960,* 12:87–93.

107. Eisenhower to George M. Humphrey, 22 July 1958, *FRUS, 1958–1960,* 11:365.

108. Kennedy's and Mansfield's remarks of 16 July 1958 are in U.S. Senate, *Executive Sessions,* 10:526–27, 550–51.

109. McClintock to State Department, 31 July 1958, State Department memorandum of conversation, 16 August 1958, and editorial note 357, *FRUS, 1958–1960,* 11:415–18, 481–85, 615.

110. Eisenhower, *Waging Peace,* 288–89; Ovendale, "Invasion of Jordan," 300–302.

111. State Department memorandum of conversation, "Middle East," 22 March 1959, *FRUS, 1958–1960,* 12:218.

The Caribbean Triangle: Betancourt, Castro, and Trujillo and U.S. Foreign Policy, 1958–1963

STEPHEN G. RABE

For historians of U.S. foreign relations, it is a revealing statement from a quotable president. As recounted by Arthur M. Schlesinger, Jr., in *A Thousand Days,* President John F. Kennedy on 7 June 1961 listed U.S. policy options for the Dominican Republic in the immediate aftermath of the assassination of dictator Rafael Trujillo. Kennedy said, "There are three possibilities in descending order of preference: a decent democratic regime, a continuation of the Trujillo regime, or a Castro regime. We ought to aim at the first, but we really can't renounce the second until we are sure that we can avoid the third."[1] In Schlesinger's judgment, Kennedy's attitude represented a notable example of his administration's enlightened anticommunism.

Beyond serving as testimony to presidential wisdom, Kennedy's statement can be used as a reliable guide for analyzing the Latin American policy of the United States. Throughout the twentieth century, the United States consistently attempted to exclude extracontinental powers from the Western Hemisphere and to maintain its political and economic hegemony in the region. Stable, orderly regimes would protect U.S. interests, for they removed a temptation for foreigners to intervene and fostered a healthy business climate. U.S. officials professed that security, prosperity, and democracy were intertwined and that decent, democratic regimes would produce the good life for all hemispheric neighbors. But promoting elections, popular participation, and respect for civil and human rights has been subordinate to the goal of preserving peace and order in Latin America. During the intense years of the Cold War, U.S. policies toward democrats, like Rómulo Betancourt, and dictators, like Trujillo and his henchmen, hinged, as President Kennedy confessed, on the tactical question of which type of government

48

and leader would be most effective in thwarting Fidel Castro. Indeed, between 1958 and 1963, U.S. officials took uncommon measures in waging the Cold War because they judged that communism in the Western Hemisphere imperiled the United States, impeded the U.S. ability to act elsewhere, and threatened to become a divisive domestic issue.

In the mid-1950s, neither democracy nor decency characterized governments throughout Latin America. Dictators like Trujillo, Fulgencio Batista of Cuba, and Marcos Pérez Jiménez of Venezuela controlled thirteen of the twenty Latin American republics. The Eisenhower administration found no fault with these tyrants, regarding them as dependable Cold War allies. The dictators vigorously backed the United States in international forums, cooperated militarily, and welcomed U.S. businessmen. President Dwight D. Eisenhower once observed to National Security Council (NSC) members that "in the long run the United States must back democracies."[2] But prior to 1959, the president avoided raising human rights issues with any dictator. In fact, he conferred the Legion of Merit, the nation's highest award for foreign personages, on Pérez Jiménez.

The Eisenhower administration's smug confidence in dictators was abruptly broken in 1958. Latin American regimes began to disintegrate in the late 1950s. The dictators failed to produce the stability and economic growth that they had promised. Latin Americans also tired of the rampant repression and corruption that characterized military rule. The dictators were replaced by leaders, such as Argentina's Arturo Frondizi, whose political base was the urban middle sections and whose programs included land reform, popular education, social services, and constitutionalism.

U.S. officials neither anticipated the mass uprisings that unseated dictators nor understood the contempt in which Latin Americans held U.S. policy. In December 1957, a month before Pérez Jiménez's overthrow, the embassy in Caracas predicted that the military dictator would hold power, for "in the absence of democratic traditions, the majority of Venezuelans have developed what appears to be an apathetic or acquiescent attitude toward their authoritarian government."[3] Venezuelans, however, proved to be anything but apathetic when, in May 1958, Vice President Richard M. Nixon reached Caracas to conclude his troubled tour of South America. Nixon had been harassed by law students in Montevideo and stoned by university students in Lima, and now he was assaulted by a mob in Caracas. The demonstrators blamed the United States for the region's social ills, charging the Eisenhower administration with supporting repressive regimes and denying Latin America economic assistance.

The administration reflexively blamed Communists for the uprisings.

Reporting to the cabinet, Nixon "emphasized that Communist inspiration was evident from the similarity of placards, slogans, and techniques." Secretary of State John Foster Dulles agreed that the Soviet Union had cleverly infiltrated mass political movements in Latin America. But CIA Director Allen W. Dulles challenged his brother's views, arguing that turmoil in Latin America transcended any possible political manipulation.[4]

Despite the CIA's findings, U.S. officials dreaded Latin America's democratic future. As Nixon told the NSC, the United States would normally be pleased about the expansion of democracy, but the phenomenon was occurring "in those Latin American countries which are completely lacking in political maturity." Nixon lamented that the dictators were being replaced not by upper-class, wealthy politicians of the past but by men, like Frondizi, who "were oriented in the direction of Marxist thinking" and who were "naive about the nature and threat of communism." The secretary of state also yearned for the old political order. Both the Middle East and Latin America were witnessing a swing away from traditional rulers and kings "in favor of a kind of dictatorship of the proletariat, which was represented by a Nasser or Sukarno, with their mass appeal."[5]

These dire predictions did not initially generate a comprehensive review of U.S. policy in Latin America. President Eisenhower responded to the Nixon/Dulles colloquy by observing that much of the world equated the term *capitalism* with *imperialism* and concluding that therefore "we should try to coin a new phrase to represent our own modern brand of capitalism." The administration's other initiatives were similarly superficial. Eisenhower and Nixon publicly stated that the United States preferred constitutional regimes, and the administration's new NSC statement on Latin America called for giving "special encouragement" to representative governments. The administration reminded itself, however, to be alert to the communists' tactic of masquerading their subversive goals by allying themselves with nationalistic and progressive parties.[6]

The administration adhered to those guidelines in its relations with Venezuela. In August 1958, President Eisenhower denounced authoritarian rule in welcoming the new Venezuelan ambassador to Washington. But the State Department coupled that welcome with warnings to the ruling junta not to legalize the Venezuelan Communist Party. The junta, led by Admiral Wolfgang Larrazábal, ignored those warnings because Venezuelans believed a united civilian front would help keep the military in the barracks. With candidates, including Larrazábal, actually accepting the support of communists during the presidential campaign, the department decided that the reform-minded but anticommunist Rómulo Betancourt must win. Through former Assistant Secretary of State Adolf Berle, who knew Betancourt well, the department offered the Venezuelan aid, including presumably covert assistance. A confident Betancourt apparently rejected the offer, won a decisive electoral victory, and took office in early 1959.[7]

Anticommunism also continued to be the predominant U.S. concern with Rafael Trujillo, although State Department officials had become exasperated with the dictator's brutality. In 1956 the dictator's henchmen kidnapped in New York City and then murdered Jesús de Galíndez, a Spanish citizen and Columbia University scholar who had written a scathing indictment of Trujillo. Trujillo's men then executed Charles Murphy, an aviator from Oregon who had piloted the plane that took de Galíndez from New York to the Dominican Republic. The murders gained national attention through the persistent efforts of Oregon congressman Charles Porter.[8]

Responding to public outrage, the State Department reluctantly investigated the murders. In one diplomat's view, the facts of the case demonstrated that the Dominican Republic's conduct was "below the level of recognized civilian nations, certainly not much above that of the communists." Nonetheless, the administration wanted amicable relations with a dictator who unfailingly backed U.S. foreign policies. In November 1958, Secretary Dulles extended an olive branch, asking the Dominican foreign minister to remind Trujillo that the United States appreciated the Dominican Republic's anticommunist leadership in the hemisphere.[9]

In 1958 officials focused neither on Venezuela nor on the Dominican Republic but on the disintegration of the Batista regime and the growing power of the 26th of July Movement led by Fidel Castro. The Eisenhower administration contested Castro and his movement because it believed that the revolutionaries threatened the substantial U.S. economic interests in Cuba and because it worried that communists had infiltrated the movement. Despite these fears, the administration made only ineffectual moves to deprive Castro of victory. In the aftermath of the Nixon trip and the public criticism of past support for dictators, the administration could hardly embrace its man in Havana. It hoped instead that it could find a "middle way" between Batista and Castro by persuading the dictator to step aside and schedule an election. But Batista stubbornly resisted all entreaties. In any case, U.S. officials misjudged the deterioration in Batista's position and the appeal of the Castro movement, with Ambassador Earl Smith repeatedly informing Washington that Castro lacked widespread popular support. As late as 4:00 P.M. on 31 December 1958, just hours before Batista fled the island, administration officials still thought they had time to find an alternative to Castro.[10]

Rafael Trujillo also dreaded Castro's triumph. In late 1958 he urged the United States to lift its arms embargo and bolster the Batista regime in order to prevent the spread of international communism. Trujillo actually shipped small arms to Cuba, and, as he had done with Pérez Jiménez, initially granted political exile to Batista. The Dominican predicted that Castro would soon attack him. On 14 June 1959, Dominican exiles, led by Enrique Jiménez Moya, landed in the Dominican Republic. Trujillo's forces routed the invaders. The exiles had been trained and equipped in Cuba, and their leader had served as an officer in the 26th of July Movement. Castro later confessed that he supported the invasion because of his friendship with Jiménez Moya and his hatred of Trujillo. Castro also knew that Trujillo armed Cuban counterrevolutionary forces.[11]

Rómulo Betancourt also plotted against Trujillo, materially supporting Dominican exiles. President Betancourt was determined to overthrow his old enemy. During the 1945–48 period, when Venezuela first experimented with democracy, Betancourt and Trujillo had feuded. Rightist Venezuelans organized in the Dominican Republic, and Dominican exiles sought haven in Venezuela. Trujillo celebrated the military *golpe de estado* of 1948 and then collaborated with Pérez Jiménez. After January 1958, Trujillo harbored right-wing Venezuelan exiles, ordered his radio stations to beam personal attacks on Betancourt, and probably authorized the planting of bombs in Caracas. In turn, Venezuela severed relations with the Dominican Republic. Venezuelans also participated in the June 1959 invasion of the Dominican Republic.[12]

Betancourt's anti-Trujillista views also reflected his political principles. As author of the Betancourt doctrine, the Venezuelan argued that it was "nonsensical" to denounce totalitarian regimes in Asia or Europe and tolerate despotic governments in the Western Hemisphere. He called for the expulsion of dictatorial states from the Organization of American States (OAS).[13]

Turmoil in the traditional U.S. sphere of influence alarmed the Eisenhower administration. As Allen Dulles informed Secretary of State Christian Herter, the United States had become associated "in the public mind of Latin America with the extreme right, especially as the friend and supporter of the Dominican dictator Trujillo." Even moderate leftists had become estranged, creating "a situation which abets the cause of those who want to bring the Caribbean political scene under Communist domination." Despite Dulles's warning, the administration rejected the Betancourt doctrine and demanded a cease-fire in the Caribbean. Hemispheric neighbors should respect the non-intervention doctrine of the OAS charter. As Assistant Secretary of State R. Richard Rubottom told Latin American diplomats, "anarchy" would ensue if groups of "liberators" undertook "from bases in other countries to launch attacks aiming to oust violently the governments they dislike."[14]

The United States tried both to reassert its hegemony and to improve its public image at a meeting of foreign ministers held in Santiago, Chile, in August 1959. The ministers met to discuss the Dominican issue and turmoil throughout the Caribbean basin. Influential OAS members, like Argentina and Mexico, enthusiastically agreed with Secretary Herter's observation that "history has shown" that democracy could not be imposed upon a country by force. Most Latin Americans, opposed to compromising the nonintervention principle, rejected the Betancourt doctrine and declined to break relations with the Dominican Republic. Herter agreed, however, to extend the Venezuelans a fig leaf to cover their diplomatic defeat. The Peace Committee, an inter-American body, would now have the power to initiate investigations of a member nation's behavior. But it would not have the power to enter the Dominican Republic without Trujillo's consent. Herter hoped that the inter-American community would hereafter focus less on Trujillo and more on Castro.[15]

The looming confrontation with Castro's Cuba, however, would force the United States to choose sides in the war between Betancourt and Trujillo. By October/November 1959 the Eisenhower administration had concluded that it could no longer abide the Castro regime. The Cuban had mocked U.S. power. He had indulged in anti-U.S. propaganda, nationalized U.S. property, proclaimed Cuba's neutralism, and worked with Cuban Communists. Unchecked, Castro would, by example, undermine the U.S. position in Latin America and weaken U.S. credibility in the world. Covert actions aimed at harming Cuba began in late 1959 and were made coherent and systematic on 17 March 1960, when President Eisenhower approved a comprehensive program to overthrow Castro.[16]

The Eisenhower administration desperately wanted regional allies in its war against Castro and now looked to Rómulo Betancourt and his doctrine. Although the administration had favored his election in 1958, it had not embraced Betancourt, for he was an economic nationalist who raised taxes on U.S. oil companies, which had over $2 billion invested in the country. Moreover, he had a suspect political past. As a youth, he had flirted with political radicalism, and in the mid-1950s he had published a scathing indictment of Pérez Jiménez and the oil companies. Such views earned Betancourt the disdain of some U.S. officials. In mid-1960, Vice President Nixon labeled Betancourt an "opportunist" who accepted the support of the pro-Castroite "left." Nixon predicted that "Betancourt would take his present line until he got his way with respect to Trujillo but he would not stay with us on Castro."[17]

Nixon was wrong; President Betancourt was a stout anticommunist. In front of U.S. diplomats, he laughed at his youthful infatuation with communism, and he ridiculed Juan José Arévalo, the former president of Guatemala, for equating anti-U.S. sentiment with anti-imperialism. He pledged that communists would not have a role in his government and that Venezuela would cooperate with the United States.[18] Ten years of exile had been a harsh and bitter experience for Betancourt. Hoping to appease Venezuela's entrenched interest groups, Betancourt now favored an evolutionary approach to reform.

Betancourt's views on Fidel Castro also caught the administration's attention. During his triumphant tour of Venezuela in January 1959, Castro met with Betancourt and startled the president by requesting a $300 million loan and oil at discount prices. Betancourt initially characterized Castro as young and inexperienced. But his attitude hardened when Castro began to criticize Latin Americans who were not revolutionaries. In March 1959, for example, Castro insulted President José Figueres of Costa Rica, Betancourt's friend and mentor, at a rally in Havana. Thereafter, Castro publicly questioned Venezuela's reformist path. Betancourt also understood that young political radicals, who fomented violent antigovernment demonstrations in Caracas in late 1960, drew inspiration from the Cuban revolution.[19]

In the name of anti-Castroism, the State Department began to woo Betancourt. In August 1959 it authorized the Justice Department to arrest Pérez Jiménez, who was now hiding out in Miami, and initiate extradition proceedings against the bearer of the Legion of Merit. It promised Venezuela economic and technical assistance. The department also made certain that attacks on Betancourt, broadcast on Cuban radio, reached his ears. And, in April 1960, it agreed that the Peace Committee should investigate Trujillo's role in the latest right-wing assault on the Venezuelan government.[20]

On 28 April 1960, the State Department formally requested Betancourt's support. The United States was "interested" in Betancourt's declaration "that he was prepared to take the lead on Cuba, which he was certain most other Latin Americans would quickly join, if the Trujillo problem was resolved with United States cooperation." The United States, however, worried that if Trujillo fell, Castroite elements might move into the power vacuum. Betancourt responded by reiterating that his first concern was Trujillo and that he doubted communist strength in the Dominican Republic. Venezuelan and U.S. officials thereafter exchanged ideas, with U.S. diplomats counseling patience. But Assistant Secretary Rubottom also observed on 11 May 1960 that "Trujillo's days are numbered."[21]

The United States had in fact already turned against the Dominican dictator. In November 1959, the same month that the Eisenhower administration had decided that constructive relations were over with Castro, Herter and Rubottom agreed that the United States would have to facilitate the post-Trujillo era. They reasoned from analogy. A tyrant in a sugar-producing island had again "liquidated and enfeebled" moderate political opponents and polarized the political milieu, thereby providing an opportunity for radicals. The United States would have to learn the lessons of history to prevent "a domino effect of Castro-like governments" throughout the Caribbean. In January 1960, the State Department developed a paper, approved in April by Eisenhower, that called for military intervention "to prevent a Castro-type government or one sympathetic to Castro."[22] But to forestall military action, the United States would persuade Trujillo to leave and would cultivate political moderates in the Dominican Republic.

The administration first tried to reason with Trujillo. During the first months of 1960, emissaries journeyed to Ciudad Trujillo to discuss with Trujillo prospects for his stepping down or permitting a free election. A comfortable exile, perhaps in Portugal or Morocco, with a "trust fund" was mentioned. But the tough old dictator resisted all blandishments, boasting that "I'll never go out of here unless I go on a stretcher."[23]

The plan to encourage a Dominican opposition movement also fell apart. In January 1960, alleging an assassination conspiracy, Trujillo ordered a roundup of prominent businessmen and professionals. Henry Dearborn, deputy chief of the U.S. mission, described for Washington the Trujillo system as "an outrage abounding in trumped-up charges, arbitrary arrests, search without warrant, and inhumane treatment of prisoners." Dearborn put the "ultimate question" to his superiors: "whether we need Trujillo's help against international communism sufficiently to support a regime characterized by such unsavory practices."[24]

Although Dearborn's colleagues in Washington agreed with him, one State Department official rejected Dearborn's point. John C. Hill, the department's liaison with the CIA, made a fact-finding mission to the Dominican Republic, concluding that it was impractical to attack Trujillo. Democratic elements were not yet strong enough to prevent communism in the post-Trujillo era. Anticipating President Kennedy's formula, Hill asserted that anticommunism had a higher priority than democracy and that "we must be prepared to jump solidly on the 'stop Castro' animal." It was an "ugly" choice, but the wrong choice would endanger national security and expose the department to virulent public criticism. Vice President Nixon seconded Hill's assessment, instructing the NSC that the primary U.S. interest in the Dominican Republic was to prevent pro-Castro groups from seizing power.[25]

Predictions of Castroism in the Dominican Republic flowed from fears and dubious historical analogies. An April 1960 National Intelligence Estimate dismissed the notion that Trujillo would be overthrown by a "Castro-like invasion or revolution," suggesting only that if turmoil ensued after the demise of Trujillo, Castro might incite a revolution and be the "ultimate victor." But intelligence analysts also understood that Castro no longer assisted exile movements or supported the Betancourt doctrine. Castro now realized that the nonintervention principles of the OAS would help protect the Cuban revolution. He further recognized that the U.S. preoccupation with Trujillo was evidence "that the North American government was maneuvering against the revolution" and "trying to establish a procedure which at any time could be turned against us."[26]

Castro reasoned well. As State Department officers noted, "the political damage resulting from a U.S. involvement in Cuba could be minimized by our first or simultaneously helping overthrow a hated dictator." Undersecretary of State C. Douglas Dillon added that "if Trujillo could be removed from power in the Dominican Republic, while pro-Castro elements were prevented from seizing power in that country, our anti-Castro campaign throughout Latin America would receive a great boost." Thus, in June 1960 the administration decided to pursue vigorous, even violent, measures to overthrow Trujillo. It accepted the Peace Committee's 3 June 1960 denunciation of Trujillo, noting that it might assist "our subsequent efforts to have the Peace Committee face up similarly to the Cuban problem." And in June it authorized a CIA proposal to make Henry Dearborn a "communications link" with Dominican dissidents who vowed to assassinate Trujillo. This authorization came shortly after President Eisenhower informed aides that he wanted Castro and Trujillo "sawed off." Thereafter, the CIA developed plans to transfer sniper rifles with telescopic sights to Dominicans.[27]

Even as the administration hatched assassination plots against both Castro and Trujillo, the Dominican counterattacked. On 24 June 1960 his agents detonated a bomb planted near President Betancourt's passing automobile; Betancourt survived, but his hands were severely burned. Trujillo also tried to undermine U.S. policy within the United States. His fifty-four consulates took out advertisements in newspapers and planted stories with friendly journalists, reminding readers that Trujillo was a staunch anticommunist. Further, he bribed U.S. officials, including congressmen who sat on committees that allocated a sugar quota to the Dominican Republic.[28] The Trujillo family controlled the island's sugar industry.

Trujillo's attack on Betancourt provided the administration with another opportunity to attack Castro. In August 1960, foreign ministers met in San

José, Costa Rica, to consider Trujillo's aggression against Venezuela. Reversing the stand he took at Santiago in 1959, Secretary of State Herter embraced the Betancourt doctrine, proposing that the OAS take control of the political machinery of the Dominican Republic, oversee the end of the Trujillo tyranny, establish political parties, and conduct a free election. As Herter explained to President Eisenhower, his plan had dual objectives. A peaceful transition of power would avoid "a revolution which might well produce a communist or Castro-type government in Santo Domingo"; further, "if we prove successful in this, a very useful precedent will have been set for possible later action when the Cuban matter is before us." Eisenhower agreed, observing that "until Trujillo is eliminated we cannot get our Latin American friends to reach a proper level of indignation in dealing with Castro."[29]

Herter's call for a renunciation of the sacred nonintervention principle shocked Latin Americans and never came to a vote. OAS members condemned the Dominican Republic for its aggression but desisted from casting judgment on the internal character of the Trujillo regime. The OAS accordingly voted to break diplomatic relations with Trujillo and impose an arms embargo.[30]

Herter also failed to attain his second objective. OAS foreign ministers declined to draw parallels between Trujillo's aggression and Castro's domestic and international policies. The ministers limited themselves to passing a bloodless resolution opposing extracontinental intervention in the hemisphere. A crestfallen Eisenhower ordered Herter not to press "weak-kneed" Latin Americans. He worried about the Cold War consequences of dividing the OAS.[31]

For the rest of 1960 the administration oscillated between various fronts in its anti-Trujillo campaign. Following the San José conclave, it broke relations with the Dominican Republic, but it maintained three consulates on the island in order to preserve bases for CIA agents. The president also imposed punitive excise taxes on imports of Dominican sugar. The president did not want Trujillo to reap a sugar windfall in the aftermath of his July 1960 decision to cut the importation of Cuban sugar. Aware that Trujillo bribed key legislators, Eisenhower acted on his own authority because the agricultural committees refused to cut the Dominican Republic's sugar quota.[32]

The CIA continued to bargain with potential assassins, but with negligible results. The Dominicans altered their requests for weapons and wavered in their determination. Their caution was justified, for in August Trujillo's security forces smashed an impending *golpe*. The administration also had second thoughts. In October 1960 Undersecretary Dillon informed the president that the United States was not taking "concrete moves" against Trujillo because it feared that his downfall would lead to "an individual of the Castro stripe in power." The administration again unsuccessfully attempted to persuade Trujillo to participate in a peaceful transition of power. Trujillo had seemingly softened his position when he appointed prominent scholar Joaquín Balaguer as president. But Henry Dearborn, who was now consul general and de facto CIA chief of station, warned Washington not to be deceived, for there was no indication that the regime planned "to abolish arbitrary arrests, prison tortures, or reprisals against its political opposition." Trujillo would continue "his political domination whether he is president or dogcatcher." Dearborn concluded: "If I were a Dominican, I would favor destroying Trujillo as the first necessary step in the salvation of my country."[33]

Such sentiments combined with renewed Venezuelan demands for action hardened U.S. resolve. President Betancourt was frustrated that his enemy lived and still meddled in Venezuela. In December 1960 he called for another OAS probe into Trujillo's conduct. He assured U.S. diplomats that he was "fully aware" of the Castro problem, that he believed Castro was in the Soviet orbit, and that Cuba inspired leftist riots in his country. And he began to criticize Castro in public addresses. But as a matter of personal dignity, he refused U.S. requests presented in "the strongest possible terms" to link Trujillo and Castro in a renewed OAS investigation. He repeated his pledge, however, to "head the movement of Latin American countries to dispose of the Castro problem once effective actions were taken against Trujillo." Betancourt further promised to dispatch troops to assist a provisional Dominican government to prevent communism.[34]

In its last days, the Eisenhower administration again accepted Betancourt's bargain, reasoning that the Venezuelan was the "best bet" to achieve U.S. goals in the region. Betancourt had publicly broken with Castro, battled leftist opponents, and embraced international capitalism. He simply believed that foreign oil companies should shoulder an appropriate tax burden. By the end of 1960 the administration had repudiated the Dulles/Nixon thesis that Latin American democrats threatened U.S. interests. President Eisenhower caught the irony in this new approach; he confided to aides that "it was strange that he used to think of Betancourt as a leftist and now he was beginning to look like a rightist in relation to pro-Castro, pro-Communist attacks against him."[35]

While embracing Betancourt, the Eisenhower administration launched its final assaults on Castro and Trujillo. It dramatically increased the size and firepower of the Cuban exile army training in Guatemala, and it pressed President-elect Kennedy to do "whatever is necessary" to overthrow Castro.

It also broke diplomatic relations with Cuba on 3 January 1961, and it recommended that the new administration invoke the Trading with the Enemy
Act. As for Trujillo, the administration banned the export of petroleum products, trucks, and truck parts to the Dominican Republic. The administration
wanted not only to fulfill Betancourt's request for additional economic pressure but also to mollify him. The United States would be legally obligated to
purchase over two hundred thousand tons of Dominican sugar during the
first three months of 1961.[36]

The administration also heeded the warning of intelligence analysts who
predicted in late 1960 that "the days of his [Trujillo's] regime appear numbered," with assassination "an increasing possibility." But they warned that
"the tide is now running against the United States and the longer the current impasse continues, the more unfavorable to U.S. interests the outcome is
likely to be when the Dominican pressure cooker finally explodes." The administration accordingly revived its covert program, with Richard M. Bissell,
Jr., the CIA's deputy director of plans, speaking on 29 December of a "decisive
stroke against Trujillo himself." Recalling the hope "to move against Trujillo
and Castro simultaneously," President Eisenhower, on 3 January 1961, ordered his national security advisers "to do as much as we can and quickly
about Trujillo." Nine days later, the 5412 Committee (the special group that
oversaw covert activities) ruled that the CIA could send small arms to Dominican dissidents. In the first months of 1961, Consul General Dearborn,
through an intermediary, passed pistols and carbines to Dominicans.[37]

President John F. Kennedy pursued Eisenhower's policies on all three Caribbean fronts. He authorized Eisenhower's invasion plan, which culminated
in the Bay of Pigs debacle of 17–19 April 1961. Thereafter, the administration
developed its own covert campaign of terrorism and sabotage—Operation
Mongoose—against Cuba. And the CIA continued to hatch anti-Castro assassination schemes. The Kennedy administration shared its predecessor's conviction that communism in the Western Hemisphere imperiled the United
States. As Attorney General Robert F. Kennedy put it to his brother on 19 April
1961, Castro's triumph at the Bay of Pigs would lead him to be "more bombas-
tic" and "more closely tied to communism." Something "forceful and determined" had to be done because "our long-range foreign policy objectives in
Cuba are tied to survival."[38]

The Kennedy administration also developed an overt anti-Castro strategy, the Alliance for Progress. Through a massive infusion of public and
private capital—ultimately $20 billion—the United States would build de-
cent, democratic, and anticommunist Latin American societies. In his March
1961 speech announcing the alliance, the president also linked Castro and

Trujillo, expressing a "special friendship to the people of Cuba and the Dominican Republic—and the hope that they will soon rejoin the society of free
men, uniting with us in our common effort."[39]

Rómulo Betancourt's Venezuela served as the model for Latin America's
democratic development. According to Kennedy's advisers, the future of
Latin America "lay between the Castro road and the Betancourt road." The
United States needed to embrace the middle-class reformers that Dulles and
Nixon had mocked in order to forestall radical change. Venezuela was the
first Latin American country that President Kennedy visited. The United
States also helped Betancourt calm urban areas, where leftist organizers
flourished, by rushing an emergency package of $100 million in economic
assistance in early 1961. Between 1962 and 1965, the United States would
provide an additional $350 million in grants and credits.[40]

Although Betancourt effusively praised the Alliance for Progress and
President Kennedy, he continued to promote his doctrine and his anti-
Trujillista views. The Kennedy administration quickly understood how it
could enlist the Venezuelan in the war against Castro. In mid-February 1961,
the president and his national security team learned from the CIA about the
ongoing covert campaign against Trujillo and that the United States had
passed small arms and sabotage equipment to Dominican dissidents. But the
administration's first move against Trujillo was an overt one. President Kennedy requested that Congress deny the Dominican Republic any "windfall"
from Cuba's sugar quota for the last nine months of 1961. With unified
support from Republican leaders, who had conferred with Eisenhower and
Nixon, the administration managed in March 1961 to push legislation out of
the agricultural committees and through Congress.[41]

Castro's rout of the Bay of Pigs invaders caused the administration to
hesitate in taking the decisive step against Trujillo. In early April the CIA had
sent machine guns through diplomatic pouch to the U.S. consulate. But, on
25 April, CIA headquarters instructed Dearborn not to pass the machine
guns and to inform the dissidents that the United States was not presently
prepared to cope with the aftermath of an assassination. The CIA cable
reflected disorder within the administration. Robert Murphy, the former
undersecretary of state for political affairs, who visited with Trujillo in mid-
April, urged the administration to make peace with the dictator because he
had been a reliable ally and because the Dominican Republic was near Cuba.
NSC Adviser McGeorge Bundy, however, warned the president that a rap-
prochement with Trujillo would undermine the Alliance for Progress. Moreover, Trujillo had begun to collaborate with the enemy. Dominican radio
stations praised the Cuban revolution and attacked U.S. "imperialism." Tru-

jillo's henchmen secretly conferred with Cuban and Soviet authorities. Notably, Havana no longer denounced Trujillo.[42]

President Kennedy took command of Dominican policy. At an NSC meeting on 5 May 1961, he ruled that the United States should not initiate the overthrow of Trujillo before knowing what government would succeed him. He also ordered the U.S. military to be prepared to invade the Dominican Republic to prevent a communist takeover. The president's ruling left Dearborn incredulous. For a year the United States had been nurturing the effort to overthrow Trujillo; it was "too late to consider whether [the] United States would initiate [the] overthrow of Trujillo." Kennedy clarified U.S. policy for Dearborn. On 25 May, "in view of the reported imminence of an attempt to assassinate Trujillo," he approved a contingency plan that authorized Dearborn to assure friendly Dominicans that they could count on U.S. military support to consolidate their hold on a post-Trujillo government. If "unfriendly elements" seized power, Dearborn had the authority to urge pro-U.S. groups to declare themselves the provisional government and request help from the United States and the OAS. The president's final word, as expressed in a cable he helped write and sent on 29 May to Dearborn, was that the United States wanted to be associated with the removal of Trujillo so as to derive credit among Dominicans and Latin American liberals but that "we must not run the risk of U.S. association with political assassination."[43]

The next evening, 30 May 1961, members of the "action group" of the Dominican dissidents ambushed and assassinated Trujillo. The aged dictator, traveling only with his chauffeur, was on his way to see his twenty-year-old mistress. The assassins apparently had with them CIA-supplied weapons.[44]

President Kennedy was perhaps surprised by at least the timing of the attack. He was in Paris meeting with President Charles de Gaulle and preparing for his meeting with Soviet premier Nikita Khrushchev in Vienna. He ordered Rusk to stay behind in the United States for a day to survey the situation. Warships, loaded with twelve thousand combat-ready troops, patrolled sixty miles off the Dominican coastline. Consul General Dearborn reported that it was "highly unsafe" for him to maintain contact with the dissidents. He and CIA personnel were quickly recalled to Washington. The State Department, however, ordered them first to destroy all records concerning contacts with dissidents but not to destroy the president's last exculpatory cable of 29 May.[45]

Although Trujillo's death sparked a short celebration in Caracas, it did not terminate the Trujillo tyranny. Trujillo's security apparatus quickly captured or killed all but two of the conspirators. The dictator's two brothers, who controlled private armies, terrorized political opponents. Trujillo's vindictive son, Rafael Leonidas Trujillo, Jr., or "Ramfis," returned from Europe, took charge of the armed forces, and supervised the torture and execution of the conspirators.

Back from Vienna, President Kennedy reviewed the Dominican situation with aides in early June and listed his famous descending order of preferences. Attorney General Kennedy proposed that the administration give Ramfis a chance to fulfill his pledge to move the nation toward democracy. Henry Dearborn, now back in Washington, responded that such promises "were the same moves that Trujillo had always made without any intended impact on the structure of his regime." He added that capable democratic groups existed on the island. In his last report from the Dominican Republic, Dearborn had recommended driving the Trujillo family out with military force. Others reminded that "we would do ourselves great harm" if the United States acted without the support of Venezuela. Despite this advice, Kennedy decided that the United States should delay action and monitor events.[46] His fear of instability and communism overwhelmed his concern for the Alliance for Progress and Betancourt.

Over the next thirty months, U.S. Dominican policy reflected Kennedy's priorities. The State Department sent John Hill, its CIA liaison, to replace Dearborn as consul general. His objectives were first to prevent "Castro/communism" and then to help establish "a friendly government as democratic as possible." Joaquín Balaguer, who remained the nominal president, was informed in July 1961 that Hill had direct access to Kennedy. What Kennedy considered of "utmost importance" was that the government move toward democracy. But the president wanted Balaguer to know that he was specifically interested in the "progress of anti-Communist laws in [the] Dominican Congress, measures taken [to] exclude [the] return of Communist and Castroist exiles, and other actions taken [to] prevent infiltration and agitation by Communist-Castroist elements." The administration also assured Balaguer that the United States would lend military support to stop a "Castroist invasion" of his nation. Hill delivered the same message to Ramfis Trujillo in a series of cordial chats with the power behind the throne. This alarm about communism in the Dominican Republic again arose from analogy. U.S. intelligence analysts largely discounted the actual threat.[47]

In deciding to work with the younger Trujillo and Balaguer, the administration assumed that their government could last until May 1962, when elections were promised. In late August, President Kennedy decided that the United States would back Balaguer because he "is our only tool" and because the "anti-Communist liberals are not strong enough." The president wistfully hoped that a Nehru-like figure would emerge who could command popular support, tame the military, and carry out socioeconomic reform. But Kennedy would take no chances, warning aides, "We don't want another Cuba to come out of the Dominican Republic." He reportedly predicted that his first year in office would be successful if neither the Congo nor the Dominican Republic was lost to international communism. In the meantime, the United States would try to facilitate an orderly transfer of power by taking up the Eisenhower scheme of establishing a trust fund to entice the Trujillos into exile.[48]

Neither Venezuelans nor Dominicans, however, were inclined to be patient. The Venezuelans sharply rejected the Kennedy administration's proposal for the partial lifting of OAS sanctions. President Betancourt emphasized that the "ouster of all the Trujillos [was] essential to full democratization" in the Dominican Republic. Dominicans similarly demanded democracy and staged massive antigovernment demonstrations when an OAS inspection team arrived on the island in mid-September. Intelligence analysts now understood that the Trujillos' leaving the island had "become an obsession" for Dominicans. Dominican democrats were losing faith in the United States with a concomitant growth of "Castro-minded influence." If the Trujillos struck a *golpe,* it would only polarize the international and domestic political milieu. The journalist John Bartlow Martin, whom Kennedy sent on a fact-finding mission, concurred, reporting that a renewed Trujillo regime would destroy the middle class, thereby ensuring that the next revolution would be "proletarian and leftist."[49]

Confronted with the collapse of his evolutionary policy, Kennedy acted boldly. In October he dispatched State Department officer George McGhee to Ciudad Trujillo to tell the Trujillos that they must leave the island. When the family balked, Secretary Rusk warned on 18 November that the United States would not "remain idle" if the Trujillos tried to "reassert dictatorial domination." Eight U.S. warships loomed on the Dominican horizon. U.S. jets buzzed the capital's shoreline, and U.S. military attaches encouraged Dominican officers to desert the Trujillos. By 20 November, the Trujillo clan had fled into exile. Over the next months, the administration would threaten and cajole Dominicans into establishing an anticommunist coalition, the Council of State.[50] With U.S. and Venezuelan assistance, the council held an election and in February 1963 transferred power to the winner, Juan Bosch, an ally of Betancourt.

The ousting of the Trujillos bolstered the administration's anti-Castro campaign, for Betancourt fulfilled his pledges. He reportedly approved of the Bay of Pigs planning, although he declined to support the invasion publicly. But with the Trujillos gone, he openly espoused the U.S. cause. As

U.S. intelligence analysts noted, Betancourt's "position at home and abroad has been strengthened by recent developments in the Dominican Republic." In November 1961 he broke relations with Castro in protest over Cuban propaganda. He then spearheaded the campaign to exclude Cuba from the OAS system. During the October 1962 missile crisis, Venezuela stoutly supported the United States at the United Nations, and Betancourt assigned two destroyers to the naval blockade of Cuba. Further, Betancourt allegedly exchanged ideas with U.S. officials on assassinating Castro.[51]

In 1963 the Venezuelan president intensified his anti-Castro crusade. In Washington for a state visit, Betancourt called for constant and unremitting actions against Cuba "to encircle it, to cut it off without ceasing and failing." President Kennedy responded by writing to the CIA that "it is obvious that the Communists in Venezuela support Castro. Do we have any information that could be presented in a public forum, such as the OAS, that would indicate that the link between the anti-Betancourt terrorists and Castro is direct."[52] That evidence surfaced on a Venezuelan beach in 1963 when Venezuela claimed that it had discovered a small cache of Cuban arms. These arms were allegedly left for leftist insurgents determined to disrupt the November 1963 presidential election.

The Cuban intervention surprised intelligence analysts in Washington, for Castro had not been exporting arms to insurgent groups. Venezuela had previously complained about arms smuggling but conceded that surplus U.S. and Western European arms came from Panama, not communist countries.[53] In fact, some have subsequently questioned the validity of the arms discovery. Joseph Burkholder Smith, who had previously served as CIA chief of station in Caracas, has implied that CIA operatives, responding to presidential pressure, engaged in a form of "black propaganda" and planted the arms. Philip Agee, a CIA agent who turned against the agency, also recalled that he immediately suspected that the Caracas station, working with Venezuelan agents, had planted the arms.[54] On the other hand, in December 1963 the CIA assured President Lyndon B. Johnson that evidence "proved absolutely that arms had been imported into Venezuela from Cuba."[55]

Whatever the source of the arms, their discovery delighted President Kennedy and provided the new Johnson administration with an opportunity to intensify the war against Castro. In July 1964, with Venezuela taking the lead, the United States obtained an OAS resolution that condemned Cuba for its aggression and called on member states to break relations and impose economic sanctions. Cuba was effectively ostracized from the hemispheric community, with only Mexico ignoring the sanctions. The investment that the United States had made in Betancourt's Venezuela in early 1960 had matured.

U.S. officials were also pleased that Betancourt was able to transfer the presidential sash to his duly elected successor, Raúl Leoni. This marked the first peaceful transfer of power in Venezuelan history. No such historical watershed characterized the Dominican Republic, however, for Juan Bosch's presidency lasted only seven months. A cabal of wealthy businessmen and right-wing military officers struck a *golpe* in September 1963, spuriously proclaiming that they were saving the nation from Castro and communism.

The United States recognized the Dominican junta, although in one final gesture to Betancourt and his doctrine it delayed recognition until after the Venezuelan election. The administration gave up on Dominican democracy because, as President Kennedy had admitted, it valued anticommunism and stability over decent, democratic regimes. Throughout 1962 and 1963, the administration discouraged the Council of State and then President Bosch from purging the Trujillistas from the Dominican armed forces. Bosch never gained effective control over the Dominican military. The administration also constantly criticized Bosch for not restricting the freedom of leftists. The U.S. ambassador complained that Bosch did not denounce communism as often as he and Dominican elites would like and once irresponsibly speculated that Bosch "has been a deep-cover communist for years." U.S. officials did not want a restoration of a Trujillo-like regime, but they ultimately spurned Bosch for refusing "to adopt a firm policy against Communism and Castro."[56]

As outlined in a newspaper article written by Assistant Secretary of State Edwin Martin shortly after Bosch's overthrow, U.S. policy had come full circle. The United States preferred tough, anticommunist democrats like Rómulo Betancourt. But it would no longer disdain military dictators. Juan Bosch and other Latin American reformers had proven inept and inexperienced. The military was a reliable anticommunist force, and Latin America needed a certain degree of authority to prevent the instability and disorder that provided opportunities for communists. Martin's article, which President Kennedy approved, reiterated the views of John Foster Dulles and Richard Nixon and anticipated the "Mann doctrine" of the Johnson administration.[57] Indeed, Martin published what the president had said privately when he listed his famous "three possibilities in descending order of preference" for the post-Trujillo Dominican Republic.

In the period from 1958 to 1963, the United States took extraordinary measures—assassination plots, bribery, embargoes, interventions, naval shows of force, grand economic schemes, propaganda, sabotage, and terrorism—in the area dubbed here the Caribbean triangle. Cold War anticommunism underlay these actions. But in pursuing these aggressive measures, officials were upholding customary U.S. policies. Throughout the twentieth century, the United States has practiced sphere-of-influence politics in the Western Hemisphere: It has tried to maintain peace and order, exclude foreign influences, expand trade and investment, and shape Latin America's development. The policies pursued by the Eisenhower, Kennedy, and subsequently Johnson administrations were rooted in that tradition.

Notes

A previous version of this essay appeared in *Diplomatic History* 20 (Winter 1996): 55–78.

1. Arthur M. Schlesinger Jr., *A Thousand Days: John F. Kennedy in the White House* (Boston, 1965), 769.

2. Memorandum of discussion at 237th meeting of NSC, 17 February 1955, U.S. Department of State, *Foreign Relations of the United States, 1955–1957* (Washington, DC, 1987), 6:2–5 (hereafter *FRUS,* with year and volume number).

3. Dempster McIntosh (U.S. ambassador to Venezuela) to State Department, 6 December 1957, *FRUS, 1955–1957,* 7:1164–67.

4. Minutes of cabinet meeting, 16 May 1958, *FRUS, 1958–1960,* 5:238–39. For Allen Dulles's views, see Dulles memorandum for secretary of state, 28 May 1958, John Foster Dulles Papers, box 8, folder: Conversations with Dulles, A. W. (Intelligence Material), Dwight D. Eisenhower Library, Abilene, KS; Allen Dulles to John Foster Dulles, 19 June 1958, Dulles Papers, Telephone Series, box 8, folder: Telephone Conversations, 6–7/58 (5).

5. Memorandum of discussion of 366th meeting of NSC, 22 May 1958, *FRUS, 1958–1960,* 5:239–46.

6. Eisenhower quoted in memorandum of discussion of 366th meeting of NSC, 22 May 1958, *FRUS, 1958–1960,* 5:244; NSC-5902/1, "Statement of U.S. Policy toward Latin America," 16 February 1959, *FRUS, 1958–1960,* 5:91–116.

7. Stephen G. Rabe, *The Road to OPEC: United States Relations with Venezuela, 1919–1976* (Austin, TX, 1982), 136–38.

8. For a widely read account of the de Galíndez-Murphy murders, see "The Story of a Dark International Conspiracy," *Life* 42 (24 February 1957): 24–31.

9. Julian P. Fromer (officer in charge of Dominican Republic affairs) to R. Richard Rubottom (assistant secretary of state), 15 February 1958, *FRUS, 1955–1957,* 6:903. See also memorandum of conversation between Dulles and Porfirio Herrera Baez (foreign minister), 7 November 1958, *FRUS, 1958–1960, Microfiche Supplement* (Washington, DC, 1991), 5:DR5.

10. Thomas G. Paterson, *Contesting Castro: The United States and the Triumph of the Cuban Revolution* (New York, 1994), 109–225; memorandum of conference in Christian Herter's office, 31 December 1958, *FRUS, 1958–1960,* 6:323–39.

11. Charles D. Ameringer, *The Democratic Left in Exile: The Antidictatorial Struggle in the Caribbean, 1945–1959* (Coral Gables, FL, 1974), 279–83. For Castro's admission of involvement, see memorandum of telephone conversation between William Wieland (director of Office of Caribbean and Mexican Affairs) and Tad Szulc (*New York Times*), 15 July 1959, *FRUS, 1958–1960,* 6:558–60.

12. Ameringer, *Democratic Left*, 56, 60, 267, 279; memorandum of conversation between Betancourt and Edward J. Sparks (U.S. ambassador), 27 April 1959, *FRUS, 1958–1960, Microfiche Supplement*, 5:VE28.

13. Rabe, *Road to OPEC*, 146–47; memorandum of conversation between Betancourt and Rubottom, 14 February 1959, *FRUS, 1958–1960, Microfiche Supplement*, 5:VE20.

14. Dulles to Herter, n.d. (but March 1959), *FRUS, 1958–1960*, 5:372–73; Rubottom quoted in enclosure 1, memorandum of conversation, State Department, 8 July 1959, in Instruction from State to All Embassies in the American Republics, 16 July 1959, *FRUS, 1958–1960*, 5:296–98.

15. Herter quoted in Department of State, *Bulletin* 41 (31 August 1959): 301–5. See also Jerome Slater, *The OAS and United States Foreign Policy* (Columbus, OH, 1967), 94–96.

16. Herter to Eisenhower, 5 November 1959, *FRUS, 1958–1960*, 6:656–58; 5412 Committee paper, "A Program of Covert Action against the Castro Regime," 16 March 1960, *FRUS, 1958–1960*, 6:850–51; Andrew J. Goodpaster memorandum of conference with president, 17 March 1960, *FRUS, 1958–1960*, 6:861–63.

17. Memorandum of discussion at 450th meeting of NSC, 7 July 1960, *FRUS, 1958–1960*, 6:984–85.

18. Memorandum of conversation between Betancourt and Sparks, 10 March 1959, *FRUS, 1958–1960, Microfiche Supplement*, 5:VE22; memorandum of conversation between Betancourt and Sparks, 27 April 1959, *FRUS, 1958–1960, Microfiche Supplement*, 5:VE28.

19. Memorandum of conversation between Betancourt and Sparks, 31 March 1959, *FRUS, 1958–1960, Microfiche Supplement*, 5:VE25; editorial note, *FRUS, 1958–1960*, 6:386–87; Ameringer, *Democratic Left*, 268, 291–92; Burrows (chargé) to State Department, 6 October 1959, *FRUS, 1958–1960, Microfiche Supplement*, 5:VE37.

20. Memorandum of conversation between Herter, Rubottom, and Pedro Arcaya (Venezuelan foreign minister), *FRUS, 1958–1960, Microfiche Supplement*, 5:VE30; Rubottom to Dennis A. Fitzgerald (International Cooperation Agency), 25 September 1959, *FRUS, 1958–1960, Microfiche Supplement*, 5:VE36; Herter to U.S. embassy in Caracas, 25 April 1960, *FRUS, 1958–1960, Microfiche Supplement*, 5:VE40; memorandum of conversation at 443rd meeting of NSC, 5 May 1960, *FRUS, 1958–1960*, 6:908.

21. Loy Henderson (acting secretary of state) to U.S. embassy in Caracas, 28 April 1960, *FRUS, 1958–1960, Microfiche Supplement*, 5:VE41; Rubottom's comment in dispatch, Herter to U.S. embassy in Caracas, 11 May 1960, *FRUS, 1958–1960, Microfiche Supplement*, 5:VE42.

22. Rubottom to Herter, 10 November 1959, *FRUS, 1958–1960, Microfiche Supplement*, 5:DR9; memorandum for president, "Possible Action to Prevent Castroist Takeover of Dominican Republic," with enclosure "Proposed Plan," 14 April 1960, Office of the Staff Secretary (OSS), Subject Series, Administrative Subseries, box 15, folder: Intelligence Matters (13 & 14), Eisenhower Library.

23. Trujillo quoted in oral history of William Pawley, Herbert Hoover Library, West Branch, IA.

24. Dearborn to State Department, 11 February 1960, *FRUS, 1958–1960, Microfiche Supplement*, 5:DR13.

25. Hill to John C. Dreier (U.S. ambassador to OAS), 15 March 1960, *FRUS, 1958–*

1960, Microfiche Supplement, 5:DR15. See also memorandum of conversation of 441st meeting of NSC, 14 April 1960, *FRUS, 1958–1960, Microfiche Supplement,* 5:DR19.

26. NIE on Dominican Republic, 26 April 1960, *FRUS, 1958–1960, Microfiche Supplement,* 5:DR21; Castro quoted in Philip Bonsal (U.S. ambassador to Cuba) to State Department, 23 April 1960, *FRUS, 1958–1960,* 6:898.

27. Edward E. Rice (Policy Planning Staff) to Gerard C. Smith (assistant secretary of state for policy planning), 13 April 1960, *FRUS, 1958–1960,* 6:892; Dillon quoted in memorandum of conversation of 441st meeting of NSC, 14 April 1960, *FRUS, 1958–1960, Microfiche Supplement,* 5:DR19; Dillon to president, 20 May 1960, *FRUS, 1958–1960, Microfiche Supplement,* 5:DR23; Eisenhower quoted in memorandum of conversation between president, Dillon, Rubottom, and Joseph Farland (U.S. ambassador to Dominican Republic), 13 May 1960, OSS, Subject Series, State Department Subseries, box 4, folder: State Department 3–5/60 (6).

28. For allegations of bribery, see memorandum of conversation between president and Herter, 30 August 1960, OSS, Subject Series, State Department Subseries, box 4, folder: State Department 8–9/60 (2).

29. Herter to president, 18 August 1960, Ann Whitman File, Dulles-Herter Series, box 11, folder 8/60 (2), Eisenhower Library; Eisenhower quoted in memorandum of conversation of 453rd meeting of NSC, 25 July 1960, *FRUS, 1958–1960, Microfiche Supplement,* 5:DR25.

30. Slater, *OAS and United States Foreign Policy,* 192.

31. Editorial notes on San José meeting, 22 to 29 August 1960, *FRUS, 1958–1960,* 6:1060–65.

32. For CIA and Dominican Republic, see telephone calls between Allen Dulles and Herter, 19 August 1960, Christian Herter Papers, Telephone Series, box 13, folder 7/1–8/31/60, Eisenhower Library; for Eisenhower's action see memorandum of conversation with legislative leaders, 23 August 1960, Whitman File, Legislative Leaders Series, box 3, folder: Legislative Leaders, 1960 (4).

33. Memorandum of conversation between president and Dillon, 13 October 1960, Whitman File, Eisenhower Diaries, box 53, folder: Staff Notes, 10/60 (1); Dearborn to State Department, 3 August 1960, *FRUS, 1958–1960, Microfiche Supplement,* 5:DR26; Dearborn to Thomas C. Mann (assistant secretary of state), 27 October 1960, *FRUS, 1958–1960, Microfiche Supplement,* 5:DR28. For CIA activities, see U.S. Congress, Senate, Select Committee to Study Governmental Operations with Respect to Intelligence Activities (hereafter Church Committee), *Alleged Assassination Plots Involving Foreign Leaders,* 94th Cong., 1st sess., 1975, S. Rept. 465, 193–96.

34. Sparks to State Department, memorandum of conversation with Betancourt, 5 December 1960, *FRUS, 1958–1960, Microfiche Supplement,* 5:VE51.

35. Allan Stewart (chargé) to State Department, 12 November 1960, *FRUS, 1958–1960, Microfiche Supplement,* 5:VE47; memorandum conversation between president and national security advisers, 29 November 1960, *FRUS, 1958–1960,* 6:1127.

36. Eisenhower quoted in Peter Wyden, *Bay of Pigs: The Untold Story* (New York, 1979), 87–88n. See also Herter to Eisenhower, 8 December 1960, *FRUS, 1958–1960, Microfiche Supplement,* 5:DR30.

37. Hugh S. Cumming (Bureau of Intelligence and Research) to Herter, 22 November 1960, *FRUS, 1958–1960, Microfiche Supplement,* 5:DR29; Bissell quoted in notes of Special Group Meeting, 29 December 1960, *FRUS, 1961–1963, Microfiche Supplement,*

10–12:234; memorandum of conversation between president, Gordon Gray, and others, 3 January 1961, Office of Special Assistant for National Security Affairs, Special Assistants Series, Presidential Subseries, box 5, folder: 1960 Meetings with President, vol. 2 (2), Eisenhower Library. See also Church Committee, *Alleged Assassination Plots*, 196–201.

38. Attorney general to president, 19 April 1961, *FRUS, 1961–1963*, 10:302–4.

39. Department of State, *Bulletin* 44 (3 April 1961): 471–74.

40. Schlesinger quoted in Tony Smith, "The Alliance for Progress: The 1960s," in *Exporting Democracy: The United States and Latin America*, ed. Abraham Lowenthal (Baltimore, 1991), 87, fn. 12. See also Rabe, *Road to OPEC*, 142–49.

41. Church Committee, *Alleged Assassination Plots*, 202–4; Dean Rusk to president, 15 February 1961, *FRUS, 1961–1963*, 12:616–18.

42. Church Committee, *Alleged Assassination Plots*, 201–7; memorandum by Murphy on 15–16 April 1961 trip, n.d. (but late April 1961), National Security File, Country File (NSFCO): Dominican Republic, box 66, folder: Subjects, Murphy Trip, 1961, John F. Kennedy Library, Boston, MA; Bundy to president, 2 May 1961, NSFCO: Dominican Republic, box 66, folder: Subjects, Murphy Trip, 1961.

43. Church Committee, *Alleged Assassination Plots*, 205–13; notes of 483rd meeting of NSC, 5 May 1961, *FRUS, 1961–1963*, 10:479–81; memorandum from Cuban Task Force of NSC to Bundy, 15 May 1961, and covering memorandum from Theodore C. Achilles (State Department) to Rusk, 26 May 1961, *FRUS, 1961–1963*, 12:629–33.

44. Church Committee, *Alleged Assassination Plots*, 213–15.

45. Dearborn's telegram in General Clifton to Bundy for president in Paris, 31 May 1961, President's Office File, Country File (POFCO): Dominican Republic, box 115A, folder: Dominican Republic Security, 2/61–9/63, Kennedy Library.

46. Dearborn and others quoted in Richard Goodwin to Bundy, 8 June 1961, NSFCO: Dominican Republic, box 66, folder: General, 1–6/61. Dearborn's recommendation in Clifton to Bundy for president in Vienna, 5 June 1961, POFCO: Dominican Republic, box 115A, folder: Dominican Republic Security, 2/61–9/63.

47. Memorandum of conversation between Robert F. Woodward (assistant secretary) and president, 10 July 1961, State Department paper, "Courses of Action in the Dominican Republic," 17 July 1961, Rusk to president on instructions to Hill, 19 July 1961, all in *FRUS, 1961–1963*, 12:644–55. See also Special National Intelligence Estimate, "The Dominican Situation," *FRUS, 1961–1963*, 12:656–59.

48. Kennedy quoted in Schlesinger, *A Thousand Days*, 770–71; Kennedy to Woodward, 10 July 1961, *FRUS, 1961–1963*, 12:646; DeLesseps S. Morrison, *Latin American Mission: An Adventure in Hemisphere Diplomacy* (New York, 1965), 113–14.

49. Teodoro Moscoso (U.S. ambassador) to Rusk, memorandum of conversation between Betancourt and Chester Bowles (undersecretary), 16 October 1961, NSFCO: Venezuela, box 192, folder 10–11/61; Roger Hilsman (Bureau of Intelligence and Research) to acting secretary of state, 20 September 1961, NSFCO: Dominican Republic, box 66, folder: General, 8–9/61; Martin report, n.d. (but September 1961), POFCO: Dominican Republic, box 115A, folder 9.

50. Rusk warning in Department of State, *Bulletin* 45 (4 December 1961): 931.

51. National Intelligence Estimate, "The Situation in Venezuela," 21 November 1961, *FRUS, 1961–1963, Microfiche Supplement*, 10–12:217. For assassination plots, see Alexsandr Fursenko and Timothy Naftali, *"One Hell of a Gamble": Khrushchev, Castro,*

and Kennedy, 1958–1964 (New York, 1997), 135–37; and Edwin McCammon Martin, *Kennedy and Latin America* (Lanham, MD, 1994), 255, fn. 10.

52. Betancourt speech to National Press Club, 20 February 1963, POFCO: Venezuela, box 128, folder: Venezuela, General, 1963; Kennedy to John McCone (CIA director), 19 February 1963, NSFCO: Venezuela, box 192, folder: Venezuela, 1–2/63.

53. Memorandum of conversation between Kennedy and Betancourt, 16 December 1961, *FRUS, 1961–1963, Microfiche Supplement,* 10–12:220; Thomas L. Hughes (Bureau of Intelligence and Research) to Rusk, 29 November 1963, NSFCO: Latin America, box 1, folder: Vol. I, Lyndon Baines Johnson Library, Austin, TX.

54. Joseph Burkholder Smith, *Portrait of a Cold Warrior* (New York, 1976), 381–84; Philip Agee, *Inside the Company: CIA Diary* (New York, 1975), 322, 364–65.

55. Meeting between McCone and Johnson on 30 November 1963, *FRUS, 1961–1963,* 11:896. See also Michael R. Beschloss, *The Crisis Years: Kennedy and Khrushchev, 1960–1963* (New York, 1991), 666–67, 692.

56. Stephen G. Rabe, *The Most Dangerous Area in the World: John F. Kennedy Confronts Communist Revolution in Latin America* (Chapel Hill, NC, 1999), 43–48.

57. Department of State, *Bulletin* 49 (4 November 1963): 698-700; Rabe, *Most Dangerous Area,* 122–23, 177–78.

"Flee! The White Giants Are Coming!": The United States, Mercenaries, and the Congo, 1964–1965

PIERO GLEIJESES

On 14 August 1964, Carl Rowan, the prominent black journalist who was the director of the United States Information Agency, wrote President Lyndon B. Johnson that there was "a real danger that in saving the present situation in the Congo we . . . could lose the longer range struggle for all of Africa." Rowan was writing in the midst of a crisis: on 5 August 1964, Stanleyville, the Congo's third largest city, had fallen to rebels, and in Washington a national intelligence estimate on the Congo had predicted "a total breakdown in governmental authority."[1]

The Congo had become independent on 30 June 1960. Unprepared for self-government, it had fallen into anarchy a few days later and been sucked into the whirlwind of the Cold War. Over the next two years the communist bloc sent money and weapons to the Congo, but its interference there was very limited compared to that of the United States. In the summer of 1960 the Eisenhower administration had concluded that Patrice Lumumba, the country's first prime minister, was an African Castro, a Soviet instrument. (Scholars now agree that he was in fact "a genuine nationalist, fanatical in his opposition to foreign control of the Congo.") For U.S. officials, he was an enemy of the most dangerous type—charismatic and popular. It would not be enough to bring him down: he would have to be eliminated. But the CIA was beaten to the punch. On 17 January 1961 Lumumba was killed by his Congolese enemies.[2]

President John F. Kennedy inherited a raging crisis as Lumumba's followers prepared to wage war to avenge their leader's death. Kennedy said that he wanted the Congolese to chart their own course and, moving beyond Eisenhower's narrow intransigence, expressed his preference for a coalition government that would include even Lumumbists. But when the Congolese parliament seemed ready to elect a Lumumbist as premier, Kennedy's response was not very different from what Eisenhower's would have been: U.S. officials bribed the parliamentarians, plotted a military coup, and succeeded in having their candidate, the lackluster Cyril Adoula, elected premier in a contest that would otherwise have been won by the Lumumbist. In time, Washington would forget this and would come to consider Adoula the true and legal expression of the parliament's will.

Adoula's election did not resolve the Congo crisis. A few days after independence had been declared, the dynamic, brave, and corrupt Moise Tshombe had led the country's richest province, Katanga, into a war of secession. As the Congo's self-proclaimed arch anticommunist, Tshombe enjoyed the sympathy of many in the United States, including members of Congress. The Kennedy administration, however, thought that Katangan independence would lead to the fragmentation of the Congo and offer opportunities to the Soviet bloc. Therefore, Washington supported sending a UN peacekeeping force to the Congo. That force finally quashed the Katangan rebellion in January 1963.

With the defeat of Lumumba's followers and the reintegration of Katanga, the Congo settled into corrupt, oppressive, pro-U.S. stability that rested on two pillars: the UN troops, numbering in the thousands, and the Congolese Army (ANC), led by General Joseph Mobutu. Therefore, in early 1964 when the UN troops prepared to leave, rebellion flared up again. Leading the revolt were the fractious followers of Lumumba, whose vague ideology was couched in Marxist jargon. "Despite the revolutionary slogans which its leaders mouthed . . . the rebels have to all intents and purposes no political programme," the British ambassador reported. "It's definitely an African and a Congolese movement but all very confused," explained the U.S. consul in Stanleyville. Ethnic rivalries, old feuds, and the fear of witchcraft added to the brew that bubbled up through the thin crust of the Pax Americana.[3]

The revolt spread "like a forest fire,"[4] taking the Johnson administration by surprise. In mid-June, Ambassador Godley had assured Assistant Secretary for African Affairs Mennen Williams that "all of us here share your optimism that the economic and political progress that has been made in the Congo during the past four years will . . . continue and that the pace will accelerate." A few weeks later the ANC had virtually collapsed. "Everywhere the soldiers of Mr. Mobutu, armed with machine-guns, flee from rebels who usually have only bows, arrows and bicycle chains," *Le Monde* reported. As they advanced, the Simbas ("lions"), as the rebels were called, seized the weapons abandoned by fleeing troops. "Refusing to face its humiliation," *Le Monde* explained, "the government claimed that the rebels were being armed by Communist China."[5]

The army's collapse was due, in part, to the troops' belief that the rebels were using witchcraft. As the foremost student of the crisis put it, "The mere announcement of their arrival terrorized the soldiers of the Congolese army, convinced as they were that their bullets would turn into water or fly back to strike them." In the words of one eyewitness, an African journalist, "This superstition has had a powerful effect on Congolese National Army troops. In many places they lay down their arms and run when the rebels advance."[6]

More than magic, however, explained the Simbas' successes, as the U.S. consul in Elisabethville, the capital of Katanga, made clear:

> There is in this and contiguous areas [a] strong, nearly universal feeling of dissatisfaction at [the] present GOC [Government of the Congo]. . . . All levels [of] population [in] this area are thoroughly disgusted with [the] first four years of Congolese independence, whose corruption, inefficiency, public violence and economic decline are in crass contrast with their original exaggerated expectations. . . . These disaffected views [are] shared also by ANC troops here. The main reason for their failure to fight is not so much lack of military capacity and superstitious fear of rebels, which of course are important factors, but that they do not want to fight.[7]

Not only were the troops unwilling to fight, but, as the U.S. embassy noted, "indiscriminate killing, looting and raping" were "normal pursuits" for the ANC. The CIA was equally blunt: "The ANC is noted for its pillaging and raping and is hated and feared. Now it is near collapse as an organized force. [It is] woefully lacking in leadership, prone to mutiny, and manned by soldiers who tend to regard their rifles as meal tickets." Therefore, Godley pointed out, the population usually welcomed the rebels, "who treat them better than [the] ANC in most cases." Rose agreed: the Simbas, he wrote, "were received with open arms" by the population.[8]

On 26 June, four days before the last UN troops left the country, the erstwhile leader of Katanga, Moise Tshombe, returned to the Congo from self-imposed exile in Spain. Tshombe "is now leading a bandwagon built of despair, disillusionment, friction and opportunism," the U.S. embassy reported. Frightened by the rebels, the country's leaders turned to their former enemy, who towered over them in vigor, courage, and charisma. ("Lumumba was probably the only Congolese who exceeded Tshombe in what is known as the charismatic quality of leadership," noted a U.S. intelligence report.) "We are all for giving Tshombe important post in gvt," cabled Godley.[9]

But neither he nor any other U.S. official expected what happened next: on 6 July, in a move that testified "to the extent of the desperation felt by President Joseph Kasavubu and General Mobutu," Tshombe was appointed prime minister. "It all happened so fast," observed the embassy's deputy chief of mission. "Before we knew it the decision had been made. It was very much a Congolese decision." Reserved at first, the U.S. reaction soon turned into warm endorsement. "Prime Minister Tshombe has brought zest and dynamism to his job," said Assistant Secretary Williams.[10]

African leaders were less impressed. Despised by many of them as "a walking museum of colonialism"[11] because of his ties with South Africans, Portuguese, and Belgians and his attempt to divide the Congo, Tshombe was also known as the moving force behind Lumumba's murder. "How could anyone imagine," the king of Morocco asked in a broadcast to his nation, "that I, the representative of my country's national conscience, could sit at a conference table or at a banquet with the man who personifies secession? How could anyone even begin to imagine that I, Hassan II . . . could observe a minute of silence in memory of our African heroes when one of their murderers is seated among us?"[12]

In the weeks that followed, the United States increased its military aid to the Congo. But neither aid nor Tshombe could stem the revolt. By late July frantic cables were reaching Washington from Leopoldville: the rebels were winning, the ANC was collapsing, and well-trained, foreign soldiers were necessary.

U.S. officials knew that the rebels were receiving very little outside assistance and thought that neither the Soviet Union nor any other communist country beside China was involved. They also realized that the Chinese role was marginal: "While the Chicoms may have contributed an element of sophistication to insurgent activity, the eastern Congo fundamentally collapsed from within. In comparison with indigenous causes of dissidence, the Chicom contribution to the collapse of central government authority probably has nowhere been more than marginal."[13] Furthermore, there was no indication that the Simbas were communists. An intelligence appraisal noted that

> while at this point it is impossible to make firm judgments about the orientation of a rebel government, it would certainly seek close links with the East and there is a good chance that it would make the position of the West in the Congo increasingly difficult. (On the other hand, given the enormous reliance of the Congo on the West and the inability of the East to duplicate Western assistance, we do not believe the position of the West would become untenable—at least not in the short run.)[14]

A rebel victory would have ended the pro-U.S. stance of the Congo that had taken four years and two U.S. administrations to establish. The loss of the Congo ("the richest country and the richest prize in Africa") could have cost Johnson votes in the presidential race.[15] The revolt had to be crushed.

Washington turned to Europe. U.S. officials badgered the Belgians, the former colonial power. The most effective measure, Ambassador Godley informed Washington, would be the "use of Belgian paratroop battalions to come in rapidly, clean up [the] situation and then withdraw as soon as possible."[16]

Secretary of State Dean Rusk and Undersecretaries Averell Harriman and George Ball agreed. On 4 August, Harriman cabled the U.S. ambassador in Brussels, Douglas MacArthur, to ask, "Under what conditions would [the] GOB [Government of Belgium] be willing to provide troops?" On 6 August, Rusk cabled the Belgian foreign minister, Paul-Henri Spaak: "Events in the Congo have reached so critical a point that you and we and all our European friends must move immediately and vigorously to prevent total collapse. . . . We must concert urgently on tangible, specific measures to save the Congo." The next day Harriman arrived in Brussels "for a final effort" to convince the Belgians to take "primary responsibility." The United States would provide the hardware; Belgium, the men. "I will tell you, but you must keep it to yourselves," Spaak later told a group of Belgian ambassadors, "they [U.S. officials] asked me if Belgium was willing to send in troops. And when Mr. Harriman came, that is what we talked about." The Belgians balked: they agreed to put more military advisers in the Congo, but no Belgian would be authorized to engage directly or indirectly in combat.[17]

U.S. policy makers were also rebuffed on a second proposal: that Belgium "take the lead in the organization . . . [of] a joint military force of the Six [European Community countries], or some of its member nations." As Harriman prepared to fly to Brussels, MacArthur had cabled Rusk that "he [Spaak] did not want to mislead us, and among other things he did not r[e]p[ea]t not see the slightest chance of getting any of the 'Six' to intervene militarily in [the] Congo. Luxembourg had no military forces and he was certain France, Germany and [the] Netherlands would refuse [to] participate in any military intervention." Further attempts in the next few days proved futile. The Europeans "had no stomach for it," Ball observed.[18]

Not only did the "gutless Belgians" fail to respond with the proper zeal, but they also seemed ready to collude with the enemy. Washington worried about the "apparent Belgian preference to try to do business with the rebels, even if Communist, rather than facing up to putting down the rebellion."[19] In fact, the Belgians were simply being practical. They had no intention of sending in troops, they did not believe that anyone else would, and they had no confidence in the ANC's ability to do the job. Moreover, they did not consider the Simbas communists and thought they could achieve a modus vivendi with them should they win. The Belgians, Ambassador Rose reported from Leopoldville, "laugh at the Americans for seeing a Communist behind every bush." In Brussels, the day before Harriman arrived, Spaak told Ambassador MacArthur that "top Belgian industrialists having [the] most extensive interests in [the] Congo . . . agreed that they could do business with . . . [the] rebel leaders since [the] latter realized Belgian economic and technical presence and assistance was essential to [the] economic life of [the] Congo." A few days later Spaak told a group of Belgian ambassadors, "My assessment of the situation . . . differs markedly from that of the Americans. People always say that I do everything the Americans want, that I always share their views, but in this affair of the Congo this is not true at all. Neither my assessment of the situation nor the remedies I proposed were similar to theirs."[20] Rusk did not mince words. He told the Belgian ambassador that he "was bitter that the European governments had refused to intervene in the Congo, even though it was above all their responsibility. He added," the ambassador reported, "that if the Congo were to be lost because of the Europeans' failure to act, it would have a profound impact on U.S.-European relations."[21]

Unlike Belgium, Washington was not interested in a modus vivendi with the Simbas. Failure to act would mean, a 6 August memo warned Johnson, "let chaos run its course, hoping the Congolese will work out an adjustment without serious Communist intrusion; and rely on [the] Congo's need for our aid and support for influence with the eventual government. This would be hard to explain politically in [the] US, but it is essentially what [the] Belgians and Europeans are doing."[22]

On 11 August, Johnson and his key advisers met in a hastily called session of the National Security Council (NSC). This was the first NSC meeting about the revolt. The mood was somber. Director of Central Intelligence John McCone stated that "Western troops would be necessary." Harriman concurred. "The Congolese army in most cases has proven useless. . . . The people in government are demoralized and Leopoldville in danger."[23]

No one challenged the basic premise: the rebels had to be defeated, and the ANC alone could not do it. Direct U.S. military involvement was considered only as "an extreme last resort," as Treasury Secretary Douglas Dillon argued. "The President said emphatically that we all share this view." Therefore, African and European troops had to be found. Harriman suggested France, Great Britain, Germany, the Netherlands, Italy, and Canada. "The job . . . should be put squarely to the Europeans as their responsibility," Rusk asserted. "We should urge them immediately to put troops into Leopoldville, using Presidential pressure if necessary." Lyndon Johnson agreed. "Time is running out and the Congo must be saved."[24]

The discussion had an air of unreality because no European government was willing to send its troops, and Washington knew it. In addition to the Europeans, the administration had already been rebuffed by Ethiopia, Nigeria, and Senegal, and in any case African troops would not have been welcome in the Congo: Mobutu and Tshombe trusted neither them nor their governments. "Despite our efforts, the Congolese Government has not so far asked any other African country for military forces save South Africa which fortunately refused," noted a U.S. official.[25]

The United States preferred a "clean solution" (European or African troops), but it would fall back on mercenaries if necessary. This had been its two-track approach from the onset. A cable from Godley on 5 August had posed the problem crisply. "There are only three places," he wrote, where the Congolese government (GOC) could turn:

a) GOC can seek direct Belgian military intervention; b) it can attempt to recruit white mercenary brigade; c) it can ask for US troops. . . . If Belgian Government refuses to accept risks of intervention . . . mercenary brigade is second best alternative. . . . From US standpoint [the] employment of mercenaries would carry advantage of being done on GOC responsibility and would reduce overt western (i.e., Belgian or U.S.) involvement. . . . It would place burden of responsibility on GOC and not on ourselves or Belgians.[26]

Washington concurred. "Tshombe and [the] GOC should proceed soonest to establish [an] effective gendarmerie-mercenary unit," Rusk had cabled Leopoldville on 6 August, as Harriman was about to leave for Brussels.[27] Tshombe was an old hand at the mercenary game: they had helped him when he had been the leader of secessionist Katanga, and he was happy to use them again.

In Brussels, on 7 August, Spaak told Harriman unequivocally that neither Belgium nor any other European country would send troops. That same day Rusk approved a proposal by Mennen Williams for an "immediate effort . . . to concert with [the] Belgians to help Tshombe to raise [a] mercenary force," and he cabled Harriman urging "Belgian help on [the] mercenary problem including recruitment of Belgians." Washington and Brussels would supply the money to pay the mercenaries and the weapons to arm them; Washington alone would supply the planes to fly them. Bowing to U.S. pressure, the Belgians embraced the mercenary option. "In fact, mercenaries were the only possible solution," wrote Colonel Frédéric Vandewalle, who would head the Belgian military mission in the Congo and was briefed by Spaak on the talks with Harriman. "In private, both Washington and Brussels admitted it." And so the United States embarked on a dual policy in the Congo. It openly provided military aid to Tshombe while it covertly financed, armed, and oversaw the mercenaries. "The Americans . . . regard white mercenaries as the essential cutting edge of the Central Government's forces," wrote a British official.[28]

The mercenaries flowed into the Congo. Most came from South Africa and Rhodesia. "Hundreds in queue for Congo army," reported the *Cape Times* from Salisbury. "They will be formed into all-White commandos." South African Prime Minister Hendrik Verwoerd said at first that his government "did not intend to interfere" in the recruitment, but he soon became concerned at the stampede. "The extent of recruiting must not get out of hand," he warned. "There is [in South Africa] a manpower shortage which has to be filled at considerable cost by State-aided immigration." The arrival of the mercenaries "is the talk of the town," wrote a Leopoldville daily.[29] By October there were, by NSC estimates, "over a thousand" mercenaries in the Congo.[30]

The U.S. embassy kept them at arm's length—in public. In private the CIA, the military attachés, and the military mission kept in close contact. The army attaché, Col. Knut Raudstein, was an admirer of their leader, Mike Hoare. "Tshombe's supporters [are] most fortunate in having [a] man of Hoare's temperament, character and capability in his position," Raudstein cabled. "He . . . conducts [him]self as [a] typical upper class Briton proud of [his] Irish extraction. Avows disagreement with some SA [South African] political concepts calling himself a moderate."[31]

Hoare's "moderate" views on race were reflected in his comment to a fellow mercenary: "I believe . . . we have a great mission here. The Africans have gotten used to the idea that they can do what they like to us whites, that they can trample on us and spit on us."[32] And they were reflected in his response to a South African black who wanted to enlist: "We only engage white mercenaries."[33]

Why did men volunteer? "For money, first of all," five freshly arrived French mercenaries told a journalist over drinks in Leopoldville. But there were loftier reasons: "Because we're ashamed of France. . . . We've lost Indochina; *le grand Charles* has tossed Algeria aside. The *fellouzes* will not get the Congo."[34]

The year 1963, a philosophical mercenary mused, "was the heyday of African unity, of the dream of African grandeur and of the expulsion of the white man from the continent." The year 1964 would be the year of the White Giants—"tall, vigorous Boers from South Africa; long-legged, slim and muscular Englishmen from Rhodesia"—who would come to the Congo and restore the white man to his proper place. "How often was I to hear the muffled drumming in the night, through forests and savannahs, 'Flee, the White Giants are coming!' "[35]

The U.S. ambassador was less romantic. The mercenaries were, he thought, "an uncontrolled lot of toughs . . . who consider looting or safe-cracking fully within their prerogatives." Their "serious excesses," the CIA reported, included "robbery, rape, murder and beatings."[36]

They were also boastful and naive. Once in the Congo, they tended to trust every white face, even that of a journalist. "These mercenaries are everywhere evident, talk frequently to the press and anybody who will listen to them," Godley complained. They talked openly, for instance, to an Italian journalist, who subsequently described their entry into the town of Boende in late October 1964. "Occupying the town," he wrote, "meant blowing out the doors with rounds of bazooka fire, going into the shops and taking anything they wanted that was movable. . . . After the looting came the killing. The shooting lasted for three days. Three days of executions, of lynchings, of tortures, of screams, and of terror."[37]

Just as tourists send postcards home, so the mercenaries sent photos of their exploits. Several found their way to the British weekly, the *Observer*. The first showed two almost naked black men, their hands tied behind their backs, ropes around their necks, being led by a white mercenary to their hanging. In the second, "smiling mercenaries" fought for the privilege of doing the "stringing up." A photograph of the swinging corpses was described but not printed. "The pictures," the *Observer* noted, "show how mercenaries not only shoot and hang their prisoners after torturing them, but use them for target practice and gamble over the number of shots needed to kill them."[38]

In a poignant two-part article in the *Cape Times,* a returning South African mercenary wrote of the mercenaries' "senseless, coldblooded killings," of their rule of never taking prisoners ("except for the odd one for questioning, after which they were executed"), of their robberies. He pleaded with his government "not to allow decent young South Africans" to enlist and become "senseless killers." In an off-the-record conversation with British journalist Colin Legum, Mike Hoare described his men "as appalling thugs."[39]

Appalling and efficient. They advanced along the paths of the Congo in mobile columns—"lightly armored Belgian jeeps mounting some automatic weapons and, for heavier work, British Ferrets [armored cars] have been [the] backbone of counterinsurgency military effort," Godley reported. Four U.S. C-130s with U.S. crews transported the mercenaries and their equipment across the Congo's immense expanses. "Nothing went by road, rail or boat—all was supplied by the C-130s," the *New York Times* journalist who covered the campaign explained.[40]

When they met resistance, the mercenaries called on the Congolese air force, which included not one Congolese. It consisted of the "21st Squadron" (seven T-6s from Italy piloted by South African and European mercenaries) and the T-28s and B-26s supplied by the United States. The State Department's official line was that the T-28s and B-26s were "provided to the Congolese government and will be flown by contract personnel engaged by that government." No U.S. citizens would be "called upon by the Congo government to engage in operational missions in the police action" under way in the country, and none therefore would fly the planes.[41] The pilots and crews of the T-28s and B-26s were Cuban exiles who, as Undersecretary Ball reassured the U.S. mission at the United Nations, were not U.S. citizens. "Guiding them into action," the *New York Times* reported, "were American 'diplomats' and other officials in apparently civilian positions. The sponsor, paymaster and director of all of them, however, was the Central Intelligence Agency. . . . Its rapid and effective provision of an 'instant air force' in the Congo was the climax of the agency's deep involvement there." It was an impressive air force, particularly against an enemy without planes or anti-aircraft guns. "The pattern," notes a careful study, "was always the same: [exile] Cuban-piloted T-28s and B-26s bombing and strafing in front of ground columns; Simbas either scattering in panic or being slaughtered by the more accurate and lethal firepower of the mercenaries." The planes, the CIA stated in November 1964, "operate over insurgent territory with impunity." This remained true throughout the war. Over the entire period, not one was downed by enemy fire.[42]

The mercenary ground offensive got under way on 1 November 1964. A mercenary column, accompanied by truckloads of ANC troops and led by Ferret armored cars, advanced from the south toward Stanleyville, the rebel capital. The CIA-controlled T-28s and B-26s "terrified the Simbas," a U.S. military officer wrote.[43] One by one, the rebel towns were recaptured, and the mercenaries closed in on Stanleyville. Then, on 24 November, as the mercenary column was approaching, Belgian paratroopers, transported in U.S. planes, raided the city, freeing about three hundred Belgian and U.S. hostages.

The raid provoked an uproar in Africa and many public pledges to help the Simbas. "We help the rebels. It is our duty," Algerian President Ben Bella proclaimed defiantly, while President Julius Nyerere of Tanzania lashed out: "In an action reminiscent of Pearl Harbour, foreign troops were flown into the Congo at the very moment that negotiations were taking place to secure the safety of all who lived in the Stanleyville area."[44]

The raid also galvanized the Soviet Union. East German reports indicate that before Stanleyville the Soviets had been reluctant to help a revolt about which they knew virtually nothing. "Our Soviet comrades do not yet have a clear idea of the present situation of the liberation movement in the Congo," the embassy of the German Democratic Republic (GDR) reported from Moscow in mid-September 1964. "They only know that . . . the leaders of the movement . . . are engaged in a power struggle that is about personal ambition, not politics." The constant, petty infighting among the rebel leaders gave the Soviets pause. A few days after the raid on Stanleyville, however, the Soviet Union decided to provide military aid to the rebels.[45]

After Stanleyville, the rebels began receiving small amounts of military aid from African countries and larger amounts of weapons from the Soviet Union and China. The weapons were, however, of little value, because the Simbas did not know how to use them. "We're not worried too much about the rebels getting small arms and ammunition," a military attaché in Leopoldville told the *New York Times* in December 1964. "We're not even worried about their getting heavier equipment, like mortars and bazookas, which they don't know how to handle any better than the Congolese army. But if they get some guerrilla veterans from outside, the war could change overnight." The CIA agreed: "The appearance in the Congo of combat 'volunteers' from the radical African states . . . [would create] a new, more ugly and dangerous situation." The radical African states, however, sent no volunteers. "The African governments that opposed Tshombe were a worthless bunch," according to Ambassador Godley. "They did nothing effective, nothing that I'm aware of."[46] As for the mythical Chinese military advisers in the eastern Congo reported by some newspapers, they turned out to be just that—a myth.

Only Cuba sent men—about 120 military instructors led by Che Guevara. They began drifting into the eastern Congo in late April 1965. By the time they fought their first skirmish, on 29 June, the back of the rebellion had been broken.[47] The mercenaries had triumphed.

Victory would have been pyrrhic, however, had it caused a backlash in Africa or at home. U.S. officials were painfully aware that the United States was vulnerable to African charges of racism despite the sincere efforts of the Johnson administration to strengthen civil rights legislation. In the summer of 1964, as the Congo operation began, intermarriage was a crime in nineteen U.S. states, segregation was rampant, and violence against blacks was apparent to anyone who opened a paper or turned on a television. On 22 July, the second summit meeting of the Organization of African Unity (OAU) unanimously approved a resolution condemning "continuing manifestations of bigotry and oppression against Negroes in the United States," while race riots in New York reminded Africans that racial hatred was not limited to "the ever-explosive Deep South."[48]

U.S. officials went to work. "I believe that there are some things that we can do to make our actions in the Congo more palatable internationally and to make ourselves less vulnerable to Communist propaganda," USIA Director Rowan told Johnson.[49] This meant polishing Tshombe's image. And it meant making the mercenary issue as politically acceptable as possible, while transforming the United States from the mercenaries' patron into a concerned onlooker.

Through reams of documents, we see senior U.S. officials trying to get Tshombe to utter the right noises and make the right gestures; they worked directly with him, and they worked through his advisers and public relations people. It was a thankless task, Ambassador Godley and his Belgian and British colleagues concluded, as they swapped stories of Tshombe's stubbornness. The man's survival depended on the United States, but he knew that his patrons also needed him. "We all agreed that dire threats should never be made unless we [are] prepared [to] accept [the] consequences and have [a] tangible alternative in mind," Godley cabled in December 1964. "For [the] moment, we can see no satisfactory person [to] replace Tshombe."[50]

The previous August, U.S. efforts at image making had faced a deadly threat. Unbeknownst to Washington, Tshombe had asked Pretoria for weapons, "white officers and white enlisted men." While sympathetic to Tshombe, the South Africans had been hesitant. They told U.S. officials that they were worried that their involvement would be "grist for the mill" for Tshombe's enemies. Washington agreed heartily, and Pretoria held back.[51]

U.S. officials would have preferred Pretoria as well as South African mercenaries to stay out of the Congo. In their stead should be Europeans. "Such a shift," Harriman and Spaak concluded during a three-hour lunch in New York, "would not in itself overcome African opposition to Tshombe but would make it easier for moderate African countries to support [the] GDRC [Government of the Congo]."[52]

Initially—in August 1964—Spaak had refused to let Belgians serve as mercenaries; he had even threatened to withdraw military assistance "if Belgian white mercenaries enter the Congo." With U.S. prodding, these reservations soon dissipated. Honored as one of the fathers of European unity, Spaak appears here in a less positive light. He looked aside while the Zairean military attaché supervised the recruitment of mercenaries in Belgium. "Several recruitment centers, of which we know the addresses, exist in Brussels and in the provinces," he cabled Ambassador de Kerchove in Leopoldville. On his behalf, de Kerchove urged Tshombe to try to recruit in Belgium "as discreetly as possible," but no one was fooled. "All this was public knowledge," remarks Colonel Vandewalle. All this was also in frank violation of a 1936 Belgian law that outlawed the recruitment of mercenaries on Belgian soil.[53]

Nevertheless, fewer than two hundred Belgians enlisted and even fewer Frenchmen; the number of Italians and Germans could be counted on one hand. U.S. officials were realistic: as long as so few Europeans volunteered, the South Africans would have to stay. In fact, for the duration of the war, South African and Rhodesian mercenaries constituted well over half the total. Godley was philosophical: while a shift to Europeans might "alleviate [the] political unacceptability [of the] mercenaries . . . none of us [the Belgian and British ambassadors and Godley] believe this would appreciably modify [the] situation." Moreover, he added, "the English-speaking mercenaries . . . have proven themselves more able than the Belgian and other heterogeneous French-speaking mercenaries."[54]

U.S. officials did what they could to package the unsavory product better. Why not call them "military technical assistance volunteers," the U.S. ambassador in Belgium asked. (Others preferred "special volunteers.") Well-meaning, repetitive suggestions rained on Godley. Rusk told him to "play down to [whatever] extent possible [the] role [of the] mercenaries." Rowan urged "more emphasis on Congolese and less on mercenaries," and Ball insisted that he take "measures to avoid publicity such as keeping mercenaries out of Leo[poldville and] impressing upon Hoare [the] necessity [of] keep[ing] quiet." Not an easy task: "Hoare can never resist the temptation to say the wrong thing to the press," the British embassy in Leopoldville remarked. The Congo "will need white troops for many years to come," he told *Le Figaro Littéraire.* "The work we have started has to be completed, and the only way to complete it is to kill all the rebels."[55]

The United States stayed in the background and built "a few fires under [the] Belgians"; as the former colonizers, they could dirty their hands. "We had to press them, cajole, yell at them," recalled a U.S. official. The Belgians were "small in resources and small in imagination," observed another.[56] U.S. policy makers wanted the Belgians to take the lead in the Congo—the lead, that is, in executing Washington's policy. The Belgians cooperated: by early 1965 their military mission in the Congo had swelled to almost 450 people, and Belgian officers were placed "in de facto command of most major Congo

Army detachments." Furthermore, it was the Belgian military advisers who openly maintained the daily contact with the mercenaries. "Overtly at least," Godley recommended, "US Reps should keep as far away from [the] mercenaries as possible." The United States wanted the mercenaries to be seen as the responsibility of the Congolese government and of Brussels. To make this unequivocally clear, "in accordance with the wishes of the American government," the mercenaries did not accept U.S. citizens.[57]

It is unlikely that U.S. public diplomacy swayed many Africans. U.S. involvement in the Congo "has resulted in a considerable strain in United States relations with a number of African countries," the British ambassador in Washington remarked. "The United States seems to have lost, in African eyes, that reputation for innocence which it once enjoyed because of its lack of colonial connection with the African continent."[58]

The governments of Algeria, Egypt, the Sudan, Guinea, Ghana, Congo Brazzaville, and Burundi lambasted U.S. support for Tshombe and the mercenaries, as did Tanzania, Kenya, and Uganda, which usually entertained cordial relations with the United States. Moreover, most of these governments provided money or weapons to the rebels or allowed aid to pass through their territory. Pragmatism, however, soon dampened their rage. With the exception of the Congo, all of these governments relied on U.S. economic aid (or, in the case of Burundi, Belgian aid)—a fact that U.S. officials did not let them forget. Moreover, from the outset England used its clout with African governments to rally support for U.S. policy in the Congo, and in early 1965 the French joined in. Finally, the mercenaries' victories could not be overlooked. "My personal relations with [President Jomo] Kenyatta healed slowly," writes the U.S. ambassador in Kenya. "But on May 5 [1965] he called me over [to] the State House, held out his hand and said, 'The Congo is finished. Now we can be friends again.' "[59]

At times, sheer luck helped the Johnson administration. Algiers had been providing some materiel to the Simbas ever since the Belgian-U.S. raid on Stanleyville. Relations between Algeria and the United States were strained, and in April Dean Rusk told the Algerian ambassador that "bilateral relations could not usefully be discussed as long as Algerian policies on Vietnam and the Congo were at such variance with those of the US." It was Ben Bella's overthrow at Boumedienne's hands in June 1965 that broke the impasse. Boumedienne, the CIA noted, "has been warm, open, and attentive with US officials." He promised that no further aid would be given to the rebels.[60]

By mid-1965, the storm was subsiding. Ghana's hostility was unchanged, but in material terms, as CIA Station Chief Larry Devlin observed, "Nkrumah did not play a role in the Congo in 1964–65, or a very limited one at most." Egypt, Burundi, Kenya, Uganda, and Guinea were "adopting a more pro-Western stance." Only Tanzania remained firm in its support for the rebels—defiant in its revulsion for the "traitor" Tshombe and his mercenaries. Tanzania, a Soviet official remarked, "is basically the only country that allows arms shipments and other assistance [for the Simbas] to pass through its borders without difficulty." The military impact of Tanzania's stand was negated, however, by one of the CIA's most successful operations: the establishment, in the spring of 1965, of the naval patrol on Lake Tanganyika, which intercepted boat traffic to the beleaguered rebels. "The trend line is going our way," the NSC specialist on Africa observed drily in June 1965.[61]

The trend was going in the right direction at home as well. The Congolese crisis had exploded at a time when the U.S. press was focusing on Vietnam. On 7 August 1964, Congress had approved the Tonkin Gulf resolution, which, as Robert McNamara remarked, "brought home the possibility of U.S. involvement in the war as never before." When a few days later, Johnson sent four C-130s with U.S. crews to the Congo and fifty-six paratroopers to guard them, the *New York Times* warned that "the United States is getting itself militarily involved in still another conflict. . . . [It] is starting with only enough arms, men and matériel to put out a little bonfire . . . but as Southeast Asia showed, bonfires can grow into great conflagrations." These fears were echoed by several members of Congress. "Today we are providing transport service," remarked Senator John Stennis (D-MS). "I cannot but wonder whether the next step will be the function of advising and training the Government forces, in the style followed in South Vietnam so that ultimately our men will be fighting and dying in combat."[62]

The administration was eager to dispel these fears. The C-130s were "mostly for evacuation purposes," George Ball assured Walter Lippmann. "We have no intention of getting . . . bogged down in the African swamp." And upon learning that the *New York Times* was "thinking of writing some editorial on the Congo situation," Ball called editorial page editor John Ochs and volunteered to send Deputy Assistant Secretary Wayne Fredericks "to N.Y. and have him talk to Ochs and [his] colleagues."[63]

It was not Ball's or Fredericks's eloquence but the mercenaries' successes that quelled the fear that the United States might be "drawn ever deeper into the Congolese jungle."[64] Through the months that followed, the U.S. press reported the obvious: "It has been the white mercenary force . . . that has contained and rolled back the insurgents." Led by the "intelligent, poetry-reading Colonel Mike Hoare," the mercenaries squared the circle: the Congo would be saved, and U.S. soldiers would not die.[65]

Nor were the mercenaries such bad chaps either, according to the U.S.

press. "They resemble rough-hewn college boys," one *Life* reporter wrote.[66] The *New York Times,* which provided more intensive coverage of the Congo crisis than any other U.S. newspaper, made only one attempt to show the U.S. people who the mercenaries were. It did so by devoting two articles to Lt. Gary Wilson, "a lean, 25-year old South African" who had enlisted, he confided, "because he believed Premier Moise Tshombe was sincerely trying to establish a multiracial society in the Congo. 'I thought that if I could help in this creation, the Congo might offer some hope, some symbol in contrast to the segregation in my own country.' "[67] We hear Wilson's distress at what he witnesses in the Congo. "It's a weird war," he muses, "frightening, brutal, sometimes comic, utterly unreal." We hear him talk about performing acts of great bravery. "He recalled the time two weeks ago when he captured [the town of] Lisala with 15 men [white mercenaries] against more than 400. . . . 'The rebs have one thing in common with our own Congolese,' he added. 'They don't take aim. They think that noise kills.' "[68] We hear his reaction to the cruelty of the Congolese—on both sides. " 'It's mass murder, it's mass murder,' " he mutters. Moreover, we hear that "his words summed up the feelings of most of his compatriots here."[69]

In its eighteen-month coverage of the war the *New York Times* reported the mercenaries' successes time and again; only on three occasions did it mention—and then ever so briefly—their transgressions. No photos like those published in the *Observer* appeared in the *Times.* Its readers learned instead of the mercenaries' efforts to protect the natives from both the rebels and the army. In a similar fashion, the *Washington Post,* the *Christian Science Monitor,* the *Wall Street Journal, Time, Newsweek, U.S. News & World Report,* and *Life* constantly assailed the rebels' atrocities and occasionally mentioned those of the army, but only exceptionally did they utter a single word of criticism of the mercenaries. They stressed instead how the mercenaries were saving the Congo from communism.

Perhaps the U.S. journalists who went to the Congo were silent about the atrocities the mercenaries committed because they were dependent on the U.S. embassy for information and transportation. Perhaps it was because the mercenaries were doing the United States's work. Perhaps it was because the mercenaries, like the journalists, were white and because they killed only blacks, while they saved the lives of white hostages (including some U.S. citizens). *Le Monde* put it well: "Western public opinion is more sensitive, one must acknowledge, to the death of one European than to the deaths of twenty blacks."[70]

Given the press's selective reporting, it is not surprising that very few whites in the United States expressed any qualms about the mercenaries.

African Americans were less placid. Malcolm X and the black Muslims lashed out at President Johnson, at his "hireling Tshombe," and his "hordes of white Nazi-type mercenaries." *Muhammad Speaks* asked: "If it is wrong for a rich individual to hire a thug to kill his enemy, does it become right for a rich country to hire killers to slaughter people of another country? . . . Or is it forgiven because the killers we hire are just 'killing niggers'?" Malcolm X called on African Americans and Africans to join together against their common enemy—in Alabama and in the Congo alike.[71]

Martin Luther King's wing of the civil rights movement was more cautious. The Call Committee of the American Negro Leadership Conference on Africa repeatedly expressed its unhappiness with U.S. policy in the Congo, called for a withdrawal of "mercenaries and other external forces," and asked that the problem be solved by negotiations. But these leaders and their constituencies were absorbed in the civil rights struggle that was raging in the United States. They had no desire to quarrel with a president whose help they needed. Insofar as they paid attention to foreign policy, they focused on issues that directly affected blacks in the United States—Vietnam, above all, where black soldiers were dying. "To them, Africa was distant, far off," remarked Congressman Charles Diggs (D-MI), one of the founders of the Black Caucus. Their interest in the Congolese drama was limited, and their complaints were somewhat perfunctory. Nevertheless, even their mild criticism provoked hostile comment. "Insofar as the civil rights leaders allow their movements to become hostage to the uncertain and confused events in Africa, they can provide heedless comfort to their enemies," the *Washington Post* lectured.[72]

The decision to rely on white mercenaries to win the civil war in the Congo did not stem from a belief that the rebels were communists or that a major Soviet or Chinese offensive was under way in the Congo but from the fact that the rebels were unfriendly to the United States. At best, their victory would have meant an unpleasant neutralist regime in a country where both the Eisenhower and Kennedy administrations had labored mightily to impose a pro-U.S. government. It came down, in the end, to a question of costs. If the cost of defeating the rebels could be kept low, then there was no incentive to explore alternative solutions, to run any risks, to accept any compromises. Had the only way to prevent a rebel victory been to dispatch U.S. troops—with its high cost at home and abroad—then U.S. officials might have allowed events in the Congo to run their course. As it was, there was very little debate among U.S. policy makers about the proper course to take, and if the administration's "doves"—Assistant Secretary Williams and his deputy, Wayne Fredericks—were uneasy, they kept their counsel.[73]

Only two newspapers, both African American, roundly denounced the United States's role "in the raising and paying of white mercenaries."[74] In the white press, the only references to any connection between the United States and the mercenaries were a phrase in *Life* about "Cuban exiles" having been "recruited by the United States" to fly the planes and three short sentences buried in a full-page article in the *Washington Post:* "The United States is flying mercenaries to the front. Better still, the United States is in effect underwriting the cost of the entire force of 'operational technicians,' as they are known in official circles. The monthly payroll: $300,000." One might have expected other newspapers to pick up the story, or *Life* and the *Washington Post* to elaborate on it. In fact, nothing happened.[75]

This reticence was not new. It had been present in 1954, at the time of the CIA covert operation in Guatemala, in 1957–58 during the covert operation against Indonesia, and in 1961, in the weeks before the Bay of Pigs. "If the leaders of the U.S. government decide that all the risks and perils of a major covert operation are required . . . it is not the business of individual newspapermen to put professional gain over that of country," Joseph Alsop explained. This "journalistic discretion," as he called it, survived the tumult of Vietnam and characterized the press's treatment of the 1975 Angolan civil war. Although aware of the U.S. covert operation there, the press maintained its silence until the failure of U.S. policy became too obvious to ignore.[76] In the Congo, however, the mercenaries were successful, and the press applauded.

It was in the Congo, in 1964 and 1965, that the United States used mercenaries in Africa for the first time, and the policy was successful at a very low cost. In late 1975, during the Angolan civil war, the Ford administration found itself in a tight spot, and again the United States turned to mercenaries. This time, history did not smile on them. This time, thousands of well-trained Cubans greeted the "White Giants." This time, the mercenaries fled. The White Giants—"who had sown death and despair in African countries in return for pay"[77]—were finally defeated.

Notes

A previous version of this essay was published in *Diplomatic History* 18 (Spring 1994): 207–37.

1. Rowan, memo for president, 14 August 1964, Confidential File, Country 29, box 7, Lyndon B. Johnson Library, Austin, TX; Director Central Intelligence (DCI), Special National Intelligence Estimate (NIE), "Short-Term Prospects for the Tshombe Government," 5 August 1964, National Security File (NSF), NIE, box 8, Johnson Li-

brary. Throughout this chapter, "Congo" refers to the former Belgian Congo, "Leopoldville" to Kinshasa, and "Stanleyville" to Kisangani.

For Congolese politics in 1964–65, see Centre de Recherche et d'Information Socio-Politiques (CRISP) of Brussels, *Congo, 1964* (1966) and *Congo, 1965* (1967); Benoit Verhaegen, *Rébellions au Congo* [Rebellion in the Congo], 2 vols. (Brussels, 1966, 1969); and Catherine Coquery-Vidrovitch, Alain Forest, and Herbert Weiss, eds., *Rébellions-Révolution au Zaïre 1963–1965* [Rebellion-revolution in Zaire], 2 vols. (Paris, 1987).

2. On U.S. policy toward the Congo in 1960–63, see Richard Mahoney, *JFK: Ordeal in Africa* (New York, 1983), 43; Madeleine Kalb, *The Congo Cables: The Cold War in Africa from Eisenhower to Kennedy* (New York, 1982); and Stephen Weissman, *American Foreign Policy in the Congo, 1960–1964* (Ithaca, NY, 1974). For the domestic situation in the Congo in 1960–63, see CRISP, *Congo, 1960* (Brussels, 1961); *Congo, 1961* (Brussels, 1962); *Congo, 1962* (Brussels, 1963); and *Congo, 1963* (Brussels, 1964).

3. Quotations from Rose, "Congo (Leopoldville): Annual Review for 1964," 12 January 1965, General Political Correspondence of the Foreign Office, Record Class FO 371, 181656, Public Record Office, Kew, England (PRO) and *Washington Post,* 25 November 1964 (quoting the consul, who had been held prisoner by the rebels for almost four months).

4. Rose, "Congo (Leopoldville)."

5. Godley to Williams, 16 June 1964, General Records of the Department of State, Record Group 59, Mennen Williams Papers, box 29, National Archives II, College Park, MD; *Le Monde,* 30 July 1964. On the alleged Chinese role, see *Le Monde,* 4 and 13 August 1964; *Le Progrès* (Kinshasa), 5 and 6 August 1964; and *Le Courrier d'Afrique* (Kinshasa), 12 August 1964.

6. Benoit Verhaegen, "La Première République" [The First Republic (1960–1965)], in *Du Congo au Zaire, 1960–1980* [From the Congo to Zaire, 1960–1980], ed. Jacques Vanderlinden (Brussels, 1984), 126; *Daily Nation* (Nairobi), 30 July 1964.

7. Dean to U.S. embassy, Leopoldville, 2 July 1964, Freedom of Information Act (FOIA), Department of State, microfiche 8503217.

8. U.S. embassy, Leopoldville, to State Department, Joint Weeka no. 10, 20 September 1964, FOIA, Department of State, microfiche 8503217; CIA, Directorate of Intelligence (DI), "The Security Situation in the Congo," 17 June 1964, FOIA 1978/135B; Godley to secretary of state, 5 August 1965, NSF Country File (NSFCF), box 81, Johnson Library; Rose, "Congo (Leopoldville)."

9. U.S. embassy, Leopoldville, to State Department, Joint Weeka no. 1, 2 July 1964, FOIA, Department of State, microfiche 8503217; Hoffacker, "What Should Be U.S. Policy vis-a-vis Tshombe in Future Contingencies?" n.d., enclosed in McElhiney to Palmer, 3 December 1964, FOIA, Department of State, microfiche 8503217; Godley to secretary of state, 1 July 1964, FOIA, Department of State, microfiche 8503217.

10. DCI, Special National Intelligence Estimate (NIE), "Short-Term Prospects for the Tshombe Government," 5 August 1964, NSF, NIE, box 8; interview with Robert Blake, Washington, DC, 21 May 1992; Williams to Harrison, 24 July 1964, RG 59, Williams Papers, box 12.

11. Ahmed Ben Bella, quoted in *Christian Science Monitor,* 17 March 1965.

12. Broadcast of 14 July 1964, quoted in CRISP, *Congo, 1964,* 456.

13. Denney to Harriman, Intelligence and Research Office of the State Department (INR), "Chinese Communist Involvement in Congolese Insurrections,"

11 August 1964, quoted, NSFCF, Congo, box 81; Hughes (INR) to secretary of state, "Appraisal of Congolese Insurgency," 7 August 1964, NSFCF, Congo, box 81; CIA, Office of Current Intelligence, weekly report, "The Situation in the Congo," NSFCF, box 87 (hereafter CIA, "Situation"), 27 August and 3 September 1964.

14. Denney to Harriman (INR), "Congo Contingency: Possible Alternatives Ahead," 15 August 1964, NSFCF, box 82.

15. *Washington Post*, editorial, 25 September 1964.

16. Godley to secretary of state, 2 August 1964, NSFCF, box 81.

17. Harriman to MacArthur, 4 August 1964, NSFCF, box 81; Rusk to U.S. embassy, Brussels, 6 August 1964, NSFCF, box 81; Brubeck, memo for president, 6 August 1964, NSFCF, box 81; Rusk to U.S. embassy, Brussels, 31 July 1964, NSFCF, box 81; "Exposé de Monsieur P. H. Spaak," 4 September 1964, Ministère des Affaires Etrangères (MAE), 149.1, Brussels, Belgium.

18. Rusk to U.S. embassy, Brussels, 6 August 1964, NSFCF, box 81; MacArthur to secretary of state, 6 August 1964, NSFCF, box 81; telephone interview with George Ball, 18 May 1992.

19. Interview with Blake; Williams to Rusk, 7 August 1964, RG 59, Williams Papers, box 12.

20. Rose to FO, 7 September 1964, FO 371, 17665; MacArthur to secretary of state, 6 August 1964, NSFCF, box 81; "Exposé de Monsieur P. H. Spaak," 4 September 1964, MAE, 149.1.

21. Scheyven to MAE, 21 August 1964, MAE, 18293 I (a).

22. Brubeck, memo for president, 6 August 1964, NSFCF, box 81.

23. "NSC Meeting on the Congo—12:30 P.M. Aug. 11, 1964," NSF, NSC Meetings File, box 1, Johnson Library.

24. Ibid.

25. Author's name deleted, memo for Bundy, 14 August 1964, NSFCF, box 81.

26. Godley to secretary of state, 5 August 1964, NSFCF, box 81.

27. Rusk to U.S. embassy, Leopoldville, 6 August 1964, NSFCF, box 81.

28. Williams to secretary of state, 7 August 1964, RG 59, Williams Papers, box 12; Rusk to Harriman, 7 August 1964, NSFCF, box 81; Frédéric Vandewalle, *L'Ommegang: Odyssée et Reconquête de Stanleyville 1964* [L'Ommegang: The odyssey and reconquest of Stanleyville, 1964] (Brussels, 1970), 201; Wilson, "White Mercenaries in the Congo," 28 August 1964, FO 371, 176683.

29. *Cape Times* (Cape Town), 25 and 27 August and 2 September 1964; *Le Courrier d'Afrique,* 28 August 1964.

30. NSF, NSC History, Congo C-130 Crisis, July 1967, box 15, Tab 1, "Background," Johnson Library.

31. USARMA Leopoldville to RUEPDA/DA, December 1964, NSFCF, box 85.

32. Hans Germani, *Weisse Söldner im schwarzen Land* [White soldiers in a black land] (Frankfurt am Main, 1966), 103.

33. The letter and the reply are in Anthony Mockler, *The Mercenaries* (New York, 1969), 244. It was not U.S. policy to exclude blacks: their inclusion was repugnant to the white mercenaries, particularly the dominant South African and Rhodesian element.

34. "Escale à Léo," *Jeune Afrique,* 8 August 1965, 19.

35. Germani, *Weisse Söldner,* 8, 60.

36. Godley to secretary of state, 13 December 1964, NSFCF, box 85; CIA, Intelligence Information Cable, "Situation Report of Stanleyville, 11–14 January 1965," NSFCF, box 85.

37. Godley to secretary of state, 26 August 1964, NSFCF, box 82; Carlo Gregoretti, "Una guerra privata in cinemascope" [A private war in cinemascope], *L'Espresso,* 20 December 1964.

38. *Observer,* 29 August 1965.

39. Peter Lloyd-Lister, "Stop Our Young Men from Going to the Congo," *Cape Times,* 14 and 21 August 1965; FO Minutes, "West Africa and the Congo. Impressions of Nigeria and the Congo by Colin Legum on his recent visit," 30 April 1965, FO 371, 181632.

40. Godley to secretary of state, 30 October 1965, NSFCF, box 85; telephone interview with Lloyd Garrison, 7 May 1992, who was the *New York Times* correspondent in the Congo in 1964–65. The best sources on the campaign are by the CIA (NSFCF, box 87). The most useful memoir by a participant is Vandewalle, *L'Ommegang.* Good secondary accounts are CRISP, *Congo, 1964,* 349–411, 535–36; CRISP, *Congo, 1965,* 43–58, 89–160; Fred Wagoner, *Dragon Rouge* (Washington, DC, 1980); and Thomas Odom, *Dragon Operations: Hostage Rescues in the Congo, 1964–1965* (Fort Leavenworth, KS, 1988).

41. Rusk to U.S. embassy, Leopoldville, 15 August 1964, NSFCF, box 81.

42. *New York Times,* 26 April 1966; Wagoner, *Dragon Rouge,* 66; CIA, "Situation," 17 November 1964.

43. Odom, *Dragon Operations,* 33.

44. Ben Bella, "Nous aidons les insurgés. C'est notre devoir" [We help the rebels. It is our duty], *Jeune Afrique,* 10 January 1965; Nyerere, *The Standard* (Dar-es-Salaam), 27 November 1964.

45. Politische Abteilung of the embassy of the German Democratic Republic (GDR), "Aktenvermerk," Moscow, 17 September 1964, quoted in AussenAmt (AA), A1154, GDR; Winzer to Ulbricht, 15 December 1964, AA, A14593.

46. *New York Times,* 13 December 1964; CIA, DI, "The Congo: Assessment and Prospects," 31 December 1964, NSFCF, box 87; telephone interview with Godley, 27 October 1992. Some Chinese aid may have arrived before Stanleyville.

47. On the Cuban presence in the Congo, see Jon Lee Anderson, *Che Guevara: A Revolutionary Life* (New York, 1997), 276–325; and Jorge Castañeda, *Compañero: The Life and Death of Che Guevara* (New York, 1997), 595–669.

48. *Le Peuple* (Algiers), 25 July 1964; *Tanganyika Standard* (Dar-es-Salaam), 27 July 1964.

49. Rowan, memo for president, 14 August 1964, Confidential File, Country 29, box 7.

50. Godley to secretary of state, 13 December 1964, NSFCF, box 85.

51. Memorandum of conversation, "Tshombe Request for South African Assistance," 11 August 1964, NSFCF, box 81.

52. Harriman to U.S. embassy, Brussels, 14 December 1964, NSFCF, box 85.

53. Williams to Harriman, 24 July 1964, RG 59, Williams Papers, box 12; Spaak to de Kerchove, 17 September 1964, MAE, 18289 (III); Kerchove to Spaak, 28 August 1964,

MAE 18288 (X); Vandewalle, *L'Ommegang*, 209. For the 1936 law, see U.S. embassy, Brussels to secretary of state, 30 January 1976, FOIA, Department of State, microfiche 8904623.

54. Godley to secretary of state, 13 December 1964, NSFCF, box 85; Godley to Department of State, 2 December 1965, FOIA, Department of State, microfiche 8503217.

55. Quotations from: MacArthur to secretary of state, 3 December 1964, NSFCF, box 85; Godley to secretary of state, 15 August 1964, NSFCF, box 81; Rusk to U.S. embassy, Leopoldville, 6 January 1965, NSFCF, box 85; Rowan to U.S. embassy, Leopoldville, 29 December 1964, NSFCF, box 85; Ball to U.S. embassy, London, 28 January 1965, NSFCF, box 85; Mason to Le Quesne, 26 June 1965, FO 371, 181705; and *Le Figaro Littéraire*, 17 December 1964.

56. Godley to secretary of state, 18 November 1965, NSFCF, box 85; interview with Robert Komer, Washington, DC, 26 September 1991, the NSC official in charge of Africa; interview with Blake.

57. CIA, "Situation," 27 January 1965; Godley to secretary of state, 26 August 1964, NSFCF, box 82. Mockler (*Mercenaries*, 247) prints the letter from which the above quotation is taken.

58. Harlech (British ambassador, Washington), "Annual Review for 1964," 1 January 1965, FO 371, 179557.

59. William Attwood, *The Twilight Struggle: Tales of the Cold War* (New York, 1987), 276.

60. Memorandum of conversation (Rusk, Guellal, et al.), 16 April 1965, NSFCF, box 79; CIA, OCI, "Consequences of Algerian Coup," 19 June 1965, NSFCF, box 79.

61. Interview with Devlin, Washington, DC, 18 June 1992; Komer, memo for president, 16 June 1965, NSFCF, box 76; *Tanganyika Standard*, 21 April 1965 (quoting Nyerere); Ronmeisl, "Auszug," Moscow, 11 August 1965, AA, A1168; Komer, memo for president, 16 June 1965, NSFCF, box 76.

62. Robert McNamara, *In Retrospect: The Tragedy and Lessons of Vietnam* (New York, 1995), 127; *New York Times*, editorial, 13 August 1964; Stennis, 14 August 1964, *Congressional Record*, 88th Cong., 2nd sess., vol. 110, pt.15: 19531.

63. Telephone conversation, Lippmann and Ball, 25 August 1964, 10:45 A.M., Ball Papers, box 2, Johnson Library; Telephone conversation, Ochs [Oakes] and Ball, 21 August 1964, 3:20 P.M., Ball Papers, box 2.

64. *New York Times*, 21 August 1964, editorial.

65. *Washington Post*, 14 March and 22 April 1965.

66. "Red Arsenals Arm the Simbas," *Life* (12 February 1965): 31.

67. *New York Times*, 25 October 1964.

68. *New York Times*, 2 October, 1964.

69. *New York Times*, 25 October 1964.

70. *Le Monde*, editorial, 28 November 1964.

71. Quotations from *Muhammad Speaks*, 18 December 1964 and 1 and 15 January 1965. See also Malcolm X with Alex Haley, *The Autobiography of Malcolm X* (New York, 1973), 347–63; and John Henrik Clarke, ed., *Malcolm X: The Man and His Times* (Trenton, NJ, 1990), 288–301, 335–42.

72. *Washington Post*, 29 November 1964; interview with Diggs, Prince George's County, MD, 18 March 1992; *Washington Post*, editorial, 1 December 1964.

73. The absence of debate on Congo policy is reflected in the documents available

at the Johnson Library and the Mennen Williams papers, and it was confirmed in interviews with Ball, Komer, Godley, and Blake.

In a letter to the author, however, Fredericks suggested that there were "differences of opinion within the USG on Congo policy" (New York, 28 May 1992). If so, they were so subtle or subterranean that U.S. policy makers were not aware of them. Thus Ball told Fredericks (who was, apparently, a dissenter) that "he and Fredericks saw eye to eye and he had complete confidence in Fredericks and his judgment" (telephone conversation, Fredericks and Ball, 11 November 1964, 3:45 P.M., Ball Papers, box 2). As for Williams, the written record shows him solidly behind the mercenary policy. The same is true for Rowan.

74. *Afro-American*, 11 September 1965 (quoted). See also 3 October 1964, 14 November, 5 December 1964, 2 and 23 January 1965. The other newspaper was *Muhammad Speaks*. (See 18 December 1964, 15 January and 19 March 1965.)

75. "Red Arsenals," 31; *Washington Post*, 15 November 1964.

76. Joseph W. Alsop with Adam Platt, *"I've Seen the Best of It": Memoirs* (New York, 1992), 443. See also Piero Gleijeses, *Shattered Hope: The Guatemalan Revolution and the United States, 1944-1954* (Princeton, NJ, 1991), 258-62, 367-70; Audrey Kahin and George Kahin, *Subversion as Foreign Policy: The Secret Eisenhower and Dulles Debacle in Indonesia* (New York, 1995), 158; Victor Bernstein and Jesse Gordon, "The Press and the Bay of Pigs," *Columbia University Forum* (Fall 1967): 5-13; James Aronson, *The Press and the Cold War* (New York, 1970), 153-69; and Harrison F. Salisbury, *Without Fear or Favor: The New York Times and Its Times* (New York, 1980), 137-64.

77. Agostinho Neto, quoted in *New York Times*, 11 July 1976.

The United States and Vietnam, 1950–1968: Capitalism, Communism, and Containment

ROBERT BUZZANCO

Throughout the Cold War the United States tried to contain or crush movements that it perceived as threats to U.S. economic or security goals in Europe, in Asia, in other parts of the so-called Third World, and at home.[1] Communists, nationalists, fellow travelers, neutralists, and activists for democracy and human rights, at various times, felt U.S. wrath in the half-century after 1945. In no place, however, did U.S. efforts to assert its own interests and thwart the will of the native population occur as intensely or tragically as in Vietnam. Though a small, underdeveloped country—haunted yet driven by a history of foreign conquest and resistance—and of little interest or concern to U.S. policy makers in the aftermath of World War II, Vietnam became the site of the most violent struggle of the Cold War era. While the country itself meant little strategically or economically in its own right, Vietnam became part of the much larger conflict that the forces of capitalism and communism were waging. In the end, by remaining ignorant of Vietnamese history, politics, and culture, by constantly pursuing a military solution despite advice to the contrary by ranking officers, by failing to address the divisions at home caused by the war, by dismissing the warnings of allies about the economic consequences of global hegemony and intervention, by failing to see Vietnamese nationalism and communism on their own terms and instead viewing those forces through the lens of the Cold War, the United States ironically managed to do to itself what its enemies had not been able to do for two decades after World War II: seriously weaken U.S. power and prestige, curb U.S. growth, and curtail U.S. hegemony in the world political economy.

Vietnam—Text and Context

As pointed out, Vietnam was part of a larger struggle, a pawn, as it were, in a geopolitical chess game. The major powers each saw in Vietnam a country that could be used to promote their own interests or those of important allies. Recall that Vietnam became an important *international* issue only after World War II. During those years in the late 1940s, U.S. officials were trying to reestablish a stable world system but at the same time restructure it according to U.S. needs. The United States believed it imperative to rebuild former enemies like Germany and Japan along capitalist and democratic lines. In this effort to create a new world (liberal) order, smaller countries, like Vietnam, became objects of interest. Future economic prosperity, if not hegemony, would depend on creating an integrated world market. Where colonial areas earlier in the twentieth century might have been attractive principally as sources of raw materials or cheap labor, in the postwar economic environment they would serve as important areas for investment and regional development. Vietnam's development along anticommunist lines, for instance, would be essential for the re-creation of capitalism in Japan and to keep the French appeased in Europe. Thus, this chapter will, more than most studies, pay attention to the economic factors involved in the Vietnam War: the need to use all of Southeast Asia, not just Vietnam, as a means of rebuilding Japan, and ultimately the drain on U.S. resources that the war would become. It will also stress the global nature of the war. In the past few years, documents from archives in ex-communist nations and from China have begun to increase our understanding of the Cold War and, in the case of places like Vietnam, the hot wars that attended it. Since Vietnam by itself was never of cardinal importance, understanding the ways in which the other powers involved—the Soviet Union and People's Republic of China (PRC), not just the United States—viewed the conflict and the respective parties at war will help provide a more satisfying explanation of the war in its broader sense. Indeed, some of the more exciting new work on the Vietnam War is beginning to be done (and will be done more and more) on the questions of the global nature of the war and its economic impact. They help us gain a more holistic sense of the United States's longest and, in most ways, most futile war.

Nationalism, Communism, Containment

Before trying to understand the U.S. war, and ultimate failure, in Vietnam, it is imperative to examine the traditions of nationalism, communism, and resistance prior to the U.S. involvement there in the wake of the Second World War. While U.S. policy makers saw Vietnam within the context of containment or capitalist growth, the Vietnamese viewed their struggle as another round in a historical process that had already lasted over two millennia. Since the second century B.C., when Chinese forces conquered Vietnam, until the twentieth century, a parade of foreign invaders—the Chinese repeatedly, Mongols, Portuguese, French, Japanese—had tried to control the states of Indochina: Vietnam, Laos, and Cambodia. All eventually met nationalist resistance and ultimately failed. U.S. policy makers, it seemed, were ignorant of this history and intervened in Vietnam expecting to get their way without undue trouble. After all, how could a small agrarian nation resist the power of a global giant like the United States?

But to the Vietnamese, the United States was, like the French or Japanese occupiers during World War II, essentially another foreign interloper. By that time also the Vietnamese had developed a rich tradition of protest against outside forces and the political organization to make resistance effective. From the late nineteenth century onward, poets and warriors—in verse and with arms—had challenged French colonialism and Japanese tyranny. As legend has it, the young Nguyen That Thanh—later known to the world as Ho Chi Minh—sat at the feet of the respected poet and nationalist Phan Boi Chau, who asked, "Shall we remain silent and thereby earn the reputation of cowards?"[2] The answer was obvious to Ho, who, as an expatriate in France and later in Beijing and Moscow, organized anticolonial groups, established the "League of East Asian Oppressed Peoples," and was a founder of the Indochinese Communist Party (ICP). Throughout the 1930s and 1940s, then, Ho was developing the foundation for both national liberation and revolution, the combined forces of which would face the U.S. forces a generation later.

Indeed, perhaps the United States's greatest blunder was its inability to recognize both the nationalist *and* socialist nature of the Vietnamese resistance, later organized as the Viet Minh. Never doctrinaire, Ho merged a class analysis and a program for land redistribution (the key issue in Vietnamese society) with popular front politics and an appeal to *all* anti-French elements to join the cause. Ho himself had no inherent animus against the United States either; in fact, encouraged by Woodrow Wilson's call for self-determination during the Great War, the expatriate in Paris had tried to get an audience with the U.S. president during the postwar conference at Versailles. In 1945, when Ho declared Vietnamese independence after the defeat of the Japanese, he had positive relations with U.S. military and intelligence officials, quoted at length from the U.S. Declaration of Independence during his own address marking Vietnamese sovereignty on 2 September 1945, and even sent telegrams to President Harry S. Truman seeking U.S. amity and recognition.[3]

To U.S. leaders, however, Vietnamese independence was not an important issue, and they saw Ho as a communist in any event. And indeed the Viet Minh was organized by most of the individuals who had established the ICP, while Ho himself had been supported by both the Soviet Union and the Chinese Communist Party in the past and would be even more so in the coming years. But Ho had never relinquished Vietnamese sovereignty to other communist parties or nations in return for aid. In fact, he had acquiesced in the restoration of French control in Indochina after World War II because, hated as the French were, the Chinese were worse. "Don't you remember your history?" he asked his comrades. "The last time the Chinese came, they stayed a thousand years. . . . Colonialism is dying. The white man is finished in Asia. But if the Chinese stay now, they will never go. As for me, I prefer to sniff French shit for five years than eat Chinese shit for the rest of my life."[4]

Ho had problems with the Soviet Union as well. While in exile in Moscow in the 1930s, Ho earned the suspicion of Stalin because he placed nationalism and peasant socialism above proletarian, Soviet-style, and Soviet-directed revolution and lobbied for a broad-based popular front against the French. In fact, Ho insisted that the ICP *not* take over the resistance but instead remain "its most loyal, active and sincere member."[5] Ho's differences with other communists were never so evident as in 1954 when—after the Vietnamese had defeated French forces in the decisive battle of Dien Bien Phu and had apparently gained independence—the Soviets and Chinese refused to support Vietnamese liberation during an international conference at Geneva, thus forcing Ho to accept the partition of the country at the seventeenth parallel, with him and the Viet Minh in control in the north and, subsequently, a U.S.-sponsored political entity in the south.

U.S. officials, however, did not appreciate Ho's distance from Stalin or Mao and treated him simply as a communist myrmidon of the other Red powers rather than as an "Asian Tito"—a term bandied about with some frequency in the 1940s and 1950s. Once World War II had ended and the U.S.-Soviet alliance had broken down, the United States, per George Frost Kennan's formulation, would pursue a strategy of containment against communism, first in Eastern Europe and then at all points along the globe. Containment really did not allow for nuance or interpretation, so Ho's communism was determinative, and his policies in the 1950s—the establishment of a centralized Communist Party in the north and land reform in particular—just hardened U.S. opposition. Even more, U.S. responses to Vietnam developed out of the larger context of the Cold War, especially the need for European security and Japanese recovery.

Though U.S. leaders had mouthed anticolonial rhetoric in World War II, the White House and State Department had supported the return of France to power in Indochina in 1945–46. Fearing the emergence of communist parties and trade union movements in Western Europe, and especially in France where the Communist Party and labor were strong, the United States would placate the French by acquiescing in their renewed control over Vietnam. For U.S. foreign policy makers, this was a no-brainer, since a French role in containing the European Left was exponentially more important than Vietnamese autonomy. Ironically, however, U.S. military officials, who agreed on the primacy of French interests, argued *against* supporting their return to Indochina, claiming that it would divert resources and attention away from their principal mission, containment at home. The civilians won out, however, and the United States began to back the French, sending about $25 million in 1950, which rose to nearly $1 billion by 1954.[6]

The Vietnamese, however, continued to resist the French, politically and militarily from 1946 to 1954, so the U.S. aid did not rescue France's position in Indochina. By 1954, then, the Viet Minh were on the verge of victory; hence the expedient agreement at Geneva to divide the country, *temporarily,* until nationwide elections could be held in 1956. That plebiscite never happened, though. Aware of Ho's popularity and support on both sides of the seventeenth parallel, U.S. officials and their Vietnamese allies canceled the vote, ensuring the continued partition of Vietnam, with a disgruntled nationalist-communist state—the Democratic Republic of Vietnam (DRV)—in the north and an artificial "country"—the Republic of Vietnam (RVN)—cobbled together by the United States in the south. Complicating U.S. efforts at containment in Vietnam, the southern regime was led by an autocratic mandarin, Ngo Dinh Diem, whose repression and corruption would be a great recruiting tool for the enemy Viet Minh. By the mid-1950s, then, the United States was on a collision course with the forces of liberation and revolution in Vietnam.

Capitalism and Communism in Asia: The Vietnam Connection

Just as Vietnam was a pawn in European politics, it had a subordinate role in Asia but was pulled into conflict due to the United States's larger goals in that region. As the United States surveyed Asia after the war, it had two major goals: to reconstruct Japan along capitalist, pro-U.S. lines, and to contain communism, especially in China. U.S. success in the first objective was offset by failure in the second as Mao Zedong's communists proclaimed the People's Republic of China (PRC) in 1949. Hence, by 1950, the United States, prompted by the need to develop markets in Southeast Asia, the area in which Indochina was located, and to keep the PRC from spreading its ideology and "exporting revolution," had assigned Vietnam a key role in its Asian policies.

The most pressing problem facing the United States after World War II was the so-called dollar gap. The United States was the only power to emerge from the hostilities stronger than it entered and was producing more goods than domestic markets could absorb (as in the 1890s). But European nations lacked adequate dollars to purchase the U.S. surplus. The United States needed to somehow get dollars into foreign hands so that other nations could in turn buy U.S. goods, but Congress, especially after appropriating $17 billion in Marshall Plan money in 1948, was reluctant to expend another huge sum of money on foreign aid. Still, without some type of support, U.S. officials feared, the Europeans would probably erect trade barriers against U.S. goods as they did during the 1930s, thereby exacerbating the Great Depression.[7]

Complicating, and connecting, such matters, the United States had also been subsidizing Japanese recovery since 1945 but by 1950 was hoping to wean Japan off U.S. funding and to connect it, as before the war, with other Far Eastern economies such as those in Southeast Asia, including Vietnam.[8] On this issue—the need for Southeast Asian markets—European and Japanese interests merged. Not only could the Japanese profit from trade with other Asians, especially since plans to link the Japanese and Chinese economies fell by the wayside with Mao's victory, but British recovery was linked to Southeast Asia as well. In the aftermath of the Second World War, British debt was growing rapidly, to a large extent because the flow of dollars from its colony in Malaya had been cut off, first because of the Japanese occupation during the war and then because of reconstruction difficulties afterward. To remedy Malaya's economic ills, the British began to pour money—£86 million between 1945 and 1949—into the country and to pressure the United States to offer economic aid and to increase imports of Malayan tin and rubber. U.S. purchases would then provide the dollars that the British could use to purchase goods from the United States.[9] As Seymour Harris, an economist on the government dole at the time, explained, "A gradual transfer of aid from Western Europe to the underdeveloped areas [such as Southeast Asia] will contribute towards a solution of the dollar problems of both Europe and the underdeveloped areas." "A vigorous foreign aid program,"

Harris concluded, was necessary "for a prosperous America."[10] Southeast Asia, then, could serve a dual purpose: providing markets and materials to Japan and helping fix the dollar gap for Europeans.

Vietnam was crucial to this process for two reasons. First, it too could provide raw materials and become a source of dollars for the French and could become a market for and offer materials to Japan. Second, the issue of communism in Asia touched directly on Vietnam. Within Southeast Asia after World War II, there were two communist insurgencies directed against European colonial powers—in Malaya against the British and in Vietnam against the French. While British leaders were not enthusiastic about France's return to Indochina, they even more feared that Ho's revolution would succeed and that Laos, Cambodia, Burma, and Thailand would then, like falling dominoes, fall to the Reds as well, thereby putting intense and direct pressure on Malaya. Once more, Ho's movement for national liberation became a target of U.S. opposition not because of events in Vietnam so much as because of the United States's need to develop a world system in which capitalist markets would be protected and nationalist-communist movements would be contained.

While the Vietnam War was being fought in the 1960s and 1970s, U.S. leaders contended that it was imperative to fight there to defeat communism.[11] But there were then, and there remain today, important questions about Ho's own version of communism, his commitment to expand Vietnamese control elsewhere, and his relationship with other communist states. In the past few years, with the opening of Chinese and Soviet archives, the work of Chinese and Soviet scholars such as Qiang Zhai, Chen Jian, and Ilya Gaiduk, and, importantly, the articles and documents put out by the Cold War International History Project, we have begun to learn more about some of these issues.[12] While Ho never accepted direction from the Soviet Union or China, he did rely upon them, especially China, for advice and support during the Viet Minh struggle against France and the later war against the United States. Through the 1950s, the Soviet Union did little to aid the Vietnamese liberation-cum-revolution, with the exceptions of recognizing the DRV in 1950 and offering light material support in the Vietnamese war against France. After Dien Bien Phu, the Viet Minh's military commander, General Vo Nguyen Giap, traveled to Beijing and met with both Chinese and Soviet military advisers, with the Soviets advising peaceful coexistence between northern and southern Vietnam and urging Hanoi to "reunify the country through peaceful means on the basis of independence and democracy."[13]

The Chinese, however, had offered important support to Ho in the war against the French (about one thousand tons of material monthly, according to U.S. military sources), though not nearly as much as the United States was giving the French, U.S. officials conceded.[14] Ho, with a traditional Vietnamese distrust of the Chinese, but also needing aid from Mao, had a somewhat ambivalent relationship with the PRC. In 1955, as the Soviets were urging compromise, Chinese military advisers told the Viet Minh to expect Western sabotage of the Geneva accords and elections planned for 1956 (they were right!) and to prepare for a protracted struggle for liberation. A year later, however, the PRC government withdrew the Chinese Military Advisory Group from Vietnam when Le Duan, a party official in the north, attacked Truong Chinh, the General Secretary of the Vietnamese Workers' Party and head of the land reform program, for applying Chinese models of agrarian reform—which had failed and led to repression and killing of Vietnamese peasants—without taking into account "Vietnamese realities." And later that year, Le Duan replaced Truong Chinh as general secretary, a possible sign of Vietnamese disaffection with the PRC. Despite that controversy over the adaptability of Chinese land reform to Vietnam, Ho continued to seek advice from PRC leaders, who were apparently paying more attention to "Vietnamese realities" when they urged the DRV to develop its agricultural sector before industrialization and to refrain from Chinese forms of agrarian collectives. As Zhou Enlai counseled, "Such changes must come step by step."[15]

In the late 1950s, both the Soviet Union and the PRC were urging Ho to be cautious with regard to any forced attempt to unify Vietnam—advice that dovetailed nicely with Ho's own conservative tendencies on that matter. After a Vietnamese request to analyze their plans for the south, Chinese communist leaders responded that the "most fundamental, the most crucial, and the most urgent" task was to rebuild and develop socialism above the seventeenth parallel. In the south, PRC officials advised Ho, the anti-Diem activists should conduct "long-term" preparations and "wait for opportunities."[16] Although dispensing advice freely, the communist powers, as General Tran Van Don, an aide to Diem in the south, conceded, were giving only limited material support to Ho, still dramatically less than the United States was supplying to the RVN. In the south, however, remnants of the Viet Minh, suffering under the Diemist repression, were pleading with the communist leadership in Hanoi to sponsor and fund an armed insurgency in the south. Ho, as William Duiker's work over the years has shown, wanted to move more slowly than the southern insurgents, and the RVN itself did not fear northern aggression below the partition line or a significant increase in DRV aid to the anti-Diem movement.[17] Apparently, the new documents show, the Chinese and Ho were on the same page.

By 1960, however, both Ho and the Chinese began to see the efficacy of armed struggle against Diem, with Hanoi acquiescing at the end of the year to the establishment of the southern-based National Liberation Front (NLF). It is not clear whether one side convinced the other or the PRC and DRV came to the same conclusion about armed insurgency on their own (which is probably more likely), but in a May 1960 meeting, Zhou Enlai, Deng Xiaoping, and the Vietnamese now saw the need for combining intensified political organization with armed struggle. By 1961, with a new U.S. president ready to significantly expand the U.S. role in Vietnam, communists in Vietnam, and China, were prepared to meet John Kennedy's challenge. During a 1961 visit by the DRV's premier, Pham Van Dong, to China, Mao Zedong expressed general support for armed struggle in southern Vietnam.[18] The war in Vietnam was about to expand.

Vietnam and the Communist Powers

As U.S. support and aid to the RVN increased and its military involvement grew correspondingly, Ho continued to make contacts with the PRC and Soviet Union and looked to them for more assistance as well. The Chinese especially had been helping the Viet Minh and NLF in the 1950s and early 1960s, providing the DRV and NLF with 270,000 guns, over 10,000 artillery pieces and millions of artillery shells, thousands of wire transmitters, over 1,000 trucks, aircraft, warships, and uniforms; in fact, one of the U.S. justifications for its own increased role in Vietnam was such PRC involvement. Thus, by 1964–65, as Qiang Zhai has shown, "Beijing perceived substantial security and ideological interests in Vietnam."[19] Remembering Korea, Mao feared a U.S. military role in Vietnam, so close to the PRC's own borders, and was ideologically committed to supporting the Vietnamese liberation movement. In mid-1964, Mao thus told officials of the northern People's Army of Vietnam (PAVN) that "our two parties and two countries must cooperate and fight the enemy together. Your business is my business and my business is your business. In other words, our two sides must deal with the enemy without conditions."[20] Beijing even placed some military units near the Vietnamese border in a state of combat readiness and sent jets to Hanoi, arranged to train Vietnamese pilots, and offered sanctuary and maintenance for DRV aircraft.

In October 1964, Pham Van Dong, Ho's closest adviser, met with Mao in Beijing and explained that his strategy was to restrict the war in the south "to the sphere of special war" (i.e. insurgency war), avoid provoking a larger U.S. intervention, and prevent the war from expanding above the seventeenth parallel. Mao was unimpressed by the U.S. potential to thwart the insurgency in the south and predicted that, if it engaged the DRV, the United States would "fight for one hundred years, and its legs will be trapped." Mao accordingly approved of the Vietnamese plans and suggested to Pham Van Dong that "you must not engage your main force in a head-to-head confrontation with [U.S. forces], and must well maintain our main force. My opinion is that so long as the green mountain is there, how can you ever lack firewood?" A few months later, Zhou Enlai elaborated on Mao's advice, telling a Vietnamese military group to attack U.S. main force units as they conducted mopping-up operations "so that the combat capacity of the enemy forces will be weakened while that of our troops will be strengthened."[21] General Giap already understood this approach and was adept throughout the war at drawing U.S. forces into battles in which the PAVN held the initiative and was able to inflict heavy casualties. Ironically, one U.S. war leader, Defense Secretary McNamara, saw the war in similar ways to Mao and Pham Van Dong. In November 1965, after the so-called victory of U.S. forces at Ia Drang, he recognized that the PAVN was avoiding main-force engagements and was attacking only at opportune moments. Even with a larger concentration of U.S. forces in Vietnam, as military commanders were requesting, Giap's strategic successes made it more likely "that we will be faced with a 'no-decision' at an even higher level."[22]

McNamara's fear, an expanded war in Southeast Asia, was, conversely, China's threat and advantage. Promising to "go to Vietnam if Vietnam is in need, as we did in Korea," Zhou warned that "the war will have no limits if the US expands it into Chinese territory. The US can fight an air war. Yet, China can also fight a ground war."[23] Lyndon Johnson understood that as well, and prudently, as Qiang Zhai correctly observes, did avoid provoking the PRC to the point of intervention. Indeed, during discussions with his military chiefs regarding reinforcements in 1967, the president asked, "At what point does the enemy ask for [Chinese] volunteers?" General Earle Wheeler, the chair of the Joint Chiefs of Staff, could not reassure Johnson, agreeing that China could easily send troops into Vietnam in support of the DRV-NLF effort.[24]

Chairman Mao, recognizing Washington's reluctance to more recklessly expand the war, was thus predisposed to help the Vietnamese more. In mid-1965, he met with Ho and agreed to help the DRV build roads to transport supplies into the south. He also recommended that the DRV "know how to escalate step by step," by destroying first a platoon and then a company, then a battalion, and then a large regiment or two.[25] Though offering advice, Mao was impressed with the Vietnamese efforts, complimenting a delegation from Hanoi that "you are fighting an excellent war. Both the South and the North are fighting well. The people of the whole world . . . are supporting you." The chairman also warned that the United States had the means to escalate the war and make things difficult. "Therefore," he urged, "there are two essential points: the first is to strive for the most favorable situation, and the second is to prepare for the worst."[26]

While counseling patience, the Chinese also believed that a late 1965 U.S. proposal to negotiate was insincere, that U.S. officials "just want to open talks to deceive public opinion." The northern Vietnamese would thus need to continue the strategy of protracted war because, as Zhou later explained, "Patience means victory. Patience can cause you more hardship, more sufferings. Yet, the sky will not collapse, the earth will not slide, and the people cannot be totally exterminated." To facilitate Vietnam's patient struggle, the PRC also agreed to send a small number of Chinese military personnel—sending in command, logistics, engineering, and political training help—to southern Vietnam. Around the same time, however, Zhou had to apologize to Pham Van Dong for a series of border crossings into Vietnam by the Red Guard, young zealots eager to fight U.S. forces during the Cultural Revolution.[27]

As the United States escalated its war in Vietnam, then, the Chinese increased their aid to the DRV—though to nowhere near the levels of U.S. support to the southern regime (the United States by the late 1960s was spending upward of $25 billion annually on Vietnam). By 1967, with over four hundred thousand U.S. troops in Vietnam, U.S. air attacks, including B-52 bombers, pounding the country on both sides of the seventeenth parallel, and both villagers and city dwellers experiencing constant hardship, it was no longer a "special war" in Vietnam but a U.S. war with growing outside communist participation. Zhou Enlai and Mao were optimistic despite the huge U.S. role. "The US is afraid of your tactics," Mao observed. "They wish that you would order your regular forces to fight, so they can destroy your main forces. But you were not deceived. Fighting a war of attrition is like having meals: [it is best] not to have too big a bite." Apparently to aid digestion, the Chinese also agreed to supply the DRV with one hundred thousand tons of rice and fifty thousand tons of corn as part of the total PRC contribution of over five hundred thousand tons of food in early 1967 already.[28]

While the PRC maintained a high level of interest in the war in Vietnam from the outset of the war of liberation in the 1950s, the other communist power, the Soviet Union (USSR), was initially more distant from the conflict. While offering recognition and some support to the DRV, the Soviets did not match the level of Chinese interest. In the aftermath of the 1962 Cuban missile crisis, U.S.-Soviet relations had improved noticeably, and the Soviets had minimized their role in Vietnam, which—along with Soviet suspicions that Ho was too close to Mao—caused a chill in the Kremlin's contacts with the DRV through 1964. That year, however, the ouster of Nikita Khrushchev and Leonid Brezhnev's assumption of power prompted the USSR to reevaluate its Vietnam policies and become more deeply involved in support of the DRV.[29] In part, the Soviets did not want to lose influence in Southeast Asia or relinquish their role as primary communist power to the PRC. Toward that end, the Soviets began to publicly denounce the "American aggression" in Vietnam and to increase their military and economic assistance to the DRV and NLF. Between 1963 and 1967, the Soviets sent over one billion rubles worth of military supplies to the Vietnamese, shipped German-, and then Soviet-, made arms to their "Vietnamese friends," and sent surface-to-air missiles, jets, rockets, field artillery, and air defense technology to Ho. Economic aid flowed as freely, with the Soviets providing 50 percent of all aid to the DRV by 1968, with a total package to that point of over 1.8 billion rubles.[30] The Vietnamese, while appreciative of Russian help, tried to exploit the friendship of both the Chinese and the Soviets. Vietnamese leaders Le Duan, Pham Van Dong, and Vo Nguyen Giap, among others, formed a working group in 1964–65 to determine ways to gain support from both communist powers while avoiding Chinese imperialism and an overreliance on the USSR. The Chinese and the Soviets recognized Vietnam's political strategy and, for their part, were using the DRV as part of their own struggle against each other. To the Soviet Union, Hanoi's interests were parochial—national liberation rather than international socialism—so the Soviets had to "drag" the Vietnamese to "greater friendship and independence [from China]." Soviet frustration was understandable, give the level of support it was giving to the DRV and NLF compared with its influence in Vietnam. As a Vietnamese journalist estimated, the USSR provided Vietnam with about three-quarters of its total outside aid, yet Soviet influence was less that 10 percent.[31]

Chinese and Soviet differences regarding Vietnam were part of a larger communist debate over the role of the two powers in developing socialism elsewhere. The PRC in the 1960s had assumed the mantle of revolution, while, as the Chinese saw it, the USSR was a stagnant bureaucratic state. Le Duan understood this and tried to take a middle path. Soviet help was "partly sincere," he told Zhou and Deng, and he disagreed with the Chinese on the nature of Soviet support. "You are saying that the Soviets are selling out Vietnam, but we don't say so," Le Duan asserted; "all other problems are rooted in this judgment." But he more strongly praised the PRC role in Vietnam, noting that there were already over one hundred Chinese military personnel in northern Vietnam and that the DRV felt confident that it could ask for several times that many if needed. Such support, Le Duan acknowledged, was based on "internationalism, especially in the context of relations between Vietnam and China. . . . We need the assistance from all socialist countries. But we hold that Chinese assistance is the most direct and extensive."[32]

And the PRC wanted to keep it that way. To Zhou Enlai, Vietnam's war against the United States was part of a larger political conflict between China and the USSR. "The closer to victory your struggle is," he told a Vietnamese delegation in Beijing, "the fiercer our struggle with the Soviet Union will be." Anticipating failure, Zhou predicted, U.S. officials would probably try to forge an agreement that would leave them in control of some parts of the RVN, a situation of "not losing totally." In this case, the "Soviet Union will give up" and not defend Vietnamese interests, just as Josef Stalin had not supported the Chinese revolution against Jiang Jieshi at the conclusion of World War II.[33] While Zhou's charges about a Soviet sellout lacked substance, it was true that the USSR was encouraging Hanoi to seek a diplomatic-political, rather than solely military, solution by 1966–67, serving as a "postman" in passing along requests and information from the United States to the DRV and acting as a "night watchman" in facilitating informal contacts between U.S. and Vietnamese officials. But the Soviet Union could not convince Ho to hold talks with the enemy to end the war. The DRV did not expect to lose, and it did not believe that the United States would accept its main demands, while, in the socialist camp, the Vietnamese did not anticipate any change in China's support for its war. Thus, the Vietnamese position on negotiations was always closer to the PRC's than the USSR's. The Soviets, however, understood Vietnam's logic and did not press Ho too much to change his approach. "China is situated close to Vietnam, whereas the Soviet Union is far away," the Soviet embassy in Hanoi acknowledged, and "Vietnam would be hard pressed to do without Chinese assistance in its struggle and in future peaceful construction. So it would be premature to ask the Vietnamese now to state their clear-cut position with respect to the USSR and China."[34]

The Chinese did expect the Vietnamese to choose, however, and even claimed "proof" of Soviet perfidy toward Vietnam. In May 1967 the USSR asked that a Soviet shipment of twenty-four fighter jets—twelve MiG-17s and twelve MiG-21s—be transshipped by air over Chinese territory. The PRC vetoed the idea, arguing that the Soviets were playing a double game—trying to publicize their support of the revolution in Vietnam but also tipping off U.S. spy planes in the area. The Soviets, China's Deputy Foreign Minister

Qiao Guanhua charged, "want to be boastful to the US" about their aid to Vietnam while "publicly revealing military secrets to the enemy." The proposal, he concluded, "has bad intentions and is a conspiracy."[35] Given such views, the Vietnamese had a difficult task in maintaining support from both the PRC and the USSR without taking an explicit stand on the conflict between the communist giants. The Vietnamese, "walking a tightrope," as Qiang Zhai put it, relied on the supply of Soviet weapons and other aid but did not want to damage their ties with the PRC or revive traditional Chinese aggression toward Vietnam.[36] Ho, the master strategist who had played off France, China, Japan, and the United States for several decades already, had once again done so, acquiring significant aid from both the Soviet Union and China but never relinquishing Vietnamese sovereignty in the process. Meanwhile, the war against the United States raged on, with the stakes for all sides increasing on a steady basis.

Vietnam and the Crisis of Capitalism

By the late 1960s, U.S. leaders had been monitoring the economic effects of military intervention in Vietnam for some time already. The war was exacerbating a deep deficit in the U.S. balance of payments (BOP)—the amount of U.S. money moving abroad, in the form of tourist dollars, investment capital, or military spending, for instance—thereby weakening the dollar and prompting foreign governments to cash in their U.S. currency for gold, which in turn undermined the international monetary structure. The eminent business historian Louis Galambos has argued that Vietnam "was the most debilitating episode in the nation's entire history, more expensive in its own special way than World Wars I and II combined."[37] An examination of the economic legacy of Vietnam in the 1960s offers ample evidence to support such claims.

After World War II, the United States had established global hegemony based on the confluence of its military power, economic growth, and political liberalism, and for a generation afterward it maintained a dominant position in the world political economy. By the mid-1960s, however, the United States's role was changing, principally as participation in the Vietnam War grew and caused greater BOP deficits and shortages in U.S. gold reserves. By 1968, the postwar system was entering a crisis phase as the Tet Offensive and the so-called gold crisis converged to transform the international system and create new political relationships at home. The events of 1967–68, it is not an exaggeration to suggest, marked the evolution of the United States's postwar role from that of unrivaled and prosperous imperial power to "first among equals" in a system of "shared hegemony." At home, the spiraling economic growth brought on by two decades of military Keynesianism could not be sustained in wartime, and U.S. capital began to flow overseas, to the detriment of domestic workers. By itself, Vietnam was calling into question the United States's military power and world leadership. At the same time, the Bretton Woods system experienced the greatest crisis since its founding. Created near the end of World War II, the Bretton Woods system established the dollar as the world's currency, fully convertible to gold at $35 per ounce and exchangeable with other currencies at stable rates based on the gold standard. Throughout the Vietnam War, however, the world monetary system was in disequilibrium or disarray, both as a result of the chronic and escalating BOP problem and, more critically, because of continuing runs on U.S. gold.

From the early 1950s onward, the United States experienced constant BOP deficits. Initially, they had a positive effect, exporting capital to facilitate European reconstruction and create markets. The so-called dollar gap, however, began to weaken the dollar, and by the early 1960s politicians began to look for ways to confront and solve the growing deficits, but attempts to pare it were futile. Although reductions occurred in 1965 and 1966, "the emergence of war in Southeast Asia," as Secretary of the Treasury Henry Fowler explained, "prevented the United States from approaching equilibrium in those years."[38] Such imbalances grew in concert with the intensified commitments to Vietnam, a war costing in the vicinity of $20 to $25 billion per annum by 1967–68, and thereby made it impossible to improve upon the shortfall or, because of the inflationary impact of the war, stem the outflow of gold from the United States. U.S. gold reserves, $23 billion in 1957, dropped to $16 billion in 1962 and decreased progressively thereafter. In 1965 alone, foreign central banks had redeemed dollars for $1.7 billion in gold.[39] At the same time, European governments began to openly criticize the U.S. war in Vietnam. French officials especially complained that Vietnam-induced BOP deficits and inflation, which averaged about 5 percent during the Vietnam era, were undermining their own economy. The British government felt likewise, prompting Johnson's national security adviser, McGeorge Bundy, to charge that the British were "constantly trying to make narrow bargains on money while they cut back on their wider political and military responsibilities. . . . There is no British flag in Vietnam."[40]

Throughout 1966 and 1967, however, the BOP deficits grew, gold continued to leave the United States, and foreign flags were still absent from Vietnam. Inflation was rising as well, causing a major increase in the cost of the war, increasing import demand, and decreasing exports. The U.S. share of world trade, which had approached 50 percent after World War II, was down to 25 percent in 1964 and fell to just 10 percent by 1968. Treasury officials also estimated that the BOP deficit would continue to soar due "entirely to our intensified effort in Southeast Asia" while "a further $200 million increase in [military] expenditures may occur next year [FY 67] and worsen the projected deficit by that amount."[41]

Then, in 1967, a full-blown monetary crisis emerged. Speculators, rather than member nations of a multinational "gold pool," were absorbing virtually all the world's new gold production, leading to a run on U.S. gold reserves—$1.2 billion in 1967 alone.[42] President Johnson, like his predecessors, vowed to maintain full convertibility at the par value of $35 per ounce. The French, more alarmed than ever about Vietnam-induced inflation, advocated a higher gold price and began cashing in their dollars. More critically, Britain devalued its pound sterling in November 1967.[43] The British devaluation—lowering the price of the pound from $2.80 to $2.40—created a monetary crisis. Speculators anticipated an increase in the official price of gold, so they withdrew $641 million—60 percent from U.S. reserves—from the gold pool in the week of 20–27 November, and National Security Adviser Walt Rostow warned the president to "expect further heavy losses this week."[44]

Facing economic pressure abroad and at home, Johnson acted on 1 January 1968, announcing a program to reduce the BOP deficit by $3 billion in 1968 by tightening regulations on the export of capital, asking U.S. citizens to travel abroad less, and cutting back on foreign and military assistance. He did not mention Vietnam, perhaps because, as Treasury officials earlier understood, the "European monetary authorities do not accept the Vietnam War as a justification" for U.S. economic distress.[45] The French nonetheless responded with "shock and surprise, sour grapes, and fear of the consequences for France and Europe," while de Gaulle personally "ran through the usual routine about the overriding power of the U.S. and the necessity of opposing the U.S. in order to help restore equilibrium in the world."[46]

At home, private sector economic experts warned of worse to come. Edward Bernstein told a Wall Street gathering that "no international monetary system can be devised under which foreign central banks can be induced to acquire unlimited amounts of dollars." The well-known economist Barbara Ward Jackson, in a memo widely circulated by Rostow, warned of "dangerous overtones of the 1929–31 disaster" in the current situation and feared that "depression and massive unemployment could occur in Europe if world trade did not stabilize."[47] Ackley and Rostow both thought Jackson's scenario was too pessimistic, but, as Rostow put it, "The overall problem Barbara has raised is real and, in one way or another, we shall have to meet it in the weeks and months ahead."[48]

1968 and the Dilemmas of Capitalism and Communism

Indeed, U.S. leaders could no longer avoid meeting the "overall problem" of Vietnam and economic calamity, and in early 1968 they had to confront the most serious U.S. crisis, military or economic, of the postwar era. In Vietnam, the enemy launched the Tet Offensive, a countrywide series of attacks that undermined Westmoreland's claim of "light at the end of the tunnel." Enemy forces, breaking a Tet holiday cease-fire, struck virtually every center of political or military significance in the RVN. Though suffering heavy losses—which U.S. officials would cite to claim victory during the offensive— the NLF and PAVN had in fact gained a major politico-strategic victory, exposing both the shaky nature of ARVN forces, who deserted in large numbers, and the bankruptcy of U.S. strategy, for U.S. forces could not even protect their own installations, even the embassy, in southern Vietnam. The shock of Tet, especially after respected newsman Walter Cronkite appeared on national television in late February 1968 urging an end to the war, forced U.S. leaders to finally reevaluate their approach to Vietnam, with the president rejecting a huge military request for new reinforcements, calling a partial bombing halt, beginning to "Vietnamize" the war, and withdrawing from the 1968 presidential race. After nearly two decades of intense efforts and the commitment of huge numbers of soldiers and money to Vietnam, Tet had made it clear that U.S. forces would not "win" in Vietnam.

But, just as importantly, the world economic crisis peaked in early 1968 as well, and money and war were on a collision course. The military's request for massive reinforcement—206,000 more troops and the activation of 280,000 reserves—McNamara warned, would require additional appropriations of $25 billion in fiscal year 1969–70 alone, without the likelihood, let alone the promise, of turning the corner in Vietnam.[49] At the same time, the Europeans, fearing the economic effects of another escalation in Vietnam, began cashing in their dollars for gold. During the last week of February, the gold pool sold $119 million in hard currency; on 3 and 4 March, losses totaled $141 million; and by early March the new chair of the Council of Economic Advisers, Arthur Okun, describing "a bad case of the shakes" in world financial markets, reported that the BOP deficit for the first week of March had risen to $321 million while gold losses soared to $395 million, including $179 million on 8 March alone.[50] Should such withdrawals continue to mount, as Thomas McCormick has explained, the depletion of gold reserves could have caused a devaluation of the dollar, which could have ignited a series of currency devaluations not unlike the 1930s. Then, with the absence of stable exchange rates, businesses would suffer globally.[51]

With the crisis intensifying, the administration scrambled for a response. An Advisory Committee established by Henry Fowler, headed by Douglas Dillon and including various leaders of the Washington and Wall Street establishments, insisted that Johnson press hard for a 10 percent surcharge on corporate and individual income taxes, a move Johnson had been hoping to avoid since late 1965; retain the $35 price of gold despite European calls for an increase; and, if the problems deepened, consider closing the gold pool. "My own feeling," Rostow admitted, "is that the moment of truth is close upon us."[52] He was right. On 14 March the gold pool lost $372 million—bringing the March losses to date to $1.26 billion—and U.S. officials anticipated that the next day's withdrawals could top $1 billion. The administration, as Rostow lamented, "can't go on as is, hoping that something will turn up."[53] The Europeans were also pressuring the United States to act, so Johnson, on the 15th, closed the London gold market for the day, a Friday—typically the heaviest trading day of the week—and called an emergency meeting of central bankers.[54] That weekend, governors of the central banks of the United States, the United Kingdom, Germany, Italy, Belgium, the Netherlands, and Switzerland—but not France—met in Washington to deliberate world monetary conditions. The governors, not for the first time, called on the United States and the United Kingdom to improve their BOP positions, urged the president to retain the official price of gold, and called for a "two-tiered" system for gold in which private markets could float their rates.[55] Perhaps the major reform emerging from the crisis was the estabishment of Special Drawing Rights (SDR). Created by the International Monetary Fund, these international reserve units—"paper" gold—provided the world monetary system with internationally managed liquid assets to avoid future massive hard currency withdrawals.[56]

While the governors had stemmed the crisis with such action, LBJ was feeling more political heat than ever. The CIA warned the White House to expect more criticism from France and continued attacks on the dollar. Rostow and Economic Adviser Ernest Goldstein told the president to anticipate additional costs for Vietnam in the $6 to $8 billion range for fiscal year 1969. And, in a biting analysis, Presidential Aide Harry McPherson berated Johnson for asking the U.S. people to keep supporting a war that was already excessively costly and had no end in sight.[57] Lyndon Johnson, however, did not have to be told how bad the situation had turned. At a 26 March meeting he lamented the "abominable" financial situation, with rising deficits and interest rates and growing danger to the pound and dollar. Worse, Westmoreland's request for 206,000 troops would cost $15 billion, which "would hurt the dollar and gold." The United States, he went on, is "demoralized." The president thus anticipated "overwhelming disapproval in the polls and elections. I will go down the drain. I don't want the whole alliance and military pulled in with it."[58]

The alliance and military survived much better than Johnson. In a 31 March speech to the nation, he announced limited reinforcements for Vietnam, curtailed bombing above the twentieth parallel, discussed the world monetary crisis, and stressed the need for a tax surcharge. At the end of his address he stunned the nation by withdrawing from the 1968 campaign.[59] Although the war in Vietnam would continue for five more years, Johnson was admitting failure in early 1968. The United States could no longer use its military and economic power in the same, often unrestrained, fashion that it had in the generation after World War II. The BOP deficit continued to grow. Without a tax bill, the administration faced back-to-back budget deficits of over $20 billion. And, as Okun emphasized, unless the world financial community regained confidence in the dollar, the "consequences for prosperity at home are incalculable."[60]

The U.S. financial community likewise understood just how seriously the war was affecting the economy. Walter Wriston, the president of Citibank, told a group of European financial leaders in January that it would be possible to overcome the monetary crisis without changing the gold standard but that "the chances would be greater if the Vietnamese war ended." Roy Reierson, senior vice president and chief economist at the Bankers Trust Company on Wall Street, complained in March that Vietnam had caused domestic inflation and had unduly burdened the BOP position. In an address amid the Tet and gold crises, a partner at Saloman Brothers, Sidney Homer, observed that "military setbacks in Southeast Asia will surely intensify attacks on the dollar." Vietnam had not alone caused the economic crises of the 1960s, Homer went on, but it had "aggravated our problems and in a sense frozen them." In a report to investors, Goldman, Sachs economists simply explained that reduced spending in Vietnam "could contribute significantly to the solution of many of the problems currently plaguing the U.S. economy." And the venerable chair of the Federal Reserve System, William McChesney Martin, lamented in late 1968 that the surtax was "18 months late. . . . Guns and butter [are both] not attainable in wartime."[61] The Bretton Woods system and military Keynesianism—which had driven economic growth in the Cold War—had been dealt a serious blow by the Vietnam War, and the United States would henceforth have to negotiate its hegemony and economic influence with Western Europe and Japan.[62]

The communist nations were not without their own crises in 1968, however, for the PRC, Soviet Union, and Vietnam all fell into conflict with each other just as the DRV-NLF war was attaining its greatest success. The Soviet Union was still trying to persuade Ho to negotiate with the United States and had denounced Hanoi for rejecting Lyndon Johnson's late 1967 "San Antonio Formula," which had promised a bombing pause if the Vietnamese would talk. The Soviet embassy even advised Moscow to inform the DRV that the USSR could not afford political brinksmanship with the United States by deepening its involvement in Vietnam and that an end to hostilities in 1968 would be in both Vietnamese and Soviet interests.[63] But the PRC, wanting to maintain a high level of antagonism between the Soviet Union and the United States, feared that negotiations could end the war, which would raise the prospects of Chinese-Vietnamese tension again and would remove the U.S. counterbalance in Asia against the Soviets.[64]

Afraid that peace might break out, Zhou, after Ho accepted LBJ's partial bombing halt as a basis for "contacts," railed against the DRV in a meeting with Pham Van Dong. To Zhou, the United States was at its weakest point, with Tet, the dollar crisis, and racial unrest provoked by the murder of Martin Luther King causing great distress in the United States. Yet the DRV's acceptance of contacts was a Vietnamese compromise, and "it helps the US solve their difficulties. . . . The situation showed that Vietnamese comrades find it easy to compromise. . . . Your position is now weaker, not stronger." To the Chinese, military means would decide victory, not negotiations, so "you have lost your initiative and fallen into a passive position," Zhou charged. U.S. officials believe that "you are eager to negotiate," Zhou added. He reminded the Vietnamese that the United States, ARVN, and other supporters had access to over one million troops and that "before their backbone has been broken, or before five or six of their fingers have been broken, they will not accept the defeat, and they will not leave." The Chinese, in concluding, also warned against bringing the USSR into the peace process, telling them, "You should not inform the Soviets about developments in the negotiations with the US because they can inform the US."[65]

For their part, the Vietnamese did not appreciate PRC pressure and began to distance themselves from the Chinese, especially during the Czech crisis of mid-1968. The USSR, believing it had to take a leadership role in global affairs regarding socialist countries, sent troops into Czechoslovakia to stem a liberalization movement there. The Chinese had repeatedly accused the

Soviet Union of deviating from the Marxist, revolutionary line and of collusion with the West, so, as Ilya Gaiduk explained, "the Kremlin had to defend
its policy not only by strong words, but also by deeds." The DRV, amid an
intense anti-Soviet campaign out of Beijing, supported the Czech invasion,
angering the Chinese but bringing praise from Moscow. Hanoi's support of
the Soviets, open and explicit, was a signal to the USSR that the DRV was
moving closer to it and remaining independent of the PRC. Thus the Soviet
Union urged—and the Vietnamese agreed—that negotiations, then under
way in Paris, should be taken seriously to try to end the war.[66]

Vietnam and the World

The events of 1968 served as an exclamation point to the previous global
crises of the decade as the various global issues being contested seemed to
converge. The U.S. war of attrition would not succeed as a result of the Tet
Offensive; U.S. economic hegemony was under siege due to the dollar-gold
crisis; the Vietnamese, under heavy pressure from the Chinese to continue
the war, avoid negotiations, and maintain distance from the Soviet Union,
instead moved closer to the Soviets and angered the PRC in the process; the
USSR tried to maintain its socialist credibility by suppressing Czechoslovakia
while conversely showing its sensibility by tempering the war in Vietnam.
What had begun in the aftermath of World War II as a war of national
liberation waged by the Viet Minh against the French Union had become a
global affair, with the world's major powers involved.

Because of the escalation of the conflict in Vietnam—by the United
States, by Vietnam, by the Soviet Union, and by China too—the world was
transformed. U.S. military and economic power, the events of the mid- to
late 1960s showed, was limited. Washington no longer had fiat over the
world as it seemed to have had in the 1940s and 1950s. Apparently unable or
unwilling to distinguish between nationalism and communism, the United
States, for reasons of credibility and capitalist expansion, tried to crush a
liberation-cum-revolution in Vietnam with dire consequences. Not only was
the United States's world position undermined, but, much worse, tens of
thousands of U.S. citizens died fighting in Indochina, while, worse still, a
small nation in Indochina was destroyed beyond feasible reconstruction.
The Vietnamese, for their part, finally reached their goal. After 1968 it was
clear that the United States did not possess the means or the will to "win" in
Vietnam, and though troops remained until 1973 and the United States supported the RVN until 1975, Tet had effectively become the U.S. obituary in
Vietnam. As for the communist world, the Vietnam War exposed divisions

between the PRC and the USSR that were evident prior to the 1960s but not as obvious. By 1968, talk of "monolithic communism" was simply absurd; the major powers were more concerned with the political war they were fighting among themselves than with the shooting war between Vietnam and the United States. And after the war, conditions in Asia returned to what seemed to be their normal state. The Vietnamese and Chinese became blood rivals once more, and in 1979, with U.S. provocation, the PRC even invaded the DRV, called the Socialist Republic of Vietnam (SRV) after its 1975 victory and the unification of the country. Inside Vietnam, one wonders if the capitalists did not win the war after all. Foreign investment in the SRV is significant, with few obstacles to outside entrepreneurs who want to exploit the people of Vietnam. While Nike—which pays its workers about $30 per month to perform what is essentially sweatshop labor—may be the most public example, such foreign business interests are commonplace. Vietnam, rather than being rebuilt "ten times more beautiful," as Ho envisioned in his final testament, remains living proof of the dangers involved in taking on the powers of the world when their interests diverge from yours.

Notes

1. There is a significant body of literature on the U.S. role in containing nationalism and communism in the Cold War, especially in "Third World" countries such as Vietnam. Some of the better works include Walter LaFeber, *Inevitable Revolutions: The United States in Central America* (New York, 1983); George M. Kahin and Audrey Kahin, *Subversion as Foreign Policy: The Secret Eisenhower and Dulles Debacle in Indonesia* (New York, 1995); Thomas Paterson, *Contesting Castro: The United States and the Triumph of the Cuban Revolution* (New York, 1994); Richard H. Immerman, *The CIA in Guatemala: The Foreign Policy of Intervention* (Austin, TX, 1983); Piero Gleijeses, *Shattered Hope: The Guatemalan Revolution and the United States, 1944–1954* (Princeton, NJ, 1991); Robert J. McMahon, *The Cold War on the Periphery: The United States, India, and Pakistan* (New York, 1994); and Mark Lytle, *The Origins of the Iranian-American Alliance* (New York, 1987).

2. In David Marr, *Vietnamese Anticolonialism, 1885–1925* (Berkeley, CA, 1971), 46.

3. Commanding General (hereafter CG), U.S. Forces, India-Burma Theatre, memorandum to War Department, CG, U.S. Forces, China Theatre, and CG, U.S. Army Liaison Section in Kandy, Ceylon, 11 September 1945, CRAX 27516, Records of the Joint Chiefs of Staff, Record Group 218, Chairman's File, Admiral Leahy, 1942–1948, National Archives II, College Park, MD (hereafter RG 218, with appropriate filing information); Gallagher, Hanoi, to General R. B. McClure, Kunming, 20 September 1945, in *Vietnam: The Definitive Documentation of Human Decisions*, ed. Gareth Porter (Stanfordville, NY, 1979), 1:77–78, doc. 41. See also Report on Office of Strategic Services' "Deer Mission" by Major Allison Thomas, 17 September 1945, in Porter, *Vietnam*, 1:74–77, doc. 40; memorandum for the record: General Gallagher's Meeting with Ho

Chi Minh, 29 September 1945, in Porter, *Vietnam,* 1:80–81, doc. 44; George McT. Kahin, *Intervention: How American Became Involved in Vietnam* (Garden City, NY, 1987), 14, 438; and U.S. Congress, House Committee on Armed Services, *United States-Vietnam Relations, 1945–1967: Study Prepared by the Department of Defense,* 12 vols. (Washington, DC, 1971), Book I, I.C.3, C-66–104 (hereafter *USVN Relations* with appropriate volume and page designations).

    4. In Stanley Karnow, *Vietnam: A History* (New York, 1983), 53.

    5. William J. Duiker, *The Communist Road to Power in Vietnam* (Boulder, CO, 1981), 31–33; William J. Duiker, *Sacred War: Nationalism and Socialism in a Divided Vietnam* (New York, 1995), 33–34.

    6. On U.S. support of France and the debate in U.S. circles over that policy, see Robert Buzzanco, *Masters of War: Military Dissent and Politics in the Vietnam Era* (New York, 1996), esp. chap. 2.

    7. See, among others, Fred Block, *The Origins of the International Economic Disorder* (Berkeley, CA, 1977), 92–96; William Borden, *The Pacific Alliance: United States Economic Policy and Japanese Trade Recovery, 1947–1955* (Madison, WI, 1984), 26–35; Thomas McCormick, *America's Half-Century: United States Foreign Policy in the Cold War and After,* 2nd ed. (Baltimore, 1995), 90–91. I would especially like to thank Curt Cardwell, whose M.A. thesis draft from California State University-Sacramento, "Making the World Safe for Capitalism: The British Sterling-Dollar Crisis of 1949–1950 and the Origins of NSC-68," was quite useful in developing these themes.

    8. Andrew Rotter, *The Path to Vietnam: Origins of the American Commitment to Southeast Asia* (Ithaca, NY, 1989), 44–46.

    9. "Implications of the Sterling Areas Crisis to the U.K. and U.S.," 18 August 1949, U.S. Department of State, *Foreign Relations of the United States, 1949* (Washington, DC, 1975), 4:806–20; Rotter, *Path to Vietnam,* 49–57.

    10. In Rotter, *Path to Vietnam,* 114.

    11. On the John Kennedy and Lyndon Johnson commitments to defeat the Left in Vietnam, see my *Masters of War.*

    12. Chen Jian, "China's Involvement in the Vietnam War, 1964–1969," *China Quarterly* 142 (June 1995): 357–87; Qiang Zhai, "Transplanting the Chinese Model: Chinese Military Advisers and the First Vietnam War, 1950–1954," *Journal of Military History* 57 (October 1993): 698–715; Qiang Zhai, "Beijing and the Vietnam Conflict, 1964–1965: New Chinese Evidence," *Cold War International History Bulletin—The Cold War in Asia* 6–7 (Winter 1995–96): 233–50; Ilya Gaiduk, "The Vietnam War and Soviet-American Relations, 1964–1973: New Russian Evidence," *Cold War International History Bulletin—The Cold War in Asia* 6–7 (Winter 1995–96): 232, 250–58; Ilya Gaiduk, *The Soviet Union and the Vietnam War* (Chicago, 1996); on the Cold War International History Project (CWIHP), consult their Web site for information on their *Bulletin* and documents: http://cwihp.si.edu.

    13. Gaiduk, "New Russian Evidence," 233; Qiang Zhai, "New Chinese Evidence."

    14. Admiral Arthur Radford and Bedell Smith in Executive Session, Senate Committee on Foreign Relations, 1954, 16 February 1954, 6:112; JCS Paper, "The Situation in Indochina," 7 February 1954, RG 218, CCS 092 Asia (6–25–48), section 57.

    15. Qiang Zhai, "New Chinese Evidence," 234.

    16. Ibid.

17. Captain W. M. Kaufman, U.S. Navy, memorandum of conversation, 13 May 1957, General Records of the Department of State, Record Group 59, file 751G.11/5-1357, National Archives II; Duiker, *The Communist Road to Power;* Duiker, *Sacred War,* 132-33.

18. Qiang Zhai, "New Chinese Evidence," 234.

19. Ibid., 243, 235.

20. Mao in ibid., 235.

21. Mao Zedong and Pham Van Dong, Beijing, 5 October 1964, CWIHP Web site, document #3 under keyword "Vietnam" (hereafter cited by document number), Zhou quoted in note 5.

22. McNamara to Johnson, 30 November 1965, Vietnam, Country File, National Security File (VN, CF, NSF), box 74-75, folder: 2EE, 1965-67, Primarily McNamara Recommendations re. Strategic Actions [1965-1966], Lyndon B. Johnson Library, Austin, TX (the 30 November memorandum was a supplement to a McNamara memo to the president of 3 November 1965 titled "Courses of Action in Vietnam," in same source as above); see also McNamara to Johnson, 6 December 1965, "Military and Political Recommendations for South Vietnam," same source as above.

23. Zhou Enlai and Nguyen Van Hieu, Nguyen Thi Binh, Beijing (The Great Hall of the People), 16 May 1965, CWIHP Web site, document #8.

24. Notes on discussion with the president, 27 April 1967, Warnke-McNaughton Files, box 2, folder: McNTN Drafts 1967 [2], Johnson Library. See also appendix to Wheeler to McNamara, 29 May 1967, VN, CF, NSF, box 81-84, folder: 3 E (1)b, 6/65-12/67, Future Military Operations in Vietnam.

25. Mao Zedong and Ho Chi Minh, Changsha (Hunan), 16 May 1965, CWIHP Web site, document #9; Mao Zedong and Hoang Van Hoan, Beijing, 16 July 1965, CWIHP Web site, document #13.

26. Mao's conversation with DRV delegation, 20 October 1965, document #6 in Qiang Zhai, "New Chinese Evidence."

27. Mao Zedong, Zhou Enlai, Pham Van Dong, Beijing, 10 April 1967, CWIHP Web site, document #25.

28. Continuing the analogy, Mao said, "In fighting the US troops, you can have a bite the size of a platoon, a company, or a battalion. With regard to the troops of the puppet regime, you can have a regiment-size bite. It means that fighting is similar to having meals, you should have one bite after another." Mao Zedong, Pham Van Dong, and Vo Nguyen Giap, Beijing, 11 April 1967, CWIHP Web site, document #26.

29. Gaiduk, "New Russian Evidence," 232, 250.

30. Ibid., 250-51.

31. Ibid., 251-52.

32. Zhou Enlai, Deng Xiaoping, Kang Shung, Le Duan, and Nguyen Duy Trinh, Beijing, 13 April 1966, CWIHP Web site, document #19.

33. Zhou then launched into an extensive explanation-cum-indictment of what he saw as the Soviet sellout of the Chinese Communists in the 1940s. Vietnamese and Chinese delegations, Beijing, 11 April 1967, CWIHP Web site, document #27.

34. Gaiduk, "New Russian Evidence," 255, Soviet embassy quote on 252.

35. Chinese Deputy Foreign Minister Qiao Guanhua and Vietnamese Ambassador Ngo Minh Loan, Beijing, 13 May 1967, CWIHP Web site, document #29.

36. Qiang Zhai, "New Chinese Evidence," 242.

37. Louis Galambos, "Paying Up: The Price of the Vietnam War," *Journal of Policy History* 8 (1996): 167.

38. Fowler to the president, late 1967, White House Central Files, Confidential Files, FO4-1, Balance of Payments (1967), Johnson Library (hereafter WHCF, Confidential Files, with appropriate filing designations).

39. Buzzanco, *Masters of War,* 237–39.

40. Bundy to the president, 28 July 1965, subj: Your Meeting with Joe Fowler, National Security File, Memos to the President, McGeorge Bundy, volume 12, Johnson Library (hereafter NSF, Memos, Bundy).

41. Fowler to the president, 26 November 1965, and Bator to the president, 29 November 1965, both in WHCF, FO4.

42. On the cost of the war, see Thomas Campagna, *The Economic Consequences of the Vietnam War* (Westport, CT, 1991); the run on gold in 1967 was similar to that of previous years: Between 1957 and 1962, U.S. gold stocks decreased from $23 to $16 billion, and in 1965 alone, foreign central banks had redeemed dollars for over $1.5 billion in gold. Gabriel Kolko, *Anatomy of a War: Vietnam, the United States, and the Modern Historical Experience* (New York: 1985), 283–90.

43. NSC synopsis, *The Gold Crisis,* Nov. 1967-Mar. 1968, National Security File, NSC History, "Gold Crisis," Book I, tabs 19–49, Johnson Library (hereafter NSC History, "Gold Crisis," with appropriate filing designations); personal message to Mr. Secretary Fowler from the Chancellor of the Exchequer, 14 October 1967, WHCF, Confidential Files, FO4, Financial Relations; Gardner, *Pay Any Price.*

44. Rostow to LBJ, 22 November 1967, NSC History, "Gold Crisis," Book I, tabs 1–18; Ackley to LBJ, 27 November 1967, NSC History, "Gold Crisis," Book I, tabs 1–18.

45. Treasury paper, "The Balance of Payments Program of New Year's Day, 1968," National Security File, NSC History, "Balance of Payments," tabs 1–3, Johnson Library (hereafter NSC History, "Balance of Payments" with appropriate filing designation); Treasury paper on international monetary situation, Fall 1967, WHCF, Confidential Files, FO4, Financial Relations.

46. Special Analysis by Lionel D. Edie and Company, "The Reactions in Paris to the American Balance of Payments Program," 16 January 1968, WHCF, Confidential Files, FO4-1, Balance of Payments (1968–1969); Bohlen to Rusk, 23 January 1968, subj: Report of the Meeting between de Gaulle and Sulzberger, NSF, Country File, France, folder: Cables, vol. XIII.

47. Edward Bernstein, "Gold and the International Monetary System," 23 January 1968, WHCF, Confidential Files, FI9, Monetary Systems; Barbara Ward Jackson memo to president, 23 January 1968, NSC History, "Gold Crisis," Book I, tabs 19–49.

48. Ackley to LBJ, 24 January and 8 February 1968, subj: Comments on the Attached Memoranda, WHCF, Confidential Files, FI9, Monetary Systems; Rostow to LBJ, 23 January 1968, subj: Prospects for Another Sterling Crisis and What It Could Mean, NSC History, "Gold Crisis," Book I, tabs 19–49.

49. McNamara in notes of meeting, 27 February 1968, VN, CF, NSF, box 127, folder: 19 March 1970.

50. Okun to LBJ, 2 and 9 March 1968, subj: Weekly Balance of Payment Report, and Fowler to LBJ, 4 March 1968, subj: Gold Problems, both in Robert Buzzanco, "The

Vietnam War and the Limits of Military Keynesianism" (paper presented at the annual meeting of the American Historical Association, New York, January 1997); Rostow to LBJ, 8 March 1968, NSC History, "Gold Crisis," Book I, tabs 19–49.

51. McCormick, *America's Half-Century,* 162.

52. Rostow to LBJ, 9 March 1968, subj: The Gold Issue, NSC History, "Gold Crisis," Book I, tabs 19–49; Rostow in Robert Collins, "The Economic Crisis of 1968 and the Waning of the American Century," *American Historical Review* 101 (April 1996): 408.

53. Rostow to LBJ, 14 March 1968, subj: Gold, in Buzzanco, "Limits of Military Keynesianism."

54. U.S. consul, Frankfort, #6686 to secretary of state, U.S. Embassy, Paris, #11520 to secretary of state, 15 March 1968, and U.S. Embassy, Paris, #11574 to secretary of state, in Buzzanco, "Limits of Military Keynesianism"; Rusk #130741 to European embassies, NSC History, "Gold Crisis," Book I, tabs 50–53.

55. Communique of meeting of central bankers, 17 March 1968, in Buzzanco, "Limits of Military Keynesianism."

56. Collins, "The Economic Crisis of 1968."

57. DCI, intelligence memorandum, "French Actions in the Recent Gold Crisis," 20 March 1968, Rostow to LBJ, 20 March 1968, Goldstein to LBJ, 22 March 1968, and McPherson to LBJ, 18 March 1968, in Buzzanco, "Limits of Military Keynesianism."

58. Note of president's meeting with Wheeler and Abrams, 26 March 1968, Tom Johnson's Notes, folder: March 26, 1968—10:30 A.M., Johnson Library.

59. President's speech of 31 March 1968, *Public Papers of the President: Lyndon B. Johnson, 1968* (Washington DC, 1969), 1:469–76.

60. Okun to LBJ, 27 April 1968, subj: Weekly Balance of Payments report, and Okun to LBJ, 23 May 1968, subj: What Fiscal Failure Means, in Buzzanco, "Limits of Military Keynesianism."

61. Address by Walter B. Wriston, 17 January 1968, and paper by Roy L. Reierson, 4 March 1968, Joseph Fowler Papers, box 82, folder: Domestic Economy: Gold, 1968 [1 of 2], Johnson Library; address by Sidney Homer, 20 March 1968, Fowler Papers, box 88, folder: Domestic Economy: Gold Crisis, Meeting with Central Bank Governors [1 of 2]; "Hope and Trouble," report by Goldman, Sachs and Company, 8 May 1968, Fowler Papers, box 78, folder: Domestic Economy: Economic Data, 1968 [2 of 2]; Martin in notes of Business Council meeting, 17–20 October 1968, Fowler Papers, box 178, folder: Government—Committees/Councils.

62. "The economic consequences of the escalating Vietnam War so exacerbated the dollar drain, the trade imbalance, and the maladies of the civilian sector," according to Thomas McCormick, "that significant tariff cuts [as in the Kennedy Round] ironically did less to help American exports than it did to open the American market to ever-more-competitive capitalists from Germany and Japan." *America's Half-Century,* 128.

63. Gaiduk, "New Russian Evidence," 255.

64. Qiang Zhai, "New Chinese Evidence," 242–43.

65. Zhou Enlai and Pham Van Dong, Beijing, 13 April 1968, CWIHP Web site, document #31; Zhou Enlai and Pham Van Dong, 19 April 1968, CWIHP Web site, document #33; conversation between Zhou Enlai, Chen Yi, and Xuan Thuy, Beijing (The Great Hall of the People), 9:45 P.M., 7 May 1968, CWIHP Web site, document #35;

"That you accepted holding talks with the US put you in a passive position. You have been trapped by the Soviets," Zhou charged. "Now, Johnson has the initiative." Conversation between Zhou Enlai and Pham Hung, Beijing, 29 June 1968, CWIHP Web site, document #37.

66. Gaiduk, *The Soviet Union,* 174–77.

Culture

Decolonization, the Cold War, and the Foreign Policy of the Peace Corps

ELIZABETH COBBS HOFFMAN

> *We are in the middle of a world revolution—and I don't mean Communism. The Communists are . . . just moving in on the crest of a wave. The revolution I'm talking about is that of the little people all over the world. They're beginning to learn what there is in life, and to learn what they are missing.*

—George C. Marshall

In July 1947, India proclaimed its independence from Great Britain, and George Kennan published his famous "Mr. X" article in *Foreign Affairs* advocating vigilant containment of the Soviet Union. Beginning (at least symbolically) in the same month, the decolonization of the Third World and the Cold War ran on parallel tracks for much of the twentieth century. While logically these events were separable, in fact they intersected constantly. Decolonizing and developing countries used the threat of communism to gain political and financial support from the West. Yet they also resented the superpowers for making their aspirations into a sideshow of the Cold War. The U.S. government recognized decolonization as an important event in its own right but nevertheless tended to interpret almost all phenomena in light of the Soviet threat. As the quote by George C. Marshall (used by Sargent Shriver to justify the Peace Corps) attests, at least some U.S. policy leaders did acknowledge the larger world revolution between North and South but found their responses to it constantly complicated by the war between East and West.[1]

The Peace Corps was born of this tension. Approved by President John F. Kennedy in March 1961 and written into law by the Congress in September, the Peace Corps owed its existence to the Cold War and to Kennedy's belief that the United States had "to do better" in competing with Moscow for the allegiance of the newly independent countries of the Third World. At the same time, the Peace Corps embodied Kennedy's genuine determination to respond to the needs of Third World nations on their own terms. Beginning with his denunciation of the French war in Algeria on the floor of the Senate in 1957, Kennedy became known for his opposition to imperialism and interest in promoting development. As chairman of the Senate Subcommittee on African Affairs (and as the heir of Irish immigrants, one might add), Kennedy warned his colleagues in the Senate that "call it nationalism, call it anti-colonialism, call it what you will, the word is out and spreading like wildfire in nearly a thousand languages and dialects—that it is no longer necessary to remain forever in bondage." In 1959 he told campaign aide Harris Wofford that he wanted to run for president to initiate "a new relationship" between the United States and the developing world.[2]

Trying to demonstrate the myopia of U.S. politicians with regard to the Cold War, historians themselves have sometimes been shortsighted. The Peace Corps story, in its full complexity, reveals the way in which this particular administration wrestled with the competing trends of history, never escaping the pull of the Cold War but managing to rise sufficiently above it to sometimes earn the respect of Third World peoples. As a foreign policy initiative, the Peace Corps was one of the most successful strategies of the post–World War II period for making friends for the United States. Justifiably or not, it earned for John F. Kennedy in countries like Nigeria and Ethiopia, Guatemala and Gabon, a reputation among the populace as "the great one," "the good man," and "the friend of the colored man everywhere."[3] In the revisionist emphasis on Kennedy as a Cold Warrior like all the others, it has been easy to dismiss the Peace Corps as a tool of the conflict and thereby to overlook the basis for Kennedy's genuine renown in the world's most impoverished and isolated regions.

Just as it requires scholars to look through and beyond the Cold War, the Peace Corps story also demonstrates how imperative it is for historians to explore their subjects beyond the bounds of U.S. policy. The Peace Corps was not the example of U.S. exceptionalism it may seem. The Third World challenged the complacency of *all* "First World" powers, large and small, after 1945. Comparing their responses to this challenge reveals the universe within which U.S. government officials weighed options and fashioned strategies. Although the United States was the preeminent leader of the post–World War II Western alliance, it also sometimes capitalized upon policy innovations to which it could not claim exclusive authorship.

While the U.S. government actively championed the use of volunteers in development, private groups in Britain, Australia, and New Zealand quietly pioneered in secular volunteering in the 1950s. And, after the founding of the Peace Corps, most European governments as well as the Israelis and the Japanese began volunteer programs modeled on the Peace Corps yet based on their own larger national policies. Between 1958 and 1965, Britain, Australia, Canada, New Zealand, the United States, France, Germany, Israel, Japan, Denmark, the Netherlands, Norway, Sweden, Italy, Argentina, Belgium, Switzerland, and even tiny Liechtenstein started volunteer programs to spread the message of economic development and international "good will." They were joined by numerous new volunteer programs in developing countries throughout Asia, Africa, and Latin America as well, which were started to promote the notion of domestic service.

It was the policy of the Peace Corps, backed by the State Department, to encourage as many nations as possible in the Western bloc to adopt volunteer development programs. In this respect, the Peace Corps stepped out in front of its predecessors in the other English-speaking nations. The goal of replication reflected the persistent, unavoidable duality of U.S. policy toward the Third World during the Cold War. On the one hand, Peace Corps director Sargent Shriver reported to his brother-in-law, the president, that inviting other countries to start their own volunteer programs would dispel "an appearance of arrogance in assuming that young Americans automatically can teach anybody else." All nations would be invited to become teachers and to contribute to the world community. Aid would be disassociated from the exercise of nationalism, and "underdeveloped" countries would benefit most. On the other hand, the Peace Corps leadership worried that the multilateral aspects of its policy had to be advanced from the start, "before the Soviets beat us to the punch."[4] *Both* Cold War preoccupations and a desire to respond effectively to the threats and opportunities of decolonization motivated the Kennedy administration. These phenomena also motivated the Europeans. After all, it was their Cold War too, and their own former colonies.

In his first communications to President Kennedy, Shriver emphasized that the United States had to take steps to show the international community that the Peace Corps was not intended as an arm of the Cold War. Chief among his proposals was that the United States relinquish any claim to exclusive ownership of the Peace Corps idea. "In presenting it to other governments and to the United Nations," Shriver recommended, "we could propose that every nation consider the formation of its own peace corps and that the United Nations sponsor the idea." Kennedy latched onto Shriver's suggestion, and in his message to Congress introducing the Peace Corps he stated, "Let us hope that other nations will mobilize the spirit and energies and skill of their people in some form of Peace Corps—making our own effort only one step in a major international effort to increase the welfare of all men."[5]

Within a month of Shriver's appointment to head the new Peace Corps, he persuaded Assistant Secretary of State Harlan Cleveland to arrange a meeting for him with Adlai Stevenson, U.S. ambassador to the United Nations. At the meeting in early April 1961, Stevenson agreed to push a two-part initiative in the United Nations. First, the Peace Corps proposed to appoint volunteers directly to UN programs, such as UNESCO. Second, the Peace Corps proposed that the United Nations give "comparable opportunities" to volunteers from other member countries.[6] To achieve this second objective, Stevenson agreed to place a motion on the agenda of the 32nd session of the UN Economic and Social Council (ECOSOC), meeting in July and August 1961.

The move to place some volunteers under international control had support in the United States among the liberal constituency on which Kennedy increasingly relied. In June 1961 hearings before the Senate Committee on Foreign Relations, a Quaker spokesman advocated that the Peace Corps "increasingly work through international organizations like the United Nations" and noted with approval Adlai Stevenson's exertions on behalf of this goal. The result, he stated, would be to "assure doubting neutrals that Peace Corps members are serving the broad interests of mankind." A spokeswoman for the Women's International League for Peace and Freedom also argued that "the league would like to see this type of project done eventually through the United Nations, so that qualified people from a wide range of countries wishing to serve could have the opportunity to do so."[7]

The U.S. resolution to "use volunteer workers in the operational programmes of the United Nations" passed the 32nd session of ECOSOC against the opposition of the Soviet Union. The innocuousness and multilateralism of the proposal stymied the Soviet effort. "The Soviets completely overplayed their hands with an hour-long attack on the Peace Corps . . . hint[ing] that all the US sought was to place spies and CIA agents throughout the underdeveloped world," the chair of the U.S. delegation noted afterward with satisfaction. Still, he cautioned, Peace Corps cooperation with the United Nations would be "watched" very carefully. "By the time that the next ECOSOC session rolls around we should be able to demonstrate that this was a sorely needed program and that it was being executed effectively," the chair counseled.[8]

Franklin Williams, deputy director of the Peace Corps and the point man to the United Nations, visited Paris a week after the end of the ECOSOC conference. Meeting with senior officials of the UNESCO secretariat, Williams spread around the idea of an eventual UN volunteer program and inquired about ways in which U.S. Peace Corps volunteers might fit into existing

UNESCO projects. A member of the U.S. embassy in Paris called Williams's visit "very successful in engendering interest and enthusiasm in the peace corps and in stimulating serious thought by the Secretariat on possible U.S. Peace Corps–UNESCO cooperation."[9]

The initiatives in the UN arena fit within a larger pattern of monitoring how the international community was receiving the Peace Corps idea. On 1 March 1961, the same day that President John Kennedy signed his executive order, Secretary of State Dean Rusk sent a memo to U.S. embassies worldwide ordering that "local reaction to [the] idea [in] all countries should be canvassed and reported." The responses that poured in from U.S. missions around the world were almost unvaryingly positive. Within a week, U.S. embassies in Austria, Britain, Cyprus, Denmark, Egypt, Ethiopia, the Netherlands, and Sweden sent word of enthusiastic newspaper and government commentary. Positive reports came even from the communist countries. The first editorial in Yugoslavia called the Peace Corps an attempt to reinvent the "petrified policy" of the United States toward the Third World but also acknowledged that it recalled "much of the old forgotten spirit of idealism and renaissance dating from the days of the American pioneer." Privately, junior Soviet officials evidenced "admiration tinged with envy."[10]

The United States Information Agency (USIA) joined in the effort to assess world reaction, demonstrating the depth of the administration's concern about international perceptions and the possibilities for transferring "some of America's aid burden to Western Europe." In June and July 1961, USIA contracted confidentially with local, private pollsters in Great Britain, France, Germany, and Italy to gauge popular responses within the allied nations without biasing responses through "knowledge of U.S. sponsorship." The survey responses revealed the strength of the perceived moral leadership of the United States in the post-World War II, pre-Vietnam era. Although each European group tended to have a high opinion of its own contributions to world aid needs and a low opinion of the contributions of other European nations, the nationalities polled evinced a consistently high regard for the efforts of the United States. Nearly a majority (48 percent) believed that the United States was either "doing more than [its] fair share" or "doing about its fair share" (37 percent had no opinion or did not believe in giving aid). The British (60 percent) and the Germans (53 percent) assessed the U.S. performance the most favorably, the French the least. But even the doubting French, only 34 percent of whom thought the United States was doing its fair share or more in the world, ranked it nearly twice as high as they ranked any of their neighbors.[11]

On the Peace Corps, the survey showed that an average of 15 percent of the populace in the four countries had heard of it by the end of Kennedy's first year in office and that 10 percent could correctly identify it as sponsored by the United States. While this hardly compares to the 50 percent of Americans who could identify the Peace Corps (its name recognition trailed that of Smokey the Bear), the fact that one in six Europeans knew of the Peace Corps attested to its appeal as a foreign policy initiative. Although the survey showed Europeans evenly divided on how much they thought the Peace Corps could accomplish, three times more people thought it was designed "to help" the Third World than thought it part of some U.S. scheme "to dominate."[12]

Undoubtedly, some of the European willingness to grant the United States the benefit of the doubt as to motives came from perceptions of their own motives. The Peace Corps was a lineal descendant of the missionary tradition originated by Christian Europeans. And, even though some would never be as well known in their own countries as the U.S. Peace Corps was, small organizations in Britain, Canada, and Australia had developed secular volunteer programs for youth even before the Peace Corps started. Imperialism's culture, as critic Edward Said describes it, contained a wealth of imagery (one need only mention Rudyard Kipling's "White Man's Burden") that explained Europeans' and North Americans' noble intentions to themselves.[13] Ironically, the Peace Corps both opposed and benefited from the cultural assumption that the West had a duty to civilize the Third World.

Following the ECOSOC resolution to encourage the use of volunteers in development, Peace Corps staff found that opportunities for volunteer placement with the United Nations were not readily forthcoming. They also found that the agency did not need UN opportunities. After Sargent Shriver's first eight-country tour of Africa and Asia during the late spring of 1961, when he met Nkrumah and Nehru, the Peace Corps received requests for volunteers from over two dozen Third World countries. Gradually, the agency dropped its early ambition to place significant numbers with the United Nations and instead focused on developing bilateral relationships with "Peace Corps countries" in Africa, Asia, and Latin America.

The Peace Corps did not cease its efforts to get other industrialized nations to adopt its model, however, nor did activists in other countries who were inspired by its example. A handful of Australian graduate students had started a volunteers-in-development scheme in Indonesia in 1951, for which they had negotiated a small amount of funding from both their own government and Sukarno's revolutionary regime. In Britain, Alec and Mora Dickson had started Voluntary Service Overseas (VSO) in 1958, and, like the Peace Corps, their first volunteers went to Ghana. In Canada, university students and faculty—some of whom knew about the Australian and British programs—lobbied their government for funds to start the same thing and sent the first Canadian volunteers to Africa the month before the Peace Corps did. The organizers of all these programs were stunned by the Kennedy initiative, especially its scope and place of prominence in the New Frontier.

Alec Dickson of VSO feared that the British were "getting hopelessly left behind in comparison" and urged his government to commit significant resources to the program. A more sanguine civil servant in the Department of Technical Cooperation observed that the size and influence of the U.S. initiative were simply a reflection of "the realities of wealth and power." The Peace Corps, he noted, was "only one of a hundred fields in which we can have no hope of keeping up with the United States."[14] The organizers of CUSO, who had autonomously conceived the idea for a volunteer service, found themselves racing to keep up with the go-go Kennedy administration. Although their volunteers reached Africa first, the rapid-fire diffusion of the Peace Corps around the globe "created difficulties," one CUSO founder noted at the time, because in many other countries "they got there first and offered a completely free service." CUSO's difficulties, especially financial ones, were further exacerbated by Prime Minister John Diefenbaker's intense dislike of President Kennedy. Concluding that the private, nonprofit Canadian program would appear as an imitation of Kennedy's initiative, Diefenbaker "dismissed it out of hand," in the words of CUSO's first chairman.[15]

Indeed, the most obviously unique characteristics of the U.S. program were its immense scale (2,816 Americans the first full year compared to 100 Canadians and 85 British around the same time) and its character as a government initiative.[16] Unlike its predecessors in other countries, or even some of the earlier private U.S. groups (such as the American Friends Service Committee, International Voluntary Service, or CARE), the Peace Corps was bankrolled by a wealthy government as an expression of its foreign policy. The Peace Corps also directly shaped foreign policy by setting new standards of language competency for foreign appointments, by legitimizing "citizen diplomacy," and by pressuring the State Department to actively encourage other governments to start similar programs.

In early 1962, Peace Corps staff began organizing the "International Conference on Middle-Level Manpower," to be held in Puerto Rico in October. Vice President Lyndon Johnson, a strong supporter of the Peace Corps who had personally lobbied Kennedy to ensure the agency's independence when the Agency for International Development threatened to swallow it up in early 1961, signed on to head the U.S. delegation. Yet State Department officials expressed "serious objections" from the start. Department members had greeted much that the Peace Corps had done over the preceding year with incredulity. "We feel confident that it is not the intention that Americans should have no special privileges . . . and should live on African standards," one diplomat wrote to Dean Rusk, before being apprised that that was exactly what the Peace Corps intended. Other officials expressed the sentiment that Shriver needed "a gentle straightening out" to bring him more into line with classic Cold War thinking—that is, to convince him to place volunteers in such hot spots as Algeria and Vietnam, which Shriver refused to do.[17]

State Department concerns about the proposed Middle-Level Manpower Conference reflected a desire to keep a tighter rein on spin-offs of the Peace Corps, which the department could hardly contain as it was. Officials particularly objected to the Peace Corps proposal that the conference end by creating an international organization to encourage other national volunteer programs. Department members instead advised a passive approach. The president had already invited other industrialized nations to undertake similar ventures. That was enough. "We hesitate to take any risks to internationalize it," one policy memo stated, especially since "Soviet participation in such international machinery would be contrary to our foreign policy objectives and . . . make it difficult for less developed countries to refuse to accept Soviet volunteers."[18]

Dean Rusk overrode his staff's objections to the Middle-Level Manpower Conference, as he had on other occasions concerning the Peace Corps. "The State Department knew we were anointed by the President," observed Warren Wiggins, Peace Corps deputy director and a former foreign service officer. "If you're in the State Department and you're dealing with somebody that's anointed by the President you treat them nice."[19]

Attended by the vice presidents or foreign ministers of forty-three nations, the International Conference on Middle-Level Manpower met in Puerto Rico in October 1962, with Lyndon Johnson presiding. The gathering voted to create an International Peace Corps Secretariat, later renamed the International Secretariat for Voluntary Services to diminish the perception of U.S. sponsorship. What the secretariat was actually to *do* was undefined, which left much to the imagination and initiative of its organizers. The French and the Swiss governments later bridled at the activist approach that the U.S.-run secretariat immediately adopted under Shriver's appointee (and former aide to the president), Richard Goodwin. The authority that the secretariat had been granted in Puerto Rico, the French foreign ministry maintained, was simply "to assemble the documents of the Conference."[20]

Nonetheless, the secretariat did a lot more than that. Goodwin went into high gear, working much of the next year to solicit funds and staff support from the United States's major allies for the "international" effort. Israel gave funds first, with the Dutch, the Germans, and again the Israelis contributing paid staff support. The Philippines, the only former colony of the United States and its major ally in the Pacific, contributed the fourth international staff person. Goodwin and his international staff also traveled around the world meeting with government officials and other potential organizers of national youth volunteer programs.

Nowhere did Goodwin meet with significant resistance. A number of countries immediately took up the idea, which had the advantage of being both popular and "noncontroversial," in the words of an observer in Italy. At Puerto Rico, twelve countries announced plans for their own overseas or domestic peace corps. In 1963, the Netherlands, Germany, Denmark, France, and Norway all started new programs. Japanese youth and student groups pressured their government to establish an equivalent. In May, the secretariat hosted representatives from thirteen countries at a two-week "Workshop for Peace Corps Development" in Washington.[21] The participants had their picture taken with President Kennedy. The glossy *International Volunteer* newsletter that the secretariat began publishing monthly in March 1963, complete with photos on every page, highlighted these developments along with the ongoing activities of the U.S., British, and Canadian programs.

The State Department fell in line with the Peace Corps initiative, which included both domestic and foreign volunteer programs. The logic behind encouraging domestic volunteering derived from the recognition that youth predominated in developing countries with high birthrates and that those youth could constitute either a positive or negative force for social change. Just as literature and films in the United States explored themes of youthful rebellion in the 1950s and early 1960s, so did policy makers. In 1961 the influential Rockefeller report *Prospect for America* noted, with reference to revolutionary Algeria, that "in a comparatively youthful population, impatience to realize rising expectations is likely to be pronounced. Extreme nationalism has often been the result."[22]

Secretary of State Dean Rusk conveyed a sense of urgency about the task of reaching youthful populations in a February 1963 memo to U.S. embassies in Latin America that was consistent with the administration's larger initiative, the Alliance for Progress. "A domestic Peace Corps in a Latin American country is essentially an effort to mobilize the youth of that country . . . in the cause of their own national development." Local volunteer opportunities, he stated, could "exert profound social and psychological influence on the thinking of youth who are frustrated in their desires to realize national goals, unable to find useful employment and who are thus easy prey for extremism or apathy."[23]

Once again Rusk urged embassies to spare the red tape and make every effort to expedite "the cause." He also instructed embassy officers to inquire if the country would accept foreign advisers from the International Peace Corps Secretariat. "If not an American, would they accept a German or Israeli or other?" Rusk queried, evidencing an awareness of the value of having a multinational staff that could be deployed strategically according to national prejudices. (Of course, it could also be a liability. The embassy in Khartoum, Sudan, warned that the Israeli staff member of the secretariat would "raise a red flag in the eyes of Arab countries," perhaps causing them to boycott the secretariat altogether.)[24] Within the year, a number of countries in Asia, Africa, and Latin America had announced plans for their own domestic programs. One of the first programs was in the Philippines, whose own volunteers in organizations like "Work a Year with the People" labored alongside an enormous Peace Corps contingent.

The programs most closely modeled on the Peace Corps, however, were those of the other industrialized countries, which sent their volunteers abroad. Between 1961 and 1965, the Peace Corps achieved its goal of multilateral proliferation. Nearly all of the governments of the industrialized "West" (including Japan and Israel) initiated or expanded their own youth corps. Why? Kennedy's Peace Corps started as a late-night, off-the-cuff campaign promise made at the end of the 1960 campaign. By 1965, the United States had 13,248 volunteers in the field, and governments were copying it worldwide. In what foreign policy contexts, for both the United States and its allies, did volunteer programs fit—so neatly and so readily?

President Kennedy bid Peace Corps recruits good luck in the Rose Garden. Queen Juliana of the Netherlands received the first Dutch volunteers at her palace and then saw them off at the airport. President Heinrich Luebke and Chancellor Konrad Adenauer invited the U.S. president to speak at the inauguration of the German volunteer program, and he did. Foreign Minister Golda Meir personally attended the Puerto Rico conference to shake hands with U.S. Vice President Lyndon Johnson, and Israel gave the secretariat its first non-American staff member. Although critics at the time questioned what possible significance these "kiddie corps" could have for Third World development, there is no doubting that the sponsoring governments staged them as high drama. Who was the intended audience?

There are four overlapping contexts that must be placed together to understand how and why these governments, beginning with the United States, undertook to send young volunteers abroad: the Cold War, the "Free World" alliance system that emerged after 1945, the phenomenon of decolonization, and the ongoing task of forging domestic consensus—that is, nation building at home. In all these contexts, volunteer programs played a role.

The Cold War

"The fifties in Holland were gray," as one Dutch volunteer later described his early youth. "The Cold War was severely felt. . . . [There was] not much space for things that were outside the most immediate necessities of life."

—Ton Nijzink, Dutch SNV[25]

In material ways, especially, the North American experience of the 1950s was dramatically different from the experience of Europe and Japan, which were rebuilding and in which individuals and families still suffered postwar privations. But even there, U.S. wealth was felt. Compared with their near neighbors, whose privations seemed to have no end, countries under the umbrella of the Marshall Plan at least had money with which to rebuild. Western Europeans also felt the chill and fear of the Cold War more intensely than did North Americans, who had the luxury of being across an ocean; but again, unlike their near neighbors in Czechoslovakia, Hungary, and Poland, at least they did not have Soviet tanks rolling down their streets. While proximity to the Soviet threat was a matter of degree, however, and postwar recovery a matter of time, the Cold War was nonetheless "severely felt" by all the countries it threatened.

In the United States the Cold War helped to end a nearly two-hundred-year-old tradition of maintaining no large standing army in peacetime. In 1950, the year after the Chinese revolution and the Soviet detonation of its first A-bomb, President Harry S. Truman approved National Security Council Paper 68 (NSC-68). The plan "meant a great military effort in time of peace," Truman later wrote. "It meant doubling or tripling the budget, increasing taxes heavily, and imposing various kinds of economic controls. It meant a great change in our normal peacetime way of doing things."[26] NSC-68 assumed that the United States would be on a wartime footing as long as the Soviet system endured. This required attention to preparedness in all its dimensions.

From its experience in World Wars I and II, the U.S. government had learned the importance of psychological warfare as one component of a coordinated defense. Wars had to be sold to the citizenry; the advantages of alliance had to be sold to neutral countries; the enemy had to be convinced of the futility of struggle and of the mercy to be expected upon surrender. In World War I, George Creel's Committee on Public Information churned out movies, posters, advertisements, and pamphlets designed to keep patriotism at "white heat." Woodrow Wilson used his famous Fourteen Points to define the war terms of the United States, establish a bargaining position with the Allies, convince Germany that the war could end in "peace without victory," and counter Bolshevik peace propaganda with his own version of the "new diplomacy."[27]

In the next war, the Office of the Coordinator of Inter-American Relations under Nelson Rockefeller began the first propaganda efforts in 1940 to convince wavering Latin Americans of the benefits of alliance with the United States. Rockefeller added a new dimension to the war of words, though—the lure of practical assistance with economic development. The Office of the Coordinator not only persuaded Walt Disney to create new cartoon characters (as in *The Three Caballeros*) and commissioned flattering busts of Latin American presidents but also sent breeding chickens, garden hoes, medicines, and an array of agricultural, health, and sanitation advisers to Latin America. To General George C. Marshall, head of the U.S. war effort, Rockefeller described his overall mission as "psychological warfare in the Hemisphere." The information division of the Office of the Coordinator subsequently became the model for the Office of War Information, once the United States officially entered the conflict on 8 December 1941.[28]

Alec Dickson, the founder of British Voluntary Service Overseas, also had responsibilities for foreign propaganda during the war. He served first in Ethiopia, in command of a platoon of the King's African Rifles. After the British routed the Italians, Dickson found himself consigned to a desk job in "Information" when the front moved to North Africa. Yet East Africa was by no means completely out of danger. The Japanese had conquered Hong Kong, Singapore, and the Dutch East Indies. Burma and Ceylon were threatened. India might fall. If a Japanese fleet appeared off the coast of Africa, what would be the reaction of black British colonials? Alec Dickson asked, and then took responsibility for running a so-called Mobile Propaganda Unit. African soldiers drawn from twenty different tribes serving in the British forces used drama and music to communicate directly and simply to villagers who had no radios and were largely illiterate. They explained the purpose of the war and that there were "different kinds" of colonizers.[29]

After World War II, the United States developed the Marshall Plan and Point Four, using economic aid to extend the nation's political influence. Countries desperate for funds eagerly accepted the assistance for the most part. In a further innovation, unpublicized for obvious reasons, Truman broadened the mandate of the new Central Intelligence Agency to include covert political warfare. The Voice of America radio network became the advance guard for overt propaganda efforts, and when the Russians jammed broadcasts and the Cold War escalated, Truman approved several efforts to diversify the nation's psychological warfare program. One of these efforts was Project TROY—named for the donated wooden horse that prompted the aphorism "Beware of Greeks bearing gifts." Project TROY brought together scientists, social scientists, and historians in a top-secret study group to develop new ways of waging "political warfare" and countering anti-U.S. propaganda. As Truman told U.S. newspaper editors, "We must make ourselves known as we really are."[30]

Project TROY floated the first trial balloon of a government Peace Corps. The TROY committee developed plans for propaganda in both Western and Eastern Europe, but when it came to areas of the world with only rudimentary technology, project members recognized the need for unusual methods. In an annex to the final report, Robert Morison of the Rockefeller Foundation suggested that "face to face contact on a wide scale" might be the only way to reach people in areas like China and Southeast Asia, which lacked modern communications systems. Morison proposed "the recruiting of a group of American youth willing and able to spend two or four years of their lives in intimate personal contact with the village people of Asia. Their primary task would be the demonstration of suitably modified western techniques of public health and agriculture. If they were the right sort of representative Americans they would also make use of their position to transmit almost automatically American ideas of cooperation in the common job, respect for individual dignity, and the free play of individual initiative."[31]

As director of the Rockefeller Foundation's medical sciences program, Morison could speak from long experience. The foundation had been bringing Americans into face-to-face contact with Asians for decades through the Peking Union Medical College.[32] Cold War necessities naturally led people like Morison to think of how the proselytizing strategies with which they were familiar—missionary outreach and philanthropic support to "underdeveloped" areas—might be applied to psychological warfare.

Throughout the 1950s, a number of prominent public figures alluded to or directly advocated the idea of a peace corps to supplement the expanding U.S. war corps. Nelson Rockefeller, special assistant for foreign affairs to President Dwight D. Eisenhower (with responsibility for assessing "the psychological aspects" of policy) and later governor of New York, was one of these men. Like George Kennan, Rockefeller emphasized that the United States had to make a convincing case of what it was for, not just what it was against.

His effort culminated in the Rockefeller Brothers Fund report *Prospect for America*. One contributor to the Rockefeller report was Max Millikin, a member of Project TROY and the author of the first policy report that John F. Kennedy solicited for the Peace Corps. The Rockefeller document helped shape the campaign platforms of both the Republicans and the Democrats in 1960. As Nelson Rockefeller noted to Henry Kissinger, he was also especially concerned that young people at home needed an outlet for the exercise of democratic values and idealism in the form of service to less privileged nations.[33]

New moves by the Soviets to strengthen their ties with the Third World undoubtedly fed Rockefeller's worries and those of many other government officials in the middle and late 1950s. Following the death of Stalin in 1953, the Soviet leadership attempted to develop a more sophisticated approach to the conflict with the West. In 1955 the Soviets expanded trade with Latin America by 34 percent, and in January 1956 Soviet Premier Nikolai Bulganin announced a program of technical assistance to the impoverished countries in the United States's traditional "backyard." (A few years earlier, Assistant Secretary of State Edward Miller had ruefully noted that the economic distress of the region was a "poor advertisement" for U.S. leadership.) In 1956 the Twentieth Communist Party Congress also declared a policy of peaceful competition with the West for the allegiance of Asia, Africa, and Latin America. Soviet officials toured the newly independent countries of Egypt, Indonesia, and India, promising lavish economic assistance programs. President Eisenhower reflected that "the new Communist line of sweetness and light was perhaps more dangerous than their propaganda in Stalin's time."[34]

Vague ideas for a youth corps that would counter the growing Soviet commitment to decolonization and foreign aid coalesced into a concerted push for new policy in 1960. In January, Congressman Henry Reuss introduced his bill to fund a feasibility study, and six months later Senator Hubert Humphrey proposed a bill to establish a "Peace Corps." When Kennedy made his early November campaign promise, he said, "Our young men and women, dedicated to freedom, are fully capable of overcoming the efforts of Mr. Khrushchev's missionaries who are dedicated to undermining that freedom." William Lederer, author of *The Ugly American* and *A Nation of Sheep*, advocated shortly thereafter the formation of a "United States Strategic Service Corps" to counter the Soviets, again fitting it into the paradigm of psychological warfare. "Having a battalion of American civil servants building native housing with their own hands, creating irrigation in deserts, rigging electrical equipment, driving cars, or as menials, bargaining for fish in the marketplace, would have a great psychological impact," he wrote in 1961.[35]

U.S. government officials were not the only ones concerned about the Cold War or aware of the potential for youth to make bridges to new allies. Keith Spicer, the Canadian founder of CUSO, later freely acknowledged that the Cold War increased his sense of urgency even though he feared that "politicians would corrupt what I thought was a good, humanitarian cause by bringing in these sordid political considerations."[36]

A 1952 letter from one of the first three Australian volunteers (who went at their own, rather than government, expense) revealed similar concerns. A young engineer, writing to his parents, revealed a patriotic sense of Australian exceptionalism and a Cold War anxiety remarkably similar to that of Peace Corps founders a few years later. The Indonesian revolutionary spirit, if broken by intransigent poverty and disease, would be followed by a loss of hope, he warned. "They'll turn to the Communists—like China." Australia, he believed, was uniquely positioned to win over the revolutionaries to the way of the West. "No country matters more to Indonesia than we do," the volunteer asserted. "Britain and Holland—NO—colonial countries. America—NO—imperialist. Russia—NO—imperialist. If Australia fails, they'll turn to China." In the same letter the volunteer also quoted an Australian chargé d'affaires: "If Indonesia fails, Australia is sunk!"[37]

The Cold War, the fear that the West might lose it, and the increasing attention to propaganda and psychological warfare in the twentieth century all provided one framework in which policy makers and even the public could readily understand the need for, and advantages of, something like the Peace Corps. For the governments that had allied with the United States in this war, starting their own "peace corps" fit into another framework as well.

The Alliance of Peace

Private individuals organized the first volunteer groups in Australia, Britain, and Canada with minimal, if any, support from their governments. In the apt phrasing of Peace Corps staff veterans David Hapgood and Meridan Bennett, "It was left to the United States to make the idea into official policy and to back that policy with the power of the national treasury." This policy might have remained unique to the United States had it not been for the importance of the post–World War II alliance system. Within this system the U.S. government strove continuously for coherence between its own domestic and foreign policies and those of its allies. Similarly, the allies, to greater and lesser extents, attempted when expedient to conform their policies to those of the acknowledged leader of the system. Cooperation in U.S.

hegemony produced many benefits.[38] European security and economic prosperity depended heavily on these benefits throughout the 1950s and into the 1960s.

Through the United Nations, and then through the International Peace Corps Secretariat, the Kennedy administration sought coherence between its new policy of using volunteers in development and the aid policies of its allies. In the first and second years of the Peace Corps, the message went out, loud and clear, that the United States wanted its allies to copy the American effort.

The speed at which the allies responded to Kennedy's appeal matched the friendliness of their relationships with his administration. The Netherlands, Britain, Germany, and Israel, all staunch allies much beholden to the United States, acted almost immediately. The sentiment in Holland, for example, corresponded to the oft-repeated reminder to Dutch youth: "They won the Second World War for us." The West Germans themselves sought ritual reassurances of unity with the United States in this period. Robert Kennedy, visiting Berlin in 1962, gently chided the encircled citizens that they "must wean themselves from the suspicion that the United States had written off its solemn obligations if a senior American official failed to visit Berlin once a month to reaffirm them." The Federal Republic started its volunteer program in mid-1963.[39]

The French and the Canadian governments, each with its own reasons for not wanting to appear too eager to follow, responded more testily to the U.S. initiative but soon joined in. The bandwagon effect was mutually reinforcing: each new forum for the peace corps idea created additional ones. The announcement of the U.S. Peace Corps, for example, gave supporters of British VSO an opportunity to start a debate in the House of Lords, which prompted a Stockholm newspaper to ask when there would be a "Swedish initiative in the same direction." The "Peace Corps has had a marked impact," one British official wrote in early 1962, creating a "climate of opinion in other countries and in international organizations [that] is further stimulating interest in Britain."[40]

The founding of peace corps by nearly all the countries of the "Free World" within four years was a testament both to the perceived inherent merit of the idea and to the prestige of the United States in the Western alliance system during the pre-Vietnam 1960s. Creating a national volunteer program was a way to keep abreast of the United States that cost little in treasure or national pride. Demonstrating solidarity with the alliance was the responsibility of each allied nation, and they all undertook to fulfill it when they could. Fortunately, the volunteer scheme also fit conveniently with the array of solutions then being considered to the thorny problems of decolonization.

Decolonization

> *If India becomes free . . . the rest will follow.*
>
> —Mohandas Gandhi to Franklin D. Roosevelt, 1942

> *Fashionable Johannesburg has tried for years to laugh at the story of the kindly housewife who asked her devoted black cook if in a "show-down" she would really kill the family of which she was virtually a part. "Oh, no, Missie," the cook is supposed to have replied, "I kill the family next door, cook next door kill you."* [41]
>
> —Allard Lowenstein, *Brutal Mandate*, 1962

One of the main events of the twentieth century—rivaling the world wars and the Cold War in its consequences for human populations—was the decolonization (broadly defined) of major parts of Africa, Asia, the Middle East, Latin America, and, as late as 1989, Eastern Europe and central Asia. By severing colonial ties with the imperial powers of Europe, or by seeking to break away from economic and military domination by the neocolonial powers of the Soviet Union and the United States, these weaker but emergent nations changed the world map and global history.

This process was not uniformly opposed by the dominant nations of the Northern Hemisphere. In fact, because of their conflicts with one another, the more powerful countries often abetted it. In World War I, Woodrow Wilson raised the hopes of submerged nationalities from Estonia to Indochina when he attempted to impose a U.S.-designed peace on the contenders in the great conflict. Eight of his Fourteen Points went directly to the principle of national self-determination. But while the victors created seven new nations out of the old Austro-Hungarian, Russian, and German empires, they did so for their own geopolitical reasons. The territory that went to the new Eastern European countries weakened Germany and created a *cordon sanitaire* against the "dirty" Bolsheviks.

In the interwar period, Britain in Africa and the United States in Latin America took unprecedented steps to ensure loyalty in the face of Hitler's challenge, promising greater freedoms and benefits to nations or territories under their sway. President Roosevelt promised to be a "good neighbor" and not to intervene militarily in the domestic problems of other hemispheric nations. Assistant Secretary of State Sumner Welles began efforts to boost Latin American economies, including the first loan for competitive industrialization ($20 million to Brazil for the tropics' first steel plant). British Colonial Secretary Malcolm MacDonald stated for the first time in Parliament in 1938 that the ultimate, if distant, aim of policy was evolution toward self-government. He also forged the proposal that resulted in Cabinet passage of a Colonial Development and Welfare Bill in 1940 at the height of the wartime emergency, when only measures of extreme national priority obtained funding. The bill's sponsors took pains to refute the notion that it was "a bribe or a reward for the Colonies' support in this supreme crisis," which was probably the best evidence of its being so.[42]

Japanese conquest of European and U.S. colonies in Asia further shook the colonial system. Nationalists in Indonesia, Vietnam, and even the Philippines gained heart (and ammunition) from the easy collapse of the Caucasians under Japanese attack. Partly to secure the assistance of guerrilla fighters like Ho Chi Minh during World War II, the United States took an officially anti-imperialist stance toward postwar arrangements. So did the Soviet Union. This heightened the expectations and political leverage of many nations attempting to overthrow a legacy of external domination, even though later policy (as in Indochina and Czechoslovakia) was sometimes completely at odds with official rhetoric.

In the United States, the policy of anti-imperialism was constrained by the Monroe Doctrine and the alliance system with Europe. On the one hand, the U.S. government refused to see any parallels between its own sphere of influence and the spheres maintained by European imperial powers. Although the United States gave up its only Asian colony before the other allies gave up theirs (the Philippines in 1946), Latin America remained a special case for the United States. The hemisphere added twenty votes to that of the United States in the sixty-member United Nations. Secretary of State Henry Stimson commented during the UN charter debate that paved the way for regional self-defense groups like the Organization of American States, "I think it's not asking too much to have our little region over here which has never bothered anybody."[43] Not only did the Monroe Doctrine represent an obvious contradiction not lost on the United States's imperialist allies, but it also gave an opening to the nation's enemies. The Soviets later used Article 51 of the UN charter to justify the Warsaw Pact.

On the other hand, the U.S. policy of self-determination also remained largely rhetorical because of the need to court European allies. France wanted to keep Indochina; Churchill vowed not to preside over the dismantling of the British Empire; the Netherlands, Belgium, and Portugal all had their stakes in Africa and Asia. During World War II, President Roosevelt refused to risk antagonizing Churchill over the question of India's independence. Instead, Roosevelt asked Gandhi to unite in the "common cause against a common enemy." Later, obtaining French consent to critical strategies of the Cold War such as the rearming of Germany became far more important to the United States than granting the principle of self-determination to Vietnam, or to any other of a bunch of raggle-taggle, would-be nations.[44]

But U.S. policy began to change as these would-be states came closer to real sovereignty. When it became clear that the Dutch could not regain control of the East Indies and that Indonesian nationalists might side with communism against the West after their impending triumph, the United States pressured the Dutch strongly to withdraw. Indonesia became independent in 1949. The most telling break with the past came when the United States sided with Egypt against the French and the British during the Suez Canal invasion of 1956. When Gamal Abdel Nasser nationalized the canal, prompting retaliatory strikes by the two European powers, President Eisenhower furiously demanded that they withdraw lest Nasser seek military support from the Soviets. U.S. officials threatened to cut off Britain's oil supply and ruin its currency if it refused. In the words of Walter LaFeber, the episode "badly split the western alliance . . . and marked the true end of the British empire."[45] It also hurt the French war effort in Algeria, where Nasser was supplying the revolutionaries.

When the hottest theaters of the Cold War moved south and east, marginal U.S. support for decolonization grew stronger in order to woo the new nations. Successful independence movements forced the United States to reorder its priorities. Just as independent Vietnam had been sacrificed in 1946 to placate France, now ten years later French interests had to be sacrificed to placate Egypt. In both cases the overarching goal remained the same: outmaneuvering the Soviet Union. Following the Suez crisis, when the movement to decolonize black Africa picked up steam, U.S. aid to the region rose from $36 million to nearly $93 million in one year. Vice President Richard Nixon attended the ceremonies marking Ghana's independence in 1957, and in travels to eleven other African nations he recommended further increases in aid to the continent.[46]

Senator John F. Kennedy nevertheless criticized the Eisenhower administration's policy toward Africa as inadequately supportive of the drive for independence. There had been a tendency, as many had noted, "to allow U.S. policy toward Africa to be formulated in the capitals of Europe." As a member of the Foreign Relations Committee, and later as chairman of the

Subcommittee on Africa, Kennedy made a name for himself worldwide by attacking the French war in Algeria in 1957 and calling for a new U.S. policy. The result, according to one historian of Africa, was ultimately to make Kennedy the most "revered" of all U.S. leaders.[47] Another result, undoubtedly, was to make Kennedy alive to African appreciation of more overt expressions of support.

Just as decolonization forced the United States to reorder its priorities in the alliance system, the imperialist nations of Europe found that they, too, had to reorder their thinking about the world. For Britain and France especially, whatever remaining claims they had to being "world" powers after 1945 were attached to their old empires. Flanked by the friendly but overbearing United States and the hostile Soviet Union, the European nations at first resisted the trend of decolonization. They also worked to develop other means for talking on equal terms with the superpowers, such as by creating the European Community and exploding their own nuclear weapons.[48]

The Dutch and the French both fought bloody wars to keep their colonies, which they ultimately lost. In 1958 the French returned Charles de Gaulle to the presidency, and he began the slow process of downsizing the Algerian war. He also began the search for new ways of responding to the cry for decolonization that would culminate in France's decision to abdicate all of its thirteen sub-Saharan black African colonies in 1960—sometimes over their objections—two years before Algerian independence. At the same time, de Gaulle sought ways of keeping the former colonies in the French orbit. Not only did their continuing allegiance enhance the "grandeur of France," but it also meant thirteen additional votes for France (and the West) in the United Nations. "We are more important than our own single country," one French foreign aid official later observed, "because we have the African countries with us."[49] French economic assistance in the transition to independence helped to sustain African allegiance. Aid that went exclusively to Francophone countries also sustained cultural ties. French continued to be taught in African schools partly because the French helped run the schools— and the hospitals.

The idea of using young volunteers to fill these positions, coming one year after the watershed of 1960, slipped easily into the overarching policy. The French Ministry of Cooperation, housed in the old, dusty colonial offices in Paris, organized the Volontaires du Progrès in 1963. The first volunteers went to Francophone Africa in January 1964 as agricultural workers who were instructed to "build their own dwellings, African style." Eventually, many of those who would go went as an alternative to the draft, but initially at least the French emphasis in volunteer selection was on recruiting peasants who could work with their hands. "The idea," according to a later Volontaires du Progrès recruiter, "was that peasant-to-peasant communication would be effective."[50]

British imperial policy had had a subtle history, evolving from outright rule in the nineteenth century to "indirect rule" at the start of the twentieth century to Commonwealth participation by the mid-twentieth century. At each step, for the most part, the British had held tightly to what they could, while yielding with greater grace than the French what they could not. They "let" India go without a fight in 1947 when it became clear they could hold on no longer, as they did in Ghana ten years later. Still, in the 1940s and 1950s the ruling British Labour Party continued to shift for new ways of persuading colonies to remain in the fold, largely through promises of economic development.[51]

The British also sought ways to strengthen links with former colonies by increasing the viability of the Commonwealth as an economic community. In January 1950 the Commonwealth nations, along with representatives of other British territories in South and Southeast Asia, met in Colombo, Ceylon, to forge a program of bilateral aid between richer and poorer members. The result was the Colombo Plan, in which participating countries undertook to respond to the specific requests of countries in the region for aid with economic development. Although the links were bilateral (from country to country), they occurred within the multilateral structure of the Commonwealth—thus informally extending Britain's influence as the leading member. Still, the former dominions could give aid independent of the mother country, and they did.

Economic and cultural ties to the former colonies not only were critical to Britain's recovery and growth and to its identity as "Britannia" but also underlay its credibility as one of the five permanent "great power" members of the UN Security Council. The Colombo Plan was Britain's answer to the Marshall Plan. Ultimately, after the 1956 Suez crisis, the Conservative Party under Harold Macmillan led the way to accelerated decolonization because of the potential otherwise for enormous bloodshed and for losing nationalist movements to the Soviet bloc. The Commonwealth model for decolonization remained important, however, since it held out hope for an enduring though diminished relationship. This particularly applied in 1962, when Britain found itself betwixt "Empire" and "Europe": denuded of its colonies and denied membership in the European Economic Community by France.[52]

The idealistic founders of VSO and CUSO argued to anyone who would listen that their organizations gave real, personal meaning to Commonwealth ties. The earliest Canadian groups that later merged into CUSO called their efforts the "Canadian Voluntary Commonwealth Service" and the "Scheme for Commonwealth Graduate Volunteers." In Britain, the Commonwealth Relations Office characterized the work of VSO as "excellent" and stated that it kept "a friendly eye on the youngsters." In 1958 the British Cabinet redesignated Empire Day as Commonwealth Day, converted the Imperial Institute into the Commonwealth Institute, and began sponsoring "Commonwealth weeks" across the country. The privately organized VSO and CUSO found a ready and comprehending audience in the councils of power—especially once Kennedy's Peace Corps also placed the volunteer movement in the context of East-West competition and the Atlantic alliance. In the mid-1960s the governments of Britain, Canada, and Australia dramatically increased their funding of VSO, CUSO, and Australian Volunteers Overseas, respectively. Volunteer programs promised to ease the transition to Commonwealth "brotherhood" and help create an environment in which the "cook next door" would not kill the family in a final showdown.[53]

Nation Building at Home

To understand the array of factors that made the Peace Corps and its international counterparts such policy "naturals" in the early 1960s, one must last consider their role in generating national consensus and solving identifiable domestic problems. Every government seeks ways of generating consensus around its policies by connecting those policies with the self-perceived identity of the nation. Since at least the time of Machiavelli, "princes" have self-consciously used foreign policy to facilitate domestic unity. Although other governments did not take up the banner of volunteering until the United States did, when they did so it fit well with the larger project of nation building at home.

For Britain and France, which experienced significant internal dissension over decolonization, volunteering could garner support simultaneously from those opposed to colonialism and those who sought to retain political and economic ties. Mora Dickson of VSO, for example, said of the British colonial experience, "We were a total reaction against all that." On the other hand, British Prime Minister Harold Macmillan told the headmaster of Eton in 1963 that he was "taking a close interest in the matter" of expanding Britain's voluntary service and wanted a plan for an increased campaign. As demonstrated by wide editorial approval in Britain at the time, volunteer programs could be a cheap, popular way of generating domestic consensus on a normally divisive subject.[54] French cabinet members told Richard Goodwin explicitly that they saw the Peace Corps idea "as a way to alleviate the disillusionment of French youth over failure in Algeria."[55]

For Canada and the Netherlands, countries not in contention for great-power status yet desirous of playing a role on the world stage, volunteering fit as well with the quest for a sense of national identity and importance. Keith Spicer, a founder of CUSO and much later the chairman of the Canadian Radio and Television Commission, argued that amidst the disintegrating forces of "too much geography," cultural dominance by the United States, and Québécois-Anglo antagonisms, Canadians had found that "helping out abroad unites us at home." As a noncolonial power, Canada made its presence felt to itself and other nations as a broker between the great powers and the Third World after 1945. Participation in the United Nations and the Colombo Plan gave Canada more weight in world counsels. It also brought recognition. Canadian Prime Minister Lester Pearson won the Nobel Peace Prize in 1956 for his leadership in the UN peacekeeping force at Suez.[56] For young people like Spicer, inspired by Pearson's outward-looking policies, volunteering naturally extended Canada's new role. Eventual government support for CUSO occurred in the same context.

Dutch identity and foreign policy also resonated well with the Peace Corps idea. Following the virtual end of Dutch colonialism in 1949, under-scored when Indonesia seized the small remains of Holland's Asian empire (Western New Guinea) in 1962, the Netherlands government had to consider what to do with its former colonial administrators and with a new generation that would not have the same socializing experiences that had reinforced Dutch nationalism in the past. Both would be funneled into the Jongeren Vrijwilligers Programma (JVP).

For the former colonial administrators who became the first staff of JVP, developing youth placements fit neatly with their previous field experience. For youth, volunteering allowed them to step into the shoes of the generations of Dutch missionaries and traders immortalized by Rembrandt. "People were used to going abroad; in every family there were people who had been abroad," one of the early Dutch volunteers said in retrospect. "We're traders," an official of SNV later commented, "and those people who sailed around Africa to Indonesia came back as heroes. In the 1960s and seventies, you could still be a hero by working for SNV." JVP, later renamed SNV, also confirmed Dutch influence in international forums. The Netherlands quickly joined the International Peace Corps Secretariat and, along with Israel and Germany, was one of the first nations to give it staff support. One Dutch political cartoon joked: "Coming soon: The Peace Corps from the Netherlands." The caption read "Holland speaks its little words."[57] The irony not to be missed was that though it was little, Holland did still have a say.

For Israel, constantly fighting for its survival in the 1950s and 1960s, domestic identity and unity were not a problem in any normal sense. Jews had always been conscious of themselves *as* Jews—and when they weren't, the world made them so. But the Peace Corps idea fit extremely well within the larger geopolitical strategy of the tiny country. Nearly encircled by hostile Arab nations, Israel under David Ben-Gurion and Golda Meir looked to build bridges to nations on the other side. Peace Corps staff member Harris Wofford, visiting Israel in 1963 after traveling through sub-Saharan Africa, wrote home that it had "leaped the Arab noose." Israel's volunteer program and other foreign aid efforts were the most effective Wofford had seen. "Because Israel is so small and so unique," he noted, "it is easier for African countries to accept advice and aid from her." For her pains, he observed, at an important gathering of African heads of state "the Arab leaders discovered how much other Africans appreciate what Israel is doing." Wofford hoped that the Jewish nation's "wide acceptance in Africa" might eventually contribute to Arab recognition of "the reality of Israel."[58]

In the United States, as in the other countries not under direct attack, the Peace Corps idea proved its usefulness many times over in promoting national identity and consensus. At a very practical level, Kennedy found in 1960 that it helped him win more of the youth vote. And while Republican front-runners like Richard Nixon and Barry Goldwater initially ridiculed the idea, when confronted with its obvious popularity they swung around to become firm supporters. But perhaps the greatest perceived contribution of the Peace Corps to domestic nation building was the opportunity it provided for ensuring, to borrow Seymour Martin Lipset's phrase, "the continued vitality of antistatist individualism."[59]

The assaults of the Cold War—the "Red threat" both at home and abroad—stimulated an unusually high degree of consciousness about the atypicality of politics in the United States and the importance of sustaining that uniqueness while reaching out to the rest of the world. A common view was that only the continued health of private associations and the national habit of voluntary action could stave off the perils of either welfare statism or communism. According to Grant McConnell, the threat of totalitarian mass movements consolidated the position after 1945 of a "body of doctrine" that exalted "the private association as an essential feature of American democracy, perhaps of any genuine democracy."[60]

While *government* support for *private* association is a contradiction in terms, there was nonetheless significant evidence of it in the postwar era, from tax laws that encouraged corporate philanthropy to the formation of the Peace Corps as a kind of private diplomacy. One early exposition on the Peace Corps in 1961 captured this sentiment by saying that the "new theorists" of foreign aid operated on the understanding that Alexis de Toqueville was right "to see a connection between the stability of the American system and our national habit of voluntary association." Through youthful volunteers, the United States could practice this habit while teaching it to others. Peace Corps director Sargent Shriver stated the problem more apocalyptically: "The character of American society itself is at stake."[61] The first director of the Peace Corps in the Philippines, Lawrence Fuchs, reflected that the Peace Corps (like the Dutch JVP) was "a product of the need of Americans to live out the ideals of their culture." That the Kennedy administration saw and responded imaginatively to this need explains at least a part of Kennedy's unique popularity—both at home and abroad.

In many, if not most, cases during the period 1945 to 1989, decolonization and development were held hostage to the Cold War. United States officials frequently found it difficult to distinguish between nationalism and communism, and not all even cared to entertain the distinction. Policy was often openly, though not rhetorically, opportunistic. In Guatemala, Iran, and Vietnam, the United States struck hard at "communist-influenced" forces. In Egypt and Indonesia, "communist-influenced" forces were treated with greater circumspection to sustain their nominal neutrality.

The Peace Corps was a singular attempt to project a nonopportunistic image and reinforce the perception of other nations that the primary objective of the United States toward the Third World was not—in the words of the 1961 USIA poll—"to dominate" but "to help." Its overwhelming success in doing this was indicated by the speed with which other Western nations adopted the same technique and applied it in their own former colonies and spheres of influence. In 1967 approximately 30 percent of foreign youth volunteers in the Third World came from France, Britain, Germany, and Canada, 10 percent came from other countries, and 60 percent came from the United States. The success of the Peace Corps mission was also indicated by the enthusiastic reception given to most U.S. contingents. Of the forty-three countries that requested U.S. volunteers between 1961 and 1965, twenty-nine nations still wanted them nearly twenty years later. The Peace Corps effectively signaled that—quite separate from the exigencies of the Cold War—Kennedy had, in the words of a Dutch observer, "less patience with countries which still have colonial aspirations than had the Eisenhower administration." He wished to side, symbolically and practically, with the new nations of the world.[62]

Of course, the Peace Corps could in no way compensate for other policies that sacrificed Third World development to the Cold War or that made the United States an obstacle to national self-determination. But it was an attempt, within the context of East-West enmity, to recognize that the greatest division "cutting across the world," according to Sargent Shriver, was that "between the economically developed northern countries and the newly developing southern continents; . . . between the white minority and the colored majority of the human race." And to the extent that the Peace Corps sustained this focus on North-South (as opposed to East-West) issues—through the policy of multilateral proliferation, through refusing to send volunteers to Vietnam, through elaborate provisions to avoid CIA infiltration, through a rhetoric of universalism rather than anticommunism—it was appreciated.

What does this mean for our understanding of the role of the United States in the era of Third World decolonization? It means that we need to embrace a reality that is more complex than one that can be explained simply by reference to the Cold War or to U.S. hegemony. Had the Cold War not occurred, decolonization would have come anyway. World War II had helped determine that outcome. Something like the Peace Corps might very well have evolved as the world's industrialized, formerly imperial nations struggled to maintain their political and economic alliances. And, in addition to the demands of realpolitik, one must consider the impulse toward solidarity with "the little people all over the world" that decolonization undeniably provoked among the hundreds of thousands of citizens who volunteered for the Peace Corps and its counterparts. For many of these youths and for the nations that welcomed their gesture, Kennedy had provided the means by which this desire could be made real.

One volunteer in Latin America wrote home after the Kennedy assassination that "many [of the local people] have told us how they wept when they heard of his death and many have pictures of him. It's so hard to explain."[63] The Peace Corps, undoubtedly, is a significant part of that explanation.

Notes

This essay was written in part at the Woodrow Wilson International Center for Scholars. I would like to thank the center for its support, as well as the College of Arts and Letters of the University of San Diego and the John F. Kennedy Library Foundation. Thanks also go to Brian Balogh, David Kennedy, Natalie Higelin, Daniel Hoffman, Leon Nower, Bruce Schulman, and the scholars of the Wilson Center for their critical comments. The essay is drawn partly from my book, *All You Need Is Love: The Peace Corps and the Spirit of the 1960s,* copyright Harvard University Press, 1998. A previous version appeared in *Diplomatic History* 20 (Winter 1996): 79–105.

1. Marshall quoted in Sargent Shriver, *Point of the Lance* (New York, 1964), 9.

2. Kennedy quoted in Gerard T. Rice, *The Bold Experiment: JFK's Peace Corps* (Notre Dame, IN, 1985), 23; Harris Wofford, Oral History Interview, 2, John F. Kennedy Library, Boston.

3. See letter of Eugene Harrington, 15 January 1965; letter of Sharry Simerl to her

family, 26 December 1963; letter of John C. Schafer to his parents, 25 November 1963; and letter of Susan Stapleton to her parents, undated (c. November 1963), all in Peace Corps Collection (PCC), box 2, file: "Letters on the Death of John F. Kennedy," files 1 and 2, Kennedy Library.

4. Sargent Shriver to John Kennedy, "Summary of Next Steps," 22 February 1961, Gerald Bush Papers, box 5, file: "Report to the President," Kennedy Library; minutes, Director's Staff Meeting, 5 April 1961, Bush Papers, box 1, file: "Decision Records, 3/9/61–5/26/61."

5. Sargent Shriver, "Summary of Report to the President on the Peace Corps," 4 March 1961, White House Staff Files, Carmine Bellino, box 1, file: "Peace Corps, General, 1961," Kennedy Library. Kennedy quoted in "Some Points for the U.S. Presentation to the UN on the Peace Corps," 7 April 1961, General Records of the Department of State, Record Group 59, file: 800.00 PC/4–161, National Archives II, College Park, MD (hereafter RG 59, with filing information). Also see Sargent Shriver to John Kennedy, "Summary of Next Steps," 22 February 1961, Bush Papers, box 5, file: "Report to the President."

6. Harlan Cleveland to Secretary of State Dean Rusk through George Ball, 14 April 1961, RG 59, 800.00 PC/4–161.

7. "Hearings before the Committee on Foreign Relations on S. 2000," U.S. Senate, 87th Cong., 1st sess., 22–23 June 1961, 115 and 154.

8. Confidential report of the chair of the U.S. delegation to the 32nd session of the United Nations Economic and Social Council (5 July–4 August 1961), attached to minutes of Director's Staff Meeting, 22 August 1961, Peace Corps Microfilm Hard Copy, box 1, file: 7/6/61–8/29/61, Kennedy Library.

9. John H. Morrow to the Department of State, 21 August 1961, RG 59, 800.00 PC/8–161.

10. Dean Rusk, 1 March 1961, Circular, RG 59, 800.00 PC/11–460; Belgrade Embassy/Rankin to secretary of state, 9 March 1961, RG 59, 800.00 PC/3–961; Moscow Embassy/Thompson to secretary of state, 16 March 1961, RG 59, 800.00 PC/3–961.

11. Research and Reference Service, "Western European Attitudes toward Economic Aid and the Peace Corps," i–ii, 2–3, December 1961, Records of the USIA Office of Research, Record Group 306, Public Opinion Barometer Reports, 1955–62; box 5, file: WE-4 (II), (hereafter "Western European Attitudes"), National Archives II.

12. Ibid.; author's interview with Warren Wiggins, 1 November 1993, Arlington, VA.

13. Edward Said, *Culture and Imperialism* (New York, 1993), xxi.

14. W. J. Smith to P. Rogers, 7 February 1962, Records of the Office of Overseas Development, Record Class OD/10/4, Public Record Office, Kew, England.

15. Quote from CUSO's first chairman, Francis Leddy, taken from "The Origins of CUSO, Personal Recollections of J. F. Leddy," 16 May 1981, Ian Smillie Papers, Ottawa, Canada (access courtesy of Mr. Smillie). The sense of urgency in getting the Canadian program under way, following Kennedy's election, is evidenced in the proposal submitted to the Canadian government by graduate student Keith Spicer, who correctly predicted that the Canadian students would get off the ground first. See Keith Spicer, "Submission to the Government of Canada on a Scheme for Commonwealth Graduate Volunteers," Canadian National Archives, Vol. 92, CUSO Papers, file: "CUSO/ SUCO History, 1959–1964 (Includes Government Relations)."

16. Figures from Gerard Rice, *Twenty Years of Peace Corps* (Washington, DC, 1961), 17 (fiscal year 1962); Ian Smillie, *The Land of Lost Content: A History of CUSO* (Toronto, 1985), 23 (1963 figures, by which time the Peace Corps had tripled to 6,646 volunteers).

17. Addis Ababa Embassy/Richards to secretary of state, 14 January 1961, RG 59, 800.00 PC/11–460; Hal (last name unidentified, initials HHS) to McGeorge Bundy, 18 January 1963, National Security Files, box 284, file: Peace Corps, 1/63–3/63, Kennedy Library. Also see U.S. Department of State, *Foreign Relations of the United States, 1964* (Washington, DC, 1992), 1:261.

18. "Scope Paper," attached to memo from Florence Kirlin to George McGhee, undersecretary of state for political affairs, 28 May 1962, RG 59, 800.00 PC/1–162.

19. Warren Wiggins interview.

20. French Ministry of Foreign Affairs to U.S. Embassy/Paris, 17 April 1963, RG 59, Central Foreign Policy File, box 3290, file: AID, 14, Peace Corps, 4/1/63.

21. Sydney Meller, Rome Embassy, to secretary of state, 31 August 1963, RG 59, Central Foreign Policy File, 1963, box 3290, file: AID, 14, Peace Corps, 7/1/63; William Haddad to McGeorge Bundy, 15 November 1962, President's Office File, box 86, file: "Peace Corps, 7/62–12/62," Kennedy Library; Tokyo Embassy to secretary of state, 6 December 1963, RG 59, Central Foreign Policy File, 1963, box 3290, file: AID, 14–1, Peace Corps Volunteers; *International Volunteer* (May–June 1963), 1, copy from the personal collection of Elizabeth Badon Ghijben, Foreign Ministry, the Netherlands. Ghijben was the Dutch staff person appointed to staff the International Peace Corps Secretariat.

22. Rockefeller Brothers Fund, *Prospect for America: The Rockefeller Panel Reports* (Garden City, NY, 1961), 170.

23. Dean Rusk to U.S. Embassy Bogota, Caracas, La Paz, Tegucigalpa, 2 February 1963, RG 59, Central Foreign Policy File, 1963, box 3290, file: AID, 14, Peace Corps, 2/1/63.

24. Dean Rusk to U.S. Embassy Bogota, Caracas, La Paz, Tegucigalpa, 2 February 1963, RG 59, Central Foreign Policy File, 1963, box 3290, file: AID, 14, Peace Corps, 2/1/63; Khartoum Embassy to secretary of state, 18 August 1963, RG 59, Central Foreign Policy File, 1963, box 3290, file: AID, 14, Peace Corps, 7/1/63. Also see *International Volunteer* (December 1963), 1, from collection of Elizabeth Badon Ghijben.

25. Author's interview with Ton Nijzink (Dutch SNV), 19 May 1994, The Hague.

26. Harry Truman as quoted in Stephen E. Ambrose, *Rise to Globalism: American Foreign Policy since 1938,* 4th ed. (Middlesex, UK, 1987), 115.

27. Creel quoted in David Kennedy, *Over Here: The First World War and American Society* (New York, 1980), 62—Creel later wrote about his efforts in *How We Advertised America* (New York, 1920); M. S. Anderson, *The Rise of Modern Diplomacy, 1450–1919* (New York, 1993), 287.

28. Nelson Rockefeller to George Marshall, 28 August 1942, RG 229, OIAA Department of Information, Content Planning Division, box 1459, file: "Content Liaison." Document obtained by author in the archives of the Centro de Pesquisa e Documentaçâo de História Contemporânea do Brasil (CPDOC), Rio de Janeiro, IAA 42.05.28; U.S. Congress, House Committee on Foreign Affairs, *International Cooperation Act of 1949 (Point Four Program)* (Washington, 1950), 84. I have written further on this subject in *The Rich Neighbor Policy: Rockefeller and Kaiser in Brazil* (New Haven, 1992).

29. Mora Dickson interview. Also see Dickson, *A Chance to Serve,* 27–28.

30. Ambrose, *Rise to Globalism*, 97; Melvyn P. Leffler, *A Preponderance of Power: National Security, the Truman Administration, and the Cold War* (Stanford, CA, 1992), 491; Truman quoted in Allan A. Needell, " 'Truth Is Our Weapon': Project TROY, Political Warfare, and Government-Academic Relations in the National Security State," *Diplomatic History* 17 (Summer 1993): 404.

31. Morison quoted in Needell, " 'Truth Is Our Weapon,' " 412.

32. Mary Brown Bullock, *An American Transplant: The Rockefeller Foundation and Peking Union Medical College* (Berkeley, CA, 1980).

33. Cobbs, *The Rich Neighbor Policy*, 245, 248–49; Peter Collier and David Horowitz, *The Rockefellers: An American Dynasty* (New York, 1976), 329. Also see Joe Alex Morris, *Nelson Rockefeller: A Biography* (New York, 1960), 292.

34. Edward G. Miller, "United States Relations with Latin America," May 1952, RG 59, lot 53D26, Office Files of the Assistant Secretary of State for Latin America, 1949–1953, file: "Business Advisory Council"; Stephen G. Rabe, *Eisenhower and Latin America: The Foreign Policy of Anticommunism* (Chapel Hill, NC, 1988), 90.

35. Kennedy quoted in Rice, *The Bold Experiment*, 15; William Lederer, *A Nation of Sheep* (New York, 1961), 154.

36. Interview, Keith Spicer, 18 May 1993, Hull, Quebec, Canada.

37. Volunteer Ollie McMichael quoted in Betty Feith, "An Episode in Education for International Understanding: The Volunteer Graduate Scheme in Indonesia, 1950–1963" (M.A. thesis, Monash University, 1984), 5–6, 50.

38. David Hapgood and Meridan Bennett, *Agents of Change: A Close Look at the Peace Corps* (Boston, 1968), 6–7. Also see Geir Lundestad, "Empire by Invitation? The United States and Western Europe, 1945–1952," SHAFR *Newsletter* 15 (September 1984): 1–21; Michael J. Hogan, *The Marshall Plan: America, Britain, and the Reconstruction of Western Europe, 1947–1952* (New York, 1987); and Richard N. Gardner, *Sterling-Dollar Diplomacy: The Origins and Prospects of Our International Economic Order*, 2nd ed. (New York, 1969).

39. Ton Nijzink interview; Willy Brandt's account of Robert Kennedy from Willy Brandt, *People and Politics: The Years 1960–1975* (Boston, 1976), 87.

40. U.S. Embassy Stockholm/Bonbright to secretary of state, 17 March 1961, RG 59, 800.00 PC/3–961; Parliamentary Debate on Voluntary Service, 12 December 1962, OD 10/35; W. J. Smith, "Service Overseas by Volunteers," 2 March 1962, OD/10/36.

41. Gandhi quoted in James Morris, *Farewell the Trumpets: An Imperial Retreat* (London, 1978), 495; Allard Lowenstein, *Brutal Mandate: A Journey to Southwest Africa* (New York, 1962), 28.

42. For an account of how Brazil took advantage of great power rivalries to increase its freedom of action, see Stanley Hilton, *Brazil and the Great Powers, 1930–1939: The Politics of Trade Rivalry* (Austin, TX, 1973); and Bernard Porter, *The Lion's Share: A Short History of British Imperialism, 1850–1970* (London, 1975), 309.

43. Abraham Lowenthal and Albert Fishlow, *Latin America's Emergence: Toward a U.S. Response* (New York, 1979), 32; Stimson quoted in David Green, *The Containment of Latin America: A History of the Myths and Realities of the Good Neighbor Policy* (Chicago, 1971), 230.

44. Roosevelt quoted in Robert Dallek, *Franklin D. Roosevelt and American Foreign Policy, 1932–1945* (New York, 1981), 360; Walter LaFeber, *The American Age: United States Foreign Policy at Home and Abroad since 1750* (New York, 1989), 415, 494. An

important distinction should be made between the significant risks the United States was willing to take from the outset to push the British to end the system of imperial trading preferences, and U.S. unwillingness to force the issue of political independence for the colonies. The first was an economic question of great interest to the post-Depression United States; the second was a matter of abstract political principle, more easily shelved.

45. LaFeber, *American Age,* 531–32.

46. Yaw Agyeman-Badu, "The Attitude of African Nations toward American Aid: The Case of Ghana and Nigeria" (Ph.D. diss., University of South Carolina, 1980), 72.

47. Ibid., 107, 112. This reality was perceived in capitals as remote as Rio de Janeiro. Maurício Nabuco, Brazilian ambassador to the United States, wrote to the Ministry of Foreign Affairs that the primary motivation for U.S. support for African colonial development was to provide resources to the imperialist nations as a complement to "European economic stabilization" under the Marshall Plan. Nabuco to Itamaraty, 3 March 1950, *Missões, Março 1950,* Archives of Itamaraty, Rio de Janeiro.

48. Miles Kahler, *Decolonization in Britain and France: The Domestic Consequences of International Relations* (Princeton, NJ, 1984), 134–36, 141.

49. Author's interview with Benôit Chadanet, French Committee for International Solidarity, French Senate, 16 May 1994, Paris. Chadanet further noted that France's possession of the atomic bomb, along with the African alliances, are what distinguishes it from countries "like Italy."

50. *International Volunteer* 2 (March 1964): 2, copy from the personal collection of Elizabeth Badon Ghijben; author's interview with Catherine de Loeper (Association Française des Volontaires du Progrés), 17 May 1994, Paris.

51. Porter, *The Lion's Share,* 187; Morris, *Farewell the Trumpets,* 507–8.

52. Only one-quarter the size of the Marshall Plan, the Colombo Plan proposed to spread resources (1.8 billion pounds sterling) over a broader area and transform countries at a much more rudimentary stage of economic development than had the Marshall Plan. Nonetheless, the British were piqued to action in their sphere of influence by the "immense scale of American generosity," according to historian Trevor Lloyd. The Marshall Plan's success in reviving Europe "encouraged everyone to believe that a few years of intense commitment to foreign aid would enable the less prosperous parts of the world to do equally well." T. O. Lloyd, *The British Empire: 1558–1983* (Oxford, UK, 1984), 332–33; Kahler, *Decolonization in Britain and France,* 130, 134–36, 144.

53. Commonwealth Relations Office to secretary of state, 14 September 1961, OD/10/3.

54. Mora Dickson interview; ARC to secretary, 10 May 1963, OD 10/5. Also see the *Times,* 23 March 1958; *Birmingham Post and Birmingham Gazette,* 12 May 1958; *Scottish Educational Journal,* 5 June 1959; *Times,* 11 September 1959; *Times,* 2 November 1960; *Scotsman,* 22 November 1960; *Daily Express,* 15 April 1961.

55. Sargent Shriver to John F. Kennedy, Weekly Report, 7 August 1962, VP Security File, box 12, file: Peace Corps Reports, Lyndon Johnson Library, Austin, TX.

56. Keith Spicer, "Canada: Values in Search of a Vision," in *Identities in North America: The Search for Community,* ed. Robert L. Earle and John D. Wirth (Stanford, CA, 1995), 13, 17, 21.

57. Author's interview with Bert Barten, 20 May 1994, Zuid-Scharwoude, Nether-

lands; author's interview with P. B. M. Knoope, 19 May 1994, The Hague; cartoon reprinted in Ton Nijzink, *Dag Vrijwilliger: Twintig Jaar SNV* (The Hague, 1985), 11.

58. Open letter from Harris Wofford, 7 January 1964, Moyers Papers, box 14, file: Peace Corps, 3 of 3, Johnson Library.

59. Seymour Martin Lipset, *Continental Divide: The Values and Institutions of the United States and Canada* (New York, 1990); Rice, *The Bold Experiment,* 16–17.

60. Grant McConnell, "The Public Values of the Private Association," in J. Roland Pennock, *Voluntary Associations, Nomos XI* (New York, 1969), 147.

61. De Toqueville quoted in Benjamin DeMott, "Objective: Local Democratic Action," reprinted from *Harper's Magazine* (September 1961) in *The Peace Corps,* ed. Pauline Madow (New York, 1964), 125; Shriver, *Point of the Lance,* 45. Corporate giving, especially, came into its own in the 1950s both because of high taxes on corporate profits and because businessmen insisted that private philanthropy was the only way "to defend and preserve" the role of the private sector in educational, scientific, and welfare activities against the encroachments of big government. See Richard Eells, *Corporation Giving in a Free Society* (New York, 1956) and Beardsley Ruml and Theodore Geiger, eds., *The Manual of Corporate Giving* (Washington, DC, 1952).

62. U.S. Embassy The Hague/Service to secretary of state, 15 March 1961, RG 59, 800.00 PC/3–961. Figures derived from Bill McWhinney and Dave Godfrey, eds., *Man Deserves Man: CUSO in Developing Countries* (Toronto, 1968), 449, appendix 2; and Rice, *Twenty Years of Peace Corps,* 4, 5, 7.

63. Quote from Sargent Shriver in *Point of the Lance,* 8–9; Susan Stapleton to parents, undated (c. November 1963), Peace Corps Collection, box 2, file: "Letters on the Death of John F. Kennedy," file 1.

The Influence of Organized Labor on U.S. Policy toward Israel, 1945-1967

PETER L. HAHN

Scholars have produced a large and distinguished body of scholarship on U.S. relations with Israel since 1948. Numerous writers have debated the relative importance of domestic political, humanitarian, diplomatic, and strategic factors behind U.S. support for the creation of the Jewish state. Others have examined the evolution of the U.S. policy toward Israel's ongoing conflict with its Arab neighbors. Various works have probed the political and economic ties between the two states.[1] Several historians have debated the idea that the United States and Israel have developed a "special relationship" over the half century of Israeli statehood.[2] Consistent with the rising popularity of new modes of inquiry in diplomatic history, a few scholars recently have probed the cultural, religious, and gender dimensions of the U.S.-Israeli relationship.[3]

Although a few scholars have examined the unofficial, nonstatist component of U.S.-Israeli relations, the important story of the interaction between major U.S. labor unions and the state of Israel has remained untold.[4] This essay explores that relationship from the late 1940s to the late 1960s. It examines, first, the degree to which leaders of U.S. labor sympathized with Israeli national interests and encouraged the government in Washington to make policy decisions favorable to Israel, especially with regard to Israel's ongoing conflict with its Arab neighbors. Second, it explores the extent to which the Israeli government and the General Federation of Labor in Israel (the Histadrut) exploited the sympathy of U.S. labor by mobilizing it as a potent political force that worked within the United States to Israel's benefit. Third, to a limited extent it also explores whether labor activism significantly affected the development of official policy by the U.S. government.

After providing evidence of the deep and personal ties between U.S. labor leaders and Israeli officials, this essay addresses these issues through a series of case studies of labor activism on Israel's behalf in the 1947–67 period.

The first twenty years of Israeli statehood coincided with a dynamic era in U.S. labor history. During the 1933–45 period, organized labor had grown in size and influence, embraced international involvement by the U.S. government, and shed its own isolationism in reaction to the foreign threats posed by fascism. For two decades after 1947, major unions dominated by the AFL-CIO strongly approved the prosecution of the Cold War by the federal government, in part because they sincerely opposed communism in principle and in part because massive government spending on defense generated substantial economic benefits for workers. Major unions collaborated with the government by battling to purge West European trade unions of communist influence. Labor remained a fairly stalwart supporter of the Cold War consensus in the 1960s, when it endorsed the government's anticommunist crusade in Vietnam.[5]

Despite its partnership with the government on foreign policy, organized labor did not enjoy consistent power and influence within U.S. domestic politics and policy. In the late 1940s, labor consolidated its partnership with the Democratic Party, securing a continuation of the New Deal by rallying behind Harry Truman and pledging loyalty in the Cold War. Although they remained well financed and professionally managed, however, major unions thereafter confronted problems such as stagnant membership rolls, declining influence on industrial relations law, and inconsistency in influencing elections. In the 1950s, conservatives dominated national elections despite labor opposition, Congress and the FBI hounded some unions over alleged corruption and Communist leanings, and public tolerance of strikes and activism waned. In the 1960s, major unions clashed with the White House over wages and inflation policy and considered the Great Society an insufficient step toward their objective of economic democracy. Students, antiwar protesters, and civil rights activists of the New Left, ironically, attacked labor because it remained committed to the war in Vietnam.[6]

Despite these limitations, organized labor in the United States attracted the attention of Israeli authorities who searched for means to influence U.S. official policy toward the Middle East. A key bridge in the relationship between Israel and U.S. labor was the General Federation of Labor in Israel, or the Histadrut. Established in December 1920, the Histadrut provided social security, military defense, and a form of political democracy to Jewish residents of Mandatory Palestine, and its agricultural settlements established a Jewish presence in the land later accorded to Israel. By some accounts it served as a government substitute before Israeli independence and thereafter remained equal to the state itself in terms of political and economic power. "Our enterprises," Histadrut's U.S. representative Moshe Bitan explained privately in 1953, "have been pioneers in agriculture, irrigation, housing, public building, transportation, and even in some industrial fields." In 1967, the union enrolled 90 percent of Israeli wage earners; it provided mutual aid and health insurance to 70 percent of Israel's population; and it owned and operated a vast network of manufacturing, agricultural, marketing, and service cooperatives that generated one-quarter of Israel's gross national product.[7]

Together with the Israeli government, Histadrut developed friendly relations with numerous U.S. labor unions. Perhaps its closest ties were to the Trade Union Division of the National Committee for Labor Israel (TUD/ NCLI)[8] and the American Trade Union Council for Histadrut (ATUCFH). In the early 1950s, the American Federation of Labor (AFL) consistently recognized the TUD/NLCI as "the living bridge between the American workers and the Israeli workers," and a decade later Histadrut Secretary General Aharon Becker applauded TUD/NLCI Director Moe Falikman for the "unflagging friendship and solidarity which had by now become a fine tradition in American-Israel labour movement relations." The ATUCFH formally described itself as "an organization representing American trade unionists of all faiths, who support the program of Histadrut." In the 1950s, its leaders often discussed with Histadrut representatives strategies for shaping U.S. policy to Israel's advantage. Prominent U.S. labor leaders were involved. In the TUD/NCLI, International Ladies Garment Workers Union (ILGWU) Vice President Joseph Breslaw served as an early chairman; AFL President William Green and Congress of Industrial Organizations (CIO) President Philip Murray served as honorary chairmen; and United Auto Workers (UAW) President Walter Reuther and AFL Vice President Matthew Woll served as honorary vice-chairmen. An early chairman of the larger NCLI was Joseph Schlossberg, former general secretary of the Amalgamated Clothing Workers of America (ACWA).[9]

One of Histadrut's best friends among U.S. labor leaders was George Meany, who occupied pivotal positions in the AFL (secretary-general from 1939 to 1952 and president from 1952 to 1955) and the AFL-CIO (president from 1955 to 1979). Meany emerged as a staunch supporter of Israel, in part because he admired the Histadrut's role in establishing the state. "There is a bond between wage earners that is like the bond between brothers and sisters," he explained in an address in 1950. "When Histadrut triumphed at last, it was natural that our hearts should swell with happiness." Meany added in a speech to the Jewish Labor Committee (JLC) in 1955 that "we have an interest, a tremendous interest, in the State of Israel—we've expressed that for many, many years by a support of Histadrut. . . . In the final analysis Histadrut is Israel."[10]

Israeli officials naturally tried to build upon the foundation of Meany's admiration for Histadrut. Representative Moshe Bitan attended annual conventions of the AFL and AFL-CIO to express his federation's admiration and to encourage AFL resolutions of amity. "Our appreciation should go to Histadrut," Israeli Foreign Minister Moshe Sharett wrote after the AFL-CIO passed a favorable resolution in 1955, "for the constant labors of its able emissaries over the years in bringing about within the American movement this full understanding of our case." Secretary General Becker reported that Meany's visit to Israel in the autumn of 1961 "was a successful one. . . . We all feel that our relationship with the AFL-CIO has been strengthened by this visit." When he toured AFL-CIO headquarters during a trip to Washington in June 1964, Prime Minister Levi Eshkol declared that "we, in Israel, derive strength from the continuous expression of your fraternal solidarity." Histadrut representative Ben-Zion Ilan concluded that this encounter "reflected the special cordiality of our relations and the high esteem in which the . . . AFL-CIO is regarded in Israel."[11]

On at least one occasion, Israeli officials exploited Meany's sympathy for their own political gain. When the government in Jerusalem wanted to influence U.S. policy toward the Arab states in late 1957, for instance, Israeli Labor Attache Nathan Bar-Yaacov briefed AFL-CIO counsel Arthur Goldberg on Israel's objectives and gave him a position paper. Goldberg then discussed the issue with Meany, who pledged to chat informally with President Dwight D. Eisenhower during a reception for a visiting foreign head of state.[12]

Occasionally, the AFL/AFL-CIO limited its support of Israel. In late 1953, Meany temporarily delayed issuing a statement criticizing State Department policy toward an Israeli-Jordanian border dispute for fear that it might damage labor interests. More important, in an address delivered during a period of rising Arab-Israeli tensions in 1955, Meany alluded to the multiethnic composition of the AFL and urged Israel to seek "real peace based on equitable adjustment of the troubles between the Arabs and the Jewish people in the old Jewish homeland." On the other hand, AFL and AFL-CIO leaders never contemplated siding with Israel's adversaries. For example, when an Egyptian labor representative protested Moshe Bitan's words at the 1954 AFL convention and requested time for a rebuttal, Meany refused even to answer his telegrams.[13]

A more serious threat to the AFL-CIO–Israeli friendship surfaced in 1964 when Israel endorsed UN membership for Communist China. Jay Lovestone of the AFL-CIO international affairs department complained to Histadrut officials that "I cannot for the life of me see why Israeli democracy . . . pursues any course which would strengthen the Mao Tse Tung dictatorship." Angrily, Lovestone added that "since I am not a diplomat, I must state frankly:— Apparently your Deputy Premier [Abba Eban] studied how to irritate friends and undermine friendship." Even after a breakfast meeting between Prime Minister Eshkol and labor leaders, Lovestone remained angry. "The breakfast was good but [showed] too much harmony, and, as you know, too much harmony is not the best dish." When he read a copy of Lovestone's invective, Eban fired back his own salvo. He defended Israel's policy toward China as designed to create "a better representation of the 'new states' of Africa and Asia in the U.N. . . . One does not win American friendship by an obsequious concealment of honestly held judgments," he added, letting his anger show. "You have no right . . . to indulge in coarse, personal discourtesy." Eban also complained to Meany, Reuther, and others in the AFL-CIO leadership about Lovestone's words.[14]

Israeli officials enjoyed a much closer relationship with David Dubinsky, president of ILGWU since 1932 and treasurer of the JLC from the 1940s to the 1960s. Israeli officials commonly included Dubinsky in a select group of U.S. Jewish leaders called upon to provide expert advice about Israel's financial problems, and they appealed to him to support Israeli bond sale drives, in hopes that "if Dubinsky [is] drawn into [the] c[a]mpaign there [is] almost no limit [to the] amounts we might get." They also routinely scheduled meetings between Dubinsky and visiting Israeli officials, including Prime Minister David Ben-Gurion in 1956 and Foreign Secretary Golda Meir in 1959, and in 1961 Ben-Gurion invited the union leader to visit his home at Sde Boqer. Dubinsky became especially close to Eliahu Elath. In 1956, he arranged a luncheon for Elath, then Israeli ambassador to London, and various U.S. labor leaders, and in the 1960s, when Elath had become president of the Hebrew University of Jerusalem, he and Dubinsky engaged in friendly correspondence. Dubinsky's sympathy paid dividends for Israel. In May 1957, to cite one example, Israeli officials recognized him for adding favorable language to a draft resolution on the Suez Canal transit issue before the AFL-CIO executive committee passed it. Foreign Minister Meir wrote to Dubinsky "to offer to you our warmest tribute for your unwavering support over many years of the causes of the Histadruth and of Israel's National redemption."[15]

Israeli and Histadrut officials also cultivated close relations with other major labor leaders. Walter Reuther, president of the UAW and president of the CIO after 1952, became a close friend. "I want you to know that your problems are our problems," Reuther wrote to Histadrut Chief of Foreign Relations Reuven Barkatt, "and Israel and the Histadrut are ever in our minds, for we realize that without Israel the forces of freedom and democracy in the Middle East will be without leadership and without foundation." The UAW also eagerly argued Israel's case on important issues. In January 1957, for example, when the writer Norman Thomas published evidence of Israeli atrocities during the Suez War, Labor Attache Bar-Yaacov drafted a letter of protest for signature by Ben B. Seligman of the UAW's International Affairs Division. Three months later, when Seligman needed information to reply to a letter about Arabs living in Israel, he secured it from the Histadrut representative.[16]

Israel also enjoyed the support of Jacob S. Potofsky, president of the ACWA and vice president of the AFL-CIO. While visiting Israel in September 1958, Potofsky declared that "the American workers in the AFL-CIO are your friends and brothers. They believe in Israel, its philosophy and its future. . . . American workers will tolerate no force of aggression, direct or indirect, by any force on the people and the state of Israel." Labor Attache Bar-Yaacov cultivated a friendship with leaders of the National Education Association, such as Paul Smith, secretary for international relations. With less success, Bar-Yaacov also tried to mobilize John L. Lewis, president of the United Mine Workers. (Lewis seemed uninterested, stressing that "he does not know anything, he has no influence with the administration, and nobody asks and he does not provide any advice.") On the other hand, Israel did enjoy the support of the United Steelworkers of America, which passed favorable resolutions in 1954 and 1958, and many other craft unions, such as the International Union of Electrical, Radio and Machine Workers (CIO). Histadrut also nurtured close relations with A. Philip Randolph, president of the Brotherhood of Sleeping Car Porters.[17]

In myriad ways, Israeli officials worked to cultivate their close friendships with U.S. labor leaders. Histadrut sponsored annual tours of Israel by leaders of AFL-CIO. "Each time I come back from a visit to Israel," Reuther wrote to Histadrut International Department Head Yehudit Simhoni, "I return with my spirit refreshed and much inspired by what I have seen and heard as you work and struggle to build the State of Israel." The NCLI awarded its "Humanitarian Award of the Histadrut" to George Meany in 1956 and Walter Reuther in 1958. (Previous winners had included such luminaries as Harry Truman and Eleanor Roosevelt.) With tremendous success, Israeli officials also sought financial donations from U.S. labor unions, whose generosity they rewarded by naming public facilities in Israel after the union leaders. In 1955, Haifa named a new soccer stadium after David Dubinsky, and the ILGWU hospital in Beersheba opened in 1959. In 1958, with AFL-CIO representatives in attendance, Israelis dedicated the Joseph Breslaw Center, a public facility in Nahora; the William Green Cultural Center, a library and meeting hall in Haifa; and the Philip Murray Memorial Center, a public building in Eilat. In the 1960s, they also erected a stadium in Haifa named for Luigi Antonini, a vice president of ILGWU; the Walter Reuther youth center in Holon; and the George Meany Stadium in Nazareth. As Histadrut Secretary General Pinhas Lavon told AFL-CIO convention delegates in 1959, "I must stress the important aid given to us by the trade unions in America. Many institutions in Israel, in city and village, have been built for the welfare of the worker and his family, thanks to the generosity of your hearts."[18]

The general friendship between U.S. labor and Israel also became evident in various unions' pro-Israel political activism in 1945–67. Labor unions consistently supported Israel at crucial crossroads in its history such as the establishment of the state in the late 1940s, the debate over providing weapons to Israel and Arab states in the early 1950s, the Suez War of 1956–57, and the Six Day War of 1967. U.S. unions also supported the Afro-Asian Institute, an indirect Israeli initiative to build political alliances in the Third World.

U.S. labor leaders vigorously supported Zionists' efforts in 1945–48 to promote immigration of Jewish refugees to Palestine and to establish an independent State of Israel. In 1945–46, William Green, David Dubinsky, and Joseph Breslaw of the TUD/NCLP publicly and privately endorsed Zionists' demands that Britain admit one hundred thousand Jewish displaced persons to Palestine. "In America, our great labor movement has been tremendously disappointed over the attitude of the party in power in Great Britain toward . . . Palestine," Green intoned in a speech at the AFL annual meeting in 1946. The convention passed resolutions demanding admission of one hundred thousand refugees and termination of British rule in Palestine and urging President Harry S. Truman to compel Britain to comply. Under Green's influence, locals such as the Wisconsin State Federation of Labor appealed to the State Department to support the Zionist demands. Histadrut Executive Joseph Sprinzak applauded these moves, and Secretary General Golda Meyerson urged Dubinsky to "use all your contacts in preventing new unnecessary tragedy for many thousands" of Jews.[19]

Labor leaders took several other steps to back Zionism. The NCLP raised $3 million for Histadrut and sponsored a pro-Zionist mass rally in New York City on 12 June 1946, and the TUD/NCLP called on U.S. labor to bolster Histadrut in its effort to absorb immigrants and develop the infrastructure of Jewish Palestine. Labor leaders also pressured the British government to accept Zionist demands. "As friends of [the] British Labor Government," Dubinsky wrote Prime Minister Clement Attlee, ILGWU members expected

British compliance. The AFL, Green declared at a May 1947 labor rally in Atlantic City, "wants to make it clear to its friends in Great Britain that it stands firm with the Palestine Federation of Labor, the Histadrut, at this moment. We, the representatives of labor, will never be satisfied, will never stop, will never cease, until the Jewish people are granted justice and accorded the right to establish their own commonwealth in Palestine, where they can safely live." The AFL passed a pro-Zionist resolution at its 1947 annual meeting, and JLC President Ben Gold and Secretary-Treasurer Max Steinberg called on the United Nations to "stop the state of warfare in Palestine precipitated by Great Britain" and to revoke Britain's mandate.[20]

U.S. labor leaders also rallied to the Zionist cause during the late 1947 UN discussion on whether to partition Palestine into Arab and Jewish states. Dubinsky, Green, and Breslaw appealed to Truman to approve the partition plan despite State Department reservations, and Matthew Woll, chair of the IAD, appealed to both Luxembourg and Haiti to vote for the plan when the UN considered it on 29 November 1947. In the winter of 1948, when the State Department proposed to shelve the partition plan and establish a trusteeship in Palestine, Green assured Histadrut Executive Sprinzak that the AFL would pressure Truman to stand by the partition resolution. Histadrut called upon trade unions, the TUC declared, "to voice [the] strongest demands that [the] United States adhere to [the] decision adopted by General Assembly and vigorously promoted by our government." With the blessing of Green and Murray, the TUC organized a general work stoppage and "huge demonstration" by labor on 14 April 1948 to protest the "shameless betrayal" of Zionism by the State Department.[21]

The appeals of organized labor were important, although not exclusive, factors in shaping the development of Truman's policy toward Israeli statehood. Truman personally offered diplomatic support to the emergence of Israel at several decisive moments, most notably by supporting partition at the United Nations in November 1947 and recognizing Israel as a state in May 1948. Although many considerations shaped his thinking about Palestine, calculations about domestic politics and public opinion were important determinants of his policy.[22] Lobbying by organized labor, which Truman considered an important political asset, contributed to the president's decisions to support Israel.

American labor leaders saluted the Israeli declaration of independence in mid-May 1948 and remained steadfast supporters of the new state thereafter. Responsive to a call from Histadrut, leaders of the AFL, TUC, and JLC pressured Truman to supply weapons to the Jewish military forces in Palestine even before independence. "It is our purpose to defend that independent country established in Palestine," Green declared to the AFL annual meeting in 1948, "and render to the Jewish people there every ounce of help and protection that we can give them." When Isaac Ben-Zvi, Histadrut representative to the convention, encouraged the AFL to support Israel, Green replied that "we will respond whole-heartedly to your request and stand with you and fight with you for the enjoyment of freedom, liberty, and democracy in that great country." The AFL resolved "to do its all to help—particularly the Histadrut, our sister labor federation—to build the Land of Israel into a thriving genuine democracy." During Israel's critical first year of independence, labor leaders pressed the Truman administration to accept Israeli views on several contentious Arab-Israeli disputes, such as the status of Jerusalem, the disposition of Arab refugees, and the demarcation of borders. They also advocated immediate de jure recognition of Israel and approval of Israel's request for a $100 million loan.[23]

Labor activism on behalf of Israel was carefully cultivated by Israeli government officials and leaders of Histadrut. For example, in November 1948, Michael S. Comay of the Israeli delegation to the UN informed Dubinsky of major issues under discussion at the UN, suggested what policy he wanted the United States to adopt on each issue, and added that "anything that can be done at this end [in the United States] to promote such a move forward would be welcome." Minister of Labor, Housing, and Public Works Golda Meyerson invited Dubinsky to provide economic advice to her government, and Ambassador to Washington Eliahu Elath, citing U.S.-Israeli differences at the Lausanne peace talks, encouraged Dubinsky to provide "friendly assistance in order to safeguard the vital interests of our young state." In August 1949, the Israeli embassy apparently supplied a position paper on major issues to Dubinsky and others. The TUC/NCLI took credit for convincing William Green to write to Truman in September 1949 opposing State Department plans to internationalize Jerusalem over Israeli objections. In 1951, Prime Minister David Ben-Gurion appealed to Dubinsky for general friendship and invited him to visit Israel.[24]

U.S. labor actively supported Israel during U.S.-Israeli discussion in 1950 about U.S. arms supply policy. Fearful of Arab aggression against Israel after Britain resumed shipments of weapons to Arab states in late 1949, Israeli officials requested comparable arms supply from the United States. When the Truman administration remained unresponsive, Foreign Minister Moshe Sharett ordered his embassy staff in Washington to initiate a vigorous publicity campaign in the United States and mobilize U.S. Jews to argue Israel's case. The Israeli embassy subtly encouraged key labor leaders and other supporters in the United States to pressure the president to modify his policy.[25]

Israeli officials briefly debated how extensively to mobilize labor to argue their case on arms. Henry Morgenthau, Jr., had arranged an audience with Truman for Green and Murray, unrelated to the arms issue, apparently in hope that the labor leaders could leverage an invitation for Ben-Gurion to visit the White House. Once the arms issue surfaced, some officials in the Israeli embassy tried to convince Morgenthau to cancel the meeting, for fear that an appeal to the White House might alienate Secretary of State Dean Acheson and other key officials in the State Department. Ambassador Elath, however, overruled his advisers and endorsed the visit, confident that a show of support by labor leaders would be worth the risk of angering Acheson. In fact, Elath also supplied Green and Murray with background briefing papers, taking care only to deliver the papers secretly through "trustworthy members" of their unions so as to avoid "undesirable effects [on] Acheson."[26]

On 10 February 1950, Murray and Green visited Truman and appealed to him to safeguard Israel and preserve Histadrut by opposing British rearmament of Arabs, by arming Israel, and by releasing economic aid to the Jewish state. Afterward, the labor leaders publicly announced that they had met Truman at the request of "the leaders of the World Jewish Movements and organizations," thus disguising Israel's role. Afterward, Murray told an Israeli official that the talk went "splendidly" and that Truman "showed sincere and friendly interest [in] Israel." Murray also informed the CIO Executive Board that Truman "promised to give every reasonable degree of consideration to the proposal of American labor." Green and Murray, the TUC announced, "deserve the utmost gratitude from all friends of Israel and of its labor organization, the Histadrut." Indeed, Pinchas Lubianiker, Histadrut secretary general, thanked Green and Murray for "this new proof [of] your unceasing support and assistance." On 17 February, Murray and Potofsky also met with Acheson to press for State Department approval of arms sales to Israel. Elath similarly briefed the two men before the meeting, and afterward they told him that Acheson seemed unconvinced of the merits in Israel's case.[27]

Despite the apparent favorable effect of Green and Murray's call on Truman, the arms situation initially remained unchanged. In April, therefore, the Israeli government mobilized Dubinsky to continue arguing its case. mbassador Elath apparently sent Dubinsky a long memorandum on Israel's view of Arab rearmament.[28] Unable to schedule a personal meeting with Acheson before he departed the country, Dubinsky, together with Jacob Potofsky, sent the State Department a long written plea to arm Israel and force the Arab states to recognize and make peace with Israel. Interestingly, the Dubinsky-Potofsky letter borrowed substantial excerpts from the memorandum by Elath, including general details about the levels of British weapons reaching Arab states as well as specific phrases such as "the good faith of the United States is involved." The union leaders made minor changes to personalize their message, such as changing "US government" in the Israeli paper to "our Government" in their letter. Assistant Secretary of State George McGhee sent Dubinsky a noncommittal reply, and Dubinsky promptly sent a copy of that letter to Elath.[29]

These appeals by labor leaders, together with similar entreaties by pro-Zionists in Congress and elsewhere within the country, convinced Truman to order the State Department to alter national policy. Initially, State Department and Pentagon officials refused Israeli requests for weapons on the grounds that Arab rearmament posed no security risk to Israel and that U.S. weapons supply to Israel would undermine vital Western security interests in Arab states. The National Security Council (NSC) approved this policy on 6 April 1950. Truman, however, who did not attend that meeting of the NSC, subsequently rejected the council's decision because it appeared "much too one-sided and . . . would cause trouble." Truman questioned the wisdom of arming Arab states and noted that "we are not doing what we should to arm the Jews appropriately." The president thus forced the State Department to improvise a new policy, manifest in the American-Anglo-French Tripartite Declaration, that sought to balance arms supply to Israel and the Arab states.[30]

U.S. labor also played a significant role during the Suez crisis of 1956–57. After months of mounting tension between Egypt and Israel, war erupted on 29 October 1956 when Israel invaded Egypt with hopes of stopping terrorist incursions from Gaza and Sinai, damaging Egypt's military capabilities before it absorbed promised Soviet weapons, and undermining the credibility of Nasser. (Israel attacked in collusion with Britain and France, which had quarreled with Nasser for months over his nationalization of the Suez Canal Company and other issues.) The crisis abated in early 1957, when Israel, under compulsion of the Eisenhower administration, conditionally withdrew its military forces from Gaza and the Sinai.

Throughout the crisis, Israeli officials sought the backing of U.S. labor. In early 1956, U.S. Jewish leaders invited Dubinsky, Potofsky, and Victor Reuther of the UAW to a conference on security threats to Israel. In June, Israeli Minister Reuven Shiloah and Labor Attache Bar-Yaacov stressed to Meany the dangers Egypt posed to Israel and encouraged him to press the Eisenhower administration to supply Israel arms. Once war broke out, the Histadrut Executive Committee promptly endorsed the Israeli government's position that the attack on Egypt was a defensive act, provoked by months of hostility emanating from Cairo. Moshe Bar-Tal, the Histadrut representative in the United States, developed a similar rationale in a letter to Walter Reuther.[31]

These appeals from Histadrut were instrumental in shaping labor's views of the crisis. In the months preceding the attack on Egypt, U.S. labor leaders had expressed a profound desire for a peaceful settlement of the Anglo-French-Egyptian controversy over the canal company.[32] Once Israel attacked Egypt, however, they rallied to Israel's side. "While action taken by Israel has been subject of grave criticism by [the] United Nations," Dubinsky wired Histadrut Secretary General Lavon, "we are keenly aware of grave provocations to which Israel has been subjected by threats and attacks by [the] Egyptian dictator and his allies. At this most critical moment we wish to assure you of our continuing solidarity and brotherly feelings and express [our] hope that out of [the] travail of [the] present situation will emerge [a] lasting peace." Lavon replied that he "deeply appreciate[d this] assurance of solidarity and brotherhood in these trying days" and asked Dubinsky so to inform "Meany and other labor leaders." In an address to a Histadrut convention on 24 November 1956, ILGWU Vice President Isidore Nagler observed that "now Israel's very existence is threatened" and pledged that "the American labor movement must rededicate ourselves and redouble our efforts to extend all aid to Israel, moral and material, not only for the duration of this emergency, but beyond that, so that the bastion of liberty may continue to thrive in peace and freedom."[33]

Other unions offered similar support. "While the invasion of Egypt was in violation of the UN Charter," the AFL-CIO Executive Committee resolved on 30 November, "it was a direct consequence of years of provocation on the part of Egypt." Even though this resolution "criticiz[ed] the invasion of Egypt," the JLC took heart that it "stressed the responsibility borne by the provocative actions of Egypt's dictator Nasser." Indeed, Bar-Yaacov listed Meany's initiatives and observed that "it is possible to say that this week was 'Israel week' for George Meany." The Transport Workers' Union and UAW also passed resolutions in November 1956 justifying Israel's resort to force and demanding that the Eisenhower administration work toward a permanent peace settlement that included Arab recognition of Israel. "Years of threat to your nation's very existence," Reuther cabled Histadrut leaders on 29 November, explaining the UAW resolution, "finally made defensive military action on the part of your nation inevitable. . . . We pledge to use all our influence in persuading our Government to take the lead in bringing about the direct negotiations that will lead to such a peace." Lavon replied that Reuther's words "are of tremendous importance to us in our struggle for peace and progress."[34]

JLC activism appears to have been even more extensive. JLC leaders resolved that Israeli military action "was a desperate and heroic action of self-defense," and they called for "a firm peace in the Middle East which should be guaranteed by the United Nations and the United States." In January 1957, the JLC took credit that "strong resolutions were passed and immediately sent to the U.S. State Department by local labor groups as well as the national AFL-CIO accusing the Arabs of provoking war tensions in the Middle East." It also compiled a long list of initiatives it undertook during the Suez crisis to mobilize national, state, and local labor groups to lobby officials in Washington on Israel's behalf. JLC leaders claimed to have secured the AFL-CIO resolution and to have distributed copies of it to every local in the nation. Such action enabled the JLC "to obtain resolutions favorable to Israel from some of the labor leadership who appeared reluctant to contradict the policies outlined by [Secretary of State John Foster] Dulles."[35]

Labor remained supportive of Israel during a showdown between the Eisenhower administration and the Ben-Gurion government over the terms of Israel's withdrawal from the Sinai and Gaza. After weeks of wrangling, Eisenhower tried to compel an unconditional Israeli withdrawal by threatening to impose economic sanctions on Israel. In a series of letters to labor leaders, Histadrut Representative Bar-Tal carefully explained Israel's case in its political, legal, and moral dimensions, and key labor leaders rallied to Israel's side. Meany issued a statement on 22 February 1957, for instance, declaring that the AFL-CIO "strongly opposed" sanctions on Israel. "We consider such a move a travesty on justice. . . . It is difficult for American labor to understand how our country ever got maneuvered into the impossible position of siding with the dictatorships and against democracy in the Middle East." Numerous local unions across the United States sent similar pro-Israel letters to the Eisenhower administration and members of Congress.[36]

In the end, Eisenhower refrained from imposing sanctions on Israel mainly because of widespread public and congressional disapproval of such a step. Eisenhower and Dulles realized that unless public opinion remained favorable, "we will lose." Dulles noted that "it was impossible to hold the line because we got no support from the Protestant elements of the country. All we get is a battering from the Jews." Israeli officials rejoiced at the groundswell of public opinion that prevented sanctions and took partial credit for causing it. "On the questions of sanctions," Y. Harry Levin of the Israeli embassy observed, "there was as close to unanimous opposition as I have ever seen here on any Israel issue."[37] The views of organized labor, of course, were a significant part of such public sentiment.

Perhaps the most novel way in which U.S. labor assisted Israel was its support of Histadrut's Institute for Training Leadership of Labor and Cooperative Movements in Newly Independent States in Africa and Asia, commonly known as the Afro-Asian Institute. "We are able to influence all the countries in Asia and Africa except China," Prime Minister David Ben-Gurion noted privately in 1958, "to bring from these countries youngsters to study." Established formally in Tel Aviv in October 1960, the institute provided intensive education in social reform and economic development to trade unionists from newly independent states, with the objective of steering such countries away from communism and promoting friendly relations between them and Israel. Seventy students from twenty-four countries enrolled in the first six-month program, and by 1967, the institute claimed 1,007 graduates from sixty-two countries throughout the Third World.[38]

Working through Histadrut, Ben-Gurion secured the full support of the AFL-CIO and other U.S. labor unions for the institute. The AFL-CIO publicly endorsed the project, as Meany explained, so that "Afro-Asian students . . . may be trained to become effective democratic fighters against Communist subversion and Soviet imperialism." Meany also hoped that the institute would "develop and strengthen free trade unions as a bulwark against despotism and tyranny." In addition, Meany accepted appointment, together with former ambassador to Washington Eliahu Elath, as co-chairman of the institute, and he in turn named Dubinsky, Reuther, Potofsky, and George M. Harrison (president of the Brotherhood of Railway Clerks) to the twelve-person board of governors.[39]

U.S. labor also backed the institute with cash. In February 1960, the AFL-CIO allocated $180,000 to the school, half its expected operating costs for its first three years. By 1965, U.S. labor unions had contributed $508,500 to the institute. Thereafter the AFL-CIO national board curtailed its funding but urged Histadrut to seek money from local unions. In 1967, in reply to urgent appeals from Histadrut, the AFL-CIO pledged $9,000 per year for three years, and members of its Executive Council individually pledged an additional $69,000 per year for three years from their own international unions.[40]

Institute and Histadrut leaders credited U.S. labor for the success of the school in Tel Aviv. In 1963, Histadrut Representative Ilan attributed much of the institute's success to the AFL-CIO's "moral and material support." The Kennedy administration, whose Peace Corps embraced some of the same ideals as the Afro-Asian Institute, expressed admiration for the school. Undersecretary of State for Political Affairs W. Averell Harriman commended the institute as "particularly outstanding. No technical assistance program is more effective in helping meet the great and growing needs of developing countries for technical skills and knowledge."[41]

U.S. labor rallied fully to Israel's side in the Arab-Israeli War of 1967. Mounting Arab-Israeli tensions escalated dramatically in May 1967, after

Egypt ordered United Nations troops to evacuate the Sinai and closed the Gulf of Aqaba to Israel-bound ships. As the United States and other countries tried diplomatically to persuade Egypt to reverse its actions, Israeli leaders decided to reopen the waterway by launching a military assault on Egypt. The attack began on 5 June, and within six days Israel defeated Egypt, Syria, and Jordan.

As early as February 1967, the AFL-CIO Executive Council issued a statement deploring Egyptian and Syrian provocations, accusing the Soviet Union of encouraging their reckless behavior, and urging the Lyndon B. Johnson administration to defend Israeli interests. On 1 June, at the height of the war scare, Meany declared that Egyptian threats against Israel were signs of Soviet expansion against the Western world. "Aided and abetted by the USSR, Nasser is fanatically rallying all Arab countries for a war to destroy Israel," he observed. "We have here the voice of Nasser, but the hand of [Soviet Premier Leonid] Brezhnev." Meany warned that failure to defend Israel would encourage Soviet aggression and imperil "the security of our country, of the entire free world." Meany's statement appeared in advertisements in major newspapers across the country.[42]

In late May, other labor groups forthrightly declared their support of Israel and called on the Johnson administration to support the Jewish state. On 22 May, the JLC cabled Johnson urging him "publically to reaffirm the United States' commitment to the territorial integrity and security of Israel." The group indicated its satisfaction when Johnson, two days later, reaffirmed the territorial integrity of all Middle East states and free transit on the Gulf of Aqaba, and it promptly urged members of Congress to endorse the president's words. The JLC also mobilized other labor groups to similar action. It convinced the New York Central Labor Council (AFL-CIO) to schedule a mass meeting on 5 June to pressure Johnson to oppose Egypt's "new threat to world peace, and to the territorial integrity and security of Israel." The JLC's local affiliates also organized mass action. For instance, its Michigan Region chapter convinced the Michigan and Wayne County AFL-CIO officers to cable Johnson, pushed a pro-Israel resolution through the Michigan House of Representatives, introduced another in the Detroit City Council, and organized a "community-wide outdoor mass meeting" to show support for the Jewish state. Similar activities were organized in every region of the country.[43]

The ATUCFH also rallied to Israel's side. Chairman Moe Falikman urged various labor leaders to declare pro-Israeli positions. ATUCFH also summoned labor leaders to a late May conference at Unity House, Pennsylvania. The conference passed a resolution "calling upon our country and all democratic countries to do everything possible to strengthen the State of Israel and to deter the hostile forces aiming to destroy it."[44]

Histadrut successfully rallied other labor unions to Israel's side as the war scare deepened in late May. On 26 May, Secretary General Becker cabled ILGWU President Louis Stulberg, Reuther, and Dubinsky, charging Egypt with breaching the peace and vowing that Israel would defend its borders and integrity with force if necessary. "We are confident," Becker stated, "that as in the past we shall have [the] support and understanding of the free labour movements throughout the world." Becker invited the labor leaders to state publicly their "great friendship and appreciation" for Israel.[45]

The ILGWU and UAW granted Becker's request. "We stand with you," Stulberg immediately replied, "in your determination to restore peace, to halt aggression, [and] to maintain your national integrity. . . . We . . . have urged our nation to use its influence and good offices to protect both peace and freedom in the Mid East." Stulberg quickly cabled Johnson as well, applauding his "forthright and courageous stand" for peace and his "efforts to summon the great powers and peace-making bodies of the world to halt the aggression against Israel." Reuther cabled Becker that "in this hour of crisis in the Middle East, on behalf of the officers and members of the UAW I send you our pledge of continued friendship and solidarity." He also telegrammed Johnson, the president's top foreign policy advisers, and members of Congress urging that the United States seek a peaceful solution consistent with Israeli interests.[46]

When Israel initiated hostilities on 5 June, Israeli government officials and Histadrut leaders sought and received the unconditional support of U.S. labor unions. In the early hours of the war, the Israeli consulate in New York sent the JLC a statement claiming that Egypt had invaded Israel, consistent with a cover story fabricated by the government in Jerusalem. When he wrote to Meany, Dubinsky, and Stulberg on 8 June, Zeev Haring, chairman of the Histadrut International Relations Department, continued to blame the war on Egypt. "We deeply believe that the international free labour movement," Haring stated, "will, as ever, lend its unqualified and unrelenting support to people whose only aim and desire is to continue with the constructive building of their land."[47]

Labor unions responded favorably to these appeals. The JLC released a statement pledging "every effort to assist the people of Israel in their struggle for survival, security, and the preservation of their national identity." Reuther observed that "the gallant and successful defense of Israel in the face of overwhelming odds has inspired people who love freedom and justice everywhere." ATUCFH "has worked for many years to get the understanding and support of the trade union movement in this country for Israel through the Histadrut," its leaders boasted on 9 June. "The present crisis has shown that we were successful to a very great degree." A month after the war ended, Meany issued another statement condemning the Soviet-Arab effort to have the UN brand Israel the aggressor in the war, and he called on local unions to send aid to Histadrut.[48]

Histadrut officials expressed clearly their appreciation of the backing of U.S. labor. Becker sent both Meany and Stulberg his "heartfelt thanks for the prompt and sincere expressions of support and desire for peace expressed in your recent communications to us directly, to the press, and to your government." Later in 1967, he told the AFL-CIO convention that "I know I am among friends, steadfast over the decades, and proven again in those fateful days we in Israel lived through in May and June of this year. . . . You stood foursquare with us in our great danger." Through NTUCFH Chairman Falikman, Histadrut expressed gratitude to New York affiliates "for the assistance they gave to labor Israel" during the war. "This was indeed an historic manifestation of international labor solidarity." ATUCFH "rejoices at the victory of Israel's heroic defense forces over the genocidal armies of Nasserism," its leaders resolved late in the year, and it "expresses its profound gratitude for the friendship manifested by the working people of America towards the people of Israel in the great emergency."[49]

This essay has demonstrated that from 1947 to 1967 U.S. labor leaders sympathized with and closely supported Israel. Much of their support stemmed from their admiration of the Histadrut, Israel's free labor federation, in building a democratic state in the Middle East. Labor showed its backing of Israel in favorable resolutions and declarations of support, financial contributions, and lobbying the U.S. government to make policy in the interests of the Jewish state. From 1947 to 1967, such support was firm and consistent.

The Israeli government and the Histadrut actively solicited labor support. On a basic level, they nurtured the innate pro-Israel disposition in labor circles by visiting union conventions, passing resolutions of friendship, and naming public facilities in Israel after U.S. labor leaders. During moments of crisis, such as those examined in detail in this essay, Histadrut and government officials sought special declarations of support from U.S. labor and encouraged it to pressure the government in Washington to shape its policy to Israel's advantage.

The critical question remains whether U.S. labor's friendship with the Histadrut and Israeli government made any differences in the evolution of official relations between the United States and Israel. Although its impact is difficult to measure, the support of labor seems to have had some influence on official policy emanating from Washington. Labor's pro-Zionist declarations in the late 1940s contributed to a political climate favorable to President Truman's support of partition and Israeli statehood and integrity. More certainly, labor and other voices compelled the president to order a change in State Department policy toward the provision of weapons to Israel and the Arab state in 1950. Labor's criticism of Eisenhower's threatened sanctions on Israel in early 1957 contributed to an atmosphere hostile to the president's intentions. During the 1967 war, labor's rally to Israel's political defense perhaps helped convince the Johnson administration to accept Israel's decision to escalate into general hostilities.

Granted, in none of these episodes was organized labor the sole or most influential public voice trying to influence official policy. Indeed, officials made policy in each case for many various reasons. Yet in all cases, even at those moments when major unions felt marginalized in U.S. political culture, the voice of organized labor joined a larger chorus of public opinion that reached the ears and shaped the decisions of key officials. Labor seemed to get what it wanted out of the administrations in Washington, and what labor wanted reflected the wishes and concerns of Israeli labor and government leaders.

Notes

1. For brief but excellent surveys of the literature, see Douglas Little, "Gideon's Band: America and the Middle East since 1945," in *America in the World: The Historiography of American Foreign Relations since 1945,* ed. Michael J. Hogan (New York, 1995), 462–500; and Burton I. Kaufman, *The Arab Middle East and the United States* (New York, 1996), 257–81.

2. Yaacov Bar-Siman-Tov, "The United States and Israel since 1948: A 'Special Relationship'?" *Diplomatic History* 22 (Spring 1998): 231–62; Peter L. Hahn, "Special Relationships," *Diplomatic History* 22:263–72; David Schoenbaum, "More Special Than Others," *Diplomatic History* 22:273–83.

3. See, for example, Paul Boyer, *When Time Shall Be No More: Prophecy Belief in Modern American Culture* (Cambridge, MA, 1992); Michael T. Benson, *Harry S. Truman and the Founding of Israel* (Westport, CT, 1997); and Michelle Mart, "Tough Guys and American Cold War Policy: Images of Israel, 1948–1960," *Diplomatic History* 20 (Summer 1990): 357–80.

4. For one notable exception, see Gerd Korman, "New Jewish Politics for an American Labor Leader: Sidney Hillman, 1942–1946," *American Jewish History* 82 (1994): 195–213.

5. John W. Roberts, *Putting Foreign Policy to Work: The Role of Organized Labor in American Foreign Relations, 1933–1941* (New York, 1995); Philip Taft, *Defending Freedom:*

American Labor and Foreign Affairs (Los Angeles, 1973); Ronald Radosh, *American Labor and United States Foreign Policy* (New York, 1969); Robert H. Zieger, *The CIO, 1935–1955* (Chapel Hill, NC, 1995); Denis MacShane, *International Labor and the Origins of the Cold War* (Oxford, UK, 1992); Stephen Burwood, *American Labour, France, and the Politics of Intervention, 1945–1952* (Lewiston, NY, 1998); Federico Romero, *The United States and the European Trade Union Movements, 1944–1951* (Chapel Hill, NC, 1992); Ronald Filippelli, *American Labor and Postwar Italy, 1943–1953: A Study of Cold War Politics* (Stanford, CA, 1989); Peter B. Levy, *The New Left and Labor in the 1960s* (Urbana, IL, 1994).

6. Ronald Radosh, *Divided They Fell: The Demise of the Democratic Party, 1964–1996* (New York, 1996); Nelson Lichtenstein, *The Most Dangerous Man in Detroit: Walter Reuther and the Fate of American Labor* (New York, 1995); Robert H. Zieger, *The CIO, 1935–1955* (Chapel Hill, NC, 1995); Kevin Boyle, *The UAW and the Heyday of American Liberalism, 1945–1968* (Ithaca, NY, 1995); Robert H. Zieger, *American Workers, American Unions,* 2nd ed. (Baltimore, 1994); Anthony Carew, *Walter Reuther* (Manchester, UK, 1993); Graham K. Wilson, *Unions in American National Politics* (London, 1979); Jong Oh Ra, *Labor at the Polls: Union Voting in Presidential Elections, 1952–1976* (Amherst, MA, 1978).

7. Bitan to Morgenthau, 1 October 1953, Records of the Office of the Minister and Director General of the Foreign Office, 2420/13, Israel State Archives, Jerusalem (hereafter RG 130.02 with appropriate file designations). See also Zachary Lockman, *Comrades and Enemies: Arab and Jewish Workers in Palestine, 1906–1948* (Berkeley, CA, 1996); and Michael Shalev, *Labour and the Political Economy in Israel* (Oxford, UK, 1992). For a simplistic explanation of Histadrut's organization and functions, see "How Histadrut Functions," *Labor in Israel Newsletter* 1:2 (February 1953). Histadrut's Secretary General Aharon Becker explained the federation's scope and size in an address to the 1967 AFL-CIO convention. See address by Becker, AFL-CIO, *Reports of Proceedings, 1967,* 189–94.

8. Until 1948, the National Committee for Labor Palestine (NCLP).

9. AFL, *Reports of Proceedings, 1951,* 306; and Becker to Moe Falikman, 11 December 1962, and "Declaration of Policy" by Executive Committee of ATUCFH, 21 September 1967, Records of Local 10, International Ladies Garment Workers Union (ILGWU), box 7, Cornell University, Ithaca, NY (hereafter Local 10 Records with appropriate file designations). See also AFL, *Reports of Proceedings, 1952,* 549, and AFL, *Reports of Proceedings, 1954,* 373–74; and paper by Bitan (Hebrew), 14 October 1954, Papers of Nachum Goldmann, Z6/834, Central Zionist Archives, Jerusalem (hereafter Goldmann Papers with appropriate file designations).

10. Address by Meany, 26 March 1950, Records of the AFL-CIO, Office of Secretary-Treasurer Files, box 7, George Meany Archives, Silver Spring, MD (hereafter AFL-CIO Papers with appropriate file designations); and address by Meany, 26 April 1955, AFL-CIO Records, Office of President Files, box 31, folder 20.

11. Sharett quoted in Bar-Tal to Meany, 19 January 1956, AFL-CIO Records, Office of President Files, box 54, folder 24; Becker to Dubinsky, 28 September 1961, Papers of David Dubinsky, box 251, Records of the ILGWU, Cornell University (hereafter Dubinsky Papers with appropriate file designations); Eshkol address, 3 June 1964, Dubinsky Papers, box 253; and Ilan to Lovestone, 4 June 1964, AFL-CIO Records, International Affairs Division (IAD) Country Files, box 10, folder 9. For examples of Histadrut activities at AFL and AFL-CIO meetings, see AFL, *Reports of Proceedings, 1953,*

457–59, and AFL, *Reports of Proceedings, 1954,* 447–48; and AFL-CIO, *Reports of Proceedings, 1957,* 487. See also Bitan to Goldmann, 31 December 1955 (Hebrew), Goldmann Papers, Z6/1084; Lovestone to Schnitzler, 14 May 1964, AFL-CIO Records, IAD Country Files, box 10, folder 9; and Dubinsky to Harman, 26 May 1964, Dubinsky Papers, box 251.

12. Bar-Yaacov to Foreign Ministry (Hebrew), 18 November 1957, Central Registry, Political Files of the Foreign Office, 3088/11, Israel State Archives (hereafter RG 130.23 with appropriate file designations).

13. Address by Meany, 26 April 1955, AFL-CIO Records, Office of President Files, box 31, folder 20. See also Lovestone to Dubinsky, 26 October 1953, Dubinsky Papers, box 253; and Alam to Meany, 21 and 23 September 1954, Goldmann Papers, Z6/834.

14. Lovestone to Ilan, 26 May 1964, Papers of Foreign Secretary Golda Meir, 4321/4, Israel State Archives (hereafter Meir Papers with appropriate file designations); Lovestone to Ilan, 9 June 1964, AFL-CIO Records, IAD Country Files, box 10, folder 9; Eban to Lovestone, 12 June 1964, Meir Papers, 4321/4. See also Eban to Meany, 2 June 1964, Meir Papers, 4321/4; Ilan to Eban (Hebrew), 29 June 1964, Ilan to Lovestone, 4 June 1964, and Morat to Simhoni, 19 August 1964, Files of the General Federation of Trade Unions (Histadrut), IV-219A-1-70-B, Lavon Center, Tel Aviv, Israel (hereafter Histadrut Papers with appropriate file designations).

15. Schwartz to Kollek, n.d. [May 1955], RG 130.02, 2420/14; Meir to Dubinsky, 17 May 1957, Meir Papers, 4321/13; Bar-Yaacov to Foreign Ministry (Hebrew), 22 May 1957, RG 130.23, 3089/5. Regarding the 1957 AFL-CIO resolution see Warburg to Dubinsky, 7 December 1953, Dubinsky Papers, box 251. See also Elath to Dubinsky, 22 May 1956, and J. Avrech to Dubinsky, 11 May 1961, Dubinsky Papers, box 251; Eban to Dubinsky, 24 December 1955, Dubinsky to Eban, 29 December 1955, Feinberg to Dubinsky, 15 May 1956, and Eban to Dubinsky, 19 February 1959, Dubinsky Papers, box 254; and Elath to Dubinsky, 24 November 1965, and Dubinsky to Elath, 3 December 1965, Dubinsky Papers, box 252.

16. W. Reuther to Barkatt, 8 January 1958, RG 130.23, 3088/11. See also Bar-Yaacov to Seligman with attachment, 30 January 1957, and Seligman to Bar-Tal, 23 April 1957, Papers of Walter Reuther, box 101, folders 15, 20, Wayne State University, Detroit, MI (hereafter Reuther Papers with appropriate file designations).

17. Potofsky speech, 18 September 1958, Records of the Amalgamated Clothing Workers of America, box 134, Cornell University (hereafter Potofsky Papers with appropriate file designations). See also Zinder to Eytan, 29 September 1949, RG 130.02, 2398/30; Bar-Yaacov to Levine (Hebrew), 18 July 1957, Bar-Yaacov to Foreign Ministry (Hebrew), 14 August 1958, and memorandum by Bar-Yaacov, 26 September 1958, RG 130.23, 3088/10, 3088/11; resolutions by steelworkers union and other unions, Goldmann Papers, Z6/834; Harman to Meir (Hebrew), 15 June 1961, Meir Papers, 4308/19; and Randolph to Simhoni, 30 October 1964, Histadrut Papers, IV-219A-1-70-B.

18. Reuther to Simhoni, 14 February 1964, Histadrut Papers, IV-219A-1-70-A; and Lavon address, AFL-CIO, *Reports of Proceedings, 1959,* 154–59. On AFL-CIO tours, see Bardacke to V. Reuther, 26 June 1957, Reuther Papers, box 102, folder 2; and Bluestone to Simhoni, 21 January 1964, Reuther to Levin, 14 February 1964, and Simhoni to Bluestone, 14 February 1964, Histadrut Papers, IV-219A-1-70-A. On the NCLI award, see Bardacke to Reuther, 27 May 1958, Reuther Papers, box 457, folder 1. On naming of public buildings, see Aba Khoushy (Mayor of Haifa) to Dubinsky, 5 August 1955, Dov

Biegun to Dubinsky, 7 July 1958, Dubinsky to Becker, 31 August 1961, and Eshkol address, 3 June 1964, Dubinsky Papers, boxes 252–53; Namir to Antonini, 23 April 1956, Namir to Meany, 28 May 1956, and Lavon to Dubinsky, 5 October 1956, Histadrut Papers, IV-208-1-8634; *Labor in Israel Newsletter* 3 (September 1955); Potofsky address, 18 September 1958, Potofsky Papers, box 134; circular memorandum by Heller, 6 October 1958, Papers of the Jewish Labor Committee, Israel & Middle East box, Memos folder, New York University, New York, NY (hereafter JLC Papers with appropriate file designations); and Becker to Meany, 9 June 1965, AFL-CIO Records, IAD Country Files, box 10, folder 8.

19. Green quoted in AFL, *Reports of Proceedings, 1946,* 376; Meyerson to Dubinsky, 27 November 1946, Dubinsky Papers, box 252. See also address by Green to International Christian Conference for Palestine, 2 November 1945, Papers of William F. Green, box 4, folder 15, Ohio Historical Society, Columbus, OH (hereafter Green Papers with appropriate file designations); Breslaw to Dubinsky, 27 May 1946, Dubinsky Papers, box 121; Green to Dubinsky, 4 June 1946, and Sprinzak to Dubinsky, n.d. [July 1946], Dubinsky Papers, box 252; and George Staberman (president, Wisconsin State Federation of Labor) to State Department, 5 June 1946, AFL-CIO Records, Department of Legislation Files, folder 10.

20. Dubinsky to Attlee, 1 July 1946, Dubinsky Papers, box 252; Green quoted in AFL, *Reports of Proceedings, 1947,* 45; and Steinberg circular letter, 10 September 1947, Records of Local 22, ILGWU, box 18, Cornell University (hereafter Local 22 Records with appropriate file designations). See also Breslaw to Charles Zimmerman (manager, Local 22, ILGWU), 17 and 28 February 1947, and Breslaw circular, 28 May 1946, Local 22 Records, box 27; and Schlossberg to Dubinsky, 26 August 1947, Dubinsky Papers, box 121.

21. Breslaw circular telegram, 31 March 1948, Records of the New York Cloak Joint Board, box 18, Cornell University (hereafter N.Y. Cloak Joint Board Records with appropriate file designations); and Breslaw circular letter, 7 April 1948, Local 22 Records, box 27. See also Dubinsky to Green, 30 September 1947, Green to Dubinsky, 1 October 1947, Breslaw circular cable, 1 October 1947, and press release by NCLP, 9 April 1948, Dubinsky Papers, box 121; Woll to Estime, 26 November 1947, and Woll to LeGallais, 28 November 1947, Dubinsky Papers, box 252; and AFL press release, 24 March 1948, AFL-CIO Records, Department of Legislation Files, box 29.

22. Benson, *Harry S. Truman;* Michael J. Cohen, *Palestine and the Great Powers, 1945–1948* (Princeton, NJ, 1982); Zvi Ganin, *Truman, American Jewry, and Israel, 1945–1948* (New York, 1982).

23. AFL, *Reports of Proceedings, 1948,* 11, 311–12, 493–94. Regarding independence, see Jewish Labor Committee to Weizmann, 17 May 1948, JLC Papers, box 1, Israel folder; Dubinsky to Weizmann, 17 May 1948, Dubinsky Papers, box 252; and Israel Feinberg to Ben-Gurion, 17 May 1948, N.Y. Cloak Joint Board Records, box 18. Regarding arms, see Breslaw to Dubinsky, 22 January 1948, Dubinsky Papers, box 121; Breslaw circular telegram, 23 January 1948, Local 22 Records, box 27; Green to Truman, 19 February 1948, and JLC to Green, 20 February 1948, JLC Papers, box 1, Israel folder. Regarding Arab-Israeli issues and U.S.-Israel relations, see Breslaw to Dubinsky, 9 and 27 September 1948, Dubinsky Papers, box 121; and Adolph Held (of JLC) to James Webb, 12 July 1949, JLC Papers, box 2–16.

24. Comay to Dubinsky, 13 November 1948, and Elath to Dubinsky, 11 August

1949, Dubinsky Papers, box 254. See also Meyerson to Dubinsky, 13 June 1949, Ben-Gurion to Dubinsky, 30 October 1951, and Dubinsky to Ben-Gurion, 28 November 1951, Dubinsky Papers, box 254; and Isaac Hamlin to Goldman[n] with attachment, 29 September 1949, and Goldmann to Hamlin, 4 October 1949, Goldmann Papers, Z6/161.

Regarding the August 1949 position paper, TUC Executive Director Isidor Iaderman sent to Dubinsky an untitled memorandum summarizing Israel's positions on major Arab-Israeli disputes. Although the authorship of the memorandum is not indicated, it clearly reflected Israel's positions, it bore "confidential" markings, and Iaderman called it "an *AUTHORITATIVE* statement." Iaderman to Dubinsky with att., 24 August 1949, Dubinsky Papers, box 121.

25. See, e.g., paper by Israeli embassy, 23 January 1950, and Keren to Kenen, 25 January 1950, Records of the Embassy in Washington, 366/12, Israel State Archives (hereafter RG 93.08 with appropriate file designations); and minutes of meeting in Foreign Office, 31 January 1950, in Israel, Israel State Archive, *Documents on the Foreign Policy of Israel* (Jerusalem, 1982), 5:82–85 (hereafter *DFPI* with volume and page citations).

26. Elath to Sharett, 7 February 1950, *DFPI*, 5:107–8. See also Epstein to Morgenthau, 6 February 1950, RG 93.08, 366/12.

27. Green-Murray statement, 10 February 1950, Dubinsky Papers, box 121; Elath to USD, 10 February 1950, *DFPI*, 5:116; minutes of meeting, 14 February 1950, Records of the Congress of Industrial Organizations, International Executive Board Proceedings, George Meany Archives (hereafter CIO Records, with appropriate file designations); circular letter by Laderman, 17 February 1950, Dubinsky Papers, box 121; and Lubianiker to Green and Murray, n.d. [c. February 1950], RG 93.08, 336/12. See also Elath to Sharett, 17 February 1950, *DFPI*, 5:134; and "summary of cables" memorandum, 19 February 1950, RG 130.20, 2474/8.

28. "Memorandum on Rearmament of Arab States," 25 April 1950, Dubinsky Papers, box 252. This memorandum in the Dubinsky Papers reveals no author, but an identical copy, sent by Elath to Local 22 leaders, is located in Local 22 Records, box 17.

29. Dubinsky and Potofsky to Acheson, 1 May 1950, Dubinsky Papers, box 252. See also Dubinsky to Acheson, 25 and 28 April 1950, Acheson to Dubinsky, 27 April 1950, McGhee to Dubinsky, 15 May 1950, Dubinsky to Elath, 17 May 1950, and Handelman to Dubinsky, Dubinsky Papers, box 252, 254.

30. Peter L. Hahn, *The United States, Great Britain, and Egypt, 1945–1956: Strategy and Diplomacy in the Early Cold War* (Chapel Hill, NC, 1991), 94–102.

31. Nahum Goldmann to V. Reuther, 11 January 1956, and Goldmann to Dubinsky, 11 January 1956, Goldmann Papers, Z6/1064; Bar-Yaacov to Meany, 27 June 1956, AFL-CIO Records, Office of President Files, box 54, folder 24; Bar-Tal to Herlitz, 10 September 1956, RG 130.02, 2409/8; *Labor in Israel Newsletter* 4 (November 1956): 1; and Bar-Tal to Reuther, 13 November 1956, Reuther Papers, box 457, folder 1.

32. See minutes of AFL-CIO Executive Council, 28 August 1956, AFL-CIO Records; and Reuther to Bar-Tal, 5 September 1956, Reuther Papers, box 457, folder 1.

33. Dubinsky to Lavon, 5 November 1956, Histadrut Papers, IV-208-1-8634; Lavon to Dubinsky, 7 November 1956, Dubinsky Papers, box 251; and Nagler address, 24 November 1956, N.Y. Cloak Joint Board Records, box 18.

34. AFL-CIO Executive Council statement, 30 November 1956, Reuther Papers,

box 101, folder 8; unsigned paper, "Work of the Jewish Labor Committee with Trade Unions on the Middle East," n.d. [c. early 1957], JLC Papers, Israel & Middle East box, Memos on Middle East folder; Bar-Yaacov to Foreign Office (Hebrew), 7 December 1956, RG 130.23, 3089/4; Reuther to Histadrut quoted in Reuther to Held, 29 November 1956, JLC Papers, box 2–42, Conference on Israel folder; and Lavon to Reuther, 2 December 1956, Histadrut Papers, IV-208-1-8634. See also UAW resolution, November 1956, and Transport Workers Union resolution, 15 November 1956, JLC Papers, Israel & Middle East box, Memos folder.

35. Declaration of JLC, n.d. [29 November 1956], JLC Papers, box 2–42, Conference on Israel folder; *JLC Outlook* 2 (January 1957): 1; unsigned paper, "Work of the Jewish Labor Committee with Trade Unions on the Middle East," n.d. [c. early 1957], JLC Papers, Israel & Middle East box, Memos on Middle East folder.

36. Meany quoted in circular memo by Philip Heller, 26 February 1957, JLC Papers, Israel & Middle East box, Memos on Middle East folder. See also Bar-Tal to V. Reuther, 9 January, 12 February, 19 March 1957, Reuther Papers, box 102, folder 2; Bar-Tal to Nagler, 10 January and 19 March 1957, N.Y. Cloak Joint Board Records, box 18; and Bar-Tal to W. Reuther, 19 March 1957, Reuther Papers, box 457, folder 1. Voluminous correspondence from the locals to Eisenhower and members of Congress is located in RG 130.23, 3088/9. It is unclear how the Israeli Foreign Office acquired copies of these letters, but their existence in the file shows that it at least monitored, if not influenced, the correspondence.

37. Record of phone call, 21 February 1957, Ann Whitman File, Eisenhower Diary Series, box 21; memorandum of conversation, 22 February 1957, U.S. Department of State, *Foreign Relations of the United States, 1955–1957* (Washington, DC, 1990), 17:239–40; Levin to Herzog, 1 March 1957, RG 130.23, 3088/9.

38. Ben-Gurion Diary (Hebrew), 23 December 1958, DBGL. See also *Labor in Israel Newsletter* 6 (December 1958); memorandum by Elath, December 1962, AFL-CIO Records, IAD Country Files, box 10, folder 8; and Executive Council Minutes, 27 February 1967, AFL-CIO Papers.

39. Meany to Avrech, 12 January 1961, AFL-CIO Records, IAD Country Files, box 10, folder 8; and Meany address, AFL-CIO, *Reports of Proceedings, 1961,* 311. See also Lovestone to Lavon, 20 January 1960, Lavon to Meany, 10 April 1960, Avrech to Meany, 22 April, 27 May 1960, Meany to Avrech, 6 June 1960, and Avrech to Meany with attachment, 19 October 1960, AFL-CIO Records, IAD Country Files, box 10, folder 8; and statement by Elath, AFL-CIO Executive Council Minutes, 28 June 1961, AFL-CIO Records.

40. Executive Council Minutes, 12 and 27 February 1960, AFL-CIO Records; Bar-Yaacov to Foreign Office (Hebrew), 17 February 1960, RG 130.23, 3924/13; Meany to Ilan, 1 May 1963, AFL-CIO Records, IAD Country Files, box 10, folder 8; Becker to Reuther, 20 April 1965, and unsigned paper on financial contributions, n.d. [late 1965], Histadrut Papers, IV-277-70-A; Reuther to Becker, 29 October 1966, and Bardacke to Haring, 5 March 1967, Histadrut Papers, IV-277-70-B; and Eger to Barash (Hebrew), 12 May 1967, Histadrut Papers, IV-277–92. Labor's financial support of the Institute continued through the 1970s. See Eger to McBride, 1 August 1978, Eger to Meany, 10 August 1978, and Eger to Chaikin, 11 August 1978, Histadrut Papers, IV-277–48.

41. Ilan to Meany, 18 April 1963, AFL-CIO Records, IAD Country Files, box 10,

folder 8; and Harriman to Ilan, 11 October 1963, Dubinsky Papers, box 253.

42. Executive Council Minutes, 24 February 1967, AFL-CIO Records; and AFL-CIO press release, 1 June 1967, Papers of Louis Stulberg, box 32, Cornell University (hereafter Stulberg Papers with appropriate file designations). See also Falikman to Meany, 2 June 1967, AFL-CIO Records, IAD Country Files, box 10, folder 12. By contrast, a broadside from the UAR Federation of Labor, arguing Cairo's version of the war scare, found in the Meany Archives, apparently went unacknowledged. UAR Federation of Labor circular memorandum, 27 May 1967, AFL-CIO Records, IAD Country Files, box 13, folder 20.

43. Circular memorandum by E. Muravchik, 23 May 1967, JLC Papers, Israel & Middle East box, Middle East folder; and Zimmerman circular memorandum, 31 May 1967, and Jack Carper to Muravchik, 31 May 1967, JLC Papers, Israel & Middle East box, Middle East folder. See also Muravchik to Held, 25 May 1967, circular letter by David Ashe, 1 June 1967, and "Confidential Report on JLC Activities in the Middle East Crisis, as of July 5, 1967," JLC Papers, Israel & Middle East box, Middle East folder.

44. Circular letter by Falikman, 1 June 1967, Stulberg Papers, box 32. See also Falikman to Reuther, 25 May 1967, Reuther Papers, box 457, folder 5; and Falikman to Stulberg, 25 May 1967, Stulberg Papers, box 32.

45. Becker to Stulberg, 26 May 1967, Stulberg Papers, box 32; Becker to Reuther, 26 May 1967, Reuther Papers, box 457, folder 5; and Becker to Dubinsky, 26 May 1967, Dubinsky Papers, box 435.

46. Stulberg to Becker, 26 May 1967, and Stulberg to Johnson, 26 May 1967, Stulberg Papers, box 32; and Reuther to Becker, 1 June 1967, Reuther Papers, box 457, folder 5. See also UAW press release, 1 June 1967, Reuther Papers, box 457, folder 5.

47. Haring circular letter, 8 June 1967, AFL-CIO Records, IAD Country Files, box 10, folder 11. Copies are found in Dubinsky Papers, box 431; and Stulberg Papers, box 31. See also statement by Consulate, JLC Papers, Israel & Middle East box, Middle East folder.

48. JLC press release, 5 June 1967, JLC Papers, Israel & Middle East box, Middle East folder; Reuther to Becker, 9 June 1967, Reuther Papers, box 457, folder 5; G. Bardacke to Stulberg, 9 June 1967, Stulberg Papers, box 31. See also International Relations Report, AFL-CIO, *Reports of Proceedings, 1967*, 91–92.

49. Becker to Stulberg, 15 June 1967, Stulberg Papers, box 32; Becker to Meany, 15 June 1967, AFL-CIO Records, IAD Country Files, box 10, folder 11; Becker quoted in AFL-CIO, *Reports of Proceedings, 1967*, 190–92; Falikman to R. Corbett, 2 October 1967, Local 10 Records, box 7; and "Declaration of Policy" by Executive Committee, 21 September 1967, Local 10 Records, box 7.

Real Men Don't Wear Pajamas: Anglo-American Cultural Perceptions of Mohammed Mossadeq and the Iranian Oil Nationalization Dispute

MARY ANN HEISS

Between 1951 and 1953, Iran struggled to gain control of its oil industry—and the considerable wealth it generated—from the British-owned Anglo-Iranian Oil Company (AIOC). The AIOC and its predecessor, the Anglo-Persian Oil Company (APOC), had run Iran's oil industry since the first decade of the twentieth century. During the First World War, the British government had purchased a large amount of APOC stock, and by the time of the oil crisis it held slightly more than half—or a controlling interest—in that company's successor. The relationship between the Iranian government and the oil company was never particularly harmonious. Financial arrangements, especially the relatively low level of royalties the company paid to Iran, the almost total lack of Iranians in high-ranking positions within the company, and the overall aura of secrecy that pervaded the company's operations, led to Iranian discontent. Added to these practical complaints was the growing sense of Iranian nationalism after the Second World War. Nationalism, rather than simply a desire for greater oil revenues, motivated Iranian policy and sustained that policy when its fruits proved bitter. It helps to explain why Iran wanted Britain to abandon its exclusive control of the Iranian oil industry and why the Iranians persisted in spite of tremendous economic hardship. It also helps to account for the decline of Western power in Iran and in other parts of the world where Western leaders failed to take nationalism as seriously as they might have.

The Anglo-Iranian oil dispute seemed irresolvable from the start. Each side saw the conflict through the prism of its own history and perspective, and neither showed much willingness to compromise. The AIOC and the British Foreign Office emphasized legal issues, denied that Iran had the right to nationalize its oil industry, and sought to protect the considerable British financial stake in Iranian oil. Between 1945 and 1950, the AIOC earned £250 million from its Iranian operations. Iran's oil fields provided Britain with twenty-two million tons of oil products and seven million tons of crude oil annually, including 85 percent of the fuel needed by the British Admiralty. In other words, the British position stressed the company's value as an economic asset of great importance and the contribution that the AIOC made to Britain's overall Middle Eastern and world position. For British officials, this last consideration was paramount, as the crux of the matter for them was the danger that Iranian nationalization posed to their nation's status as a great power. As Britain's largest overseas investment, the refinery at Abadan and the AIOC's Iranian operations symbolized Britain's power in the Middle East. Losing control of these assets would be a deadly blow to British prestige the world over, especially considering Britain's recent withdrawals from India and Palestine. It might also imperil other British holdings around the world, foremost among them the Suez Canal. At a time when British policy makers were keenly aware of their diminishing status as a global power, it is not surprising that they were sensitive to anything that might undermine their position in Iran, particularly surrendering control of the nation's oil industry to the Iranians. Accordingly, from the very beginning of the oil dispute, British officials expressed their frustration at what they termed the "growing Near East practice of twisting the lion's tail." The Iranian nationalization campaign, they believed, struck at the foundations of British pride and Great Britain's "efforts to re-establish [itself] as [an] equal partner" with the United States around the world.[1]

By way of contrast, the Iranian stance during the oil dispute stressed politics and national independence. Although Iranian nationalists complained bitterly about the relatively small profits they received from the AIOC's Iranian operations—their royalties between 1945 and 1950 totaled only £90 million, slightly more than one-third of what the AIOC earned from its Iranian operations—what most galled them was the imperious way the company used its oil concession to dominate and control their nation almost as a colony. Convinced that the AIOC and the British government had interfered in Iran's internal affairs for decades by bribing legislators, influencing elections, and essentially holding the country hostage financially, nationalists like Prime Minister Mohammed Mossadeq asserted that such interference would stop only after Iran had gained control of its rich oil holdings. Mossadeq was ultimately willing to make concessions on price, production levels, and other technical details, but he would not budge on the central point that operational control of the oil industry had to rest in Iranian hands. Unless British officials were willing to concede that point, the prime minister was prepared to see his nation's oil industry shut down. "Tant pis pour nous. Too bad for us," was his usual response when Anglo-American officials warned him that his refusal to reach a resolution of the oil dispute might shut down the industry.[2] To his way of thinking, Iran would be better off leaving its oil in the ground than allowing the British to remain in control. The nation's "independence," he said, was more important than "economics."[3]

It was the inability of the British and the Iranians to resolve the oil dispute on their own that ultimately brought the United States into the conflict. U.S. officials saw the oil crisis as a potentially destabilizing force in Iran—and perhaps throughout the entire Middle East—that could lead to communist advances and provide the Soviets with an inroad to the oil-rich Persian Gulf. As the only direct land barrier between the Soviet Union and the Persian Gulf, Iran served as a vital link in the Western security chain; Soviet control of its territory would make the defense of Greece, Turkey, and the eastern Mediterranean all but impossible. Compounding Iran's importance were its rich oil reserves, which U.S. officials considered crucial to the reconstruction and rearmament of Western Europe. Loss of these resources would have dire consequences. In the short term, it would create serious shortages of aviation gasoline and other fuels needed for the military effort in Korea and would raise the specter of civilian rationing in the United States and throughout the West. In the long term it might compromise the West's ability to fight a protracted war with the Soviets, force augmentation of its military establishments, and result in an expansion of Soviet military bases in the Middle East.

Initially, the Truman administration acted as an honest broker in the search for a settlement that paid lip service to the idea of nationalization but also recognized the contractual rights of the AIOC. On the one hand, U.S. policy makers called for a firm, commercially acceptable agreement that did not set a dangerous precedent or encourage nationalization elsewhere. On the other, they advocated a flexible approach to the nationalization dispute that would make a settlement possible before Iran collapsed internally or succumbed to Soviet penetration. To this end, President Harry S. Truman and his secretary of state, Dean Acheson, lobbied for concessions from both sides, warning that "too much 'take'" on the part of the Iranians was as dangerous as "too little 'give'" on the part of the British.[4]

As the dispute dragged on, however, and as the chance of destabilization in Iran became increasingly likely, officials in the Truman administration abandoned their middle-of-the-road stance and decided to prop up the British position in Iran, just as they were doing in Egypt and would soon do for the French in Indochina. By the summer of 1952, Truman went so far as to join British Prime Minister Winston S. Churchill in a joint Anglo-American proposal to Mossadeq than wedded the U.S. government to the British position in Iran. President Dwight D. Eisenhower and Secretary of State John Foster Dulles continued this pro-British position when they assumed office in January 1953, ultimately joining the British in a covert operation against Mossadeq late that summer. Administration officials justified this coup as necessary to save Iran from communism. The prolonged oil crisis was beginning to take its toll on the Iranian economy, and economic dislocation was spawning mass demonstrations that U.S. officials feared would grow into full-scale revolution. Making matters worse, Mossadeq was forging closer ties with the Communist Tudeh Party and moving his country closer to the Soviet Union through new trade agreements. He was even threatening to sell Iranian oil to the Soviet Union and its satellites. In truth, Mossadeq was a staunch anticommunist who hoped such moves would win U.S. assistance for his financially strapped government. Given the anticommunist hysteria of the early 1950s, however, officials in Washington could not easily dismiss the prime minister's apparent flirtation with communism. To them, he was a dangerous radical whose policies could lead Iran into the Soviet bloc. Accordingly, they felt they had no choice but to get rid of him. Just weeks after assuming office, Dulles and Eisenhower approved a British plan for joint action against Mossadeq.

In addition to collaborating to remove Mossadeq from office, over the course of the oil dispute, Anglo-American officials came to a common way of looking at Mossadeq that used many of his personal characteristics, habits, and negotiating tactics, as well as some of his policy positions themselves, to justify a view of him as unmanly and unfit for office. Because Anglo-American officials did not view Mossadeq as their equal, they found it easy to dismiss him as an unworthy adversary whose position did not matter. Although these Anglo-American conceptions and descriptions of Mossadeq were not the sole, or even the most important, factor influencing policy, they deserve scholarly consideration because they helped to shape the context within which officials formulated policy. They buttressed claims of Western superiority over Iranian and other Middle Eastern peoples by perpetuating the idea that those peoples were weak and incapable. And their cumulative effect was to paint Mossadeq and others like him in unfavorable ways that rationalized and justified Western control.

The discussion of the Anglo-Iranian oil crisis in this chapter will use gender—and to a lesser extent culture—as its organizing construct. Rather than examining the major episodes of the oil crisis or providing a general overview of its development, the essay will focus on the ways that Anglo-American officials viewed, described, and dealt with Mossadeq. It is a central proposition of this essay that the ways government officials describe each other have import, and that while these descriptions do not in and of themselves determine policy, they are nonetheless influential.

Historians of U.S. foreign relations are just beginning to undertake this sort of analysis, although, as Emily S. Rosenberg has maintained, "examination of [the] gendered overtones of . . . foreign policy language and symbolism can provide fresh, provocative insights into the wellsprings of policy formulation and public legitimation."[5] To date, valuable work in this area has been undertaken by Andrew J. Rotter, Frank Costigliola, Robert D. Dean, and Kristin Hoganson, among others. Andrew Rotter's work on U.S. perceptions of Indian and Pakistani officials during the early Cold War, which is included in this volume, highlights the value of gender as an analytical category and serves as a model for this essay.[6] Frank Costigliola and Robert Dean have analyzed the gendered images that often permeated U.S. foreign policy pronouncements in their work on George F. Kennan's Long Telegram and the Kennedy administration's "ideology of masculinity," respectively.[7] And Kristin Hoganson has recently traced the gendered notions that propelled the United States toward war with Spain in 1898.[8] Sociologist John Foran has even gotten into the act by comparing press images of Mossadeq and the shah at the time of the joint Anglo-American operation against the former in August 1953.[9] As all of these scholars make clear, U.S. officials shared common gender-based assumptions that shaped their worldviews and influenced how they dealt with the world around them. Although none of these scholars would argue that gendered assumptions constituted the sole source of U.S. foreign policy, they would all maintain that these assumptions merit scholarly consideration because they formed part of the context within which U.S. foreign policy was made.

The analysis presented in this essay is intended to complement the work of these and other historians. It postulates that Anglo-American officials joined to formulate a gender-based view of Mossadeq that denigrated him for departing from what they considered to be acceptable Western norms and that worked against their stated goal of seeking a resolution to the vexing oil imbroglio. It should not be construed as a complete picture of the Iranian oil crisis, and it certainly does not purport to be the only way of looking at what happened in Iran during the early 1950s. On the contrary, it utilizes the concepts of gender and culture as tools for examining the oil crisis in new ways.

When *Time* magazine designated Mossadeq as its 1951 Man of the Year, it proclaimed the Iranian prime minister to be "by Western standards an appalling caricature of a statesman." "His tears, his tantrums," and "his grotesque antics" led the magazine to dub Mossadeq a "dizzy old wizard" who "put Scheherazade in the petroleum business" by nationalizing the Anglo-Iranian Oil Company in the spring of 1951.[10] *Time*'s editors accurately reflected the prevailing sentiment in the West and unknowingly echoed what British and U.S. government officials had been telling each other for quite some time.[11] Influenced by long-standing stereotypes that justified Western superiority and sought to maintain Western control, Anglo-American policy makers consistently employed what Edward Said has termed "Orientalism" when dealing with Mossadeq, whom they considered inferior, childlike, and feminine.[12] They often referred to him with gendered language that revealed their conviction that he was neither manly enough for international politics nor fit to hold the office of prime minister. They condemned as unacceptable examples of Mossadeq's unmanliness what were accepted forms of behavior in Iran, failed to see Mossadeq as their equal, and dismissed him as an unworthy adversary whose position did not matter. Their cables, reports, and other private documents, intended only for internal consumption and not released to the public for decades, judged Mossadeq by their own standards of acceptable behavior instead of measuring his behavior against prevailing Iranian norms and considering him within the context of the society of which he was a part. As a result, Mossadeq's appearance, behavior, and policies never quite measured up to Western norms or conformed to what Western leaders found acceptable. The end result of the Orientalization of Mossadeq was an increasingly rigid Anglo-American position on the oil crisis that eschewed compromise or concessions and ultimately saw removing him from office as the only acceptable course of action.

Anglo-American officials found Mossadeq different from themselves in many ways, and these differences affected the way they dealt with him during his premiership. One startling difference concerned the way the prime minister dressed and his preferred place of conducting business. Because of his age and poor health, Mossadeq usually worked from his bed while dressed in pajamas, thereby presenting Anglo-American officials with a situation so strange that they took to including the color of his pajamas in their reports home. Some days, in fact, they noted that the prime minister wore two sets of pajamas on top of each other—khaki and green one day, blue and khaki another.[13] Officials also thought it significant to note, sometimes with veiled sarcasm, those occasions when Mossadeq was up and about. U.S. ambassador Loy Henderson, for example, described one meeting in which Mossadeq "received me fully dressed (not pajama clad) as though for [a] ceremonial occasion."[14] Officials from the International Bank for Reconstruction and Development, who went to Iran seeking to arrange an oil settlement in 1952, made the same point by expressing shock one day to find the prime minister "alert" and "on his feet." On another occasion they were astonished that Mossadeq actually "got out of bed, put on his slippers, and escorted us to the hall," as if the prime minister and his iron-framed bed had somehow become conjoined.[15] The cultural assumptions behind such remarks are clear: Real leaders are expected to wear suits or other professional attire when conducting business, not pajamas,[16] and they are expected to conduct their business from an upright position, not while reclining in their beds. Never mind that Winston Churchill often wore pajamas and worked from his bed. That Mossadeq did so marked him as an "eccentric" at best, a "lunatic" at worst, and contributed to a mounting Anglo-American conviction that what Mossadeq had to say from his bed was unimportant.[17]

Another thing that U.S. and British officials had difficultly dealing with was what they termed Mossadeq's "fragile" and "emotional" temperament.[18] On many occasions throughout his premiership, Mossadeq became teary eyed when speaking of the plight of the Iranian people, sometimes during private discussions, sometimes during public appearances.[19] In part, these outbursts were genuine reflections of his outrage at the sufferings wrought upon the Iranians by the "evil" Anglo-Iranian Oil Company.[20] In part, though, these episodes were carefully choreographed plays to the balcony designed to garner important popular support for the prime minister during the long and economically devastating oil crisis. Anglo-American officials did not give enough credence to the possibility that Mossadeq's tears might have stemmed from something other than uncontrolled emotionalism. To them, they were signs of weakness and effeminacy that diminished Mossadeq's standing as a statesman and absolved them of the responsibility of dealing with him as an equal.[21]

Mossadeq's tears were not the only thing that made him feminine in Western eyes. The prime minister also displayed a host of other traits that earned him the opprobrium of officials in the Foreign Office and State Department and that yielded descriptions thick with gender-coded language. He was "moody," "impractical," and "unrealistic," they said.[22] He lacked the capacity "to carry on complicated negotiations for any length of time in a single direction."[23] He had a tendency "to change his mind, to forget, to become confused."[24] He approached "international politics from [an] emotional point of view" rather than from a "rational" one.[25] All of these descriptions painted Mossadeq in feminine terms and seemed to brand him unworthy of playing the role of an international statesman. Sometimes Anglo-American officials even went beyond simply gender-coded language to explicit and obvious characterization, as when they railed against the prime minister's "negative and feminine [negotiating] tactics."[26] This description came during the failed mission of British Lord Privy Seal Sir Richard Stokes to arrange an oil settlement during the summer of 1952 and apparently meant that like most women, Mossadeq had trouble making up his mind, sought to avoid final decisions, and always wanted something better. The cumulative result of such characterizations was the conclusion that Mossadeq was an irrational and fickle adversary who was prone to emotional outbursts, often changed his mind, and could not be trusted. It seemed to follow that any permanent, realistic settlement required his removal from office and the appointment of a more reasonable and reliable prime minister.

Many of Mossadeq's policies contributed to Western descriptions of him as weak and incapable. By eschewing the economic gains that would come from a compromise settlement and insisting on total Iranian control of the oil industry, even if that meant operating at a reduced output, Mossadeq saw himself as safeguarding his nation's independence against the rapacious imperialism of the West. Anglo-American officials, however, saw things differently. For them, such a stance was further proof of Mossadeq's simple mind and unfitness for office. He was living in a "dream world" if he thought that "the simple passage of legislation nationalizing [the Iranian] oil industry [would create a] profitable business" and "'ludicrously misinformed'" if he thought other countries would step in to help when the AIOC demonstrated its opposition to nationalization by instituting a boycott of Iranian oil purchases by the other international oil companies, including the U.S. majors.[27] If Mossadeq thought he could play the U.S. firms off against the AIOC, he was sadly mistaken.

Mossadeq's effort to steer a middle course in the Cold War, which at the time took the name of "negative equilibrium," also made him look weak in Western eyes. Such a course turned the traditional Iranian policy of playing the Great Powers against each other on its head by proclaiming instead that no foreign power should have influence in Iran. As the prime minister saw it, what would later come to be called "nonalignment" was the only way to protect Iran from the kind of interference that the AIOC had practiced throughout Iran and thereby to ensure the attainment of the nation's true independence.[28] For U.S. officials, though, refusing to stand with the West against the communist menace was unmanly, even perfidious. In the "if you're not with us you're against us" climate that characterized the early 1950s, especially once the Republicans returned to power in 1953, Mossadeq's neutralism only further confirmed suspicions that his regime was leading Iran toward disaster.[29]

Also telling were the frequent Anglo-American references to Mossadeq's childishness and immaturity and the attendant assumption that the West needed to save Iran from his unrealistic and naive policies. The prime minister was called "insolent" and "intransigent" when he refused to accept British and U.S. plans for resolving the oil crisis, and during negotiations he allegedly had to be "humored" like "a fractious child."[30] In contrast to the British, who had been " 'saints' " throughout the oil crisis, Mossadeq had " 'been the naughty boy' " who needed to be disciplined.[31] Such descriptions were dripping with the arrogance and superiority of Western colonialism and are prefect examples of the Orientalist thinking that pervaded Western policy-making circles. They denigrated Mossadeq's capacities, questioned his fitness for office, and justified Anglo-American opposition to his regime—opposition, of course, that ultimately resulted in the coup that overthrew him in August 1953.

Anglo-American officials used yet another category of descriptors to denigrate and dismiss Mossadeq: the language of psychology and mental illness. The documentary record on the oil crisis is replete with references to Mossadeq as "crazy," "sick," "mad," "hysterical," "neurotic," "demented," "periodically unstable," and "not quite sane."[32] Because he was "suspicious" and "entirely impervious to reason," the "ordinary rules [of] logic" were useless when dealing with him.[33] In the discourse of the 1950s, terms like *hysterical* and *neurotic* were usually reserved for females, and their use in this context reflects an Anglo-American proclivity to see Mossadeq as feminine as well as demented—and indeed to link the two, to consider Mossadeq's supposed effeminacy and his apparent mental illness as part and parcel of the same problem and to see both as reasons for dismissing him and what he had to say. Anglo-American references to Mossadeq's mental state also reflected a tendency by British and U.S. officials to practice pop psychology on the prime minister, to ascribe to him medical conditions they were certainly not qualified to diagnose, and to use those diagnoses to justify their refusal to take what he said very seriously. "If Mr. Moussadiq is as mad as he seems," they concluded, talking and reasoning with him were futile.[34] These characterizations of Mossadeq as mentally ill continued through the planning for the coup that ultimately overthrew him: Secretary of State John Foster Dulles reportedly exclaimed, "So this is how we get rid of that madman Mossadegh" when the operation was laid out for him in June 1953.[35] Mossadeq's "madness," it seemed, truly was grounds for the Anglo-American operation against him.

Finally, Anglo-American officials revealed their cultural biases when describing Iranian society and the Iranian people in general. Mossadeq's supporters were termed little more than "mad and suicidal . . . lemmings" who needed to be saved from their folly by Western benevolence.[36] It was difficult to negotiate an agreement with Tehran because of "characteristic defects in the Persian mode of conducting business."[37] And any thought that the Iranians could operate the Abadan refinery in the absence of British technicians was roundly dismissed by Averell Harriman, sent by President Truman to arrange an oil settlement in the summer of 1951, as "lunacy."[38] Anglo-American officials also wrote often about the "Iranian mentality" and the "Oriental mind," vague, undefined terms that became all-too-easy rationalizations for the failure to reach an acceptable oil agreement and prevented Western officials from searching for the real root of the impasse in oil talks. Blaming the inability to reach a settlement on inherent differences between the Iranians and themselves offered Anglo-American officials what they considered an honorable way to escape responsibility for the continued stalemate.[39] It wasn't their fault there was no oil agreement; the fault lay with the Iranians, whose way of thinking was so different from the Anglo-American one that no settlement was possible. As Frank Costigliola has pointed out, George Kennan used the same specious logic to explain in the Long Telegram why it was pointless to try to negotiate with the Soviet Union.[40] Not surprisingly, descriptions of Mossadeq fit in with these general assessments of the Iranian people. The prime minister was a "wily Oriental" whose approach to the oil question was "almost purely mystical."[41] Patronizing remarks about the Iranian people's inability to choose and follow the right leader, assertions that they lacked the intelligence to operate the oil industry on their own, and stereotypical remarks about the mysterious East did more than reveal the cultural biases of Anglo-American officials. By assuming an air of Western superiority, they also suggested, at least implicitly, an imperialist mentality that questioned Iranian fitness for self-government and ultimately justified Western intervention to save the Iranians from self-destruction.

In characterizing Mossadeq as feminine and incapable, Anglo-American officials made two serious mistakes. One was their failure to recognize that Iranian standards of acceptable and normal behavior differed greatly from those that prevailed in the West. Whereas Mossadeq's tears symbolized weakness and emotionalism to them, for the Iranian people they were proof of Mossadeq's deep concern for the welfare of the country, concern that was so strong that he was driven to tears when he thought about the plight of his fellow countrymen. Whereas his proclivity to conduct business from his bed while dressed in pajamas proved his quirkiness to Westerners, for the Iranians these things were, as Andrew F. Westwood has noted, "deeply symbolic . . . of their personal plight and that of their nation, symbolic of the frailty of righteousness beset by powerful forces of evil." And whereas his fainting spells were for the Anglo-Americans something to mock and laugh about, they were the kinds of public displays of emotion and feeling that Iranians expected from a leader.[42] In other words, the Iranian people found nothing wrong with Mossadeq's behavior. On the contrary, they respected and admired him for being so concerned about the plight of his nation that he was driven to faint and cry about it.

Anglo-American officials also erred by not giving enough weight to the possibility that Mossadeq's emotionalism might have been intentional, something he employed to serve his own ends: Maybe he fainted and cried on purpose. In fact, there is evidence to suggest that this is precisely what the prime minister did. The best example of the depth of Mossadeq's theatrical talent came from a Majlis deputy who related the following personal experience. One day during an emotional speech on the floor of the Majlis, Mossadeq collapsed in a heap. Fearing that the elderly premier had suffered a heart attack, the deputy, who also happened to be a medical doctor, rushed to check Mossadeq's pulse, which he expected to find weak and fluttering. He was quite surprised when it was strong and regular, and even more surprised when the prime minister opened one eye and winked at him, as if to say, "My trick has worked. You were taken in, and so were the others. I have won you over."[43] Officials in the State Department and Foreign Office failed to seriously consider Mossadeq's deliberate use of tears and fainting. And even had they done so, they would have judged such tactics inappropriate for the political realm.

As *Time's* editors asserted, and as official descriptions and accounts revealed, when judged by Western standards, Mossadeq clearly did not measure up. He wept in public; he wore pajamas to work; he apparently did not understand the intricacies of the international oil industry; he eschewed involvement in the Cold War. These were not things real men did, and they set Mossadeq apart from the Anglo-Americans.

Like all of us, policy makers in London and Washington judged others, including Mossadeq, in relation to how they saw themselves. They developed in their own minds standards of acceptable behavior, action, and appearance and used these standards as a yardstick to measure others. Those who met the minimum were respected as equals; those who did not were denigrated and dismissed. As scholars such as Carol Cohn and Emily Rosenberg have noted, these standards consisted largely of opposing pairs of traits and behaviors with the positive element of each pair denoting acceptable (or Western) norms and the negative element signifying unacceptable (or Other) norms. For Westerners, the positive traits were coded as male, the negative traits as female.[44] Thus, in the pairs "strong and weak," "rational and irrational," and "realistic and emotional," "strong," "rational," and "realistic" were seen as male, and therefore desirable, traits, while "weak," "irrational," and "emotional" were seen as female, and therefore undesirable, traits.

In the case of Mossadeq, everything he did fed Western perceptions of him as weak and unmanly, which in turn made it much easier for Anglo-American officials to discount his position—and that of his country. Because Mossadeq neither looked nor acted like a Western leader and refused to kowtow to Western pressures for continued control of Iran's oil industry, he was described as an irrational lunatic unfit to hold the office of prime minister.

An indication that it was Mossadeq's behavior, dress, and personal beliefs that fueled Western condemnation of him and not the fact that he was Iranian is that some Iranians did receive positive press from British and U.S. officials. One member of the Iranian opposition who was willing to see the British return to Iran "as partners in the oil industry," for example, was praised for his "physical and mental" strength and for an ability to drink "his whisky manfully" (always the mark of a competent leader).[45] Mossadeq's successor as prime minister, Fazlollah Zahedi, also won plaudits as "a realistic man who [could] recognize a need to cooperate with the West in order to obtain revenue from sales of Iranian oil."[46] In accepting the necessity of Western influence in and control over Iranian affairs and in displaying other traits that Western officials admired, these men differed from Mossadeq. They went along with Western schemes and tacitly accepted the idea of Western superiority that was built into the Orientalist thinking that so condemned and denigrated Mossadeq. In other words, in order to win Western acceptance, they had put aside their Iranianness and embraced Westernness. They had abandoned the idea of national independence that spurred Mossadeq to defy the Anglo-Americans in order to receive Western support and assistance.

Assessing the immediate influence of Western characterizations of Mossadeq on the formulation of Anglo-American policy is tricky because it is not possible to determine a direct causal relationship between Anglo-American perceptions and prejudices and specific events. We cannot say, for example, that Western stereotypes led linearly to the coup that removed Mossadeq from office in the summer of 1953. But this does not mean that these stereotypes were unimportant. On the contrary, by shaping the mind-set of Anglo-American officials, they were part of the context within which those officials formulated policy. They buttressed claims of Western superiority over Iranian and other Middle Eastern peoples by perpetuating the idea that those peoples were weak and incapable. And their cumulative effect was to paint Mossadeq and others like him in unfavorable ways that rationalized and justified Western control.

The British and U.S. officials charged with negotiating an oil settlement with Mossadeq were probably not aware of the role cultural perceptions played in circumscribing their ability to reach such a settlement. But as this essay has demonstrated, those perceptions did constitute important obstacles to a negotiated resolution of the oil crisis on terms that Western officials would have considered acceptable. To be sure, there were many other contexts surrounding the oil crisis besides gender and culture—the East-West Cold War, Anglo-American relations, and decolonization and the rise of Third World nationalism, to name only three—and each of these contexts provided its own obstacles to an acceptable oil agreement. But in seeking a complete understanding of the Anglo-Iranian oil crisis, and especially the reasons why resolution proved so difficult, scholars should not discount the role of cultural perceptions. Without a doubt, by judging Mossadeq according to Western standards rather than accepting him on his own terms, Anglo-American officials demonstrated their own cultural arrogance and greatly reduced their chances of reaching a negotiated oil settlement.

In conclusion, this essay makes clear that the question of perceptions—or, perhaps more accurately, misperceptions—proved to be an important one throughout the Iranian oil crisis. Without question, Mossadeq committed his own errors of perception. He misread the willingness of U.S. officials to come to Iran's assistance in its struggle against Britain, the difficulties of selling nationalized oil on the open market, and the degree of British opposition to surrendering control of Iranian oil. He also miscalculated the usefulness of communism as a way to win U.S. support. But of much greater consequence were the misperceptions of British and U.S. officials about Mossadeq—that he was senile, mentally unbalanced, and unfit for office. Because key U.S. Foreign Service officers had little understanding of Iranian history, culture, or tradition, they did not appreciate the role that emotion or public tears played in the political culture of Iran or why Mossadeq might have worn pajamas and worked from his bed. Instead of taking Mossadeq on his own terms, Western leaders chose to judge him according to their own standards and to dismiss him when he failed to measure up to expectations. This tendency was not unique to Iran, of course, but applied throughout the world's developing countries. It reflected an Anglo-American sense of cultural superiority over developing world leaders who sought to maintain their nations' independence and helps to explain why the Anglo-Iranian oil crisis, which was at its heart a North-South conflict, ultimately proved so difficult to resolve.

Notes

1. Foreign Office telegram 2103 to British Embassy, Washington, 18 May 1951, Foreign Office General Political Correspondence, Record Class FO 371, 91535/EP1531/354, Public Record Office, Kew, England (hereafter FO 371, with filing information); Gifford telegram 5774 to State Department, 5 May 1951, General Records of the Department of State, Record Group 59, file 888.2553AIOC/5-2651, National Archives II, College Park, MD (hereafter RG 59, with file number).

2. Memorandum of conversation between Mossadeq and Anglo-American officials, 31 May 1951, in U.S. Department of State, *Foreign Relations of the United States, 1952-1954* (Washington, DC, 1989), 10:57-59 (hereafter *FRUS*, with year and volume number).

3. Mossadeq quoted in Grady dispatch 1159 to State Department, 29 June 1951, RG 59, 788.00/6-2951.

4. Acting Secretary of State James E. Webb to U.S. Embassy, London, 22 May 1950, *FRUS, 1950,* 5:550-51.

5. Emily S. Rosenberg, "Walking the Borders," in *Explaining the History of American Foreign Relations,* ed. Michael J. Hogan and Thomas G. Paterson (New York, 1992), 32. See also Emily S. Rosenberg, "Gender," in "A Round Table: Explaining the History of American Foreign Relations," *Journal of American History* 77 (June 1990): 116-24.

6. See Andrew Rotter, "Gender Relations, Foreign Relations: The United States and South Asia, 1947-1964," in this volume.

7. See Frank Costigliola, " 'Unceasing Pressure for Penetration': Gender, Pathology, and Emotion in George Kennan's Formation of the Cold War," *Journal of American History* 83 (March 1997): 1309-39; and Robert D. Dean, "Masculinity as Ideology: John F. Kennedy and the Domestic Politics of Foreign Policy," *Diplomatic History* 22 (Winter 1998): 29-62. Additional work along these lines may be found in Frank Costigliola, "The Nuclear Family: Tropes of Gender and Pathology in the Western Alliance," *Diplomatic History* 21 (Spring 1997): 163-83.

8. See Kristin L. Hoganson, *Fighting for American Manhood: How Gender Politics Provoked the Spanish-American and Philippine-American Wars* (New Haven, CT, 1998).

9. See John Foran, "Discursive Subversions: *Time* Magazine, the CIA Overthrow of

Mussadiq, and the Installation of the Shah," in *Cold War Constructions: The Political Culture of United States Imperialism, 1945–1966,* ed. Christian G. Appy (Amherst, 2000), 157–82.

10. "Man of the Year," *Time,* 7 January 1952, 18–21. Other contenders for Man of the Year honors included Dwight Eisenhower, Douglas MacArthur, Winston Churchill, and John Foster Dulles.

11. Because British and U.S. officials shared common cultural assumptions regarding Iran and the Middle East—and especially because U.S. officials learned much of what they knew about the Middle East from the British—for the purposes of this essay the two will be considered together.

12. Edward Said, *Orientalism* (New York, 1978). For an excellent exploration of the use of such stereotypes regarding India, see Rotter, "Gender Relations, Foreign Relations."

13. For two instances of reporting on Mossadeq's pajama color see Shepherd despatch 164 to Foreign Office, 3 June 1951, FO 371, 91545/EP1531/609; and Shepherd to R. J. Bowker, 22 May 1951, FO 371, 91542/EP1531/547.

14. Henderson telegram 384 to State Department, 18 August 1953, *FRUS, 1952–1954,* 10:748.

15. Hector Prud'homme to Robert Garner, 1 January 1952, and Prud'homme to Henderson, 14 January 1952, both in WBGA, Central Files, 1946–1971: Operational Correspondence, Iran, box 31, folder: 10, World Bank, New York City. I am grateful to Amy L. S. Staples for providing me with copies of her research in the records of the World Bank.

16. See Andrew Rotter's essay in this volume for the importance U.S. officials placed on dress with regard to Indian and Pakistani leaders.

17. Shepherd to Bowker, 22 May 1951, FO 371, 91542/EP1531/547.

18. Acheson memorandum for the president, "Luncheon Meeting with Prime Minister Mosadeq," 22 October 1951, Harry S. Truman Papers, President's Secretary's File—Subject File, box 180, folder: Iran—W. Averell Harriman, Harry S. Truman Library, Independence, MO.

19. For two references to Mossadeq's tears, see Arthur L. Richards (counselor, U.S. embassy, Tehran) despatch 1006 transmitting Mossadeq's 25 May 1951 statement to the press, 26 May 1951, RG 59, 788.13/5-2651; and Henry F. Grady (U.S. ambassador, Tehran) telegram 3255 to State Department, 13 June 1951, RG 59, 888.2553AIOC/6-1351.

20. Richards despatch 1006 transmitting Mossadeq's 25 May 1951 statement to the press, 26 May 1951, RG 59, 788.13/5-2651.

21. Although previous accounts of the Anglo-Iranian oil crisis have noted Mossadeq's tendency to weep, they have not made much of how the prime minister's tears affected Western officials. See, e.g., Daniel Yergin, *The Prize: The Epic Quest for Oil, Money, and Power* (New York, 1991), chap. 23; and H. W. Brands, *Inside the Cold War: Loy Henderson and the Rise of American Empire* (New York, 1991), chap. 16.

22. Henderson telegram 3178 to State Department, 13 February 1953, RG 59, 888.2553/2-1353; Acheson memorandum for the president, "Luncheon Meeting with Prime Minister Mosadeq," 22 October 1951, Truman Papers, PSF—Subject File, box 180, folder: Iran—W. Averell Harriman.

23. Henderson telegram 2803 to State Department, 19 January 1953, RG 59, 888.2553/1-1953.

24. Ibid.

25. Henderson telegram 2727 to State Department, 16 January 1953, RG 59, 888.2553/1-1653.

26. Ramsbotham to Logan, 20 August 1951, FO 371, 91580/EP1531/1391.

27. Harriman telegram 736 to State Department, 22 August 191, RG 59, 888.2553/8-2251; Gifford telegram 5748 to State Department, 4 May 1951, RG 59, 888.2553AIOC/5-451.

28. For good discussions of Mossadeq's "negative equilibrium" see Farhad Diba, *Mohammed Mossadegh: A Political Biography* (London, 1986), 84-90; and Sepehr Zabih, *The Mossadegh Era: Roots of the Iranian Revolution* (Chicago, 1982), chap. 6.

29. For an examination of how Indian neutralism evoked similar condemnations from U.S. officials see Rotter, "Gender Relations, Foreign Relations."

30. D. A. Logan, "Brief for the Minister of State for the meeting of the Cabinet on the 26th of September 1952," w/enclosed annex, "Persian Reply to Joint U.S./U.K. Offer," 25 September 1952, FO 371, 98700/EP15314/412; P. E. Ramsbotham minute, "Persia: Oil," 8 September 1952, FO 371, 98697/EP15314/332; Henderson telegram 422 to State Department, 28 July 1952, *FRUS, 1952-1954*, 10:417; C.(52)275, "Political Developments in Persia: Note by the Secretary of State for Foreign Affairs," 5 August 1952, Cabinet Papers, Record Class CAB 129/54, Public Record Office.

31. Walter S. Gifford (U.S. ambassador, London) telegram 1698 to State Department, 5 October 1951, *FRUS, 1952-1954*, 10:205. *Time*'s editors echoed these characterizations of Mossadeq, comparing him to a "wilful little boy" who tried to get his own way by threatening to hold his breath until he was "blue in the face." See "Man of the Year," 18.

32. William Strang minute, 23 June 1951, FO 371, 91556/EP1531/884; Henderson telegram 2462 to State Department, 4 January 1952, *FRUS, 1952-1954*, 10:302; Sir Francis Shepherd (British ambassador, Tehran) despatch 253 to Foreign Office, 15 September 1951, FO 371, 91589/EP1531/1591; Henderson telegram 514 to State Department, 3 August 1952, RG 59, 788.00/80352; Steel telegram 1952 to Foreign Office, 25 June 1951, FO 371, 91551/EP1531/736; Henderson telegram 422 to State Department, 28 July 1952, *FRUS, 1952-1954*, 10:417.

33. Unsigned memorandum, 19 January 1953, FO 371, 104610/EP1531/113; R. J. Bowker minute, 4 May 1951, FO 371, 91534/EP1531/327; Henderson telegram 3627 to State Department, 10 March 1953, *FRUS, 1952-1954*, 10:707.

34. E. A. Berthoud minute, 6 June 1951, FO 371, 91551/EP1531/733.

35. Dulles purportedly quoted in Kermit Roosevelt, *Countercoup: The Struggle for the Control of Iran* (New York, 1979), 8. Roosevelt tells a good story, but readers should proceed with caution, as he tends to exaggerate and may even at times misrepresent the events. A good scholarly account of the coup that makes excellent use of interviews with participants is Mark J. Gasiorowski, *U.S. Foreign Policy and the Shah: Building a Client State in Iran* (Ithaca, NY, 1991).

36. Henderson telegram 377 to State Department, 24 July 1952, RG 59, 788.00/7-2452.

37. Shepherd dispatch 376 to FO, "Conduct of the Anglo-Persian Question: Anal-

ysis of Persian Objections to the Supplemental Oil Agreement and Suggested Future Policy," 31 December 1950, FO 371, 91521/EP1531/7.

38. Harriman quoted in Sir Richard Stokes note on his 8 August 1951 meeting with the shah, 12 August 1951, FO 371, 91578/EP1531/1342.

39. H. Freeman Matthews memorandum of conversation, 2 August 1951, Papers of Dean Acheson, box 66, folder: Memoranda of Conversations, Aug 1951, Truman Library; C. Steel (Washington) telegram 2321 to Foreign Office, 19 December 1952, FO 371, 98704/EP15314/528.

40. See Costigliola, " 'Unceasing Pressure for Penetration.' "

41. Foreign Office telegram 1576 to British ambassador, United Nations, 10 October 1951, FO 371, 91606/EP1531/1988; Middleton (Tehran) telegram 189 to Foreign Office, 23 February 1952, FO 371, 98707/EP15317/1.

42. Andrew F. Westwood, "Politics of Distrust in Iran," *Annals of the American Academy of Political and Social Sciences* 358 (March 1965): 127. See also Sattareh Farman Farmaian, with Dona Munker, *Daughter of Persia: A Woman's Journey from Her Father's Harem through the Islamic Revolution* (New York, 1992), 173.

43. For one recounting of this famous tale see Yergin, *The Prize,* 457.

44. See Carol Cohn, "Wars, Wimps, and Women: Talking Gender and Thinking War," in *Gendering War Talk,* ed. Miriam Cooke and Angela Woollacott (Princeton, NJ, 1993), 227–46; and Rosenberg, "Gender."

45. George Middleton to A. D. M. Ross (Eastern Department, FO), 16 June 1952, FO 371, 98707/EP15317/8.

46. Henry A. Byroade (assistant secretary of state for Near Eastern, South Asian, and African affairs) memorandum to Robert Bowie (director, Policy Planning Staff), "Iran," 21 August 1953, *FRUS, 1952–1954,* 10:761.

Gender Relations, Foreign Relations: The United States and South Asia, 1947–1964

ANDREW J. ROTTER

In 1951, four years after India and Pakistan became independent nations, the prominent Democrat Chester Bowles approached President Harry S. Truman and asked to have the ambassadorship to India, if the job was available. Bowles described Truman's reaction: "The president was appalled at the thought of anyone wanting to go to India and he said, 'Well, I thought India was pretty jammed with poor people and cows wandering around the streets, witch doctors and people sitting on hot coals and bathing in the Ganges, and so on, but I did not realize that anyone thought it was important.'"[1] Equally irresistible is the confession of Truman's worldly secretary of state, Dean Acheson, who confided in his memoirs: "I have never been able to escape wholly from a childhood illusion that, if the world is round, the Indians must be standing on their heads—or, perhaps, vice versa."[2]

Historically, the U.S. understanding of India evolved as a part of what Edward Said has called Orientalism, a way of conceptualizing Asia that presupposed Western superiority and undergirded Western domination. Orientalism was a "discourse," principally "a British and French cultural enterprise," that encompassed "such disparate realms as the imagination itself, the whole of India and the Levant . . . colonial armies and . . . colonial administrators, a formidable scholarly corpus, innumerable Oriental 'experts' and 'hands,' . . . a complex array of 'Oriental' ideas (Oriental despotism, Oriental splendor, cruelty, sensuality), many Eastern sects, philosophies, and wisdom domesticated for local European use—the list [Said concludes] can be extended more or less indefinitely." What was for nearly two centuries a European enterprise became after World War II a U.S. one.[3]

Gender is a discourse in its own right and a constituent element of the

195

more general discourse of Orientalism. Given the expansive content of Orientalist discourse, however, it is perhaps most useful to focus on Said's description of it as a "cultural enterprise." Although *culture* "is one of the two or three most complicated words in the English language," as Raymond Williams put it, these days it has nothing on *discourse*.[4] In the formulation of Max Weber and Clifford Geertz, culture consists of the "webs of significance" (in Weber's phrase) spun by human beings.[5] Everyone, even the shapers of U.S. foreign policy, is affected by culture and deploys webs of significance in order to understand the world outside the self. At the policy-making level, this is political culture. Some webs are inherited, being the property of institutions rather than the individuals who move in and out of them. Other webs come with those who staff these institutions. People are not only the makers of webs but their subtle victims because they can become enmeshed in the skeins that they or others have made and become dependent on the sustenance and security that their webs provide. Significantly, no matter what others' webs look like, we perceive them through our own. Our understanding of others thus comes from our views of ourselves.[6]

The focus of this essay is on gender, one of the critical skeins in the web of significance deployed by U.S. policy makers and used to explain India. An analysis of gender illuminates important aspects of relations between nations; here the concern is with the United States, India, and, tangentially, Pakistan. Mrinalini Sinha has written, "Empires and nations are gendered ideological constructs," to which one might add that nations also construct each other.[7] For the purposes of this essay, gender, or "gendering," is not a static idea but a transnational process: it is the assignment of certain characteristics based on prevailing ideas of masculinity and femininity to a people and nation by another people and nation. Masculinity and femininity are not, in this view, biologically determined categories but culturally and socially conditioned constructs. Nations and the people who constitute them become "gendered," and this affects the policies that other nations pursue toward them.

The history of U.S. foreign relations is not generally held to be susceptible to gender analysis. The makers of U.S. foreign policy, almost all of them men, do not talk explicitly about gender issues or intentionally use a vocabulary of gender when they discuss their policies toward other countries. They talk about strategy and geopolitics, economics and access to raw materials, and systems, ours versus theirs. Because of this, as Joan Scott has written, most historians believe that gender "refers only to those areas . . . involving relations between the sexes. Because, on the face of it, war, diplomacy, and high politics have not been explicitly about those relationships, gender seems not to apply and so continues to be irrelevant to the thinking of historians concerned with issues of politics and power."[8]

Increasing numbers of diplomatic historians have pursued Scott's argument that "high politics itself is a gendered concept."[9] In two important essays, Emily S. Rosenberg has suggested that historians of U.S. foreign relations undertake "a quest to understand the ever-changing ideologies related to gender, and their social and political implications."[10] This essay takes up that quest in an effort to discover how ideas about gender, many of them found in popular culture, affected policy makers in Washington and New Delhi as they considered each other, especially during the period 1947–64.

Examination of the gender issue requires in the first place the use of sources not often studied by diplomatic historians, among them anthropology and psychology texts, photographs, popular literature, travelers' accounts, films, and plays. The study also demands an unconventional reading of conventional sources on policy making. One must look at the usual published documents, in the State Department's *Foreign Relations* volumes and elsewhere, as well as consult the holdings of the U.S. presidential libraries and the national archives of the United States, Great Britain, and India. But the researcher with gender in mind must look for odd things in the documents: stray remarks about personal style or gesture, for example, or comments about a people's alleged "emotionalism" or "effeminacy," and even references to the kinds of parties U.S. hosts put on for their Indian or Pakistani guests. What for most diplomatic historians would be a collection of marginalia becomes for someone interested in culture a treasure trove of information demanding thick description.

Begin with the Western idea, which persists over time, that India is a female country. One of the most influential books ever written about India by a Westerner was Katherine Mayo's *Mother India* (1927), a scathing attack on Hindu customs and practices.[11] Mayo's choice of title was no accident; it built on a long tradition of representing India, the place, as female. The early twentieth-century U.S. traveler Sydney Greenbie noted, apparently without irony, that on a map India "looked like the ponderous milk-bags of a cow holding the very living essence of Asia."[12] Writers contrasted the West and India in ways that evoked gender. The West was grasping, materialistic, scientific, and calculating; India was spiritual, impulsive, even irrational. "The masculine science of the West," wrote Greenbie, "has found out and wooed and loved or scourged this sleepy maiden of mysticism."[13] In the discourse of India's relations with the West, concludes Richard Cronin, "one metaphor emerges as dominant. The West is a man, the East is a woman."[14]

The Western representation of India as female worked to confer effeminacy on most Indian men. Caught in the enervating web of Hinduism, which was regarded by Westerners as less a religion than a pathology, the majority of Indian men had been deprived of their manliness and their virility. In the context of gender, it is possible to discern three features that Westerners historically assigned to most Indian men. The first of these was passivity and its more exaggerated forms; the second was emotionalism; the third was a lack of heterosexual energy. All were associated with femininity, which Westerners regarded as effeminacy if exhibited by a man, and all involved the application to India of Western constructions of the feminine and the masculine.

The first of these features, in this case a cluster of characteristics, included passivity, servility, and cowardice. Nothing, argued Westerners, could stir Hindu men out of their passive torpor. Indian men could endure anything, evidently without suffering from a sense of shame about their inaction. They did not resist oppressors but regarded them with stupefying indifference. During the 1920s and 1930s, there was a Hindu craze in the United States, and thousands of U.S. citizens became familiar with the "three levels of conduct" of Vedanta, the type of Hinduism most often brought to the country by Indian swamis. Level one was "obedient activity," level two was "desireless activity," and the third and highest level was "pure passivity."[15] The terms could have been borrowed from a primer on behavior written for proper U.S. women, now projected onto allegedly effeminate Others.

The exaggerated form of passivity was servility. This, Westerners declared, Hindu men had in abundance. Many subscribed at least implicitly to John Stuart Mill's dictum that "in truth, the Hindu, like the eunuch, excels in the qualities of the slave."[16] The traveler Henry M. Field was astonished and delighted with the apparent servility of Indian men. He was "surrounded and waited upon by soft-footed Hindoos, who glided about noiselessly like cats, watching every look, eager to anticipate every wish before they heard the word of command." Everyone called him "sahib," a title of respect, and the servants automatically rose in his presence. "I never knew before how great a being I was," Field wrote. "There is nothing like going far away from home, to the other side of the world, among Hindoos or Hottentots, to be fully appreciated."[17]

Beyond servility was cowardice. Westerners asserted that Hindu men were unwilling to stand and fight and that this explained the apparent ease with which they had been conquered. First the Muslims, then the British, had found the Hindu population relatively unresisting, especially in Bengal.[18] To make this argument, particularly after Bengalis were heavily involved in the Sepoy Rebellion of 1857, required tortuous reasoning, but Katherine Mayo was up to the task. She claimed that acts of Hindu resistance were cowardly because they relied on treachery, not confrontation. "If only he need not face his enemy," she wrote of the Bengali male. "If only he may creep up behind and take his enemy in the back."[19]

The idea that Indian men were passive, servile, and cowardly persisted into the Cold War period. U.S. policy makers condemned Indian foreign policy makers for their unwillingness to take a stand in the conflict between the United States and the Soviet Union and believed that Indian neutralism got its comeuppance in the fall of 1962, when Communist Chinese troops smashed through Indian defenses on the northeast frontier and pushed deep into Indian territory. Roger Hilsman, an assistant secretary of state who came to New Delhi with a high-level delegation to offer India help, could not refrain from a sharp observation: "We were ushered into the Prime Ministerial residence through the reception hall lined with photographs of all the neutral and unaligned Chiefs of States who have so notably failed to come to India's support during the present crisis. The irony was more than funny—it was oppressive."[20]

A second trait that according to U.S. officials and Westerners revealed the effeminacy of Hindu men was emotionalism, usually associated with hypersensitivity. Rather than deal with issues logically and coolly, Hindu men flew off the handle—just as U.S. women were allegedly apt to do. U.S. policy makers claimed constantly to find verification for the cliche that the West was rational and tough, while the East was emotional and sensitive. In a 1948 profile, the CIA described the Indian prime minister: "Nehru is a man of broad vision and of integrity, but his character is weakened by a tendency toward emotionalism which at times destroys his sense of values. He is gracious as well as brilliant, but volatile and quick-tempered."[21] A sense of pride came naturally with independence, but the Indians were an especially sensitive people—or so claimed ambassadors to India Loy Henderson (1948-51) and Chester Bowles (1951-53).[22] In 1954, the law partner of Secretary of State John Foster Dulles wrote that Indians had "an almost feminine hypersensitiveness with respect to the prestige of their country."[23] President Eisenhower agreed. Reading of Indian objections to the administration's plan to provide arms for Pakistan, Eisenhower wrote Dulles: "This is one area of the world where, even more than most cases, emotion rather than reason seems to dictate policy."[24]

Finally, U.S. officials believed that Hindu men failed to show a healthy sexual interest in women. This failure was not, of course, a characteristic of U.S. women, but of unmanly U.S. men. Hindu men seemed inclined to homosexuality or, like the great nationalist leader Mohandas Gandhi, sexual renunciation. Visitors to India noticed Indian men holding hands, as they do still. They saw sculptures of beings that were bifurcated into male and female halves, adding to the apparent confusion of gender roles in India. In the mid-1950s, Harold Isaacs surveyed 181 prominent U.S. citizens, including several foreign policy makers, about their attitudes toward India. Respondents offered a host of gendered, and censorious, descriptors: Indian men were "servile," "cringing," "submissive," "effete," "weak," and "effeminate." They were characterized by "passivity," "inertia," and "docility," and they lacked "vigor," "industry," "stamina," "virility," and "muscles." Most revealing is the diatribe of a distinguished (though anonymous) scholar: "Indians? I think of fakiry, spelled both ways. It's the same thing. It means deception. . . . Somehow I am almost tempted to use the word feminine. I feel a certain effeminateness about Indians that bothers me, although I am not bothered in general by homosexuals. . . . Effete is a word I think of."[25]

U.S. officials learned much of what they knew about empire from the British. Of course, the United States became an imperialist nation in its own right, but like the British raj the U.S. empire was undergirded by perceptions based on gender. When U.S. policy makers looked abroad in the late nineteenth century, they beheld nations whose populations seemed to cry out for the protection, guidance, and discipline only white men could provide. As Emily Rosenberg notes, "Women, nonwhite races, and tropical countries often received the same kinds of symbolic characterizations from white male policy makers: emotional, irrational, irresponsible, unbusinesslike, unstable, and childlike."[26] Concerned, perhaps, that their own masculinity was at risk—a concern of U.S. men at least as far back as the Revolution, when Tom Paine had charged men to awaken from "fatal and unmanly slumbers"[27]—policy makers developed patriarchal designs on the weaker members of the family of nations. There were figurative children out there who needed help, and there were figurative women who were too soft or emotional to take care of themselves. This view applied to Latin America, the countries of which were frequently depicted as women in distress, victims (like Cuba and Puerto Rico) of Spanish villainy. Delicate Chinese mandarins required protection against the brutalities of men from Europe, Russia, and Japan. Theodore Roosevelt's emphasis on the strenuous life and the manly virtues of combat gave rhetorical substance to images of Others based on gender.[28]

U.S. officials also learned most of what they knew about India from the British. During the nineteenth and early twentieth centuries, they watched with interest as the British played the "Great Game" against Russia, trying to block tsarist expansion through the Khyber Pass into South Asia. They struggled to compete with the British for markets in the region. And they adopted the gendered British view of the peoples of India. The mid-nineteenth-century U.S. traveler Robert Ninturn thought that Indian soldiers lacked only one thing—"manly courage." India itself was a "rich and fertile country," but it was "inhabited by a cowardly and effeminate race."[29] Nearly a century later, John K. Fairbank, stationed in British India during the Second World War, found Indians "timorous cowering creatures, too delicate to fight like the Chinese."[30] The United States did not become an imperialist nation in India, but it replaced Great Britain as the principal Western power in South Asia, and U.S. officials brought with them many British assumptions, some of them founded on perceptions of gender.

There was another reason why U.S. policy makers saw Hindu men, and India itself, as feminine. In the U.S. view, there are sharp lines drawn between the genders. As Susan Jeffords has argued, while the U.S. definition of masculinity may change over time, "it remains consistently opposed to the 'feminine,' those characteristics that must be discarded in order to actualize masculinity."[31] Hindu men, however, subscribe to codes of masculinity that are not the same as Western ones. In ancient Hindu myth, pride of place is reserved for feminine principles. The cosmos was the creation of Shakti, or energy, which has a feminine gender in Sanskrit. The first mortal couple were the twins Yama and Yami. The woman, Yami, was not derived from Yama, as Eve was derived from Adam, but had her own, powerful identity.[32] The leading Indian hero of the 1857 Rebellion was a twenty-year-old princess, the Rani of Jansi. She remains widely admired and was the subject of a popular movie released in India in 1953.[33]

Hindu ideas of how men should look and what they should be incorporate what most Westerners would regard as a female aesthetic. In India, a boy or a man can be called the equivalent of beautiful without embarrassment. The ideal man, wrote Krishnalal Shridharani, has "regular features, eyes that move languidly, lashes that fringe, hair that resembles velvet." In contrast, U.S. "girls favor men with jutting chins, hair that stands on end [this was the early 1940s], bulging nostrils, hands that can break down doors, and one-way eyes that express Harpo-Marxian intensity."[34] In general, the line drawn in the West between masculine and feminine behavior is drawn in a different place in India, and by incorporating so-called female attributes into their personalities, Hindu men fulfill themselves, round themselves off.[35] Androgyny is not a pathology but a virtue; bisexuality can be "an indicator of saintliness and yogic accomplishments."[36] As for homosexuality, it is worth recording an excerpt from a song called "The Wounded Heart," sung by the hearty, Pushtu-speaking Muslim men of the far northwest: "There's a boy across the river with a bottom like a peach/But, alas, I cannot swim."[37]

India's Mahatma Gandhi personified the distortion of gender categories as Westerners understood them. In his own life Gandhi practiced *brahma-charya,* or self-control, which included not only a limited diet and rigorous mental discipline but abstinence from sexual relations with his wife (and refusal of self-made sexual temptation). He hoped to achieve in his sexual life what Lloyd and Susanne Hoeber Rudolph, in a phrase that is revealing to a diplomatic historian, call "the serenity of neutrality." More to the point, Gandhi turned Western gender discourse to his own purposes. He deliberately challenged this discourse in order to attack both British colonialism and the Indian caste system. As Ashis Nandy writes, Gandhi "rejected the British as well as the Brahmanic-Kshatriya [ruling caste] equation between manhood and dominance, between masculinity and legitimate violence, and between femininity and passive submissiveness." Gandhi's political activism was inspired by what he and his followers called *satyagraha,* popularly construed as "passive resistance." Gandhi disliked the translation, preferring "truth force," but the sight of Indian nationalists walking calmly into beatings and arrests by the police suggested to Westerners a kind of resignation. In fact, Gandhi hoped to separate bravery, which the nationalists had in abundance, from aggressiveness, a trait associated with Western maleness. Gandhi opened the ranks of the movement to women, and *satayagraha* embodied what Gandhi held to be the peculiar strengths of women—compassion, endurance, and courage. This position, as Nandy contends, challenged patriarchy and thus negated the very basis of colonial culture.[38]

Some Westerners, of course, flocked to Gandhi's banner; a good number of them were women. But Gandhi's appeal perplexed many Westerners. The popular New York columnist Arthur Brisbane voiced his scorn for Gandhi's methods: "In these days, you only get justice when you fight for it. Even then it is slow."[39] On board a ship bound for the United States in 1943, Nehru's nieces, Nayantara and Lekha Sahgal, talked to some marines about Gandhi. "Our talk of non-violence only made them laugh," Nayantara remembered. " 'This guy Gandhi must be crazy. Suppose a man came along and killed his sister; would he sit still and not do anything about it?' "[40] The Mahatma's unwillingness to take up cudgels for his cause seemed proof that he was insufficiently manly. His opponents were made to feel ashamed and guilty for using force against those who seemed to glory in their quiet courage. Shame and guilt are weapons of the cunning, not the physically strong.

The Congress Party led the Indian government through Nehru's ministry and beyond. Though most of its members, including Nehru, rejected Gandhi's plans for an agrarian, localized economy, they carried with them the movement's conviction that courage in world affairs need not be confused with Western definitions of manliness. In fact, they cultivated the gendered view that India was a female still at risk, despite its independent status, of seduction or brutalization by the West. The prime minister had long believed this. Writing to a U.S. friend in 1938, Nehru declared: "India is a feminine country. . . . Anyway she has certain feminine virtues and certainly the feminine vices."[41] It was an image the prime minister never abandoned. The United States in particular had to be watched. It was "a blundering giant with no finer feelings or regard for Asian sentiment," the inheritor of "rapacious tendencies" previously attributed to the British.[42] Indians found the United States "a kind of loathsome Uncle Sam seeking to seduce the lovely virgin India."[43] As it had with the British, the characterization of U.S. Others as sexually aggressive served a useful purpose for Indian leaders: it rallied a diverse people around the defense of the motherland, and by representing the state as weak it elevated unity and self-defense to a high moral plane.

The femaleness associated by Westerners with India did not have the same implications for all the people who lived in India. While Westerners commonly judged Hindu men, especially Bengalis, to be effeminate, allegedly passive, cowardly, servile, emotional, and bi- or homosexual, they represented Indian women differently. Indian woman were alleged to be seductresses, waiting to lure unsuspecting men into danger. The practice of purdah, or the seclusion of women, supposedly functioned as a way of tempting men, driving them to distraction without the promise of sexual fulfillment. As Sydney Greenbie saw it, "Forty million women live in seclusion, and all their inexperience, all their ignorance, all their suppressed desires, deny and condemn and withhold from men the fullness of life which they crave."[44] Westerners also regarded Indian women as glorified housekeepers incapable of loving their husbands, superstitious lightweights whose heads were turned by pseudoreligions and shiny baubles, or harridans who could not control their passions.[45]

The most dominant Western representation held that Indian women were heartless, domineering, and emasculating. This representation emerged most strongly with reference to Hindu gods, the most compelling of whom is the goddess Kali, one of the forms of the god Shiva's wife. Kali is a frightening figure to a Western man. Over the years, she has appeared in a variety of U.S. media. In the March 1950 issue of *Fate* magazine—a kind of occult *Reader's Digest* with stories such as "They Eat Dirt and Like It"—Kali is depicted as a beautiful but cruel destroyer of men. She has four arms: one holds a bloody cutlass, a second a man's head that the cutlass has severed, and a third a pan into which drips blood from the head. She stands on the chest of another man, who is intact but seemingly comatose. She wears a belt made of human arms; around her neck is a wreath of heads of the giants she has slain. This image of Kali would not be unfamiliar to an Indian viewer. But the text of the article goes on: "Before her goddess each worshipper is a Kali herself, and she would recognize no male in the presence of Kali." Here is a totalizing image, in which all Indian women are conflated with the bloody-minded, emasculating deity they venerate.[46]

If she is not killing men, the Kali of Western construction is making them do terrible things in her name. The sensationalist paperback *Woman of Kali*, published by Gold Medal Books in 1954, had as its title character "Sharita, high priestess of the cult of death" in "barbaric India, land of languor, intrigue, strange appetites, exotic women, cruel, and scheming men!" Sharita's army of Thugs carries out her murderous wishes.[47] So do the Thugs seen in the 1939 film *Gunga Din* and the recent *Indiana Jones and the Temple of Doom*, though these movie Thugs worship Kali directly. In the latter film Kali has hordes of male slaves, who lose their free will when they drink her blood.

What has any of this to do with U.S.–South Asia relations during the Nehru period? The contention here is that ideas about gender, particularly the U.S. belief that Indian men were effeminate, conditioned U.S. policy toward India as the Cold War developed in South Asia during the 1940s, 1950s, and 1960s, dovetailing as they did with U.S. strategic concerns and ideas about race, religion, and caste or class, among others. This occurred in good measure because Nehru, who was not only prime minister but foreign minister from 1947 to his death in 1964, seemed to inherit from Gandhi qualities that U.S. men considered feminine. Partly this was a matter of Nehru's style. He wore the traditional north Indian shirt, the kurta, that flowed past his hips like a skirt. He loved flowers. He was rarely seen without a small rose in his lapel, and on birthdays he exchanged bouquets with other male government leaders.[48] Nehru drank fruit juice, never alcohol.[49] Admirers and critics alike noted Nehru's supposed feminine qualities. Harold Isaacs's respondents characterized the prime minister as "naive" and "fluffheaded," among other things.[50] "Nehru is so delicate and graceful that he makes one feel awkward," confessed C. L. Sulzberger.[51] Christopher Isherwood likened Nehru to "a tremendous nanny," and Eleanor Roosevelt thought him "sensitive and gentle."[52]

But it was not just style that made Nehru seem effeminate. Nehru's foreign policy was designed to keep India out of the Cold War. The nation would follow the path of neutralism, moving between the contending power blocs, committed to neither. Faced with the enormous task of unifying his country and providing for his people, Nehru hoped to avoid an expensive and dangerous arms race. He sought a role as mediator, choosing to act as an impartial referee who would keep disputes between the powers from erupting into global war. Drawing on a long Indian tradition of arbitration and mediation, Nehru worked to resolve conflicts outside the subcontinent without resort to war, or to limit wars that had already broken out. India played a leading part in promoting negotiations in Korea from 1950 on, served on the International Control Commission sent to monitor the Geneva Agreements on Vietnam, and tried to coax the United States and the People's Republic of China away from unremitting mutual hostility during the 1950s.[53]

To U.S. policy makers, there was something wrong with all this mediating. It smacked of naivete, cowardice, and moral evasiveness. There was a right side and a wrong side in the Cold War, and it was deceitful for Nehru to pretend otherwise. Nehru detected the disapproval of the West, and he responded to it: "A strong country," he told a U.S. audience in 1961, "would not lose its strength in gentle approaches to solving the cold war issues of the day."[54] U.S. policy makers were unconvinced. They believed that India, in its foreign policy, was acting just like a frightened woman.

The three state visits Nehru made to the United States—in the fall of 1949, December 1956, and November 1961—gave the Truman, Eisenhower, and Kennedy administrations opportunities for close examination of the Indian leader. Each encounter illustrates the influence of gender thinking on U.S. explanations of the man who personified India for nearly two decades. President Truman was not unsympathetic to Indian problems, and a week before Nehru arrived in the United States, Ambassador Loy Henderson made an eloquent plea to the State Department for a generous program of economic aid for India.[55] But Henderson had previously expressed reservations about the president's imminent guest. "Nehru," Henderson had written, "is a vain, sensitive, emotional and complicated person." While in school in England, Nehru had adopted the attitudes of "a group of rather supercilious upper middle-class young men who fancied themselves rather precious"— here is the barely concealed vocabulary of scorn for the supposed effeminacy of the Oxbridge dandy.[56] Truman himself had spent over four years demonstrating that he was "not afraid of the Russians" and that it was essential to "stand firm" and not "baby" the adversary. In Nehru he beheld a man with a rose in his lapel who reviewed the U.S. honor guard arrayed at the airport with evident distaste. The two men simply did not click. Truman found Nehru uncommunicative and suspicious. The reason, Nehru later confided, was that he had been put off by the president's extended discussion of the merits of Kentucky bourbon with Vice President Alben Barkley.[57] As Nehru's biographer Sarvepalli Gopal put it, "Truman's cocky vulgarity had grated" on the prime minister.[58]

Gender perceptions also played a role in Dwight Eisenhower's meetings with Nehru in late 1956. On the basis of ideology alone, there was no reason to suspect that Eisenhower and Nehru would get along. Eisenhower's secretary of state, John Foster Dulles, was a staunch opponent of Indian neutralism and an advocate of military alliances, in two of which resided Pakistan. Eisenhower had of course approved these arrangements. But the president knew of Nehru's dislike of military pacts and deliberately soft-pedaled their importance. In fact, Eisenhower seemed largely untroubled by Indian neutralism.[59] Though he concurred with Dulles and others that Indians were "emotional," he was neither threatened by this nor stirred to acts of paternalism. Eisenhower was a grandfatherly figure. His manhood had been established by his successful generalship during World War II. He felt no need to "stand up to the Soviets" merely for the sake of posturing. There was something "strange, even feminine" about the president that made him attractive, editorialized the *Eastern Economist* of New Delhi.[60] Rather than try to impress Nehru with the pomp and glitter of Washington, Eisenhower took the prime minister off to his Gettysburg farm, where the two men talked intimately for hours. They disagreed on many issues, including arms for Pakistan, the disposition of Kashmir, and the relative strength of nationalism and communism. But Eisenhower listened affably and never lectured his guest about the moral failings of neutralism.[61] Even before the visit, the *Chicago Tribune* found the president's policy incomprehensible; "every Indian kick [it complained] is rewarded by us with another favor. The Administration's behavior is neither manly nor sensible."[62] Nehru told reporters that the president was "thoroughly honest" and had "a certain moral quality."[63] "Of the American Presidents of his time, it was, curiously, Eisenhower with whom Nehru got on best," Gopal observes.[64] The attraction is least curious if the relationship is analyzed in terms of gender.

The Nehru-Eisenhower relationship stood in compelling contrast to the one that emerged between Nehru and John F. Kennedy. On the basis of ideology alone, there was every reason to suspect that Kennedy and Nehru would get along. The president had long supported economic aid for India, and in 1958 he was one of two senatorial sponsors of a bill that would have increased significantly the U.S. economic commitment to India.[65] For his part Nehru, urged on by Kennedy's ambassador in New Delhi John Kenneth Galbraith, looked forward to meeting the president; much excitement preceded the prime minister's visit to the United States in November 1961. As with Truman and Nehru, however, something failed to work. Kennedy seemed insecure, in a way that was exacerbated rather than concealed by his determination to act with vigor in the world. He would not promise to forbear from testing nuclear weapons or from intervening militarily in Vietnam. Particularly after the Bay of Pigs fiasco in April 1961, Kennedy felt the need to stand up to the Soviets, to show that he was neither callow nor cowardly—to prove he was a man. " 'Toughness,' " Henry Fairlie has written, "was one of the most prominent words in the vocabulary of the New Frontier; perhaps no other quality was so highly regarded."[66] "That son of bitch won't listen to words," Kennedy said of Soviet leader Nikita Khrushchev. "He has to see you move." Nehru thought Kennedy "brash, aggressive and inexperienced."[67] For the president, the meeting was even more disappointing. Nehru, who flinched visibly with each shot from a welcoming gun salute, was "passive and inward looking" and "simply did not respond" to the president's attempts to draw him out.[68] Kennedy later called the encounter "the worst head of state visit I have had."[69] Nehru seemed to confirm his long-standing reputation in policy-making circles as a man without vigor, determination, or spine.

In contrast, policy makers noted with approval the "manly" behavior of leaders in India's neighbor and rival, Pakistan. U.S. officials inherited from the British the idea that Muslims were more aggressive, more direct, and otherwise more masculine than Hindus. "From the very beginning," recalled Elbert G. Mathews, who directed the State Department's Office of South Asian Affairs from 1948 to 1951, "there was, in the U.S. Government . . . a strong view, based on the reading of Kipling, that the martial races of India were in the north, and much was now Pakistan. And therefore, the sensible thing for us to do was to cozy up to these martial races; they would be a great value to us in the fight against communism."[70] Harold Isaacs summarized ideas about Muslims and Hindus elicited by his interviews: "Even the poor Muslim is a vigorous man, while the poor Hindu is buckling at the knees; Pakistanis seemed energetic Western types, easier to talk to; . . . I hear from people that the Pakistanis are up and coming, good people, good fighters, whereas the Hindus are said to be mystics, dreamers, hypocrites; . . . Muslim faith is more dynamic . . . [has] more masculinity."[71] This is not just the language of gender, but it is hard to resist altogether the impression that these adjectives convey the long-standing concerns of U.S. men about how they and other men are supposed to act, and supposed not to.

U.S. statesmen, generally uncomfortable with Nehru, embraced a succession of Pakistani leaders. George McGhee, assistant secretary of state for Near Eastern, South Asian, and African affairs, was impressed with Prime Minister Liaquat Ali Khan when he met him in Karachi in 1949. "He was a big, strong, confident man with considerable international stature," McGhee remembered. "I liked him, as a man you could do business with."[72] Loy Henderson had described Nehru as "vain, sensitive, emotional and complicated";

according to a State Department profile, Liaquat's characteristics included "calmness, imperturbability, industry, energy, [and] perseverance."[73] The general Mohammed Ayub Khan, who came to power in a coup in 1958, was a favorite of Eisenhower, despite the president's sympathy for Nehru. When Eisenhower learned that Ayub was planning to switch the greens on the Rawalpindi golf course from sand to grass, he sent the general enough nursery stock of a grass called Tifgreen to do the job.[74] In the meantime, Ayub played a round of golf with Generals Nathan Twining and Omar Bradley at Burning Tree Country Club outside Washington. "During play Twining kept talking to Bradley about Pakistan and our armed forces in warm terms," Ayub noted with obvious satisfaction.[75] On a tour of South and Southeast Asia in 1961, Vice President Lyndon Johnson wrote to President Kennedy that Ayub was "seasoned as a leader where others are not; confident, straightforward and I would judge dependable."[76] What might be called the gestures of diplomacy reveal much about gender roles and the U.S.-Pakistani relationship. On visits to the United States, Pakistani officials, all of them men, wore suits and ties and openly drank alcohol, in defiance of the Muslim prohibition. Unlike Nehru, Liaquat seemed to relish reviewing the troops at the airport. When prime minister H. S. Suhrawardy came to Washington in 1957, Eisenhower hosted a stag luncheon for him.[77]

It was too much for Chester Bowles. On his second tour as ambassador to India in 1963, Bowles let loose his frustrations in his diary. "For fifteen years," he wrote, "our relationship with South Asia has suffered from our habit of sending important personages to this area who have no knowledge of the forces at work here. They come convinced that all Asians are 'inscrutable' products of the 'Inscrutable East.' And then in Karachi they meet Asians they can really understand, Asians who argue the advantages of an olive over an onion in a martini and who know friends they know in London. Here at last," Bowles went on, "are Asians who make sense, who understand our problems, who face up to the realities, who understand the menace of whatever may worry us at the moment. And so we agree to more F-104's or C130's or whatever may be currently required as political therapy to ease wounded Pakistani feelings."[78]

Most of all, as Bowles pointed out, the Pakistanis respected and valued armaments and were quite willing to take the United States's side in the Cold War in order to get them. Beginning in the early 1950s, the United States favored Pakistan as the most reliable nation in South Asia. The two countries signed an arms agreement in 1954, and the Eisenhower administration induced Pakistan to join two defense organizations: the Southeast Asia Treaty Organization (SEATO) in 1954 and the Baghdad Pact (later the Central Treaty

Organization, or CENTO) in 1955. There were strategic reasons for these alliances.[79] But it was also true that U.S. officials felt most comfortable standing with real men against the menace of communism. Pakistani leaders, who ate meat, drank liquor, and knew the value of a well-tuned military machine, were real men.

Indian men were not. Westerners had long represented Hindus as cowardly and morally phlegmatic. Gandhi and Nehru were effeminate, soft on communism, and too squeamish to take a forceful stand against evil. Ironically, this won for India's chief female leader, Nehru's daughter Indira Gandhi, a measure of Western respect. Gandhi was India's prime minister from 1966 to 1977 and again from 1980 until her assassination in 1984. Even before she took office she was admired for her toughness; as the British high commissioner in India put it in 1960, "Indira is the best man in India."[80] Despite policy differences with the Gandhi government, U.S. policy makers grudgingly admired the prime minister's backbone. Henry Kissinger noted that Richard Nixon disliked Indira Gandhi personally but "had an understanding for leaders who operated on an unsentimental assessment of the national interest. Once one cut through the strident, self-righteous rhetoric, Mrs. Gandhi had few peers in the cold-blooded calculation of the elements of power."[81]

Notes

An earlier version of this essay appeared in *Journal of American History* 81 (September 1994): 518–42.

1. Columbia Oral History Interview with Chester Bowles (1963), Chester Bowles Papers, box 396, folder 177, 480, Yale University Library, New Haven, CT.

2. Dean Acheson, *Present at the Creation: My Years in the State Department* (New York, 1969), 420.

3. Edward Said, *Orientalism* (New York, 1978), 1–9.

4. Raymond Williams, *Keywords: A Vocabulary of Culture and Society,* rev. ed. (New York, 1983), 87.

5. Clifford Geertz, *The Interpretations of Cultures* (New York, 1973), 5. The image is not inconsistent with Said's rendering of Orientalist discourse, which he refers to at one point as "an accepted grid for filtering through the Orient in Western consciousness." *Orientalism,* 6.

6. See Alan Roland, *In Search of Self in India and Japan* (Princeton, NJ, 1988), 4; and Sander L. Gilman, *Difference and Pathology: Stereotypes of Sexuality, Race, and Madness* (Ithaca, NY, 1985), 19–25.

7. Mrinalini Sinha, "Reading Mother India: Empire, Nation, and the Female Voice" (paper presented at the annual meeting of the American Historical Association, Chicago, December 1991).

8. Joan W. Scott, *Gender and the Politics of History* (New York, 1988), 32.

9. Ibid., 48.

10. Emily S. Rosenberg, "Gender," *Journal of American History* 77 (June 1990): 116–24; Emily S. Rosenberg, "Walking the Borders," *Diplomatic History* 14 (Fall 1990): 565–73; Emily S. Rosenberg, "Revisiting Dollar Diplomacy: Narratives of Money and Manliness," *Diplomatic History* 22 (Spring 1998): 155–76; Michelle Mart, "Tough Guys and American Cold War Policy: Images of Israel, 1948–1960," *Diplomatic History* 20 (Summer 1996): 357–80; Frank Costigliola, "The Nuclear Family: Tropes of Gender and Pathology in the Western Alliance," *Diplomatic History* 21 (Spring 1997): 163–83; Frank Costigliola, "'Unceasing Pressure for Penetration': Gender, Pathology, and Emotion in George Kennan's Formulation of the Cold War," *Journal of American History* 83 (March 1997): 1309–39; Robert D. Dean, "Masculinity as Ideology: John F. Kennedy and the Domestic Politics of Foreign Policy," *Diplomatic History* 22 (Winter 1998): 29–62; Kristin Hoganson, *Fighting for American Manhood: How Gender Politics Provoked the Spanish-American and Philippine-American Wars* (New Haven, CT, 1998).

11. Katherine Mayo, *Mother India* (New York, 1927).

12. Sydney Greenbie, *The Romantic East* (New York, 1930), 15.

13. Ibid., 124.

14. Richard Cronin, *Imagining India* (New York, 1989), 147. The connections between colonialism and patriarchy, including the representation of India as a woman's body, are explored by Laura E. Donaldson, *Decolonizing Feminisms: Race, Gender, and Empire-Building* (Chapel Hill, NC, 1992), 88–101.

15. Wendell Thomas, *Hinduism Invades America* (New York, 1930), 98.

16. Quoted in Lloyd I. Rudolph, "Gandhi in the Mind of America," in *Conflicting Images: India and the United States,* ed. Sulochana Raghavan Glazer and Nathan Glazer (Glenn Dale, MD, 1990), 159.

17. Henry N. Field, *From Egypt to Japan* (New York, 1877), 118–19.

18. Robert Minturn, Jr., *From New York to Delhi* (New York, 1858), 234.

19. Katherine Mayo, *The Face of Mother India* (New York, 1935), 38.

20. Roger Hilsman memorandum for the record, 22 November 1962, Hilsman Papers, box 1, John F. Kennedy Library, Boston, MA.

21. Central Intelligence Agency, Situation Report (SR)-21, "India-Pakistan," 16 September 1948, President's Secretary's Files (PSF), box 260, Harry S. Truman Library, Independence, MO.

22. Henderson to Dean Acheson, 7 April 1951, U.S. Department of State, *Foreign Relations of the United States, 1951* (Washington, 1977), 6:2139–40 (hereafter *FRUS,* with year and volume number); Bowles to Acheson, 6 December 1951, *FRUS, 1951,* 6:2191–2202.

23. Eustace Seligman to Dulles, 4 November 1954, John Foster Dulles Papers, General Correspondence and Memoranda Series, box 3, Dwight D. Eisenhower Library, Abilene, KS.

24. Eisenhower to Dulles, 16 November 1953, General Records of the Department of State, Record Group 59, file 611.90D/11–1653, National Archives II, College Park, MD.

25. Harold Isaacs, *Scratches on Our Minds: American Views of China and India* (New York, 1958), 274–75, 359–60.

26. Rosenberg, "Gender," 119.

27. "Common Sense" in *Major Problems in American Foreign Policy,* ed. Thomas G.

Paterson, 3rd ed. (Lexington, MA, 1989), 1:30–33. See also Philip Greven, *The Protestant Temperament* (New York, 1977), 351–52; Drew McCoy, *The Elusive Republic: Political Economy in Jeffersonian America* (New York, 1982), 102–3; and Clyde Griffen, "Reconstructing Masculinity from the Evangelical Revival to the Waning of Progressivism: A Speculative Synthesis," in *Meanings for Manhood: Constructions of Masculinity in Victorian America,* ed. Mark C. Carnes and Clyde Griffen (Chicago, 1990), 189.

28. Michael H. Hunt, *Ideology and American Foreign Policy* (New Haven, CT, 1987), 60–62, 66–67, 70, 75, 126, 142; John E. Johnson, *Latin America in Caricature* (Austin, TX, 1980).

29. Minturn, *From New York to Delhi,* 180, 206–7.

30. Quoted in Nathan Glazer, "Introduction," in Glazer and Glazer, *Conflicting Images,* 14. See also Rudolph, "Gandhi in the Mind of America," 159.

31. Susan Jeffords, *The Remasculinization of America: Gender and the Vietnam War* (Bloomington, IN, 1989), xii.

32. Krishnalal Shridharani, *My India, My America* (Garden City, NY, 1943), 198, 201.

33. Chester Bowles, *Ambassador's Report* (New York, 1954), 54.

34. Shridharani, *My India, My America,* 178.

35. Roland, *In Search of Self,* 267; Lloyd I. Rudolph and Susanne Hoeber Rudolph, *The Modernity of Tradition: Political Developments in India* (Chicago, 1967), 215–16; Ashis Nandy, *At the Edge of Psychology: Essays in Politics and Culture* (Oxford, UK, 1980), 37; Ashis Nandy, *The Intimate Enemy: Loss and Recovery of Self under Colonialism* (New Delhi, 1983), 4–10.

36. Nandy, *At the Edge of Psychology,* 38.

37. Charles Allen, ed., *Plain Tales from the Raj* (New York, 1985), 144. In 1948, the journalist John Frederick Muehl traveled in Maharashtra state with a circus troupe. He noted that "the percentage of homosexuality in the troupe was enormous. . . . Indians are generally quite tolerant of inversions, and it was not at all uncommon to see two men keeping house together and behaving quite like a married couple." John Frederick Muehl, *Interview with India* (New York, 1950), 168.

38. Rudolph and Rudolph, *The Modernity of Tradition,* 191–92, 214–15; Nandy, *The Intimate Enemy,* 54; Nandy, *At the Edge of Psychology,* 47–98; N. K. Gandhi, *An Autobiography, or the Story of My Experiments with Truth* (Ahmedabad, 1927), 263–75.

39. Quoted in Joan Jensen, *Passage from India: Asian Indian Immigrants in North America* (New Haven, CT, 1988), 272.

40. Nayantara Sahgal, *Prison and Chocolate Cake* (New York, 1954), 16.

41. Nehru to Frances Gunther, 8 May 1938, in *The Selected Works of Jawaharlal Nehru,* ed. Sarvepalli Gopal, series 1 (New Delhi, 1982), 14:629. One of the most popular movies ever made in India is *Mother India,* though it had nothing to do with Katherine Mayo's book. See Rosie Thomas, "Sanctity and Scandal: The Mythologization of Mother India," *Quarterly Review of Film and Video* 11 (October 1989): 11–30.

42. U.K. high commissioner in India (Sir Archibald Rye), "Review of Events in India, June–September Quarter," 27 October 1950, Foreign Office Political Correspondence, Record Class FO 371, 84204/FL1013/96, Public Record Office, Kew, England; CIA, Situation Report (SR)-21, "India-Pakistan," 16 September 1948, PSF, box 260.

43. Chester Bowles, typescript "New Delhi Diary," entry for 18 September 1963, Bowles Papers, box 392, folder 159.

44. Greenbie, *The Romantic East,* 95.

45. Veena Das, "The Imaging of Indian Women: Missionaries and Journalists," in Glazer and Glazer, *Conflicting Images,* 208–11.

46. Dr. Harland Wilson, "Kali–Dread Goddess of Life and Death," *Fate* 3 (March 1950): 10–15. In the wake of the postpartition riots, a *Time* magazine cover depicted the subcontinent itself as Kali, stabbing herself in the heart. *Time,* 27 October 1947.

47. Isaacs, *Scratches on Our Minds,* 280–81.

48. *The Times of India,* 15 November and 4 December 1953.

49. Robert Trumbull, *As I See India* (New York, 1956), 122.

50. Isaacs, *Scratches on Our Minds,* 312.

51. C. L. Sulzberger, *A Long Row of Candles* (Toronto, 1969), 794.

52. Sarvepalli Gopal, *Jawaharlal Nehru, A Biography,* vol. 3, *1956–1964* (New Delhi, 1984), 189–90. According to his personal secretary, Nehru had an active heterosexual social life. M. O. Mathai, *Reminiscences of the Nehru Age* (New Delhi, 1978), 201–11.

53. *Times of India,* 14 December 1953; G. Morris Carstairs, *The Twice-Born: A Study of a Community of High-Caste Hindus* (London, 1957), 46–47; Myron Weiner, "India: Two Political Cultures," in *Political Culture and Political Development,* ed. Lucian Pye and Sydney Verba (Princeton, NJ, 1965), 214.

54. Nehru's address to the Los Angeles World Affairs Council, 14 November 1961, quoted in the *Times of India,* 15 November 1961.

55. Dennis Merrill, *Bread and the Ballot: The United States and India's Economic Development, 1947–1963* (Chapel Hill, NC, 1990), 40.

56. Henderson to Dean Acheson, 18 June 1949, Henderson Papers, box 8, Library of Congress, Washington, DC.

57. Ann C. Whitman to John Foster Dulles, 30 August 1956, Dulles Papers, Memoranda Series, box 5, Eisenhower Library; George McGhee, *Envoy to the Middle World: Adventures in Diplomacy* (New York, 1983), 47; Selig S. Harrison, "Nehru's Visit in Retrospect," *New Republic,* 31 December 1956, 7–8.

58. Gopal, *Jawaharlal Nehru,* 3:190.

59. H. W. Brands, *The Specter of Neutralism: The United States and the Emergence of the Third World, 1947–1960* (New York, 1989), 128–32.

60. "Indo-American Relations: Second Thoughts," *Eastern Economist* 26 (13 January 1956): 45–46.

61. Eisenhower memorandum of conversations with Prime Minister Nehru, 17–18 December 1956, Eisenhower Papers, Ann Whitman File, International Series, box 28, Eisenhower Library.

62. Reported in J. R. A. Bottomley (British embassy, Washington) to J. O. McCormick (Foreign Office), 18 September 1956, FO 371, 123588/DL10345/24.

63. *Times of India,* 19 December 1956.

64. Gopal, *Jawaharlal Nehru,* 3:190.

65. Walt W. Rostow, *Eisenhower, Kennedy, and Foreign Aid* (Austin, TX, 1985), chap. 1.

66. Henry Fairlie, *The Kennedy Promise* (Garden City, NY, 1973), 185.

67. Gopal, *Jawaharlal Nehru,* 3:189.

68. Ibid., 189–90; the *Hindu,* 9 November 1961; John Kenneth Galbraith, *Ambassador's Journal* (New York, 1969), 227.

69. Arthur M. Schlesinger, Jr., *A Thousand Days* (Boston, 1965), 526.

70. Oral History Interview with Elbert G. Mathews, 42–43, Truman Library.

71. Isaacs, *Scratches on our Minds*, 276–77.

72. McGhee, *Envoy to the Middle World*, 93.

73. Henderson to Acheson, 18 June 1949, Henderson Papers, box 8; Department of State, "Background Memoranda on Visit to the United States of Liaquat Ali Khan," 14 April 1950, RG 59, lot file 54D341, "Records of Office of South Asian Affairs, 1939–1953."

74. Eisenhower to Mohammed Ayub Khan, 7 December 1960, Whitman File, International Series, box 38.

75. Mohammed Ayub Khan, *Friends Not Masters: A Political Autobiography* (New York, 1967), 59.

76. Johnson to Kennedy, 23 May 1961, President's Office Files, Special Correspondence Series, box 80, Kennedy Library.

77. Dulles to Eisenhower, 8 July 1957, *Declassified Documents Reference System*, 1989: 000863.

78. Chester Bowles, typescript "New Delhi Diary," entry for 9 August 1963, Bowles Papers, box 392, folder 159.

79. Robert J. McMahon, "United States Cold War Strategy in South Asia: Making a Military Commitment to Pakistan, 1947–1954," *Journal of American History* 75 (December 1988): 812–40.

80. Malcolm MacDonald, quoted in Taya Zinkin, *Reporting India* (London, 1962), 13.

81. Henry Kissinger, *White House Years* (Boston, 1979), 848.

Economic Development

Like Boxing with Joe Louis:
Nelson Rockefeller in Venezuela, 1945–1948

DARLENE RIVAS

The congressional debate was impassioned. At issue was the role of a North American capitalist in a Latin American nation whose economy was woefully dependent on a single product. In revulsion, delegates hurled epithets at the Yankee. He was a "Drácula," a "venerable gangster," an "imperialist at our doors." Furthermore, this capitalist was the grandson of an infamous robber baron. As one delegate warned, "The heirs of this international filibuster are those who come into Venezuela to save us from ruin, they are men in whom the [government] has placed the exploitation of agriculture, of livestock, of fish, and that which is most grave, the distribution and importation of food." Members of the ruling party responded by insisting that they would vigilantly protect the national interest. Many delegates remained unconvinced. "A man can be very brave, but if he confronts a tiger, the tiger will scratch him," warned one delegate. A leading Communist representative, Juan Bautista Fuenmayor, suggested another vivid metaphor: Venezuela tangling with Nelson Rockefeller was "like boxing with Joe Louis."[1]

This abbreviated account of a Venezuelan event in 1948 highlights common stereotypes of U.S.–Latin American relations. U.S. private interests endangered Latin American nations' economic sovereignty, Latin American governments refused to recognize the threat, and the defense of the national interest against U.S. imperial domination was led by indigenous communists or others on the left. There is truth in this portrait, but it is also a source of much confusion. Since the advent of Roosevelt's Good Neighbor policy in the 1930s and World War II, the United States had encouraged private interests to acknowledge the sovereignty of Latin American governments over their natural resources. As James Park has shown, the 1930s Depression momentarily checked U.S. confidence about the nation's ability to shape poor "backward" nations in its image, leading to efforts at cooperation rather than confrontation or manipulation. Indeed, some in the United States acknowledged the legitimacy of Latin American complaints of exploitation and supported attempts to industrialize and diversify national economies.[2] During World War II, the United States led Latin American governments to believe that cooperation in the wartime alliance would bring economic rewards after the war in the form of loans and technical assistance for that purpose. In the immediate aftermath of the war, however, Washington again left individuals and corporations to shape the relationship between the United States and Latin America. These private groups pursued their ambiguous mixture of self-interest and altruistic goals much as they had for decades. Nevertheless, there were differences. While Allied victory restored U.S. optimism in nation building, some Americans demonstrated a greater sensitivity to nationalist aspirations in what would soon be called the "Third World." Private U.S. interests and State Department and embassy officials in the 1940s, well aware of increasing "economic nationalism," formulated views on its meaning to U.S. interests and often responded by making concessions in order to maintain some influence. For some, certain expressions of economic nationalism were a justified response to past exploitation by U.S. interests and governments.

Scholars, on the other hand, have often identified economic nationalism in the Third World as a "force" that U.S. leaders "misunderstood," mistaking it for communism or socialism.[3] This portrayal implies that nationalism is a monolithic phenomenon across the developing world, that it arose from the left wing of the political spectrum alone, and that it took much the same form in varying regions and nations. It also suggests that Americans were consistently shortsighted in confronting nationalism. This vagueness in identifying the sources of nationalism obscures understanding of exactly what was "misunderstood" as well as the variety of U.S. responses. Important questions to ask include: Were there distinctive sources of economic nationalism? How did North Americans respond to competing expressions of economic nationalism, and what other options might they have had? How do national cases compare? Examination of domestic politics of Third World nations reveals differences of opinion within their societies about the best means to develop their economies and societies. Debate within developing countries on relations with the United States and the world economy often took place in the context of internal struggles for power. Historians such as Kyle Longley have paid close attention to domestic politics, observing more closely the sources and complexity of economic nationalism and the varied U.S. responses to nationalist expressions. Such works complicate the image of the United States as consistently misunderstanding Third World nationalism.[4]

Unfortunately, there is little scholarly focus on the immediate post–World War II era. There are important studies of the Eisenhower administration's role in toppling the Jacobo Arbenz government in 1954 (and the role of private interests in that case), that same administration's support of dictators, and U.S. hostility to the communist turn of Castro's Cuban revolution.[5] One reason for the interest in the Eisenhower administration is the clear impact of the Cold War on relations with Latin America during the 1950s. Additionally, the emphasis of diplomatic historians on government policy not surprisingly leaves them relatively uninterested in an era in which U.S. government attention to the region decreased dramatically after the high points of Roosevelt's administration, with its Good Neighbor policy, and World War II, with its imperatives of managing hemispheric solidarity. The gap in the literature is unfortunate, for at least two reasons. The leap to the 1950s neglects continuities in U.S. policies and in domestic Latin American politics from the 1930s to the 1960s and beyond. Moreover, historians of foreign relations have bypassed a significant moment in Latin American history. Leslie Bethel and Ian Roxborough have called the critical immediate postwar period an important "conjuncture" in the region. Their work describes a wave of democratic-leftist movements that swept into power in 1944–45, creating a window of opportunity for social democracy on the continent.[6] The implication is that for social democracy to endure, U.S. officials needed to respond to rising aspirations for national economic development. Instead, the United States repeatedly delayed a hemispheric economic conference and insisted that Latin Americans rely on private investment to develop their economies. The United States did little to prevent the turn to dictatorship in the late 1940s.[7] A further implication is that the United States could and should have prevented this shift.

This chapter examines this important era through one case study: the postwar activities of Nelson Rockefeller in Venezuela. Rockefeller's awareness of Latin American aspirations for national economic development dated from personal experience in the 1930s and World War II. Shortly after the war, he embarked on projects designed to promote economic development in the region. He focused on two nations of vital importance to the United States: Brazil, with its strategic location and tremendous size, and Venezuela, with its vast reserves of oil.[8] This essay details Rockefeller's relationship with Venezuela's postwar government, headed by the nationalist and democratic leftist party Acción Democática (AD) during the *trienio* (1945–48). The AD-led government is a classic case supporting Bethel and Roxborough's "conjuncture" thesis. This essay argues that Rockefeller and AD leaders shared a vision for the national economic development of Venezuela. Although important differences between them existed, they believed in technical solutions to human problems and a pragmatic approach to questions of political economy. Their vision for Venezuela's future as a liberal democracy with a modern, diversified economy necessitated a nonexploitative, reformed capitalism. Furthermore, despite, and because of, Venezuelan government support for his projects, Rockefeller faced intense pressure from other forms of economic nationalism that differed from the views of AD leaders. This pressure affected Rockefeller's projects, contributing to their partial failure. Although U.S. policy regarding economic development in Latin America required that Latin Americans look to private investment, U.S. officials, preoccupied with their expanding commitments in Europe and Asia, only half-heartedly encouraged innovative approaches to private development efforts.

The rise of economic nationalism in Venezuela dates from 1928, when student protests erupted against dictator Juan Vicente Gómez (1908–1935). Disturbed by Gómez's unscrupulous dealings with the foreign-owned oil companies that flocked to Venezuela in the 1920s, many young Venezuelans who would come of age politically in the postwar era critiqued Venezuela's dependence on foreign interests.[9] As time went on they were particularly disturbed by the economic distortions caused by Venezuela's "monoculture," in this case reliance on petroleum revenues. After Gómez's death in 1935, governments and government opponents alike decried the decline of agriculture, including the traditionally strong livestock, coffee, and cacao sectors, and the movement of agricultural laborers from fields to oil camps and nearby shanty towns. The rallying cry of economic nationalists was "sembrar el petróleo" or "sow the oil." Venezuela needed to rebuild and protect the agricultural sector by harnessing oil company profits.[10]

It was in this environment that Nelson Rockefeller first came to Venezuela in 1937 as a director of Creole Petroleum, the Venezuelan subsidiary of Standard Oil of New Jersey. The critique against foreign-owned oil companies convinced Rockefeller that Creole needed to provide for the well-being of its employees and act to ameliorate some of the appalling conditions near the oil camps. Mexico's expropriation of foreign oil companies in 1938 made an impression, as did the New Deal political milieu at home. The message seemed clear: if business did not consider the economic welfare of all people, social pressure would move states toward planned economies, and if American businesses wished to continue to find open markets for investment abroad, corporations would have to change their behavior and improve their images. While he convinced Creole executives to make some effort to improve their public relations, the company primarily responded to government demands for improved conditions for workers.[11]

The ambitious, confident, and idealistic young Rockefeller even created his own company to contribute to economic diversification, the Compañía de Fomento Venezolano or Venezuelan Development Company. He hoped to make money while establishing a reputation as a progressive businessman with sound entrepreneurial instincts and a social conscience. As he sought opportunities, he encountered obstacles. In one case with implications for his postwar experiences, he halted plans for a "socially responsible" food retail center, designed to counteract the tradition of hoarding food for the purpose of speculation. Consultants advised that political backlash from angry commercial groups would be too severe. Despite such setbacks, during this period Rockefeller developed a fascination with Latin America, its people and its cultures.[12]

War interrupted Rockefeller's Venezuelan plans. Concerned over Axis political and economic influence in Latin America, he served as the coordinator of the Office of Inter-American Affairs (OIAA) in the Roosevelt administration and as assistant secretary of state for Latin American affairs in 1945. During his stay in Washington, Rockefeller identified with individuals he viewed as sympathetic to the needs of Latin America, such as President Franklin D. Roosevelt and Vice President Henry A. Wallace. Despite other more visible activities, one of Rockefeller's most important accomplishments was the founding by the OIAA of a government corporation, the Institute of Inter-American Affairs (IIAA), that represented a new departure in government-sponsored technical assistance for development. Previous programs had emphasized the development of strategic materials, such as rubber, or complementary products, such as coffee, that would not compete with North American agriculture. In 1943, the IIAA created a "Basic Economy" department, which encouraged the development of agriculture based on a country's food needs rather than its place in the international market. Based on Rockefeller Foundation principles of self-help, the IIAA emphasized cooperative projects in such areas as food supply, health, and sanitation, for which foreign assistance would be phased out, leaving the assisted nation with programs it could continue to fund and operate on its own.[13]

As the war ended, Rockefeller's wartime experiences refined his prewar strategy to promote economic development. He decided to serve as an example to other private interests, leading the way in filling the gap left by the reduction in U.S. government interest and involvement in Latin America. He wanted to combine the nonprofit activities of the traditional philanthropic organization with a new set: profit-making companies with social objectives. He envisioned these companies as small model enterprises that would reinvest earnings to increase production and reduce prices. He and his associates, most of whom had experience with the wartime OIAA, eventually decided on two distinct programs, the nonprofit American International Association (AIA) and the for-profit International Basic Economy Corporation (IBEC).[14] The AIA would follow the cooperative model established by the IIAA. IBEC projects would serve as models to local and foreign investors, using modern techniques to demonstrate that profits could be derived in previously low-profit sectors of a nation's basic economy.

After initial planning for programs in Venezuela and Brazil, Rockefeller and his associates began their activities in Brazil. Then, in late 1946, they stepped up their Venezuelan efforts, developing a program with significant differences. First, Rockefeller viewed the Venezuelan program as something of an emergency measure, a direct response to a perceived food crisis that threatened to destabilize the new government.[15] Second, the oil companies in Venezuela put up large amounts of the capital involved. This provided the means for larger, more ambitious projects. Third, the negotiations for entry occurred at the highest levels of the federal government in Venezuela. Last, the Venezuelan government participated directly in the IBEC venture through its development agency, the Corporación Venezolano de Fomento (CVF). Armed with greater available resources and more extensive contacts at the national level than in Brazil, Rockefeller believed he could have a more significant impact on the smaller Venezuelan economy.

The new government was led by Provisional President Rómulo Betancourt and leaders of his political party, Acción Democrática (AD).[16] They came to power after participating with young army colonels in overturning the progressive but oligarchic Isaías Medina Angarita administration. While they asserted power by force, AD leaders proposed to expand representative democracy by franchising previously excluded groups, which led in December 1947 to the election of the first truly "popular" president in Venezuelan history, novelist Rómulo Gallegos. AD's success was directly attributable to Betancourt. His former career included arrest and exile by President Gómez in 1928, membership in the Costa Rican Communist Party, and a subsequent break with the communists. A brilliant organizer, he guided AD's growth through its legalization under President Medina and its active recruitment of a multiclass coalition throughout all regions of Venezuela. He built his reputation in part through harsh criticism of U.S. oil companies and the government's subservience to international capital. Indeed, in 1939, Betancourt had written derisively of the visiting Nelson Rockefeller as "Johnny Ten Cents," a hypocrite pretending to play a humanitarian role while oblivious to the real needs of the Venezuelan people.[17]

Once in power, Betancourt and AD responded to conditions of economic dependency and distorted economic development through policies designed to promote economic self-sufficiency and greater economic bargaining power in Venezuela's foreign relations. The government extended the work of previous administrations in gaining greater revenues from foreign-owned oil companies by enforcing the 50–50 profit-sharing policy of the Medina administration. In addition, the government negotiated with the oil companies to build refineries on Venezuelan territory and attempted to barter oil for Argentine meat. They established a Greater Colombian Merchant Fleet with Colombia and Ecuador to reduce dependence on the U.S. Merchant Marine. The government also established an independent development agency, the Corporación Venezolana de Fomento, modeled loosely on a Chilean development agency.

The CVF's purpose was to use the state to modernize the economy through both industrial and agricultural projects. The CVF, under the leadership of its president Alejandro Oropeza Castillo and the minister of development, Juan Pablo Pérez Alfonso, attempted to develop aspects of the economy either that they viewed as unsuitable for private investment or in which private capital was reluctant to invest. The CVF's methods reflected Betancourt's assumptions regarding Venezuela's capitalists. He viewed them as parasites, speculative and untrustworthy, lacking sufficient nationalist feeling to invest in productive enterprises for the public good. In contrast, he saw elements of foreign capital as progressive. One aim of the CVF was to show local capitalists that investments could provide social benefits. In the long term Betancourt hoped to reduce Venezuela's dependence on foreign capital; for the short term he had more faith in the government's ability to harness foreign than domestic capital for economic development.[18]

In light of these views, Betancourt moderated his anti-imperialist rhetoric. He and AD leaders immediately assured U.S. embassy officials and U.S. and British oil company executives that they had no plans for major changes in oil policy. Betancourt believed that in the short term Venezuela lacked sufficient technical knowledge and skills to run the petroleum companies. He actively sought private foreign capital to assist in the development of other aspects of Venezuela's economy, from steel to grain elevators. He also attempted to pursue a policy of "social peace." To reassure powerful economic groups, in 1946 he established an "Economic Council" composed of business and financial leaders to advise the government on economic policy.

While the AD-led government pursued controversial land and education reform, promoted further organization of labor, and unlike most other democratic-leftist movements of the period, promoted the organization of peasants, Betancourt discouraged strikes.[19]

In 1946, two urgent and intransigent problems faced the new government: a food shortage and the high cost of living. In Venezuela, the booming oil industry pumped petroleum revenues into the economy, generating wage disparities and the highest cost of living in the Western Hemisphere. A rapidly expanding population and the difficulties of postwar economic adjustment contributed to a food shortage.[20] Betancourt pursued a variety of avenues to increase imports and local food production, most of them with little success.[21] He looked to the United States for assistance. In addition to petroleum revenues, Venezuela, like other Latin American nations immediately following World War II, had dollar reserves from sales to the Allies. The CVF attempted to import agricultural machinery, steel, and other equipment to modernize its agriculture.[22] Such equipment was largely unavailable.

Disappointed by their failed attempts to purchase capital equipment and by quotas limiting food imports from the United States, AD leaders asked Rockefeller to serve as an intermediary between the U.S. government, U.S. firms, and the Venezuelan government. Rockefeller could only repeat what U.S. officials had already told AD leaders: Venezuela's food needs were carefully considered in light of the high demands on the world's food supply, and reconversion to peacetime production proceeded apace, but domestic and international demand for equipment was high. Similar refrains frustrated other Latin American governments.[23] While reluctant to take on the role of go-between, Rockefeller welcomed discussions about fishing, farming, food distribution, and other projects that matched his goals for IBEC. From Betancourt's perspective, Rockefeller's IBEC provided a means to approach both the food problem and a goal of AD petroleum policy: persuading the oil companies to use some of their profits to address social and economic problems. It was this aim that facilitated Rockefeller's plans to undertake his projects in Venezuela, since oil company executives agreed to contribute capital.[24] In January 1947, Rockefeller came to Venezuela to work out a mutually acceptable arrangement.[25]

The venture appealed to U.S. embassy officials and prominent AD economic development planners because it seemed to promise a reformed and reforming capitalism. The New Deal ethos of a capitalism leashed by government to benefit all people, whatever its basis in reality, still had a strong appeal in Venezuela, and U.S. officials understood this. An embassy memo to the State Department noted, "The impression conveyed by Rockefeller that

permanent values of democratic political institutions can and must be pre-
served by constructive adjustment of the economic structure gave the people
a new concept of capital's functions."[26] Enthusiastic representatives of the
government, including Betancourt, Oropeza, and Pérez Alfonso, seemed to
concur. Betancourt assured Rockefeller that only a "liberal democratic approach" rather than the approaches of the "communists or reactionaries"
could meet Venezuela's needs.[27] Oropeza wrote of his "great hopes" for their
cooperation, adding that intelligent leaders could save "the capitalistic regime from the misfortunes which it suffers from the overwhelming social
upheaval throughout the world." Pérez Alfonso considered gaining Rockefeller's assistance a "triumph for Venezuela" and praised the "technical and
administrative aid of the North American people" in assisting the people of
Latin America.[28]

Despite this support from influential AD leaders, opposition to Rockefeller's plans emerged. From critics on both the right and the left, and among
members of AD, came questions regarding both Rockefeller's intentions and
the motives of the participating oil companies.[29] Prominent local businessmen objected to extensive government investment. Opponents on both the
right and the left expressed concern that Rockefeller and the oil companies
would gain what they called a "monopolistic" control of the economy because of the extension of foreign-financed activities into agriculture and
industry. In response, in May the government prepared a "Joint Memorandum," outlining conditions for cooperation with the Rockefeller ventures.[30]

In the memo the government asked that the Venezuela Basic Economy
Corporation (VBEC, IBEC's Venezuelan subsidiary) reserve to itself only 50
percent of its capital, the remainder to be provided by Venezuelan private
investors and the CVF. It also demanded that dividends be limited to 6
percent. Betancourt and Perez Alfonso later argued that just as the U.S. government limited profits on public utilities, the Venezuelan public should be
protected by their government against unfair markups on basic goods. They
also required that within ten years after VBEC established the companies,
control of them should be sold to Venezuelan investors.[31]

Rockefeller responded quickly to protect what he considered the fundamental basis of free enterprise—the growth of private initiative through the
profit incentive. He also objected to carving out an economic sphere subject
to limited profits by private investors. This would set a precedent that might
be extended to other sectors, such as the oil industry. He pointed out that the
oil companies were already limited to 4 percent of earnings from VBEC.[32]
Rockefeller agreed to offer 50–50 capital participation through ownership of
preferred stock by CVF, with later sale of common stock to the public. While

he hoped to set an example of privately capitalized development, Rockefeller accepted government investment for political reasons. He even preferred government to extensive private Venezuelan investment until the projects' success seemed assured. Rockefeller's prewar experiences with a hotel venture in Venezuela made him apprehensive about the response of local investors if the companies failed or were slow to take off.[38] But a proviso that government-held stock would later be sold to the Venezuelan public reflected his concern that state involvement be only a temporary measure. In private, Rockefeller had asserted that he hoped to "halt the trend" of a South American "tendency to leave all developmental work to government agencies." Rockefeller had great faith in a capitalist system with a social conscience. He was optimistic that such a system would demonstrate its value over a state-dominated economy.[33]

Rockefeller also assured the Venezuelan negotiators that he would keep capital funds in Venezuela and would eventually offer the majority of common stock to Venezuelan private investors. For their part, the Venezuelans conceded the vital issue of unlimited profits and VBEC control of any companies created. Rockefeller believed he had not compromised his "basic principles," and AD leaders decided that the deal addressed their major concerns. Probably more important, they had a political defense against charges that the government was carelessly giving up Venezuela's economic sovereignty.[34]

For the next eight months or so, the public response to Rockefeller's activities fell into a predictable pattern. In general, left editorials were harshly critical of the Rockefeller presence. From the right came occasional criticism of government investment in the projects, but general satisfaction with the agreement. Even the presidential campaign in the fall of 1947 fit into this pattern. Leaders of the moderate-to-conservative Christian Democratic Comite de Organización Política Electoral Independiente (COPEI) said little about Rockefeller during the campaign; they and AD were absorbed in mutual recriminations regarding outbreaks of physical violence between COPEI and AD members. The center-to-left Unión República Democrática (URD) and the two factions of the Communist Party in Venezuela continued to express their concerns about Rockefeller. To URD leader Jóvito Villalba, the Rockefeller enterprises were "a demonstration of the imperialistic policy of the Government" and "a step backward for the country."[35]

AD won a resounding victory at the polls on 14 December with the election of Gallegos to the presidency.[36] With confidence, VBEC released publicity on 16 January and 4 February regarding the organization of the farming (Productora Agropecuaria Compañía Anónima, PACA) and fishing (Pesquerías Caribe Compañía Anónima, PESCA) companies. U.S. Ambassador Walter Donnelly reported to the State Department that "today's press coverage is simply the public announcement of an accomplished fact." Betancourt told Donnelly that he had full confidence in VBEC and blamed renewed opposition attacks on communists.[37] At this point, most criticism was indeed from the left of AD, although not only from communists. It is significant that the fishing and farming projects posed little threat to Venezuelan business interests. The government and VBEC were the only groups attempting to organize and modernize the fishing industry beyond the efforts of individual fishermen. Further, as an editorial in the centrist *El Universal* observed, the farms were located on so-called abandoned lands, and the initial risk was potentially great. The editorial noted that few Venezuelans would risk capital on enterprises with such low profit margins. In addition, business and financial interests approved of the provision that private Venezuelan capital would eventually displace foreign capital and the fact that the CVF's ownership through preferred stock meant the government corporation would not run a risk with public money.[38]

For a time, then, it seemed that intrusive political problems were minimal. While in Venezuela to attend the 15 February inauguration of Gallegos, Rockefeller and CVF President Oropeza reached a tentative agreement on CVF participation in a food distribution company, Compañia Anónima Distribuidora de Alimentos (CADA), pending approval by the CVF directors. Rockefeller envisioned CADA as a network of warehouses and supermarkets supplied through both imports and local production. VBEC officials hoped CADA would meet the demands of AD and the oil companies for more and cheaper imports of food in the short term to supply the expanding food deficit. As early as July 1947, Pérez Alfonso and Oropeza had given "informal approval," expressing their hope that the company could begin operations quickly.[39] Then, during the election campaign, AD leaders had developed a cautious approach to CADA and a possible deal with a regional milk company, which they correctly saw as subject to greater political attack than the farming and fishing companies. The CVF had pressed VBEC officials to wait to organize CADA for "obvious reasons." VBEC officials reluctantly agreed, although they feared delays would mean heavy losses since they had already purchased land and equipment.[40]

After the election but before final approval came on CADA, a major crisis occurred in VBEC's public relations. On 9 March Caracas newspapers published articles on CADA. The source of information was a press release from Houston, Texas, announcing plans for the distribution company and explaining that it would import products through a Houston firm, Henke and Pilot. The news that Rockefeller would begin his efforts to increase the food supply not by purchase of local products but through imports mobilized Rockefeller opponents.

Much of the criticism now came from the commercial sector. The Sindicato Patronal de Comerciantes (Commercial Employers' Association) announced that it opposed Rockefeller because CADA enjoyed unfair influence in gaining imports: "A competitor like Rockefeller, with international political influence, with power to influence transportation of all kinds, with possibilities of investing millions even at risk of loss, cannot be resisted by criollo [Venezuelan] commerce."[41] A representative of the Corporación de Comercio Mayorista (Wholesale Trade Corporation), made similar claims. Rockefeller could provision the market cheaply, he suggested, but the cost would be "the ruin of thousands of Venezuelans and the domination of our markets by foreign capital."[42] An article in the editorially conservative *Últimas Notícias* noted growing collaboration between the Wholesale Trade Corporation and the government's National Supply Commission; Venezuelans did not need "foreign intervention or its capital."[43]

The government and AD leaders did their part to minimize the damage. When the Commercial Employers' Association in a 12 March meeting passed resolutions "to petition the President, Congress, and the Municipal Council to declare [VBEC personnel] 'persona non grata' in the country," the Senate and Municipal Council four days later voted along party lines to deny the petitions.[44] The AD-dominated and largest labor organization, Confederación de Trabajores Venezolanos (CTV), approved the agreement. An editorial in the party organ, *El País,* accused VBEC's opponents of "political maneuvering, energized by the Communist Party in fulfillment of international orders and with the help of URD."[45]

While AD attacked the extreme left by suggesting it was under Soviet influence, which also had the advantage of highlighting AD's pursuit of national as opposed to foreign interests, it pursued a strategy of appeasement with the right. AD leaders scheduled meetings for VBEC officials with the Fedecamaras (Chamber of Commerce) and the Economic Council.[46] When Venezuelan importers expressed concern that Rockefeller would use up part of their nation's U.S. export quotas on essential agricultural products, VBEC official Bill Coles reassured importers "emphatically that all of our export permits had been procured outside of the Venezuelan quota." The council then approved the CADA program.[47]

After the March crisis Rockefeller traveled almost monthly to Venezuela for discussion with VBEC personnel, government officials, and businessmen. He agreed to cooperate with other distribution organizations in the outlying areas of the country, promised to assist Venezuelan importers in establishing connections in the United States, and reassured them that the United States had given him "encouraging promises" that Venezuela would continue to receive basic products beyond its assigned quota. VBEC now began to find Venezuelan partners, such as the previously anti-Rockefeller Wholesale Trade Corporation, for its distribution company.[48]

Rockefeller's public relations generally improved, but the Gallegos government faced escalating attacks from the press and the opposition parties and growing restlessness among military leaders. Even the centrist papers found little to praise and much to disparage regarding AD policy and performance. AD's oil policy, agrarian reform, and labor policy worried influential Venezuelans, and the political parties complained of AD's domination of the government. The press published accusations of corruption and misuse of public monies.[49]

As the political crisis intensified and neared its climax, AD's opponents had an opportunity to scrutinize the Rockefeller relationship with the government. At an extraordinary joint session on 28 October, the Venezuelan Congress debated and voted on the *Memória y Cuenta* (annual report, including plans and budget for the following year) of the Ministry of Development. While the VBEC projects were a small portion of the entire Development Ministry's program, AD's opposition turned the "Rockefeller Plan" into a central focus of the debate. The debate highlighted the main trends in the criticism of Rockefeller/government collaboration that had developed during the preceding two years. Regardless of the particulars, there was an undercurrent of frustration and opposition to AD and its strategies of governance.

Pérez Alfonso and AD Secretary of Organization Alberto Carnevali defended the government by pointing to the conditions placed on VBEC, namely, the ten-year proviso, the 50 percent Venezuelan ownership rule, and the general oversight by the CVF through its participation in the projects. They argued that a diligent national government, unlike the corrupt ones of the past, could prevent exploitative practices by foreign investors; under AD oversight, Rockefeller could not monopolize Venezuela's basic economy.[50] Opponents from all the other parties continued to raise doubts about the ability of the government to manage Rockefeller or hold him to the conditions. The tiger and pugilist metaphors exemplify the intensity with which opponents illustrated the danger Rockefeller presumably posed.

The stormy debate demonstrated the fault lines on the question of Venezuela's economic development. URD and the communists opposed in principle any foreign investment outside the petroleum sector; AD and COPEI agreed that Venezuela lacked needed technical expertise and capital, but COPEI members questioned the need for foreign investment in competition with Venezuelan nationals in commerce and agriculture. Indeed, the perceived threat to Venezuelan merchants through competitive advantages concerned members of all the opposition parties. COPEI and URD delegates alike observed that, while some Venezuelan importers and wholesalers were not acting in the national interest, many loyal, "democratic" Venezuelan merchants were. Jóvito Villalba complained that the government should stop speculators itself, not bring in Rockefeller to deal with them.[51]

The debate had no real significance for AD policy. The new 1947 constitution, like previous Venezuelan ones, provided for a strong executive. Rule by decree was the norm. AD dominated the bureaucracy, particularly the Ministry of Development. Besides, AD's vast majorities and party discipline ensured passage of its legislation. In the case of the *Memória,* the opposition could merely insist that their objections be noted.

One group possessed significant means to alter the balance of power. The military pressed the Gallegos government to replace cabinet members. Gallegos refused and suspended constitutional guarantees on 20 November. On 24 November 1948, the military overthrew the Gallegos government. Despite AD's popular following there was little resistance; most Venezuelans did not anticipate that the event represented the beginning of ten years of increasingly harsh military dictatorship. The three-man military junta, composed of Lt. Colonels Carlos Delgado Chalbaud, Marcos Pérez Jiménez, and Felipe Llovera Páez, announced its reasons for the coup as the political turmoil of AD rule, the monopolistic control of offices by AD and its interference with the military, and its incitement to unrest of workers and peasants. URD, which initially favored the coup, insisted that the collaboration of AD with Nelson Rockefeller demonstrated AD's failure to govern in Venezuela's national interest.[52]

Gallegos mishandled the growing opposition from the military. And AD alienated the other parties by refusing to share power in significant ways. In light of AD's huge popular support—it received over 70 percent of the vote in elections for the Constituent Assembly in 1946, for the president in 1947, and for the Municipal Council in 1948—the other parties felt shut out from power. In their party organs before the coup, URD and COPEI indirectly suggested military intervention.[53] As for the communists, the faction known as the Blacks supported the coup and were later favored by the military government as a counter to AD among labor unions. The scholarly consensus is that the military, uneasy with the intensity of political conflict and concerned about the direction of AD's policies and "one-party rule," found support (or at least no opposition) from the other parties, economic elites, and the Catholic Church.[54]

Gallegos charged the U.S. government and the oil companies with complicity in the coup; he retracted his statement after reassurances from President Truman. Scholars generally agree that the United States undertook no direct involvement. Regarding the respective role of U.S. and domestic interests, Stephen Rabe concludes, "If they [adecos] had respected the power of Venezuela's traditional elites as much as they respected U.S. power, the adecos perhaps would not have suffered a decade of exile."[55] The large oil companies did not support the coup, but they pushed for U.S. recognition of the military junta to promote stability. In the end, their interests were temporarily served, since the military halted the gradual trend toward greater national control of Venezuela's oil. In Latin America, and in Europe, the labor-left was in retreat. As the conflict between the United States and the Soviet Union intensified, the Truman administration was loath to antagonize potential allies by refusing recognition.[56]

In the coup's aftermath, VBEC officials debated the future of their projects under the military junta. Not unlike the Truman administration, they worried about how quickly to establish a working relationship with the new government.[57] Junta President Delgado Chalbaud assured Ambassador Donnelly that the government supported the Rockefeller projects.[58] But VBEC-government relations were strained. When Rockefeller entertained Betancourt in his New York home in Pocantico Hills, news of the dinner reached Venezuela; VBEC officials scrambled to explain. Thereafter, Rockefeller maintained a cordial but distant friendship with Betancourt.[59] Actually, the new government did not place a high priority on VBEC. In a June discussion on VBEC's future, Miguel Moreno, secretary of the junta, admitted he knew little about the details of the VBEC-government relationship. He noted the dismal financial picture of the enterprises and continued attacks on them. Characteristically for the "unity"-minded junta, he observed that the government wished "to divest VBEC from all politics." After a reorganization, the CVF would formulate a policy on VBEC. (Of course, this reorganization would purge the CVF of AD members and sympathizers.) VBEC representative Bill Coles departed with the perception that "in view of the attacks (on VBEC), the Government is somewhat embarrassed at being a partner of VBEC's and . . . they might want to alter the fundamental agreements at sometime in the future."[60] After prolonged negotiation, the government sold its preferred stock to VBEC in 1950 and 1951 in exchange for cash and some fixed assets. The government came out about even, while the oil companies bore the brunt of the losses.[61] Rockefeller consolidated the holdings, continuing operation of the milk and supermarket companies on a much smaller scale.

VBEC's weak showing was partly caused by poor decisions by Rockefeller and VBEC officials as well as the difficulty of pioneering in the establishment of modern, productive, and profitable agricultural enterprises in Venezuela in the late 1940s. It was also the result of the interplay of these factors and the nationalist politics faced by VBEC. Rockefeller was eager to work with AD leaders in projects of mutual interest and prove that his companies could make profits *and* solve Venezuelan needs. In the ensuing haste to achieve these objectives and forgetting his goal of developing small enterprises, Rockefeller's company struggled to pursue "sound" business policies, stay out of political controversies, and manage public relations. A volatile mix resulted from the spotlight of attention and opposition: both mistakes and high expectations. The companies overextended financially, burdening themselves with costly assets from hasty purchasing. Nationalist politics contributed to the severe financial difficulties, causing delays in the organization of CADA and capitalization of Frigorífica, C.A., created with 75 percent CVF ownership to hold the property that CADA then leased. The rationale behind this company was that CADA would benefit from government capital without the political risks. The government also declined to contribute capital to the milk company for political reasons.[62]

One of the most significant aspects of the nationalist opposition in Venezuela was that Rockefeller and AD leaders found themselves squeezed between the left and the right. The left, including the left-of-center URD and extreme left Communist representatives, constantly challenged AD leaders to remember their roots as anti-imperialist nationalists before coming to power. CVF participation in VBEC and the conditions of the May joint memo represented AD's attempts to address charges from the left, which included some members of AD. On the other hand, the right questioned the association of the state with private foreign capital and, perhaps more important, what they viewed as special privileges provided to foreigners. They had no objection to foreign investment and expertise so long as it did not provide competition with Venezuelans. AD leaders avoided participation with CADA to appease the right, only to face charges that it lacked control over CADA from the left. On other issues as well, AD leaders ultimately understood that to maintain power they must make some effort to placate dominant economic groups.[63] But AD's efforts to moderate its policies and to indicate its support for private foreign capital proved frustrating to the left and inadequate in appeasing the right.

Rockefeller could not resolve the tension between using the profit motive to mobilize Venezuelan capital and pursuing social objectives more in tune with the goals of the democratic left. Despite his goal of serving as a model to Venezuelan capitalists, he found that many of them did not share his flexibility regarding strategies for increasing production. They were skeptical of his motives and viewed him merely as a dangerous competitor. Rockefeller's goals of reforming business attitudes seemed more likely to be achieved, not through persuasion, but through results. Given VBEC's poor financial showing, Rockefeller had little impact on the Venezuelan business culture of high-profit–low-risk investment. Venezuelan capitalists, and most U.S. investors, did not share his view that self-interest demanded direct action to raise living standards by focusing on the "basic economy," primarily food production and distribution. Significantly, by the latter part of the 1950s, Rockefeller's successes in milk processing and supermarkets led to Venezuelan competitors in those businesses, as he had originally intended. Success for Rockefeller's "social objectives" seemed most likely through alliance with AD leaders. They possessed political power, and because of their modernization plans, they were eager to work with foreign capital when they believed that cooperation furthered their ends. Their practical approach and willingness to experiment in promoting Venezuelan economic development appealed to Rockefeller. While he hoped to wean them from their preference for state-directed action, he did not see their "economic nationalism" as a mortal threat to U.S. interests. As Nick Cullather has shown for Taiwan, while official U.S. policy supported nonstatist development policies, Americans deeply involved in individual national cases often showed flexibility to local conditions.[64] During the politically volatile *trienio,* however, cooperation came to naught, since there was too little time and too much outspoken and powerful internal opposition to AD.

The Venezuelan experience demonstrates, too, the need for policy makers and historians to assess "economic nationalism" on a nation-by-nation basis. The reaction to Rockefeller in Venezuela contrasts with the quieter response to his projects in Brazil. Elizabeth Cobbs notes that Rockefeller's name "became a convenient synonym for *North American Imperialism.*" She minimizes political opposition to Rockefeller, however. Of press attacks, she remarks, "The tempests were invariably short-lived. Considering Brazilian nationalism and the connotations of the Rockefeller name, reaction against IBEC and AIA was remarkably mild."[65] There are several reasons for the milder opposition to Rockefeller in Brazil than in Venezuela. IBEC ventures in Brazil were smaller, generally well conceived, and, on the whole, more successful. IBEC officials recognized the difference and longed to translate their Brazilian successes in Venezuela.[66] The Brazilian state never participated directly in IBEC. It might have made no difference if it had, since Brazil pursued statist economic policies throughout the 1940s and 1950s and was in the main receptive to foreign capital. Regardless, Rockefeller's for-profit projects were never as closely identified with Brazil's government. Finally, Rockefeller could never overcome the negative baggage from his Standard Oil connection in Venezuela. The family ghosts he faced in the oil-rich nation remained ever present. Similarly, the oil companies' contributions to VBEC created another target. This points to the strength of economic nationalism in Venezuela relative to Brazil. Despite growing frustration with U.S. policy, many Brazilians continued to believe that their nation shared a special relationship with the United States. Brazil had a more diversified economy and greater distance than the Caribbean nation had from the United States. In contrast, Venezuela in the early postwar period relied on petroleum for 90 percent of its export earnings; petroleum revenues accounted for around 70 percent of its budget. Venezuela was simply more dependent on the United States, and that dependence bred hostility.

The U.S. policy of promoting private enterprise for economic development meant encouraging Latin American governments to provide an atmosphere congenial for private foreign investment. Since AD provided such an environment—indeed, eagerly sought foreign investment to diversify and modernize Venezuela's economy—the State Department was content. Active cooperation between the oil companies and the State Department occurred because of the strategic nature of the oil industry and the goal of U.S. oil policy, maintaining control of foreign oil by U.S. companies. The Truman administration, like Roosevelt's, responded to AD's nationalist oil policy by indicating its approval of Venezuelan efforts to increase its share of wealth from petroleum profits. But the United States discouraged attempts by Venezuela designed to exert more control over petroleum, such as taking royalties in petroleum and establishing a government oil agency.[67] Issues in oil development were priorities in U.S.-Venezuelan relations. While this was to be expected, Venezuelan leaders were frustrated by the lack of attention to broader economic development from Washington. At the April 1948 Bógota Conference to set up the Organization of American States (OAS), Venezuelan delegate Betancourt led the futile call of Latin American leaders for a Marshall Plan for Latin America. The United States was interested in gaining support on a resolution condemning totalitarianism and attempted to head off economic questions. Still, it is not clear what impact greater economic aid might have had in this period. Had the U.S. government been more forthcoming in economic assistance to the Betancourt and Gallegos administrations, it is unlikely that AD would have survived its domestic challenges given the character of the political opposition to AD's policies.

While the United States was not inclined to provide a large-scale plan for Latin American economic development, it also made little effort to address Latin American concerns in smaller matters. Rockefeller's contacts based on his government service during the war and previous activities at the embassy in Caracas facilitated his gaining support for his projects. But his "experiments" were viewed as good works that required little active support. IBEC officials used the deterioration of the political situation in the late summer of 1948 in their argument for continued approval to import goods into Venezuela beyond that nation's quota. IBEC had received special project status in part through Rockefeller's personal connections, but the criterion for this status was that food should go to ensure adequate nutrition for U.S. workers employed in the production of strategic materials. Since VBEC's products were intended to help Venezuelan consumers, not just American workers employed in the production of petroleum, representatives of the Commerce and Agriculture Departments questioned special project status renewal. The State Department declined to intervene.[68]

In 1952, Rockefeller criticized U.S. economic development policy. In November 1950 Truman had appointed Rockefeller chairman of International Development Advisory Board (IDAB), charged with examining U.S. foreign economic policy, particularly Point Four technical assistance. Rockefeller recommended a centralized agency to coordinate public and private aid. His personal experiences had led him to believe that greater state cooperation with private interests would facilitate development projects like the ones he had initiated in Venezuela. The administration's consolidation of foreign economic assistance programs in the Mutual Security Agency was not what Rockefeller had envisioned. Moreover, Rockefeller argued, it was bad "public relations" to tie U.S. defense interests to foreign assistance for economic development: "Efforts to use economic assistance as a means of buying political friends or military cooperation only undermine and corrupt our long-term relations with other nations." Rockefeller sensed the world was at "a unique moment in history," when "the basic spiritual forces, democratic concepts, and economic necessities which stirred this country to revolt 175 years ago are stirring again today among peoples throughout the world."[69] Despite Rockefeller's rhetorical claim that common goals existed between North American revolutionaries in the 1770s and Third World nationalists in the 1940s and 1950s, neither the Truman nor the Eisenhower administrations pursued Rockefeller's ideas as Cold War concerns increasingly colored U.S. foreign relations. Latin American aspirations for national economic development continued to rise, despite the ebbing of democracy.

The end of the Cold War permits an opportunity to revisit questions that were obscured both by the emergence of the Cold War and by Cold War–dominated historiography. Now, with the increasing priority given to open markets and investment in U.S. foreign relations, a reexamination of

Rockefeller's ideas and the challenges he faced may provide insight for those interested in moderating the political, social, and economic impact of the United States in the countries of the Third World.

Notes

I gratefully acknowledge the Society for Historians of American Foreign Relations for the W. Stull Holt Fellowship, which financed my travel to Venezuela.

1. *Gaceta del Congreso de los Estados Unidos de Venezuela (Sesiónes Extraordinárias),* Caracas, 29 October 1948, Mes VII, No. 18, 1007–49.

2. James W. Park, *Latin American Underdevelopment: A History of Perspectives in the United States, 1870–1965* (Baton Rouge, 1995), 149–51, 176–82.

3. See, e.g., Robert McMahon, "Eisenhower and Third World Nationalism: A Critique of the Revisionists," *Political Science Quarterly* 101 (Fall 1986): 453–73; and Dennis Merrill, "America Encounters the Third World," *Diplomatic History* 16 (Spring 1992): 325–27.

4. See Kyle Longley, "Resistance and Accommodation: The United States and the Nationalism of José Figuéres, 1953–1957," *Diplomatic History* 18 (Winter 1994): 1–28; and Kenneth Lehman, "Revolutions and Attributions: Making Sense of Eisenhower Administration Policies in Bolivia and Guatemala," *Diplomatic History* 21 (Spring 1997): 185–213. Perceived differences behind economic nationalist goals in Guatemala and Bolivia led the Eisenhower administration to pursue different policies in response to reforming governments. Lehman argues that the administration failed to account for the similarities in the two cases; the policy choices were not the result of systematic analysis.

5. See, e.g., Richard H. Immerman, *The CIA in Guatemala: The Foreign Policy of Intervention* (Austin, TX, 1982); Stephen G. Rabe, *Eisenhower and Latin America: The Foreign Policy of Anticommunism* (Chapel Hill, NC, 1988); and Burton I. Kaufman, *Trade and Aid: Eisenhower's Foreign Economic Policy, 1953–1961* (Baltimore, 1982). For the Truman administration, historians have relied heavily on David Green, *The Containment of Latin America: A History of Myths and Realities of the Good Neighbor Policy* (Chicago, 1971), which provides an interpretive account of U.S. relations with the entire Latin American region, largely on the basis of U.S. documents. Part of the problem is a larger one in U.S.–Latin American relations, tremendous gaps in the literature. See Richard V. Salisbury, "Good Neighbors: The United States and Latin America in the Twentieth Century" in *American Foreign Relations: A Historiographical Review,* ed. Gerald K. Haines and J. Samuel Walker (Westport, CT, 1981), 311–34; Stephen Rabe, "Marching Ahead (Slowly): The Historiography of Inter-American Relations," *Diplomatic History* 13 (Summer 1989): 297–316; and Mark T. Gilderhus, "An Emerging Synthesis? U.S.–Latin American Relations since the Second World War," *Diplomatic History* 16 (Summer 1992): 429–52.

6. Leslie Bethell and Ian Roxborough, eds., *Latin America between the Second World War and the Cold War, 1944–1948* (New York, 1992), 1–2, 10–19. For a discussion of the question of continuity and change, and the relative impact of domestic and inter-

national factors in shaping Latin American politics, see David Rock, ed., *Latin America in the 1940s: War and Postwar Transitions* (Berkeley, CA, 1994).

7. Stephen Rabe, "The Elusive Conference: United States Economic Relations with Latin America, 1945–1952," *Diplomatic History* 2 (Summer 1978): 279–94.

8. Elizabeth Cobbs, *The Rich Neighbor Policy: Rockefeller and Kaiser in Brazil* (New Haven, CT, 1992).

9. Michael L. Krenn, *U.S. Policy toward Economic Nationalism in Latin America, 1917–1929* (Wilmington, DE, 1990).

10. For the best synthesis of twentieth-century Venezuelan history, see Judith Ewell, *Venezuela: A Century of Change* (Stanford, CA, 1984).

11. Joe Alex Morris, *Nelson Rockefeller: A Biography* (New York, 1960), 111–12, 122–23; interview with Margot Boulton de Bottome, Caracas, Venezuela, October 1993; interview with David Rockefeller, New York, 4 May 1994. The best biography is Cary Reich, *The Life of Nelson Rockefeller: Worlds to Conquer, 1908–1958* (New York, 1996).

12. "Compañía de Fomento Venezolano, S.A.," 27 March 1940, RG 3, Business Interests, 109:817, Rockefeller Archive Center (RAC); Morris, *Nelson Rockefeller*, 126–27.

13. Claude Curtis Erb, "Nelson Rockefeller and United States–Latin American Relations, 1940–1945" (Ph.D. diss., Clark University, 1982); Allen Brewster Maxwell, "Evoking Latin American Collaboration in the Second World War: A Study of the Office of the Coordinator of Inter-American Affairs" (Ph.D. diss., Tufts University, 1971); Peter Bales, "Nelson Rockefeller and His Quest for Inter-American Unity" (Ph.D. diss., State University of New York at Stony Brook, 1992); Gerald K. Haines, "Under the Eagles Wing: The Franklin Roosevelt Administration Forges an American Hemisphere," *Diplomatic History* 1 (Fall 1977): 373–88; Darlene Rivas, "Missionary Capitalist: Nelson Rockefeller in Venezuela" (Ph.D. diss., Vanderbilt University, 1996).

14. "Minutes of Meeting on December 17, 1946," memo dated 3 January 1947, p. 4, R. G. 4, NAR: Personal, AIA-IBEC, 1:1, RAC.

15. Ibid. The first Brazilian project was an emergency one designed to deal with a hog cholera epidemic, but other AIA-IBEC projects in Brazil did not have this emergency character. The sense of urgency was clearly expressed by AD leaders. See Memória y Cuenta de la Corporación de Fomento (Caracas, 1947), 121.

16. As subjects, Betancourt and his political party, Acción Democrática, have spawned a huge literature. In English, see Robert J. Alexander's biography of Betancourt, *Rómulo Betancourt and the Transformation of Venezuela* (New Brunswick, NJ, 1982) and Alexander's *Venezuela's Voice for Democracy: Conversations and Correspondence with Rómulo Betancourt* (New York, 1990); Daniel Hellinger, *Venezuela: Tarnished Democracy* (Boulder, 1991); and Glen L. Kolb, *Democracy and Dictatorship in Venezuela, 1945–1958* (Hamden, CT, 1974). For U.S.-Venezuelan relations, see Stephen G. Rabe, *The Road to OPEC: United States Relations with Venezuela, 1919–1976* (Austin, TX, 1982), esp. chap. 5, "The *Trienio*," 94–116. See also Judith Ewell, *Venezuela and the United States: From Monroe's Hemisphere to Petroleum's Empire* (Athens, GA, 1996).

17. "Nelson Rockefeller está en Venezuela," editorial of 23 February 1939 in Rómulo Betancourt, *Problemas Venezolanos* (Santiago de Chile, 1940), 48. This book is a collection of Betancourt's articles in *Ahora* from 1937 through 1939.

18. "Tendéncias Parasitárias Del Capital Nacional," editorial in *Ahora,* 21 May 1939, in Betancourt, *Problemas*, 343–46; *Memória y Cuenta de la Corporación de Fomento*

(Caracas, 1946), 8–9; Rómulo Betancourt, *Venezuela: Oil and Politics,* trans. Everett Bauman (Boston, 1979), 314; Kolb, *Democracy,* 30–31.

19. Hellinger, *Tarnished Democracy,* 50–53, 60–64.

20. Since the late 1930s, Venezuela had been the largest exporter of petroleum in the world and had vied with the Soviet Union for second place in the production of petroleum behind the United States. In 1945 the United States produced 1,714 million barrels of oil; the Soviet Union, 149 million; and Venezuela, 323 million. President Medina's 1943 petroleum legislation ensured that Venezuela received a significant share of oil industry profits. Edwin Lieuwen, *Petroleum in Venezuela: A History* (Berkeley, CA, 1954), 121.

21. Kolb, *Democracy,* 39. Agricultural production declined between 1945 and 1947, despite increased agricultural subsidies and CVF operations. In 1945 agricultural production was 95 percent of 1938 production; it dropped to 91 percent in 1947, rebounding to 103 percent in 1948. Jorge Salazar-Carillo, *Oil in the Economic Development of Venezuela* (New York, 1976), 89–90.

22. Conversation between Dawson and Betancourt, Corrigan to secretary of state, airgram A395, 30 October 1945, General Records of the Department of State, Record Group 59, file 831.00/10–3045, National Archives II, College Park, MD (hereafter RG 59, with file number).

23. J. Jennen to NAR, 26 and 27 February 1947, NAR Papers: Personal, Countries, box 69:592; Oropeza to NAR, 30 November 1946, NAR Papers: Personal, Countries, box 70:609; NAR to Oropeza, 13 March 1947, NAR Papers: Personal, Countries, box 70:609.

24. Betancourt, *Oil and Politics,* 145–46. The large companies participated in AIA-IBEC: Creole Petroleum, Shell, Caribbean Petroleum, Mene Grande, and Socony Vacuum contributed $12,840,800 to VBEC, the CVF provided about $4.5 million, and Rockefeller and his brothers put up about $1,000,000. Wayne G. Broehl, *The International Basic Economy Corporation,* NPA Series on United States Business Performance Abroad (National Planning Association, 1968), 44–45.

25. Policy Committee Meeting of 4 February 1947, NAR: Personal, AIA-IBEC, box 12:116.

26. Memo, "Venezuelan Reaction to Rockefeller Visit," 17 February 1947, RG 59, 811.503131/1–2947; memo re Trip to Venezuela, 7 February 1947, NAR: Personal, AIA-IBEC, box 14:144.

27. Memo re Trip to Venezuela, 7 February 1947, NAR: Personal, AIA-IBEC, box 14:144.

28. Oropeza-Castillo to NAR, 11 February 1947, and Juan Pablo Pérez Alfonso to NAR, 19 February 1947, both in IBEC unprocessed, box 21, folder, Public Relations: Letters of Introduction, RAC. Pérez Alfonso later played a major role in the establishment of OPEC.

29. A faction within AD argued throughout the *trienio* that foreign investors needed careful government supervision. According to Steven Ellner, "These 'left' AD members frequently clashed with those who feared that stringent regulations on investments would discourage capital from abroad." Steven Ellner, "Populism in Venezuela, 1935–1948: Betancourt and Acción Democrática," in *Latin American Populism in Comparative Perspective,* ed. Michael L. Coniff (Albuquerque, NM, 1982), 135–49.

30. Betancourt, *Oil and Politics,* 275–77; Alexander, *Rómulo Betancourt,* 286.

31. Coles to NAR, 30 May 1947, and "Joint Memorandum," 29 May 1947, both in NAR: Personal, AIA-IBEC, box 9:90.

32. "Report by Nelson A. Rockefeller on Negotiations with the Venezuelan Government in connection with the Venezuelan Basic Economy Corporation (VBEC) Investment Policy Agreement," 27 June 1947, "Outline for Meeting with President," Exhibit D, and "VBEC: Capital Structure and Agreements with Regard to Operating Companies," Exhibit B of "Report by NAR," all in NAR: Personal, AIA-IBEC, box 9:91.

33. Rockefeller's prewar development company built a luxury hotel in Caracas at the behest of President López Contreras. When wartime exigencies threatened to derail the project, some Venezuelan investors sold their stock to the Rockefellers. While the stock purchase was intended to prevent both hard feelings and losses on the part of the local investors, they later cried foul when the venture proved successful; "Minutes of Special Meeting of Board of Directors (VBEC)," 12 June 1947, Broehl Papers, box 4: VBEC: Corporate Papers and Minutes, 1947–1949, RAC.

34. "Report by NAR." AD used the agreements to answer criticism. See Betancourt to Pedro René Barboza and Juan R. Hernández W., 23 July 1947, Archivo Histórico de Miraflores: Sección Cartas, L725-C (Caracas) in which Betancourt insists that AD is protecting Venezuela from foreign domination, bolstering his argument by sending copies of the Rockefeller agreements.

35. Memo "Jóvito Villalba," Flor Brennan to NAR, 24 April 1948; Ambassador Corrigan to Department of State, 20 August 1947, RG 59, 831.00/8-2047; memo "Election Campaign of Communist Party and Culminating Demonstration in Nuevo Circo," 5 December 1947, enclosure to U.S. Embassy, Caracas, to secretary of state, 18 December 1947, RG 59, 831.00/12-1847. Report by Jofre, 4 November 1947 quoted in memo "Venezuelan Political Parties, URD and Copei," Brennan to NAR, 4 November 1947, NAR: Personal, Countries, box 72:627.

36. Gallegos received 871,752 votes; COPEI candidate Rafael Caldera, 262,204 votes; Communist candidate Gustavo Machado, 36,514. URD did not field a presidential candidate. In the congressional elections, AD received 70.83 percent, Copei, 20.48 percent, URD, 4.34 percent, and the Communists, 3.64 percent. Robert Alexander, *Rómulo Betancourt*, 251.

37. Donnelly to State Department, 16 January 1948, RG 59, 831.5034/1-1648; Donnelly to State Department, 23 January 1948, RG 59, 831.5018/1-2348.

38. Documento 1167, *El Universal*, 18 January 1948, *Gobierno y época del presidente Rómulo Gallegos: la opinion política a traves de la prensa*, 94 (Caracas, 1992).

39. Memo, Coles to NAR, 30 July 1947, Broehl Papers, box 2: Operations.

40. Coles to NAR, 27 November 1947, NAR: Personal, AIA-IBEC, box 14:140; VBEC Progress Report, November 1947; Broehl Papers, box 2: Operations.

41. Doc. 1170, *Últimas Noticias*, Caracas, 12 March 1948.

42. Doc. 1171, *El País*, 13 March 1948.

43. Doc. 1175, *Últimas Noticias*, 14 March 1948.

44. March Report, 2 April 1948, Broehl Papers, box 2: Operations; doc. 1174, *El Universal*, 14 March 1948.

45. Doc. 1187, *La Esfera*, 19 March 1948; doc. 1185, *El País*, 18 March 1948.

46. March Report, 1 April 1948, Broehl Papers, box 2: Operations.

47. April Report, 15 May 1948, March Report, 1 April 1948, Broehl Papers, box 2: Operations; doc 1198, *El Heraldo*, 9 April 1948; doc 1201, *La Esfera*, 15 April 1948; doc

1194, *El Universal,* 28 March 1948. Due to world food shortages after World War II, the United States placed country quotas on exports of essential agricultural products based on its determination of the needs of each trading nation. Rockefeller obtained special project status to import food beyond Venezuela's quota. Memo of conversation, "Requirements of VBEC, Food Production and Distribution Project," 2 March 1948, RG 59, 831.501/3–248; Samuel P. Hays, Jr., to Mr. Norman Armour, 9 July 1948, RG 59, 831.6582/7–948.

48. Doc. 1207, *El País,* 27 April 1948; doc. 1208, *Últimas Notícias,* 29 April 1948; May Report, 16 June 1948, and June Report, 7 July 1948, Broehl Papers, box 2: Operations; doc. 1185, *El País,* 18 March 1948.

49. Kolb, *Democracy,* 44; memo from Controlled Source, Political Revolutionary Movement Against the Venezuelan Government, 4 June 1948, RG 59, 831.00/6–448.

50. *Gaceta del Congreso,* 1007–48, 1072.

51. Ibid., 1049, 1051.

52. *Documentos oficiales relativos al movimiento del 24 de Noviembre de 1948* (Caracas, 1949), 72.

53. Alexander, *Rómulo Betancourt,* 314–15, 341–45.

54. Winfield J. Burrggraff, *The Venezuelan Armed Forces in Politics, 1935–1959* (Columbia, MO, 1972), 116–38; Rabe, *Road to OPEC,* 112–16; Hellinger, *Tarnished Democracy,* 48–50.

55. Rabe, *Road to OPEC,* 116.

56. Steven Ellner insists that the U.S. government and the oil companies bear indirect blame since they knew of the military plotting and did nothing. U.S. recognition of Peru's government after a similar coup a few days earlier signaled the Venezuela military that it had nothing to fear from the United States. Steven Ellner, "Venezuela," in Bethell and Roxborough, *Latin America,* 165–66.

57. 10:30 Meetings, 10 January 1949, 22, 24, and 26 November 1948: NAR: Personal, AIA-IBEC, box 22:239. It could be said that VBEC contributed to the charged political atmosphere that brought on the coup by providing a convenient target for AD's political opponents. This certainly was unintentional. Rockefeller had a great deal to lose by the coup. Both VBEC and AIA personnel had built working relations with appropriate Venezuelan ministry officials. Each subsequent reorganization of the various ministries by the military government required renewed efforts to establish contacts, repeated recitations of goals and strategies, and general frustration and loss of morale for AIA and VBEC employees. Despite these problems, AIA remained in cooperation with the Venezuelan government through dictatorship and democracy until 1968.

58. Memo of conversation between Ambassador Donnelly and Delgado Chalbaud, 3 December 1948, RG 59, 831.00/12–848.

59. Coles to Rockefeller, 23 July 1949, and Rockefeller to Coles, 26 July 1949, NAR: Personal, Countries, box 68:583; U.S. Embassy, Caracas, to State Department, 8 June 1949, RG 59, 831.5034/6–849.

60. Memo to files from Coles, 3 June 1949, enclosure to U.S. Embassy, Caracas, State Department, 8 June 1949, RG 59, 831.5034/6–849.

61. Progress Report for April 15–May 15, 24 May 1950 (Frigorífica), December Report, 22 January 1952 (PACA), both in Broehl Papers, box 2: Operations.

62. Coles to NAR, 27 November 1947, NAR: Personal, AIA-IBEC, box 14:140. Also

VBEC Progress Reports, November 1947, March Report, 1 April 1948, May Report, 16 June 1948, and June Report, 16 July 1948, all in Broehl Papers box 2: Operations; and 10:30 meeting, 26 January 1948, NAR: Personal, AIA-IBEC, box 22:238.

63. AD leaders refused to move to the right as APRA did in Peru. Ellner, "Venezuela," 169.

64. Nick Cullather, " 'Fuel for the Good Dragon': The United States and Industrial Policy in Taiwan, 1950-1965," in this volume.

65. Cobbs, *The Rich Neighbor Policy,* 176-77.

66. Venezuelan matters dominated the agendas at IBEC meetings in New York. See the 10:30 Meetings, NAR: Personal, AIA-IBEC, box 22.

67. Rabe, *Road to OPEC,* 103; David S. Painter, *Oil and the American Century: The Political Economy of U.S. Foreign Oil Policy, 1941-1954* (Baltimore, 1986), 128, 134.

68. Samuel P. Hays, Jr., to Mr. Norman Armour, 9 July 1948, RG 59, 831.6582/7-948.

69. Speech by NAR, 7 April 1952, Conference on International Economic and Social Development, George Elsey Papers, box 61: Foreign Relations, Point Four Conference, Harry S. Truman Library, Independence, MO. By 1968 Rockefeller had moderated his views on the links between economic and military assistance. Disappointed by the failure of the Alliance for Progress and the virtual absence of political democracy on the continent, Rockefeller became convinced that military leaders had a developing "social" vision for their countries. *Rockefeller Report on the Americas* (Chicago, 1969).

"Fuel for the Good Dragon": The United States and Industrial Policy in Taiwan, 1950–1965

NICK CULLATHER

In the summer of 1965 the Agency for International Development (AID) celebrated a small victory. Ambassador Jerauld Wright formally closed the aid office in Taipei and declared Taiwan the first country to "graduate" from U.S. foreign assistance. After fifteen years and $1.5 billion in economic aid, Taiwan was now a going concern, its growth, according to Wright, "one of the marvels of the present age." "What has happened on Taiwan is what we want to see happen throughout Africa and Asia and Latin America," AID chief David Bell affirmed. "Taiwan is an especially impressive case." American and Taiwanese officials stressed the contrast between communist failures on the mainland and the Republic of China's successful development through "free institutions" and "private enterprise," a theme echoed by journalists covering the event. *Reader's Digest* heralded "Asia's newest economic miracle" and offered Taiwan as "proof of the wisdom of depending mainly upon private enterprise for economic growth."[1]

In the 1980s and early 1990s, when the Asian miracle seemed truly miraculous, scholars and bankers feuded over the meaning of Taiwan's rapid development. The World Bank reaffirmed AID's interpretation: Taiwan's liberalization, its reliance on private enterprise, and its adherence to economic "fundamentals" had catapulted it into the ranks of the world's richest nations. But area specialists pointed out that Taiwan only appeared liberal. The state, not markets, controlled virtually every economic variable, and this supervision accounted for Taiwan's industrial surge. Alice Amsden, Stephan Haggard, and other "state-oriented" theorists argued that Taiwan, along with South Korea and Japan, had improved on free enterprise. By crossbreeding capitalism and socialism, it had created a hybrid that confounded both classical development theory and dependency theory.[2]

The debate turned on a historical question: how successfully did U.S. officials push market-oriented reforms in the 1950s? Taiwan emulated the U.S. model, according to neoclassical interpretations, reshaping its economy with the help of AID's funds and advice. State-oriented theorists replied that Chinese officials took the money but ignored the recommendations. Confucian traditions and internal politics guided Taiwan's development. "All that is certain," according to Amsden, "is that freer trade and freer enterprise (including freer foreign enterprise) were preached by the American aid mission. In view of the preferences of its major benefactor, the extent to which the Guomindang government persisted in its 'etatisme' is all the more impressive."[3]

Amsden's certainty rests on an assumption that the United States has urged liberalization more or less consistently throughout the long history of its international development efforts. Writings on modernization on the left and the right characteristically focus on strategies rather than on the developers who devise them or the historical circumstances in which they arise. Typically, according to Michael Cowen and Robert Shenton, "the origin of the *intention* to develop is omitted from discussion."[4] Other parts of the story disappear too. Because development scholars are concerned with replicable features in any case study, they pass over unique personalities and events that cannot be reproduced elsewhere. Without personalities, motives, or events, history dissolves, and the "Taiwan model" discussed and debated by development scholars starts to look less like Taiwan.

The debate over the lessons of the Taiwan miracle has been premised largely on an account in which the Straits Crises, the Cold War, the fears and ambitions of U.S. and Chinese officials, and even the officials themselves have been obscured behind the abstractions of modernization theory. Shortly after Taiwan's graduation, AID published a study by Neil Jacoby, a former member of the Council of Economic Advisers and a consultant to aid missions in India and Laos. It remains the most authoritative on the subject. Following the official line, it discounted the importance of state guidance and emphasized the success of U.S.-sponsored private sector expansion. "By far the most important consequence of U.S. influence," it concluded, "was the creation in Taiwan of a booming private enterprise system."[5] Analysts of Taiwan's development policy cite Jacoby to show that the United States either discouraged or overlooked Taiwan's statist tactics.

In Jacoby's account, Taiwan confirmed the assumptions of both develop-

ment theory and U.S. policy, assumptions that linked U.S. aid to liberalization and growth. But more importantly from the agency's perspective, it
contradicted the 1963 report of the Clay Commission, which attacked AID
for designing programs "without regard . . . to the historic form, character
and interest of our own economic system." The presidential commission
condemned AID's support for state enterprises in competition with private
(sometimes U.S.) firms and its failure to encourage recipient countries to
see their "essential choice between totalitarian, inefficient, state-controlled
economies on the one hand and an economically and politically freer system on the other."[6] The report provoked cutbacks and a revision of policy,
but it should also have raised questions about Jacoby's interpretation. The
newly opened papers of U.S. aid agencies confirm that the United States was
far from dogmatic in promoting market-oriented reforms. In the pursuit of
short-term economic and strategic goals—price stability, job growth, or more
military spending—aid officials often found that direct action by the state
worked better and faster. The United States supported state-oriented policies
systematically, not by tolerating Taiwanese backsliding. On closer examination, Taiwan's system of state guidance looks less Confucian and more like a
collaborative project.

Taiwan's story reveals the breadth of the gap between development policy and its execution. While official pronouncements seldom strayed from
the liberal developmentalist creed, in actual practice U.S. aid and advice
often responded creatively to particular threats and opportunities. Dennis
Merrill and Linda Wills Qaimmaqami, for example, find that strategic imperatives led U.S. officials to back state planning schemes in India and Iran,
respectively. In the Philippines, Argentina, and Turkey, according to Sylvia
Maxfield and James Nolt, the United States supported import substitution, a
strategy it officially opposed. Instead of reproducing a single model of political economy around the world, U.S. aid officials, faced with local crises,
experimented. "You cannot hold fixed ideas," a member of the China aid
mission discovered. "You must keep fluid, face things as they are rather than
as you would like them to be." In Taiwan, U.S. officials were forced to jettison
free-market nostrums from the start and collaborate with Chinese officials in
creating a type of political economy that would only later be described as an
"Asian" development model incompatible with "Western" models.[7]

From the beginning, officials of the Economic Cooperation Administration (ECA) recognized that they would not find in Asia the same combina-
tion of ingredients that made the Marshall Plan a success. The European
experience, one observer noted, "was far less relevant than had been supposed. Advice from foreigners was not awaited with bated breath. Pat solu-

tions toppled like tenpins." Meeting at the Brookings Institution in April 1948, economists from the State and Treasury Departments, the Bretton Woods institutions, U.S. aid agencies, and the Federal Reserve conceded that "a fundamental contrast exist[ed] between 'recovery' in Europe and 'development' in Asia." Except for Japan, none of the Asian countries had a corporate or banking structure to support a program like the Marshall Plan. Without private institutions, development efforts would have to be organized around other "political and social bases. . . . Governments will have to play a considerable role in developing trade in the immediate future. When trade has been started, private traders may step in on the heels of governments."[8] For the moment, circumstances favored a state-centered strategy.

But Chiang Kai-shek's tottering state could do little to help relief efforts in 1948. In the Nationalists' shrinking zone on the mainland, army confiscations and thousands of refugees fueled a hyperinflation that undermined the ECA mission's efforts. Administrators Roger Lapham and R. Allen Griffin concentrated their energies on Shanghai, distributing commodities and buying gold in an attempt to ease the panic, but to no avail. Speaking to Congress in February 1948, Secretary of State George C. Marshall warned that little could be accomplished in China, even with the $570 million that had just been appropriated. He urged aid officials to avoid undertaking projects that would connect the United States with the Nationalists' defeat. By April 1949 Griffin conceded that "from the beginning the cards were stacked against us. . . . All that is left to do is to conduct an orderly liquidation of our affairs in the midst of a situation that is, in other respects, in disorder."[9]

Anticipating a longer struggle on the mainland, ECA had dispatched dozens of experts to China on the eve of the Nationalists' collapse. Land reform specialists formed a Joint Commission on Rural Reconstruction (JCRR) to set up cooperatives in the Yangtze Valley. Five engineers from the J.G. White Engineering Corporation, a New York firm specializing in colossal, government-funded projects, arrived at Shanghai with an ambitious program for industrial expansion. In late 1948, these experts moved to Taiwan, where they began surveying the island's resources and potential for development. What they saw looked promising. The Japanese Empire's agricultural heartland before 1945, Taiwan had the most literate population in Asia, a commercialized agricultural system geared for export, rail and road networks, and a small but important industrial base. Port facilities, fertilizer and cement factories, the oil refinery, and the aluminum smelter had all been damaged by Allied bombing during World War II, but skilled machinists and engineers stood ready to run them once they had been repaired. The loss of the mainland, officials recognized, might simplify the ECA's problems. When President Harry S. Truman announced his Point Four economic aid program in January 1949, Harlan Cleveland, chief of the ECA's Far Eastern Division, suggested Taiwan as an ideal site for a pilot program that could be "successful enough to serve as a model" for the rest of Asia.[10]

But the ECA's optimism was no match for the State Department's despair. Diplomatic officials recognized that Taiwan was an unlikely sanctuary for the Nationalists, who had treated the islanders like defeated enemies since 1945. When the Japanese left, Chiang's armies seized all Japanese-owned businesses—almost the entire industrial economy—and imposed trade restrictions and heavy taxes on native Formosans, merchants and landowners who had migrated from China in the nineteenth century. In February 1947 the government-controlled Bank of Taiwan moved to confiscate the remaining independent businesses by recalling loans to private merchants. The actions of the hated Monopoly Bureau provoked an incident on 28 February that soon led to open revolt across the island. Reinforcements arrived from the mainland on 8 March and suppressed the uprising, killing over six thousand Taiwanese, many of them from the business and professional classes.[11] An uneasy peace settled over the island during the next two years, but as thousands of undisciplined troops, corrupt bureaucrats, and refugees streamed into the island in the spring of 1949, U.S. observers considered another rebellion likely.

For most of 1949, the ECA redirected fertilizer, petroleum, and cotton shipments from the mainland to Taiwan while J.G. White engineers refurbished the aged factories. In July, Shanghai fell, and Chiang Kai-shek, now in "retirement," moved to Taiwan with thirty-seven tons of gold. For the rest of the year, Secretary of State Dean Acheson maneuvered to salvage as much as he could from the China disaster. Anxious to preserve both Taiwan and Hong Kong, and seeing advantages in recognizing the People's Republic, he hoped to establish a UN trusteeship in Taiwan with the help of a Formosan independence movement or Nationalist defectors. To keep his options open, he wanted the ECA to remain in place, but without helping Chiang, arousing the communists, or encouraging more refugees to flee to the island. In January 1950 Truman confirmed the "hands-off" policy, and Taiwan-bound shipments stopped. Aid workers held no brief for Chiang or his cronies, but they refused to stand idle while the economy deteriorated. Valery de Beausset, J. G. White's lead engineer, scorned the State Department's predictions of collapse. "Suppose we act as if we really believe in what we hope and do what we started to do and not act so much like God?"[12] Using the supplies they had, the engineers and ECA officials began to lay the groundwork for a viable economy.

The Nationalists' reaction to defeat heartened ECA officials. On Taiwan,

Chiang purged the ranks of the Kuomintang (KMT) Party, reducing graft and factionalism and elevating younger leaders favored by the United States. K. C. Wu, a civilian reformer, became governor of Taiwan. Ch'en Ch'eng, Joseph Stilwell's favorite general, took the posts of premier and head of the central reform committee. Yen Chia-kan, a missionary-trained economist, became finance minister and head of the Committee on U.S. Aid (CUSA).[13] Yin Chung-jung, an engineer who had headed the Chinese procurement mission in New York during the war, led the key planning and resource allocation agencies, the Taiwan Production Board and the Central Trust.

The new leaders acted decisively to shore up the island's economy, enforcing controls on imports and foreign exchange. In a bid to raise agricultural yields, the government reduced farm rents and distributed land that had been confiscated from the Japanese. At the same time, it continued confiscations of manufacturing enterprises owned by Formosans. In one case, Chiang seized a factory after exiling the owner and threatening the general manager with arrest.[14]

Although versed in Anglo-American economics, none of the reformers advocated liberalization as an answer to Taiwan's problems. All agreed with the KMT's program of a "planned free economy" in which the state would direct economic activity while permitting a degree of "enterprise freedom." Ch'en likened the program to the socialism of the British Labour Party, while Yin drew analogies to Japanese development in the Meiji period. Both subscribed to Chiang's interpretation of the "Min-Sheng" principle: that restricting capital on behalf of the people's welfare was a primary function of the state.[15] Conflict between mainlanders and Formosan natives reinforced this ideology. State control meant control by mainlanders and the KMT, while "private" meant Formosan. Economic reforms coincided with a crackdown on Formosans believed to be sympathetic with Acheson's trusteeship plan.[16] By mid-1950 most of the economy was in government hands, and it was safe to allow private concerns some freedom in nonthreatening sectors. This "liberalization," however, did not signal a new commitment to free enterprise, only a move from cruder to more sophisticated methods of state manipulation.

By contrast with their KMT counterparts, U.S. officials addressed questions of development strategy in a more heterodox spirit. The ECA's authorizing legislation committed it to look first for solutions that employed private investment, but aid administrators refused to allow a technicality to delay the attainment of practical objectives.[17] The aid mission reinforced Taiwan's statist direction in four ways: by shoring up collapsing state enterprises, pioneering new methods of state control, strengthening the institutional base for planning, and co-opting groups—mainly the military—that opposed or disrupted change. Working within political and material constraints, ECA officials and J.G. White engineers restored state-owned factories to prewar production levels and collaborated with Chinese planners in creating the textile industry, one of the early triumphs of the Taiwan miracle.

Yin Chung-jung and J.G. White engineers Val de Beausset and Sidney L. Buffington together devised a program of "entrustment" under which the ECA furnished raw cotton directly to spinning mills. CUSA then purchased the finished yarn and sold it to weaving mills at fixed prices, likewise purchasing finished cloth and garments to be sold through government distribution networks. ECA officials liked the plan because at each step it generated "counterpart" funds, proceeds from the sale of U.S.-supplied goods in the form of local currency. These funds could be used to reduce the government deficit and hold down inflation. To maximize counterpart, they encouraged vertical integration and economies of scale. But the plan also served important KMT political objectives. It drew public and private manufacturers together under a program that allowed the state to fix prices, employment, profits, and production levels. Mills could be privately owned, but, with the state as sole supplier and client, control remained with the KMT. Textile manufacturing catapulted ahead of Taiwan's other industries. Within two years, Yin and other KMT officials were using it as a model for how the state could incubate new industries by controlling imports and prices. The ECA had shown the KMT how to defy the laws of the market.[18]

Not satisfied to furnish commodities and tinker with industries, aid workers wanted a hand in setting government policy on budgets, imports, and exchange. Mission chief Raymond Moyer appealed through the embassy for a more flexible policy, but Acheson and Assistant Secretary of State Dean Rusk feared becoming implicated in Chiang's final failure. Congress meanwhile continued to approve larger sums of aid for Taiwan. On 5 June, Truman signed a bill providing $94 million for the next fiscal year. Twenty days later, war erupted in Korea, and on the 27th, Truman ordered the Seventh Fleet to guard the Taiwan Straits. But the State Department still hesitated to let the ECA take a more active part in Taiwan's economic policy making. In July, Moyer, with Cleveland's backing, asked to be allowed to set up a joint Economic Stabilization Board (ESB), to build aid around long-term plans, and to set targets for taxes and spending. The military situation and the magnitude of the assistance demanded a more active role, he argued, and the Nationalists were receptive, even eager, for U.S. advice. Rusk refused. For now the program would remain unchanged, he explained, but the administration was examining the situation and might soon decide differently.[19]

ECA participation in industrial and budget planning did not become imperative until the Truman administration proposed a substantial program of military aid. Between December and February, as a balance-of-payments crisis emptied the Nationalist treasury, a Pentagon survey team found Chiang's armies in urgent need of $500 million worth of supplies. The Korean War and the approval of National Security Council Paper 68 (NSC-68) made aid on this scale possible, and by early March 1951 the Joint Chiefs of Staff (JCS) could imagine scenarios in which Nationalist troops would be used in raids on the mainland. As the JCS sent emergency aid and a military mission (MAAG) to Taiwan, ECA officials warned that these actions could tip Taiwan's economy over the edge. Huge budget deficits and drought-shrunken farm exports already threatened to destabilize the New Taiwan Dollar. To prevent a ruinous inflation, the government had cashed its gold hoard, and while the JCS deliberated, the Bank of Taiwan was packing $1.7 million in gold—the last of its reserves—aboard planes bound for New York. A sudden increase in military spending would send prices into a death spiral. On 19 March Rusk ordered Griffin to proceed with plans for economic stabilization.[20]

ECA officials were ready to move ahead with the industrial program. Over the previous six months they had quietly expanded the list of U.S.-supplied commodities to include tinplate, iron, steel, sulfur, and bauxite, which arrived in crates and sacks emblazoned "Fuel for the Good Dragon." Moyer's Economic Stabilization Board met for the first time on 19 March, and although Rusk admonished the mission to "advise but not give direction to the Chinese," U.S. advisers did most of the talking at the first three weekly meetings. Yin, Yen, Ch'en, and other Chinese officials listened as a U.S. adviser explained that over the past eight months Taiwan had been hemorrhaging dollars and gold at a monthly rate of $2 million. In another two months, hyperinflation would set in unless the government implemented "rigorous" exchange controls. "These actions are drastic and necessary," he urged, "but they are dangerous."[21] On 9 April, the Executive Yuan implemented a dual exchange rate.

In the following months, the State Department urged the ECA to expand its role in directing Taiwan's recovery. Chester Morrill, a monetary policy expert dispatched to Taiwan by the Federal Reserve, consulted with Rusk and his deputy, Livingston Merchant, in May and found the department's position nearly the reverse of what it had been three months earlier. "It now appeared possible," Rusk explained, "that we might employ the Chinese forces where they could best serve in the world in the event of a general conflagration. In consequence, we were now raising our sights to somewhat longer-range programs." Morrill asked if the department still favored reducing the size of Chiang's army. No, Merchant replied. If Taiwan employed its full resources, it could develop a self-sustaining economy "and still maintain a military establishment no larger in proportion to [the] total population than were the United States and United Kingdom World War II establishments." Military Keynesianism had come to Taiwan. On 9 May, Rusk rescinded his order to refrain from giving directions. The mission should "exert its influence vigorously and firmly, in the Economic Stabilization Board and elsewhere."[22]

Over the next four months, the ECA placed advisers in virtually every branch of Taiwan's government and industry. MAAG closely supervised military spending. A visiting Senate mission noted that the ECA had "a hand, sometimes large, sometimes small, in the setting up of a national budget, revision of the tax structure to increase revenues, [and the] institution of a more austere import program" and that aid officials participated "in day-to-day decisions concerning such matters as banking and currency, individual applications for foreign exchange, and overall national economic planning." Morrill worked with KMT officials to set up a banking structure more firmly under state control. Taiwan should avoid modeling its central bank on the United States's, he cautioned, since the Federal Reserve was too indecisive and susceptible to democratic pressures. The Bank of Taiwan, with the Fed's cooperation, became a pillar of the statist economy, chief financier to the army and its client firms.[23]

U.S. chargé Karl Rankin presented Chiang with an aide-memoire on 20 July demanding that U.S. officials be allowed to supervise Taiwan's budget. Chiang complied by forming a joint budget review committee, and by 7 August, Griffin could tell Congress that the Chinese "spend their full foreign exchange earnings now, we believe, pretty much under our guidance and direction."[24]

The state's broad economic powers augmented the effectiveness of the mission's advice. An aide to Senator Pat McCarran who visited Taiwan in August learned from Raymond Moyer that the ECA's decisions affected every corner of the economy. "Admittedly, implementation of these decisions is facilitated by the Government ownership or control of almost every significant economic activity: banks, railroads, electric power, large sugar plantations, major industrial installations, communications." Moyer explained that since "the government controls credit, imports, exports, and production, . . . once ECA has hurdled the barrier of government consent, it has a relatively clear course, devoid of the obstacles of independent labor or independent management to its goal."[25]

But the ECA had more than one reason for supporting state monopolies.

State corporations were nearly the sole source of government revenue, four-fifths of which went to the army. Through bond purchases, taxes, and requisitions, government enterprises met the army's daily food, clothing, and payroll requirements. It was this revenue base that made U.S. military aid to Taiwan a bargain. General William H. Chase, the chief military adviser, explained that "the cost of each soldier of the Chinese armed forces was about $300 for maintenance, training, etc.," a figure that compared favorably with "an estimated $5000 for each member of the United States armed forces." As Rankin later observed, "in strictly military and financial terms . . . the United States is getting a strategic bargain in its support of Free China." The mission placed a "management control advisor" in each of the principal monopolies and put J. G. White engineers at their disposal.[26]

These actions upset U.S. businesses and violated the State Department's liberal developmentalist principles, but ECA saw no alternative. A regional director of the Standard Vacuum Oil Company advised the ECA to "get the government to sell the large number of industries it now owns. The situation is worse than it was in England at any time under the Labour government." Rankin sympathized. "In connection with state-owned or controlled industrial and commercial enterprises," he wrote the mission chief, "I hope that we can help the Chinese to avoid some of the pitfalls of uneconomic Socialism." But as far as the ECA was concerned, private enterprise was not an option. Domestic investors had vanished, and foreign capital was almost as scarce. Hong Kong speculators were unwilling to rely on mainland China's forbearance. In 1952 U.S. investment in Taiwan consisted of "several small export-import companies and an airline office." Those few investors who expressed an interest presented proposals that upset ECA's priorities. Reynolds Aluminum and Westinghouse tried to obtain U.S. and Chinese approval for a plant that would produce aluminum ingots for export, but Chinese economists objected that it would use scarce electric power. Instead, the ECA helped Taiwan build its own aluminum rolling mill and fabricating plant, both owned by the state.[27]

Under U.S. guidance, Taiwan employed a development strategy now known as "import substitution." Throughout the 1950s, external trade (chiefly sugar and other farm goods) remained small, never reaching above a third of the island's prewar levels. Japan remained the principal partner, but Tokyo's own import restrictions prevented it from absorbing more of Taiwan's produce. The island's efforts were directed inward, toward developing domestic resources, markets, and manufacturing for home consumption. A barrier of import and exchange controls protected domestic firms from foreign competition and indirectly subsidized industry. The differential between the two exchange rates funneled 40 percent of the earnings from farm exports to manufacturers through artificially low prices for imported machinery and raw materials. The United States mediated between this sheltered economy and the world market, making up the inevitable exchange shortfall and adding its own subsidies. To lighten its own burden, the United States tried to reduce Taiwan's reliance on imported goods.[28] Military advisers and aid officials worked closely to build an economy capable of supporting Taiwan's military establishment.

Anticipating reductions in military and economic assistance, the Truman administration encouraged the Economic Stabilization Board to draft long-range plans. As the Korean War stabilized in 1952, the Truman administration reconsidered the value of Chiang's army as an auxiliary to U.S. forces in the Far East. Despite aid and controls, Taiwan's economy remained perilously unstable, and Congress could not be expected to subsidize it forever. CIA Deputy Chief Allen Dulles and Paul Nitze, head of the Policy Planning Staff, urged that in the years remaining, aid should be used "to develop policies which will assure Formosa as an asset." This meant reducing the economic burden of Chiang's six-hundred-thousand-man army, which required the ECA to devote its resources to generating counterpart funds and supporting consumption and state enterprises. If the military burden could become smaller and more predictable, aid could subsidize imports of capital goods—machine tools, dynamos, fabricators—equipment that could be used to make Taiwan's economy support itself.[29]

The last shipments of military hardware were scheduled to arrive in 1956, and the ECA (now called MSA) began planning to terminate economic aid the same year. In August 1952 the mission consulted with the Economic Stabilization Board on preparations for the ending of aid. "An essential corollary of this effort," according to a State Department official, "is a shift in type of economic aid from saleable commodities to generate counterpart over to industrial and capital repair, expansion, and development." At MSA's request, the ESB presented a first draft of a four-year plan on 26 September, beginning a practice that has guided industrial growth in Taiwan ever since. A collage of earlier applications for grants and loans, the plan requested $242 million in U.S. aid before 1957, when all aid (except military assistance) would end. The section on industry closely copied an industrial program prepared earlier by de Beausset, using his estimates and production targets. Under the plan, Taiwan would use import restrictions and exchange controls to shift foreign buying from commodities to capital machinery while continuing to protect textiles and other light manufacturing. Economists distinguish Taiwan's "indicative" plans from the "command" plans of the USSR, since Taiwan attained its goals with the help of incentives as well as penalties. But by manipulating investment, exchange, imports, prices, and wages, Taiwan seldom missed a target.[30] By strengthening and institutionalizing the planning function, the United States gave Taiwan a powerful tool for guiding development.

In announcing the plan, Chinese officials acknowledged that Taiwan had departed from the course of laissez-faire and private enterprise. On 31 December 1953, all of Taiwan's major dailies carried an article by Yin Chung-jung, "A Discussion on Industrial Policy for Taiwan," which declared that in the immediate future, Taiwan must face the near certainty of war with the mainland and the termination of U.S. aid. Both factors made necessary an intensive industrialization effort proceeding as quickly as possible and without wasting resources. "These two aims, however, cannot be achieved under a 'laissez faire' economy," Yin explained. "Their achievement must depend upon the active participation of the government in the economic activities of the island through deliberate plans and its supervision of their execution." The textile program offered a model, he argued, of how the government could guide investment, prices, supply, and demand to create industries from scratch. Private firms that worked "hand in hand with good government policy" would be rewarded; those who failed would be placed under "temporary control." The article excited little disagreement in the controlled press. "Mr. Yin's 'Discussion' on industrial policy, both in spirit and in substance . . . advocates controlled economy," Taiwan's *United Daily News* noted. Most writers approved. As one observed, "Progress spearheaded by the government is bound to be more rapid than [progress] promoted by the people alone." The public discussion only hinted at divisions in the government over whether industry or the military should have first claim on resources and manpower.[31]

Strategic refinements that followed the election of Dwight D. Eisenhower enlarged the aid pool, allowing industrial growth to proceed without reducing Taiwan's military budget. During the campaign Eisenhower had criticized containment, arguing that Chiang should be "unleashed" to attack the mainland. On 2 January 1953, he followed through, announcing revised orders for the Seventh Fleet permitting Taiwanese offensive operations. The move was mainly bluff (Chiang secretly promised not to attack), but it meant a reprieve for Taiwan. Levels of military aid climbed—from $24 million in 1953 to $36 million in 1954 and $37 million the following year—forcing economic aid to keep pace in order to forestall inflation. Talk of aid termination momentarily ceased, and the industrial program continued without cutbacks or competing demands from the military.[32]

Businessmen in Eisenhower's cabinet raised concerns about the statist direction of aid policy, but the administration remained pragmatic. Defense Secretary Charles E. Wilson, a former General Motors executive, complained in 1955 that by building government-run factories, the United States was "helping these countries to proceed down the road which led to state socialism or Communism." Undersecretary of State Herbert Hoover, Jr., agreed that "in many instances our assistance programs were actually subsidizing state socialism." The Soviet economic offensive in the Third World focused the National Security Council's attention on the issue in January 1956. Treasury Secretary George Humphrey argued that the Soviet initiative made it imperative that U.S. aid programs not be allowed to "create and maintain other government-controlled economies in the underdeveloped nations of Asia and Africa." But the president disagreed. "We did not need to fear a socialized state as something inimical to us in itself," Eisenhower observed. Sweden and Norway were socialist but also strong allies. Only socialized states tied to Moscow posed a danger. Vice President Richard M. Nixon pointed out that in most of Asia "there is no private enterprise which can be developed. . . . We cannot let these Asian nations go down the drain and be swallowed up by the Soviet Union while we are engaged in a campaign to support the ideals of free enterprise." Harold Stassen, director of the foreign aid program, suggested that the United States ought at least to appear to back private firms.[33]

In stressing the essential choice between a planned and a market economy, Humphrey and Wilson were simply repeating a widely accepted axiom of development theory. But other officials—from Eisenhower down—saw the situational imperatives shaping Taiwan's political economy and were ready to discard theory if the circumstances justified it. Stassen, Rankin, and advisers close to the Taiwan aid mission would have preferred market-oriented solutions, but none seemed available. They complained that Taiwan's state enterprises were inefficient, riddled with nepotism, sinecures, and "mysterious" bookkeeping. But they recognized that Taiwan had few entrepreneurs and even fewer outside investors. Stassen had to admit that "private capital, both local and foreign, has not responded to the call." "Obviously it is desirable that private investment be encouraged" to lighten the aid burden, Rankin acknowledged, but even with U.S. guarantees, Taiwan's uncertain future kept investors away. "We are dealing with a problem that cannot wholly be solved by financial mechanisms," explained John J. McCloy, the governor of the World Bank. "Government capital can be directed, but private capital movements . . . can only be induced." U.S. officials in Taipei concurred. When Christian Herter, a visiting aid official, questioned the necessity for multiple exchange rates and state corporations, the embassy's economic officer pointed out the futility "of applying generalized free enterprise truisms to the peculiarities of the Chinese situation."[34] This kind of situational economics drew fire from Congress and critics within the administration, but aid officials continued to act on circumstances instead of theory.

Sensitive to U.S. criticism, the Taiwanese took pains to appear at least to move toward liberalization. In 1952 aid workers had urged KMT officials to pay for the proposed final stage of land reform, the "Land to the Tiller" program, by giving landlords shares in public corporations. "Non-productive corporations would be at least partially removed from government ownership," a U.S. official explained. The firms "would presumably improve in productivity, while at the same time, the means would have been found for the re-purchase of land." Some analysts have since identified the program as a genuine move toward privatization; but as it was implemented in 1954, it looked more like a power grab. The state compelled landlords to surrender their property in return for overvalued shares in four public enterprises. Most shares immediately lost half their value. Shareholders enjoyed no proprietary privileges, and the firms continued under the same management with as much guidance from the state as ever. Aid officials noted that the shabby treatment of stockholders frightened potential investors more than ever.[35]

The aid mission may have strengthened the state's entrepreneurial role with its policy of incubating new "private" ventures. The mission encouraged Taiwanese planners to identify promising fields and to make investments even when no private companies offered to participate. Factories would be built with U.S. aid and then turned over to a hand-picked "entrepreneur" who would administer the company as a private concern. The mixture of state guidance and private ownership fit the political imperatives guiding U.S. policy: privatization co-opted Formosans into the system, while Chiang's government kept control of resources and revenue. In 1955 the mission initiated a $1.5 million project to manufacture plastic resins that were then being imported from a Japanese subsidiary of Monsanto. Despite congressional opposition in the United States, the project went ahead. J.G. White and Taiwanese planners both identified plastics as a desirable venture, and Yin Chung-jung took a personal interest in the proposal. Using the state's access to bank records, Yin identified Y. C. Wang as a suitable entrepreneur and "told" him to take over the plant when it was completed in 1957. The company went on to become the Formosa Plastics Group, a Fortune 500 company with subsidiaries in the United States. In Taiwan, establishing firms under state tutelage became standard practice as U.S. policies encouraged ever more complex and sophisticated linkages between corporations and the state.[36]

U.S.-Taiwan relations did not always run smoothly, but economic dis-
agreements often appeared to be quarrels over military strategy. After their
initial enthusiasm, Eisenhower's aides soon recognized that the United
States could not support Chiang's oversized army indefinitely. The largest
army in proportion to population in the world, it consumed 80 percent of
Taiwan's budget, yet only a third of its soldiers were combat effective.[37] In
1956, MAAG encouraged Chiang to strike a more defensive posture, rely
more on U.S.-supplied Matador missiles and Sabrejet fighters, and shrink the
army. If military consumption could be reduced, aid officials could divert
sufficient resources to capital formation to allow Taiwan to become self-
supporting in a few years.[38] But Chiang stubbornly refused. Believing a reduction in military consumption would weaken mainlander control, the
Bank of Taiwan, heads of state enterprises, and KMT officials joined ranks in
upholding the pledge to return to the mainland, a mythic mission that
justified the perpetual regimentation of the economy.[39] For the heads of
state monopolies, the stakes were huge. The military was their source of
credit and largest customer, buying 65 percent of the island's output of petroleum products and 40 percent of its cement.[40] U.S. officials argued, but
they learned to design programs allowing the industrial program to continue without endangering the privileges of the military and state firms.[41]

To accelerate the industrial program, the aid mission first had to give the
military a stake in industrial development. Instead of diverting the military
budget into capital formation, aid officials advised sacrificing consumer
spending. The mission found that the "standard of living on Taiwan, although miserably low by U.S. standards, is quite good by Asian standards."
With Taiwan's 3.4 percent population growth, the State Department agreed,
"a considerable portion of increased economic activity will have to be *prevented* from improving standards of living in order to help reduce imports"
and government spending.[42] The mission advised keeping wages in check,
resting its calculations partly on the assumption that the Formosan majority
had little capacity for dissent.[43]

The mission also included the army in the industrial program by em-
ploying it to build infrastructure, committing a substantial portion of the
aid budget after 1956 to an East-West highway built by retired soldiers. To get
Chiang to reduce his forces and recruit younger Formosan troops, the United
States created the Vocational Assistance Committee for Retired Servicemen
(VACRS) to employ overage soldiers in building the highway and developing mines, businesses, and timberlands along its route. VACRS enjoyed first
claim on machinery imports and investment capital, privileges it continues
to enjoy today. Now a conglomerate of some forty firms, VACRS is Taiwan's

largest "private" business.[44] By ensuring the military and its client firms dominance over resources and attractive sectors, the mission co-opted the army into the industrialization drive.

Taiwan's economy moved rapidly ahead in the last years of the decade. With the help of generous applications of chemical fertilizer and DDT, farm exports tripled, and nearly every available hectare was brought into production. Hydroelectric dams made Taiwan's power among the world's cheapest and most abundant. Manufacturing grew eight-fold from 1950 to 1959, flooding local markets with aluminum pans, textiles, and electrical parts.[45] The *Wall Street Journal* found Taipei "bustling and sprawling with the raw energy of an American frontier town."[46] But as U.S. aid passed the $1 billion mark in mid-1958, aid officials knew import substitution had reached its limit. The inward-looking manufacturing sector remained at the mercy of the U.S. Congress, and export earnings—from sugar, pineapple, and other farm goods—suffered from Cuban and even U.S. competition.[47] Continued growth depended on finding new investment and sources of exchange.

U.S. advisers had long seen manufactured exports as a solution to Taiwan's critical shortage of foreign exchange. In 1952, de Beausset had urged manufacturers to exploit shortages created by the Korean War to corner markets in Southeast Asia. The opportunity drew more attention in 1954, when overproduction provoked a crisis in the textile industry. Mills were forced to close for more than a month owing to the saturation of the home market, a condition afflicting other industries as well. China gave officials in Washington and Taipei a second reason to push exports. In 1955, the People's Republic had reopened the Burma Road and launched a campaign to capture markets in Southeast Asia. KMT and State Department officials worried that trade might enlarge Communist China's influence, particularly in the region's overseas Chinese communities. In December 1956, Chiang and Secretary of State John Foster Dulles had agreed on an export program to counteract this "cultural penetration." Nonetheless, import substitution had created powerful interests bent on preserving the system. Instead of exports, Finance Minister Hsu Peh-yuan and army officials proposed diverting resources into new import-substituting ventures, like plastics and autos. But faced with increasing pressure from the United States, domestic manufacturers, and the KMT leadership, the opposition broke in April 1958. Hsu resigned, clearing the way for export-oriented reform.[48]

Between 1958 and 1961 the government imposed a series of reforms known as the Nineteen Points, replacing multiple exchange rates with a single rate; relaxing import controls and tariffs; offering rebates, tax incentives, credit, and subsidies to manufacturers producing for export; and allowing foreign firms to remit profits for the first time.[49] Neoclassical economists see this as Taiwan's turning point, its rejection of counterproductive, interventionist policies. But state-oriented analysts point to the selective nature of the reforms, which applied only to targeted sectors, industries like aluminum and textiles that were ready for international competition.[50] Import substitution continued for most of the economy. Reform did not even mean an end to intervention in the export sectors, since government subsidies, credits, and rebates remained the key to success for private firms. Once again, the mechanisms of control simply became more sophisticated.

Taiwan's military success during the August 1958 Straits Crisis reinforced the shift toward an export-based strategy. When communist forces began shelling Quemoy island on 23 August, Taiwanese Sabrejets took to the skies and inflicted heavy losses on the air force of the People's Republic. On 6 October the shelling stopped, and two weeks later Chiang and Secretary of State John Foster Dulles signed a joint communiqué renouncing the use of force to reconquer the mainland. The communiqué promised no reductions in China's armed forces, but the crisis demonstrated that Taiwan's defense rested on air supremacy, which in turn rested on earnings of foreign exchange. The Sabrejets required $5 to $6 million worth of imported fuel and parts each year, an amount that could only be earned with manufactured exports.[51] Two weeks after the communiqué, Taiwan implemented exchange rate reforms.

Export orientation did not make things easier for private firms or outside investors. The government still controlled prices and interest rates, and without official sponsorship private firms remained vulnerable to sudden shifts. The most conspicuous victim was Tang Rong, a privately owned steel firm undergoing rapid expansion when it was caught overextended by a sudden rise in interest rates in 1960. The military had a strong interest in steel, and two years later the government stepped in to reorganize Tang Rong as a public enterprise.[52] But private firms that collaborated with the state enjoyed favored access to investment capital, as well as almost guaranteed profits and market share. TaTung Engineering, a manufacturer of electric fans, expanded with the help of U.S. aid and the Taiwanese government into the production of electrical meters, motors, and switches for export under licenses from Westinghouse and Toshiba. Lin Ting-sheng, the company president and a member of the KMT central committee, explained that "money is no problem. The problem is how to spend it wisely."[53] For both the United States and Taiwan, choices between public and private sector solutions were guided less by theory than by considerations of control, politics, and cost.

Continued restrictions, official and unofficial, discouraged foreign direct investment and encouraged arrangements favorable to Taiwanese companies. U.S. investment accelerated after the reforms, growing from just over $2 million in 1959 to around $50 million by 1965, but U.S. businessmen still felt harassed. *Fortune* noted that Taiwan's "prevailing philosophy, inherited from Sun Yat-sen, if not exactly anti-capitalist, was in important respects not pro-capitalist."[54] A congressional delegation visited Taiwan in 1960 and found businessmen skeptical about reform, accusing the government of "extreme interference in the conduct of business, whether domestic or foreign." Public corporations competed with private ones, and officials persecuted foreign firms. The delegation found one unfortunate U.S. businessman whose plant had been shut by the Keelung city government and who, weeks later, had yet to discover why it was closed and who could reopen it.[55]

The economic ministry screened applicants for investment permits and employed a variety of devices to induce foreign firms to accept local partners (or partnership with a state enterprise) and transfer ownership to Taiwan after a set period. No fully foreign-owned subsidiaries were allowed.[56] Faced with these restrictions, many foreign investors found it easier to allow Taiwanese firms to manufacture products under license, an arrangement by which U.S. and Japanese firms transferred technology and capital to a Taiwanese company in return for royalties. Japanese firms worked chiefly through licensing agreements, and between 1960 and 1965 a growing number of U.S. firms employed this option. It allowed Taiwan to retain domestic control of key industries and compelled foreign firms to share technology. Not until the erection in 1965 of the first export-processing zone, a constructed platform in Kaohsiung harbor that physically and symbolically segregated foreign firms from the domestic economy, did U.S. firms enjoy a degree of autonomy. Even then, a government Investment Commission kept a close eye on their operations.[57] Embassy officials were fully aware of the restrictions hampering U.S. investors, but there is no evidence that they made a concerted effort to change matters.

The aid mission could not undo what it had done. U.S. programs had given life to a plexus of government-corporate linkages too tangled even for AID officials to figure out. In the early 1960s, an AID official tried to discern the scale and complexity of links between the ministries, state enterprises, and private firms by interviewing managers and bureaucrats. His first visits provoked an official protest, and he was ordered to stop.[58] Most U.S. officials saw few reasons to quarrel with success. With its low inflation, high rate of capital formation, and solid support for defense, Taiwan stood apart from other clients. Undersecretary of State C. Douglas Dillon found its prospects for "rapid and sustained growth . . . quite exceptional."[59]

By the first years of the Kennedy administration, both governments were advertising Taiwan as a private enterprise success story. KMT officials presented it as a showcase of enlightened Nationalist rule and hinted that Taiwan's growing prosperity could incite rebellion on the mainland.[60] Kennedy, who had criticized Eisenhower's aid programs, touted Taiwan as an exemplar of noncommunist development.[61] AID held up Taiwan's success as a shield against criticism. Release in 1958 of *The Ugly American,* a best-selling account of bungling aid officials, opened a series of congressional probes, funding cutbacks, and restrictions that only intensified during the Kennedy years. Senators Mike Mansfield (D-MT) and Jacob Javitz (R-NY) pushed for termination deadlines and a "private enterprise" approach to aid policy, positions ratified by the Clay Commission in 1963. The same year, Congress created an Advisory Committee on Private Enterprise in Foreign Aid and instructed it to suggest a program of reforms by July 1965.[62] In January 1965 AID responded by announcing Taiwan's impending graduation and the commissioning of the Jacoby study.[63]

Jacoby's study defended AID at its most vulnerable points. While critical of procedural details, it congratulated AID for sticking to free-market fundamentals. "Both through its allocation of aid funds . . . and through its influence on Chinese policies, AID helped make private enterprise flower. It did not 'build socialism' in the Republic of China." Bell called the report "a milestone in the study of economic development."[64] At least temporarily, it mollified the critics. The advisory committee produced a report milder than that of the Clay Commission, but AID's prestige was only partly restored.[65] As the *New York Times* observed, "the 'graduation' of one client state . . . denotes virtually nothing about the progress of the other major clients or about the needs and American obligations in all the rest of the world."[66]

Taiwan did not pursue "etatism" in spite of U.S. advice but partly because of it. The aid mission and Nationalist officials together invented institutions and patterns of government activity that some analysts today identify as ingredients of Taiwan's success. U.S. engineers and aid officials carefully steered the Nationalist government around political obstacles that might have prevented or delayed industrialization, appeasing the military and improving the efficiency of state enterprises instead of trying to eliminate them. They chose solutions based not on fixed ideas but on circumstances and military necessity.

Aid officials saw the Nationalists' preference for statist solutions not as a cultural characteristic but as a reasonable response to political and economic circumstances: the absence of entrepreneurs, the needs of the military, the shortage of export revenue. Instead of waiting for the cascades of capitalist development to reach Taiwan, the aid mission made its own waves. U.S. officials only later came to regard such tactics as counterproductive, and not because of their own experience but because of pressure from Congress to adopt strategies that would create the proper climate for U.S. direct investment abroad. After the mid-1960s, in a vain bid to appease its critics, AID justified its massive interventions in foreign markets in the name of preventing government intervention in foreign markets. But by then Taiwan had already graduated.

From the start, the foreign aid program suffered from a shortage of steady supporters and a surplus of conflicting rationales. Policy makers were never sure what the program's aims were: stability or social revolution, inoculation against communism or opportunities for U.S. investors. The great irony, according to one former AID official, was that this conceptual confusion in Washington was often coupled with remarkable competence in the field. Behind the theoretical debate, "the actual practice of foreign assistance ultimately comes down to the rather elementary matter of transferring resources and skills from one polity to another."[67] Taiwan's success owed less to a philosophy than to the talents of those immediately involved, and its lessons should be learned from their perspective.

Notes

I am indebted to Dennis Merrill, Stephan Haggard, Robert McMahon, David Painter, and Su-Ya Chang for their valuable suggestions. An earlier version of this essay appeared in *Diplomatic History* 20 (Winter 1996): 1–25.

1. Max Frankel, "U.S. Economic Aid to Taiwan Ended; 'Graduation' Hailed," *New York Times*, 1 July 1965; *Congressional Record*, 89th Cong., 1st sess., 14 July 1965, A3759; David E. Bell, "The Challenge to the Developing Countries," Department of State, *Bulletin* 53 (26 July 1965): 175; Keyes Beach and Clarence W. Hall, "Formosa: Asia's Heartening Success Story," *Reader's Digest*, February 1966, 142.

2. International Bank for Reconstruction and Development, *The East Asian Miracle: Economic Growth and Public Policy* (New York, 1993), 354–55, 366. For other neoclassical views, see David Aikman, *The Pacific Rim: Area of Change, Area of Opportunity* (Boston, 1986), 22; and Milton Friedman and Rose Friedman, *Free to Choose: A Personal Statement* (New York, 1980), 57. For state-oriented interpretations, see Alice H. Amsden, "Taiwan's Economic History: A Case of Etatisme and a Challenge to Dependency Theory," *Modern China* 5 (July 1979): 341–80; Alice H. Amsden, "The State and Taiwan's Economic Development," in *Bringing the State Back In*, ed. Peter Evans, Dietrich Rueschemeyer, and Theda Skocpol (New York, 1985), 78–106; Chalmers Johnson, "Political Institutions and Economic Performance: The Government-Business Relationship in Japan, South Korea, and Taiwan," in *The Political Economy of the New Asian Industrialism*, ed. Frederic C. Deyo (Ithaca, NY, 1987), 136–64; Johnson quoted by

Gregory Noble, "Between Competition and Cooperation: Collective Action in the Industrial Policy of Japan and Taiwan" (Ph.D. diss., Harvard University, 1988), 3; Robert Wade, *Governing the Market: Economic Theory and the Role of Government in East Asian Industrialization* (Princeton, NJ, 1990); and Stephan Haggard, *Pathways from the Periphery: The Politics of Growth in the Newly Industrializing Countries* (Ithaca, NY, 1990).

3. Amsden, "The State," 91.

4. Michael P. Cowen and Robert W. Shenton, *Doctrines of Development* (London, 1996), 440.

5. Neil H. Jacoby, *U.S. Aid to Taiwan: A Study of Foreign Aid, Self-Help, and Development* (New York, 1966), 138. Nancy Bernkopf Tucker "depends heavily on the outstanding work of Neil H. Jacoby." Her account also employs the work of the state-oriented theorists, particularly Wade, Gold, and Haggard. She concludes that the United States was partly successful in imposing market-oriented reforms, and that this partial success accounts for Taiwan's growth. Tucker, *Taiwan, Hong Kong, and the United States, 1945–1992* (New York, 1994), 56–72.

6. Committee to Strengthen the Security of the Free World, *The Scope and Distribution of United States Military and Economic Assistance Programs* (Washington, DC, 1963), 5, 12–13. Headed by Lucius Clay, the committee was appointed by President Kennedy in December 1962 to review foreign military and economic aid programs. It amplified the criticisms of William J. Lederer and Eugene Burdick's *The Ugly American* (New York, 1958), which attacked aid officials' preference for colossal state-controlled projects over small, private ones.

7. Emily Rosenberg notes that after World War II, "policymakers tended to apply their liberal canons selectively," allowing actual policy to diverge from developmentalist dogmas; Emily S. Rosenberg, *Spreading the American Dream: American Economic and Cultural Expansion, 1890–1945* (New York, 1982), 231; Dennis Merrill, *Bread and the Ballot: The United States and India's Economic Development, 1947–1963* (Chapel Hill, NC, 1990), 161–67; Linda Wills Qaimmaqami, "The Catalyst of Nationalization: Max Thornburg and the Failure of Private Sector Developmentalism in Iran, 1947–1951," *Diplomatic History* 19 (Winter 1995): 1–31; Sylvia Maxfield and James H. Nolt, "Protectionism and the Internationalization of Capital: U.S. Sponsorship of Import Substitution Industrialization in the Philippines, Turkey, and Argentina," *International Studies Quarterly* 34, no. 1 (1990): 49–81; Roger D. Lapham to Paul Hoffman, 30 June 1949, U.S. Department of State, *Foreign Relations of the United States, 1949* (Washington, DC, 1974), 9:666–67 (hereafter *FRUS*, with year and volume number). On the emerging Confucian bloc, see Samuel P. Huntington, "The Clash of Civilizations?" *Foreign Affairs* 72 (Summer 1993): 28.

8. Harry B. Price, quoted in Robert A. Packenham, *Liberal America and the Third World* (Princeton, NJ, 1973), 39; A. B. Hersey to J. Burke Knapp, "Summary of Discussion at IPR Dinner Meeting, Brookings Institution, April 20, 1948," 22 April 1948, Records of the Board of Governors of the U.S. Federal Reserve, Country Files: Asia, Australia, and New Zealand—General, U.S. Federal Reserve, Washington, DC.

9. The ECA took over aid operations in June 1948. Roger Lapham to Paul Hoffman, 30 June 1949, *FRUS, 1949*, 9:656–67; "Statement by Secretary Marshall," Department of State, *Bulletin* 18 (29 February 1948): 270–71; Robert Allen Griffin to Harlan Cleveland, 14 April 1949, Records of the U.S. Foreign Assistance Agencies, Office of the

Administrator, Country Subject Files, 1948–50, Record Group 286, box 1, National Archives II, College Park, MD (hereafter RG 286, with filing information).

10. One of the nation's leading civil engineering firms since World War I, J. G. White had constructed naval bases, airfields, and the Muscle Shoals steam-generating plant for the U.S. government as well as hydroelectric dams in Chile and irrigation projects in the Sudan. Its president, Gano Dunn, defined an engineer as someone "who can do with one dollar what any fool can do with two." "Gano Dunn is Dead," *New York Times*, 11 April 1953; Harlan Cleveland to Paul G. Hoffman, "China Aid Program," 22 July 1949, RG 286, box 1; Harlan Cleveland to Paul G. Hoffman, "Taiwan," 27 January 1949, RG 286, box 1. State Department officials were less enthusiastic about Taiwan's economic prospects in 1948 but thought the island could be made viable as a sort of agricultural hinterland for Japan. State Department, Office of Intelligence and Research [OIR], "Prospects in Formosa, November 1948," 22 November 1948, General Records of the Department of State, Record Group 59, R&A Report No. 4807, National Archives II.

11. George H. Kerr, *Formosa Betrayed* (Boston, 1965), 248, 257–315; Tucker, *Taiwan, Hong Kong*, 28; Lai Tse-Han, Ramon. H. Myers, and Wei Wou, *A Tragic Beginning: The Taiwan Uprising of February 28, 1947* (Stanford, CA, 1991), particularly chap. 3, reveals how the mainlanders' heavy-handed economic policies provoked the uprising.

12. Hsu Chen-kuo, "The Political Base of Changing Strategy toward Private Enterprise in Taiwan, 1945–1955" (Ph.D. diss., Ohio State University, 1987), 134; Cleveland to Hoffman, "China Aid Program," 22 July 1949, RG 286, box 1. The debates on Taiwan's predicament are described in Ronald L. McGlothlen, *Controlling the Waves: Dean Acheson and U.S. Foreign Policy in Asia* (New York, 1993), 86–134; Acheson to Edgar, 30 March 1949, *FRUS, 1949*, 9:305–6; "United States Policy toward Formosa," Department of State, *Bulletin* 22 (16 January 1950): 79–81; and De Beausset diary, 15 February 1950, Val de Beausset Papers, Westcroft Farm, Grosse Ile, MI.

13. Bruce J. Dickson, "The Lessons of Defeat: The Reorganization of the Kuomintang on Taiwan, 1950–52," *China Quarterly* 133 (March 1993): 56–84. For biographies of Chinese officials, see Chien-kuo Pang, "The State and Economic Transformation: The Taiwan Case" (Ph.D. diss., Brown University, 1988), 317.

14. Thomas B. Gold, *State and Society in the Taiwan Miracle* (Armonk, NY, 1986), 65; K. C. Wu, "Your Money has Built a Police State in Formosa," *Look*, 29 June 1954, 39–45.

15. Yin visited Japan at the height of the reverse course in 1950 and came to regard its mix of state guidance and export-oriented conglomerates as the model for Asian development. Hsu, "Political Base," 183–84, 230–36. *Min-Sheng*, the third of Sun Yat-sen's principles, is sometimes translated as "people's livelihood" and other times as "socialism." For Chiang's interpretation with respect to economic planning, see Taiwan Provincial Government, Department of Information, *Taiwan: A Model Province of the Republic of China Based on the Three Principles of the People* (Taipei, June 1971), 56.

16. Kerr, *Formosa Betrayed*, 416–26; OIR, "Graphic Summary of the Formosa Situation," 21 August 1950, RG 59, State Department R&A Report No. 5320; Haggard, *Pathways*, 88. Each of the reforms increased the economic power of the mainlander-dominated state while reducing the power and wealth of potential rivals. Farm rent reduction, for instance, was followed by increases in taxes and the price of fertilizer

supplied by a state monopoly. The income of Formosan landholders was thus simply transferred to the state.

17. *U.S. Statutes at Large* 64 (1950–51): 205.

18. Textiles remain Taiwan's most important industry, generating more jobs, exchange, and production value than any other enterprise. Thomas B. Gold, "Dependent Development in Taiwan" (Ph.D. diss., Harvard University, 1981), 97–106, provides a detailed account of the industry's origins. See also Hsu, "Political Base," 166; and Alan P. L. Liu, *Phoenix and the Lame Lion: Modernization in Taiwan and Mainland China, 1950–1980* (Stanford, CA, 1987), 52–54, 123.

19. Strong to Acheson, 21 January 1950, RG 59, 894A.00R/1–250; Moyer to Cleveland, 12 July 1950, RG 59, 894A.00R/7–2650; Rusk to Cleveland, 11 August 1950, RG 59, 894A.00R/8–1150. Rusk's position softened slightly after the National Security Council approved NSC-37/10, "Immediate United States Courses of Action with Respect to Formosa" (3 August 1950, *FRUS, 1950* [Washington, 1976], 6:413–14), which ordered a military survey to determine the usefulness of the armies on Taiwan. Memorandum of conversation, "Policy Guidance for ECA Mission Taipei," 8 September 1950, RG 59, 894A.00R/9–850. Rusk allowed that while avoiding "very long range projects, ECA on Formosa need not keep looking over its shoulder" and could think about suggesting projects for approval.

20. Karl Rankin to Clubb, 24 January 1951, *FRUS, 1951* (Washington, 1983), 7:1523–27; memorandum of conversation, Department of State-JCS meeting, 6 February 1951, *FRUS, 1951*, 7:1566–68; JCS, "Courses of Action Relative to Communist China and Korea," 14 March 1951, *FRUS, 1951*, 7:1598–1605; Hsu, "Political Base," 146; Rusk to Griffin, 19 March 1951, *FRUS, 1951*, 7:1596–97.

21. OIR, "The Current Situation on Taiwan," 4 May 1951, RG 59, State Department R&A Report No. 5529; Yen Chia-kan to William Foster, 23 January 1951, Records of the U.S. Federal Reserve, Country Files, Taiwan—General; Rusk to Griffin, 19 March 1951, *FRUS, 1951*, 7:1596–97; minutes of the second meeting of the Economic Stabilization Board, 22 March 1951, RG 59, 894A.131/4–1051; minutes of the third meeting of the Economic Stabilization Board, 28 March 1951, RG 59, 894A.131/4–1051.

22. Memorandum of conversation, "Projected Assignment of Mr. Morrill to Formosa," 14 May 1951, RG 59, 894A.10A/5–1451; Rusk to Griffin, 9 May 1951, *FRUS, 1951*, 7:1664–65.

23. Senate Appropriations Committee, Special Subcommittee on Foreign Economic Cooperation, *United States Aid to Formosa*, 82nd Cong., 1st sess., August 1951, 4–6; Morrill recommended a "European type" central bank that could steer investment into socially desirable industries. "One of the weaknesses of [U.S.] central banking in the past," he explained, "has been that the monetary authority has just gone along with economic changes instead of anticipating and formulating ideas on how they might be dealt with before they arise." Twenty-seventh meeting of the Economic Stabilization Board, 6 September 1951, RG 59, 894A.14/9-1551. The Bank of Taiwan did not make a single loan to a private firm until 1955, and until 1965 its lending to the private sector remained insignificant. Chi Huang, "The State and Foreign Capital: A Case Study of Taiwan" (Ph.D. diss., Indiana University, 1986), 123.

24. Acheson to Rankin, 22 June 1951, *FRUS, 1951*, 7:1715–16. Rankin became ambassador in April 1953; U.S. Senate, Committee on Foreign Relations, *Mutual Security Act of 1951*, 82nd Cong., 1st sess., 1951, 536.

25. Senate Appropriations Committee, *United States Aid to Formosa*, 6.

26. Laura Hughes to Fred Bunting, "Activities of the China Mission in the Economic Field," 12 May 1952, *Records of the Office of Chinese Affairs, 1945–1955*, microfilm (Wilmington, DE, 1989), reel 16; memorandum of conversation, "Conference with Maj. Gen. William H. Chase, Chief of Military Assistance Advisory Group, Formosa," 20 February 1952, *FRUS, 1952–1954*, 14:10; Karl M. Rankin, "Report on Foreign Economic Policy Discussions Between United States Officials in the Far East and Clarence B. Randall and Associates," 18 December 1956, *Declassified Documents Reference System, 1990*, 0443 (hereafter DDRS); Hughes to Bunting, "Activities of the China Mission in the Economic Field," 12 May 1952, *Records of the Office of Chinese Affairs, 1945–1955*, reel 16; National Security Council, "U.S. Economic Assistance to Formosa," 28 May 1952, *FRUS, 1952–1954*, 14:58.

27. L. B. Pearson to Department of State, 16 June 1952, *Records of the Office of Chinese Affairs, 1945–1955*, reel 16; Rankin to Schenck, 14 January 1952, *Records of the Office of Chinese Affairs, 1945–1955*, reel 16; OIR, "Private U.S. Investments As Sources of Friction in Selected Countries: The Far East," 31 December 1952, RG 59, State Department R&A Report No. 5985.2; Burton Crane, "Formosa Changing Form of Economy," *New York Times*, 8 February 1950.

28. Ching-yuan Lin, *Industrialization in Taiwan, 1946–72: Trade and Import Substitution Policies for Developing Countries* (New York, 1973), 70–72; U.S. Department of Commerce, "Licensing and Exchange Controls, Taiwan," World Trade Information Service Operations Report No. 56–10 (Washington, DC, January 1956); H. K. Kao, "Foreign Exchange and Trade Control in Free China," *Far Eastern Economic Review*, 13 January 1955; Igor Oganesoff, "Formosa Invasion Peril Spotlights U.S. Aid to Army, Economy," *Wall Street Journal*, 27 August 1958.

29. Memorandum of conversation, Department of State-JCS Meeting, 9 April 1952, *FRUS, 1952–1954*, 14:39.

30. Walter P. McConaughy to Allison, "Program Analysis: MSA Formosa," 22 August 1952, *Records of the Office of Chinese Affairs, 1945–1955*, reel 16. Taiwan had six four-year plans between 1953 and 1975, a six-year plan (1976–81) and a ten-year plan (1980–89). Johnson, "Political Institutions and Economic Performance," 142. The first four-year plan remains secret in Taiwan but has been released in the Records of the Office of Chinese Affairs. De Beausset chose a four-year cycle to coincide with the term of J. G. White's contract. C. L. Terrell to MSA, "Economic Aid to China," 30 September 1952, *Records of the Office of Chinese Affairs, 1945–1955*, reel 16; Hope to McConaughy, "Request for Clearance on Press Release Regarding Chinese Four-Year Plan," 3 December 1952, *Records of the Office of Chinese Affairs, 1945–1955*, reel 16; interview with Val de Beausset, 31 May 1995; memorandum of conversation with Martin Wong, 9 December 1955, RG 59, Records of the Office of Chinese Affairs, 1954–56, lot 60D171, box 5; Gold, "Dependent Development," 250.

31. K. Y. Yin, "A Discussion of Industrial Policy for Taiwan," *Industry of Free China* 1 (May 1954): 1–14; "Road to Taiwan's Industrial Reconstruction," *Industry of Free China* 1 (May 1954): 29–36.

32. Karl Rankin to Walter P. McConaughy, 10 April 1953, *FRUS, 1952–1954*, 14:184; memorandum of conversation No. 230, "Chinese Government Budgetary Problems and Interest in IBRD Loan," 21 September 1953, in *FRUS: Secretary of State's Memoranda of Conversation, November 1952–December 1954, Microfiche Supplement* (Washington,

DC, 1992); memorandum of conversation with Martin Wong (secretary general Council for U.S. Aid), 9 December 1955, RG 59, Records of the Office of Chinese Affairs, 1954–1956, lot 60D171, box 5.

33. Minutes of the 266th meeting of the NSC, 15 November 1955, *FRUS, 1955–1957*, 10:29–30; minutes of the 273rd meeting of the NSC, 18 January 1956, *FRUS, 1955–1957*, 10:64–66.

34. Joseph Schumpeter and Max Weber are largely responsible for the market/planning dualism; see Chalmers Johnson, *MITI and the Japanese Miracle: The Growth of Industrial Policy, 1925–1975* (Stanford, CA, 1982), 18; Nathan Godfried, *Bridging the Gap between Rich and Poor: American Economic Development Policy toward the Arab East, 1942–1949* (New York, 1987), 12–13; Foreign Operations Administration (FOA), *Conclusions and Recommendations of the International Development Advisory Board* (Washington, DC, 1953), 18; Karl M. Rankin, "Report on Foreign Economic Policy Discussions between United States Officials in the Far East and Clarence B. Randall and Associates," 18 December 1956, *DDRS, 1990*, 0443; FOA, *Conclusions*, 18; and A. Guy Hope to Rankin, 14 January 1955, RG 59, Records of the Office of Chinese Affairs, 1954–1956, lot 60D171, box 4.

35. Troy L. Perkins to Mr. Johnson, "MSA Proposals for a Joint Commission for Industrial Development and a China Development Corporation," 18 July 1952, RG 59, 894A.00/7–1852; Nicholas H. Riegg, "The Role of Fiscal and Monetary Policies in Taiwan's Economic Development" (Ph.D. diss., University of Connecticut, 1978), 38; Igor Oganesoff, "A Tale of Two Lins: Land Reform Narrows Formosan Social Gap," *Wall Street Journal*, 15 April 1960. Of the four firms, only Taiwan Cement appreciated in value, and it began to show a return only after several years. Industry officials sought assurances that relations with government would remain as before. See the discussion on privatization in *Industry of Free China* 1 (1954); and Joseph L. Brent, "Report on Foreign Economic Policy Discussions between United States Officials in the Far East and Clarence B. Randall and Associates," December 1956, *DDRS, 1990*, 0444.

36. House Committee on Foreign Affairs, *Interim Report of the Subcommittee for Review of the Mutual Security Programs*, 86th Cong., 1st sess., 15 February 1959, 5; Alfred E. Moon to Stassen, "Secretary Hoover's Request for Information on the Proposed Plastics Plant for Formosa," 13 May 1955, and D. A. Fitzgerald to Stassen, "Polyvinyl Chloride Project in Formosa," 7 July 1955, Records of U.S. Foreign Assistance Agencies, Geographic Files of the Director, RG 469, box 26, National Archives II; Wade, *Governing the Market*, 80.

37. Walter P. McConaughy to Mr. Allison, "Program Analysis: MSA Formosa," 22 August 1952, *Records of the Office of Chinese Affairs, 1945–1955*, reel 16.

38. Rankin to Radford, 3 January 1956, RG 59, Records of the Office of Chinese Affairs, 1954–1956, lot 60D171, box 18. The military hampered the industrial effort by running up budgetary deficits that siphoned off savings and investment through taxes and high interest rates. The military also had first claim on skilled technicians, electric power, petroleum, and cement.

39. Haggard, *Pathways*, 87; memorandum of conversation, Karl Arndt and Herbert Prochnow, "Discussion on Taiwan Economy in Taipei, October 10, 1955," RG 59, Records of the Office of Chinese Affairs, 1954–1956, lot 60D171, box 12.

40. Operations Coordinating Board, "Report on Taiwan and the Government of

the Republic of China," 16 April 1958, Eisenhower Papers, NSC Series, Policy Papers, Dwight D. Eisenhower Library, Abilene, KS.

41. NSC-5610, "Report by the Interdepartmental Committee on Certain U.S. Aid Programs," 3 August 1956, Eisenhower Papers, NSC Series, Policy Papers.

42. T. R. Bowden to Laura B. Hughes, 7 February 1956, Records of the Office of Chinese Affairs, 1954–1956, lot 60D171, box 12 (emphasis in original).

43. OIR, "Attitudes toward Aid Programs." This assumption was proved wrong on 24 May 1957, when a mob sacked the U.S. embassy in Taipei after the acquittal (by a U.S. military court) of a U.S. officer accused of murdering a Taiwanese man. The high living standards of U.S. servicemen partly accounted for the rioters' anger. Tucker, *Taiwan, Hong Kong*, 90–92.

44. House Committee on Government Operations, *Foreign Aid and Construction Projects*, 85th Cong., 2nd sess., 1958, 852; Republic of China, *China Yearbook, 1960–1961* (Taipei, 1960), 10; Robert H. Silin, *Leadership and Values: The Organization of Large-Scale Taiwanese Enterprises* (Cambridge, MA, 1976), 21. VACRS was originally called the Retser program.

45. "Taiwan Electric Power Industry," *Far Eastern Economic Review*, 21 October 1954, 529; House Special Committee to Study the Foreign Aid Program, *Korea, Japan, Taiwan, and the Philippines: A Report on United States Foreign Assistance Programs*, 85th Cong., 1st sess., March 1957, 17.

46. Vermont Royster, "Island in the Sun: Formosa Grows Prosperous and Tries not to Look Back," *Wall Street Journal*, 26 March 1959.

47. H. K. Kao, "Foreign Exchange and Trade Control in Free China," *Far Eastern Economic Review*, 13 January 1955.

48. Val de Beausset to File, "Value of Aluminum Company to Taiwan," 19 February 1952, RG 469, Records of U.S. Foreign Assistance Agencies, Mission to China, Organizations and Individuals, 1948–54, box 2; The Economist Intelligence Unit, *Quarterly Economic Review of China and Hong Kong* No. 9, March 1955, 8; George K. C. Yeh to Karl Rankin, "A Plan for Sino-American Cooperation to Combat Communist Penetration in Asia," 1 December 1956, *DDRS, 1994, 1929*; Stephan Haggard and Chien-Kuo Pang, "The Transition to Export-Led Growth in Taiwan," in *The Role of the State in Taiwan's Development*, ed. Joel Aberbach, David Dollar, and Kenneth Sokoloff (Armonk, NY, 1994), 73–74.

49. U.S. Department of Commerce, Bureau of Foreign Commerce, "Licensing and Exchange Controls, Taiwan," *World Trade Information Service Operations Report No. 59–12* (Washington, DC, February 1959).

50. Wade, *Governing the Market*, 52–55; Haggard, *Pathways*, 92–93.

51. Harold Stassen to Struve Hansel, "Approval of FY1950–54 Mutual Defense Assistance Revised Material and Training Programs," 29 December 1954, RG 59, Records of the Office of Chinese Affairs, 1954–1956, lot 60D171, box 5; Operations Coordinating Board, "Report on Taiwan and the Government of the Republic of China," 15 April 1959, Eisenhower Papers, NSC Series, Policy Papers.

52. Gregory W. Noble, "Between Competition and Cooperation: Collective Action in the Industrial Policy of Japan and Taiwan" (Ph.D. diss., Harvard University, 1988), 133.

53. "Formosa: The Remarkable Message," *Fortune*, June 1959, 224; "Industries to

Be Visited by Herter Party," 13 September 1957, RG 469, Records of the U.S. Foreign Assistance Agencies, Mission to China, Industrial Development Division, Subject Files, 1956–61, box 14.

54. P. W. Colm and C. B. Bongard, "Taiwan: U.S. Policy Problems," 10 January 1966, *DDRS, 1993,* 2117; "Formosa: The Remarkable Message," 220, 226; Robert Keatley, "Prosperous Taiwan Is on Way to Becoming Big Factory Center," *Wall Street Journal,* 2 August 1965.

55. Senate Committee on Interstate and Foreign Commerce, *Foreign Commerce Study,* 86th Cong., 2nd sess., 1960, 7.

56. For the full list of restrictions on foreign investment see Chi Huang, "The State and Foreign Capital."

57. P. W. Colm and C. B. Bongard, "Taiwan: U.S. Policy Problems," 10 January 1966, *DDRS, 1993,* 2117; Haggard, *Pathways,* 198–99.

58. Allan B. Cole, "Political Roles of Taiwanese Entrepreneurs," *Asian Survey* 7 (September 1967): 645.

59. Douglas Dillon to Robert B. Anderson, 3 December 1959, RG 59, 894A.00/12–359.

60. Seymour Topping, "Taiwan Shifting Emphasis from War to Prosperity," *New York Times,* 21 December 1964.

61. Kennedy to Chiang, 17 April 1961, in *President John F. Kennedy's Office Files, 1961–1963,* part 5, *Countries File,* ed. Paul Kesaris and Robert E. Lester (Bethesda, MD, 1989), microfilm, reel 4; Rostow to Kennedy, 31 July 1961, ibid.

62. *Congressional Record,* 88th Cong., 2nd sess., 1963, 110, pt. 9:11906.

63. Felix Belair, Jr., "U.S. to Publicize Effects of Aid on Boom in Taiwan," *New York Times,* 13 January 1965.

64. Jacoby, *U.S. Aid to Taiwan,* 245, vi.

65. Advisory Committee on Private Enterprise in Foreign Aid, *Foreign Aid through Private Initiative* (Washington, DC, July 1965).

66. Max Frankel, "U.S. Economic Aid to Taiwan Ended; 'Graduation' Hailed," *New York Times,* 1 July 1965.

67. Lucian W. Pye, "Foreign Aid and America's Involvement in the Developing World," in *The Vietnam Legacy: The War, American Society and the Future of American Foreign Policy,* ed. Anthony Lake (New York, 1976), 375–78.

Conclusion

PETER L. HAHN AND MARY ANN HEISS

During the several decades of the Cold War, scholarship on U.S. foreign relations concentrated on the political, strategic, and economic confrontation between the United States and the Soviet Union. By comparison, U.S. policy toward the Third World paled in popularity. Some peripheral areas, such as Latin America and East Asia, attracted a fair amount of scholarly attention, in the case of the former because of traditional U.S. dominance but in the case of the latter because Cold War tensions were played out in China, Korea, and Vietnam. Diplomatic historians showed much less interest in the Middle East and especially Africa, and much of the limited research done on such areas considered the unfolding of the Cold War there.[1]

The end of the Cold War in 1991 stimulated new approaches to the study of diplomatic history. While some scholars anticipated that the opening of Soviet, Chinese, and East European archives would shed new light on the traditional questions about the origins and duration of the Cold War, others adopted new methodologies and borrowed approaches from related disciplines to examine U.S. foreign experiences in fresh light. Elizabeth Cobbs Hoffman observed the emergence in the 1990s of a "new diplomatic history" that examined the U.S. national experience in a global context on the basis of multinational research. The new diplomatic history also widened the scope of research beyond the Cold War and national security issues into matters of race, culture, gender, and other issues to a degree unprecedented in the history of the field. These innovations in scholarly research have deeply affected the study of U.S. policy in the Third World.[2]

The essays in this volume demonstrate the breadth, depth, and range of recent scholarship on U.S. relations with the Third World. Collectively, the essays include traditional accounts of diplomacy and policy making and innovative studies based on culture, gender, labor activism, economic development, and international reformism. They examine policy-making elites based in Washington, government officials assigned to overseas posts, private citizens who became involved in shaping foreign relations, and the officials and citizens of foreign states, and they place the evolution of U.S. policy in the context of local, regional, and domestic circumstances. Geographically, three essays deal with the Middle East, three with Asia, two with Latin America, one with Africa, and one with the Third World as a whole. All focus on the 1940s through the 1960s—the decades in which the United States first faced the challenge of decolonization and Cold War in the Third World, and the decades for which sufficient documentary sources are available—although some essays examine small spans of time with acute precision while others reveal trends that unfolded over longer time periods. In short, the scholarship in this volume shows that the study of U.S. relations with the Third World, if a bit eclectic, is also innovative and vibrant.

Despite the diverse approaches, several major and unifying themes emerge from the essays in this volume. The Cold War, for example, recurs frequently, not surprisingly given the extent to which it remained the dominant issue in international relations in the 1940s–1960s. Robert Buzzanco finds that U.S. officials shaped policy toward Vietnam primarily on the basis of Cold War considerations. Importantly, however, the other essays collectively provide a more nuanced view than the traditional notion that U.S. officials always followed Cold War dictates when making decisions about the Third World. To be sure, the Cold War figured prominently in U.S. thinking about certain issues, but in other situations the Cold War actually faded in importance in the determination of U.S. policy.

At times, for example, U.S. policy was primarily designed to support pro-U.S. regimes in other countries or to thwart potentially dangerous Third World nationalism. As Piero Gleijeses acknowledges, U.S. officials were determined to preserve a friendly government in the Congo in large part to deny open and easy access to that strategically important land to Cold War adversaries. Chinese and Soviet intervention in the Congo, however, followed rather than preceded U.S. involvement, which, in Gleijeses's judgment, stemmed from the calculation that the United States could help preserve a friendly regime at minimal cost or risk. In a similar vein, Douglas Little views the Cold War as a driving force in some U.S. policies in the Middle East, such as arms supply, but finds that U.S. officials formulated the Eisenhower Doctrine as an antinationalist measure unrelated to their concerns with communist expansionism, despite their public rationalization of it on anti-communist grounds.

Other essays in this volume also suggest that U.S. policy was motivated by more than simply Cold War considerations. Stephen Rabe concedes that anticommunism became a crucial factor in U.S. decisions between democracy and dictatorship as the best means to thwart Castroism, but he contends that U.S. policies were deeply rooted in traditional concerns—such as maintaining closed-door, sphere-of-influence economic opportunity for U.S. business interests—that had long antedated the communist threat. Elizabeth Cobbs Hoffman acknowledges that the Peace Corps was designed to project a favorable image of the United States on the global screen, and she places in it a historical context of U.S. psychological warfare operations designed to advance national security aims. But she argues that the impact of the Cold War is often exaggerated by historians who cynically consider the Peace Corps a Cold War measure. In Cobbs Hoffman's view, the Peace Corps reflected John F. Kennedy's genuinely idealistic drive to improve the world. It would have developed even without the Cold War, she contends, as a mechanism by which colonial powers would have tried to manage the transition from empire to independence in the Third World.

Some of the contributors to this volume suggest that the Cold War remained in the shadows for many officials who participated in the formulation of U.S. policy. Darlene Rivas detects a tendency in the years immediately following World War II for U.S. officials and businessmen to mesh their own New Deal reformism with the nationalist impulses of Venezuelans, with little regard for the Cold War emerging in the Eastern Hemisphere. Nick Cullather downplays the importance of the great power confrontation in the worldviews of U.S. officials stationed in Taiwan. Rather than reflexively opposing socialism, communism, and Soviet or Chinese communist power, aid officials in Taiwan promoted economic development models with statist controls and encouraged the Nationalist Chinese to demobilize their enormous military force for economic reasons. Cullather even ascribes to Eisenhower the attitude that the United States should not uniformly oppose socialism but should encourage it where useful in containing Soviet power. (Ironically, the studies by Mary Ann Heiss, Andrew Rotter, and Peter L. Hahn, which focus the least on political, economic, and security issues, concede that Cold War security concerns formed an integral part of policy making before they explore hidden dimensions of U.S. foreign relations.)

A second common theme that runs through this volume is the way in which allied states complicated U.S. policy in the Third World. As the world's greatest prewar empire and the United States's closest partner in the Cold War, Britain figured prominently in U.S. deliberations about the dynamics of the Cold War and decolonization in the Third World. Little finds that Eisenhower consulted closely with officials in London while planning military interventions in Lebanon and Jordan and positioning warships near Kuwait. Heiss observes that Truman abandoned his early, moderate position of playing honest broker between Iran and Britain and sided with his ally as the Anglo-Iranian oil deadlock hardened and that Eisenhower embraced a full partnership with Britain, including collaboration to overthrow Mossadeq. Heiss and Rotter suggest that U.S. and British officials made many similar, culture-bound assumptions and observations about Iranians and Indians. In Rotter's view, decades of British Orientalism profoundly shaped official and private U.S. views of India.

Britain was not the only allied power to appear in U.S. thinking. Buzzanco suggests that U.S. calculations about the economic livelihood of all European allies and Japan drove U.S. officials to intervene in Indochina. In the case of the Congo, Gleijeses reveals, the United States pressured Belgium, as the former colonial power, to defend the government in Leopoldville (Kinshasa) by approving a mercenary initiative, allowing Belgian citizens to serve as combatants, dispatching Belgian paratroopers to rescue Western hostages, and maintaining a vast personnel force to supervise the overt side of the mercenary initiative. Cobbs Hoffman details in great depth the official cooperation and the unofficial symmetry between the Peace Corps and the overseas service programs of other countries. Numerous Western allies joined the international voluntary movement in response to U.S. leadership, and even states like the Philippines and Israel found reasons to participate in programs resembling the Peace Corps.

The U.S. response to the rise of revolutionary nationalism in the Third World forms a third major theme of this volume. Scholars critical of U.S. policy in the Third World have traditionally advanced the notion that U.S. officials frequently misunderstood and misinterpreted Third World nationalism and blindly and errantly equated it with communism.[3]

To a certain extent, evidence presented in this volume confirms this critical interpretation of U.S. policy. In one sense, U.S. officials of the 1950s and 1960s displayed symptoms of what might be called "democraphobia." While espousing democratic ideology, they feared the rise of mass-based revolutions targeting conservative national regimes that advanced U.S. interests in the Third World. On occasion, U.S. officials feared that new-style democratic leaders were at worst closet communists or at best novices who were naive about communism's sinister ability to take over their countries once they uprooted older regimes. Unlike the conservative, wealthy, older men with whom the United States had grown comfortable, the new leaders were often young radicals who commanded enormous popular appeal. Such fears drove U.S. officials to oppose Ho Chi Minh, Gamal Abdel Nasser, Mohammed Mossadeq, Patrice Lumumba, Fidel Castro, and, briefly, Rómulo Betancourt. Kennedy refrained from pushing for full democratic reform in the Dominican Republic after the assassination of Trujillo, Rabe suggests, because he feared that Castroism might take hold there.

On balance, however, the essays in this volume present a more nuanced assessment of the U.S. response to nationalism than the traditional, critical interpretation. They posit that U.S. officials fairly accurately perceived nationalism, understood its differences from communism, and took steps to mollify it on terms consistent with important U.S. objectives. They also detail important and distinctive features of nationalism and suggest that leaders of Third World states often responded to it more conservatively than U.S. officials.

According to Little, for example, officials of the Eisenhower administration correctly perceived the powerful appeal of nationalism among Arab peoples, understood that masses of them endorsed Nasserism, and accurately anticipated the likely nationalistic reactions to gunboat diplomacy. Moreover, conservative regimes in Saudi Arabia, Jordan, Kuwait, and Morocco clamored for Western military intervention in Iraq and Lebanon even in the face of U.S. reluctance. Eisenhower privately distinguished nationalism from communism, Little contends, and publicly associated the two phenomena only when necessary to build consensus at home sufficient to support his reluctant military interventionism in Lebanon.

Rabe concedes that U.S. officials were originally ignorant about Latin American nationalism and dismissed it as communist inspired. By the late 1950s, however, officials in Washington realized that a tide of nationalism was sweeping the region and challenging the dominant constellation of rightist, pro-U.S., authoritarian regimes. Eisenhower consciously decided to embrace democracy with a leftist slant, as manifest in Betancourt's Venezuela, over rightist dictatorship as practiced in Trujillo's Dominican Republic, if he could do so without risking extreme leftist revolution as evident in Castro's Cuba.

Other examples abound. Gleijeses discovers an awareness among U.S. officials that nationalism burned brightly in the Congo and that the anti-Mobutu revolt was a Congolese movement lacking a strong leaning toward communism or Communist China. In Cobbs Hoffman's judgment, Peace Corps officers successfully mitigated the more hostile anti-U.S. impulses of nationalism in the Third World by co-opting the people of the beneficiary nations, requiring volunteers to learn the languages and cultures of their host states, promoting a universalist sense of international connectedness, downplaying anticommunism as a political weapon, and assiduously avoiding connections to intelligence agencies. Before Cold War security concerns forced them to take extreme measures against Mossadeq, Heiss suggests, U.S. officials initially recognized that Iranian nationalism had deep and legitimate aspirations to which Britain should make concessions.

Evidence emerges in this volume that some Third World nations actually welcomed U.S. involvement. In Venezuela, Rivas notes, economic nationalists encouraged foreign capital investment under certain conditions as the best means to modernize and stabilize their economy. Private businessman Nelson Rockefeller showed sensitivity to nationalist concerns by modifying his capitalist practices to promote popular welfare (and thereby stabilize Venezuela and preserve capitalism there). State Department officials likewise believed it prudent to make some concessions to economic nationalists. Rockefeller collaborated with a government led by a democratic leftist party to build a postwar economy featuring private capital investment, technical expertise, pragmatism, and diversification. Similarly, Cullather finds that Taiwanese leaders eagerly welcomed U.S. officials, who provided not only a security shield against attack from mainland China but also the economic aid and expertise needed to invigorate their infant economy. By the early 1950s, Taiwan accepted U.S. advisers in all major branches of government and industry and resisted only when the advisers urged sharp and prompt reductions in the size of the nation's military.

Several essays in this volume also reveal that concern among U.S. officials and citizens with the "Other" occasionally shaped their perceptions of the Third World. Most noticeably, Rotter finds that U.S. officials consistently characterized Indian leaders as feminine, weak, passive, and unmanly, traits that were opposite to the qualities they attributed to themselves. For such cultural reasons, U.S. officials found it difficult, during decades of crucial political change, to relate to Indian leaders or to understand policies that emanated from long-held Indian cultural values. According to Heiss, Western officials who dealt with Mossadeq drew similar distinctions between the Iranian leader and themselves. U.S. officials judged Mossadeq by Western instead of Iranian standards and therefore found disreputable certain of his behaviors that Iranian culture viewed in a positive light.

Although it is probably not intended, other contributors present evidence of similar modes of thinking among U.S. officials dealing with other states. U.S. attitudes toward the Congo, in light of Gleijeses's findings, appear to have been shaped by perceptions that the Congolese were ignorant and unskilled bush people under the sway of witchcraft and superstition and by subconscious fears that mass black rebellion in the Congo portended a mass black movement within the United States. The instinctive dislike of communists, nationalists, and anti-Zionists, as portrayed in several other essays, reveals that U.S. policy makers possessed irrational fears of people different from themselves.

U.S. officials often showed a propensity to view Third World leaders in metaphors based on gender and strength. According to Little and Rabe, U.S. leaders worried about "weak-kneed" leaders in the Middle East and Lebanon, and Gleijeses finds that U.S. officials denounced Europeans who refused to send mercenaries to the Congo as "gutless." U.S. and British officials spoke dismissively of their adversary Mossadeq in gendered terms, Heiss argues. They denigrated his dress, behavior, conduct, temperament, strength, maturity, and mental health, and they characterized him in feminine terms, not only to show their disdain but also to justify their determination to oust him from power. Rotter argues that U.S. perceptions of passivity, emotionalism, and femininity among Indian men contributed to U.S. distaste for Indian neutralism. U.S. officials also made clear what type of foreign figures they preferred. They liked the "zest and dynamism" of Congolese Prime Minister Moise Tshombe, Gleijeses finds, and celebrated the mercenaries, despite their frequent excesses such as murder, rape, and robbery, as "tall, vigorous Boers from South Africa," "long-legged, slim, and muscular Englishmen from Rhodesia," and "rough-hewn college boys." Rotter and Heiss discover that U.S. officials preferred leaders in Pakistan and Iran who dressed, behaved, and consumed whiskey like Western men.

Collectively, the essays in this volume also present evidence that U.S. officials frequently tried to export their own cultural values and institutions to other nations in the Third World. According to Little, U.S. officials spoke of implementing a new deal for the Arab states, and according to Rivas, the State Department endorsed Rockefeller's initiatives to create a reformist capitalism in Venezuela, with the state harnessing capitalism for public good on the model of the New Deal. While U.S. economic aid officials in Taiwan showed flexibility in adapting to local circumstances, Cullather contends, they also followed economic development models that had worked well in the United States and in Europe under the Marshall Plan. Cobbs Hoffman argues thematically that Peace Corps volunteers sought to export their cultural values and institutions for the benefit of Third World peoples, while Hahn suggests that leaders of private U.S. labor unions intended to preserve and promote in Israel a political economy that was democratic and sympathetic to labor, like the one they aspired to establish in the United States.

The essays in this volume also find that a common theme of U.S. policy in the Third World was the propensity of officials to engage in covert operations. Little uncovers evidence of the CIA spending cash to influence

Lebanon's elections and attempting some kind of undercover operation in Syria. Rabe recounts how the CIA offered money to Betancourt in Venezeulan elections, delivered arms to dissidents in the Dominican Republic, launched the Bay of Pigs invasion, and apparently tried to discredit Castro by planting Cuban weapons in Venezuela. In the Congo, according to Gleijeses, the CIA interfered in elections in 1961; supervised, armed, transported, and paid hundreds of mercenaries from Europe and southern Africa; and established an air force and a naval patrol on Lake Tanganyika. In Iran, the CIA partnered with British intelligence to overthrow Mossadeq.

Lest it appear that only the CIA conducted such activities, Rabe observes that Trujillo engaged in covert operations against Venezuela and that Betancourt worked overtly to undermine Castro. Hahn finds that Israeli government officials and U.S. labor leaders engaged in secret initiatives to change U.S. official policy, albeit without the sinister dimension of cloak-and-dagger operations. And lest it appear that the CIA was omnipresent, Cobbs Hoffman maintains that the Peace Corps assiduously avoided any taint of intelligence work, and Rivas asserts that the United States was not involved in the coup in Venezuela in November 1948.

The essays in this volume reach a range of conclusions on the degree of success U.S. officials achieved in the Third World. Some contributors portray U.S. officials as achieving their goals at what they considered to be tolerable cost. Gleijeses believes that the United States accomplished its objective of crushing a rebellion against the government of the Congo without substantial detriment to itself. Cobbs Hoffman credits the Peace Corps with dramatic success at its stated mission of earning for the United States universal admiration, evident in the extent to which many other states tried to replicate the U.S. program and in the worldwide mourning at the death of Kennedy. Cullather credits U.S. economic aid officials stationed in Taiwan for showing the innovation, wisdom, and flexibility needed to adapt their ideology of private development to actual circumstances in Taiwan. By practicing "situational economics" in Taiwan, they created an infrastructure and a corporatist conglomerate of public-private enterprises that produced an economic miracle. In the private realm, in Hahn's analysis, U.S. labor leaders usually got what they wanted in regard to Washington's official policy toward Israel.

Other scholars more critically conclude that U.S. policy in the Third World produced failures. Buzzanco concludes that the American experience in Vietnam failed militarily and politically and caused unprecedented dislocation to the U.S. economy. Little finds that short-term achievement in Lebanon was offset by long-term costs, including the provocation of Arab nationalism and the dangerous precedent of deploying troops without congressional consent. To stabilize the Dominican Republic, Rabe suggests, the United States backed a dictator, engaged in covert operations, and discouraged democracy. Rivas finds that Rockefeller's private initiatives fell short of their target, the result of poor business decisions on his part and the collapse of the centrist government that had welcomed him. Heiss censures U.S. policy in Iran as a complete failure featuring a morally questionable covert operation that was driven in part by cultural misperceptions, ignorance, and arrogance. Likewise, Rotter concludes that U.S. officials failed to understand the culture of India and made policy choices on the basis of subjective feelings.

After 1945, the Third World experienced the momentous processes of decolonization and modernization. Drawn to Asia, Africa, the Middle East, and Latin America by various factors, the United States interacted with the governments and peoples of these regions in a variety of ways. Recently, scholars have used both traditional and pioneering methodologies to capture the U.S. experience in the Third World in all its breadth and diversity. Although not in complete agreement on conceptual, methodological, and interpretive issues, the essays in this volume collectively reveal the dynamism and innovation of recent scholarship. By representing various, viable modes of inquiry, these essays should serve as models and stimuli for further research on U.S. policy in the Third World.

After the end of the Cold War, some scholars escaped the common fixation on the Cold War and examined U.S. foreign policy in the Third World on its own merits. Their scholarship recognizes that U.S. officials and citizens confronted a special set of challenges and opportunities in the Third World that were influenced only in part by the Cold War. This realization would not have surprised some practitioners of U.S. foreign policy, such as Secretary of Defense Charles E. Wilson. "The collapse of colonialism had been too rapid," he observed to the National Security Council in August 1956, "and was having as much effect on the world as the rise of Communism."[4] This volume has sought to reveal how the government, institutions, and people of the United States reacted to the "collapse of colonialism" and to the other dynamics of change in the Third World since 1945.

Notes

1. Dennis Merrill, "The United States and the Rise of the Third World," in *American Foreign Relations Reconsidered, 1890–1993,* ed. Gordon Martel (New York, 1994), 166–86; David S. Painter, "Explaining U.S. Relations with the Third World," *Diplomatic*

History 19 (Summer 1995): 525–48; Mark T. Gilderhus, "An Emerging Synthesis?: U.S.–Latin American Relations since the Second World War," in *America in the World: The Historiography of American Foreign Relations since 1941*, ed. Michael J. Hogan (New York, 1995), 424–61; Douglas Little, "Gideon's Band: America and the Middle East since 1945," in Hogan, *America in the World*, 462–500; Robert J. McMahon, "The Cold War in Asia: The Elusive Synthesis," in Hogan, *America in the World*, 501–35; Thomas Borstelmann, "Africa and the United States," *Diplomatic History* 20 (Fall 1996): 681–84.

    2. Elizabeth Cobbs Hoffman, "Diplomatic History and the Meaning of Life: Toward a Global American History," *Diplomatic History* 21 (Fall 1997): 499–518; Melvyn P. Leffler, "The Interpretive Wars over the Cold War, 1945–60," in Martel, *American Foreign Relations Reconsidered*, 106–24; Michael J. Hogan, "State of the Art: An Introduction," in Hogan, *America in the World*, 3–19.

    3. Robert J. McMahon, "Eisenhower and Third World Nationalism: A Critique of the Revisionists," *Political Science Quarterly* 101 (Fall 1986): 453–73; Bonnie F. Saunders, *The United States and Arab Nationalism: The Syrian Case, 1953–1960* (Westport, CT, 1996).

    4. Minutes of meeting, 9 August 1956, U.S. Department of State, *Foreign Relations of the United States, 1955–1957* (Washington, DC, 1990), 16:173.

BIBLIOGRAPHICAL ESSAY

MARY ANN HEISS AND PETER L. HAHN

This brief essay is not designed to be an exhaustive listing of everything currently in print on the United States and the Third World. Rather, it is a selected list of sources related to the topics covered in this book. Readers are advised to consult the notes for the individual essays in this volume for additional titles.

Several broad histories of U.S. foreign relations include accounts of U.S. policy toward the Third World. Among the best are Thomas J. McCormick, *America's Half-Century: United States Foreign Policy in the Cold War and After*, 2nd ed. (Baltimore, 1995); Walter LaFeber, *America, Russia, and the Cold War*, 7th ed. (New York, 1993); and Stephen E. Ambrose and Douglas G. Brinkley, *Rise to Globalism: American Foreign Policy since 1938*, 8th rev. ed. (New York, 1997). Melvyn P. Leffler, *A Preponderance of Power: National Security, the Truman Administration, and the Cold War* (Stanford, 1992), is an outstanding account on a crucial period. An excellent volume that traces the historiography of recent U.S. foreign relations, including policy toward the Third World, is Michael J. Hogan, ed., *America in the World: The Historiography of American Foreign Relations since 1941* (New York, 1995). An older, but still valuable, historiographical contribution is Gerald K. Haines and J. Samuel Walker, eds., *American Foreign Relations: A Historiographical Review* (Westport, CT, 1981).

General studies of U.S. foreign policy toward the Third World include H. W. Brands, *The Specter of Neutralism: The United States and the Emergence of the Third World, 1947–1960* (New York, 1990), which focuses on Egypt, India, and Yugoslavia, the principal nonaligned nations in the early Cold War; Richard J. Barnet, *Intervention and Revolution: The United States and the Third World* (New York, 1968), a highly critical account; Douglas J. Macdonald, *Adventures in Chaos: American Intervention for Reform in the Third World* (Cambridge, MA, 1992), Jonathan Kwitny, *Endless Enemies: The Making of an Unfriendly World* (New York, 1986), John L. S. Girling, *America and the Third World: Revolution and Intervention* (London, 1980), and Melvin Gurtov, *The United States against the Third World: Antinationalism and Intervention* (New York, 1974), all of which emphasize U.S. interventionism;

Robert A. Packenham, *Liberal America and the Third World: Political Development Ideas in Foreign Aid and Social Science* (Princeton, NJ, 1973), which links domestic thinking with foreign policy; and S. Neil McFarlane, *Superpower Rivalry and Third World Radicalism: The Idea of National Liberation* (Baltimore, 1985), with an emphasis on Third World independence. An excellent introduction to the emergence of the Third World is Scott L. Bills, *Empire and Cold War: The Roots of U.S.- Third World Antagonism, 1945-1947* (New York, 1990). See also Geir Lundestad, *The American "Empire" and Other Studies of U.S. Foreign Policy in a Comparative Perspective* (New York, 1990). An account that is highly critical of U.S. policy is Gabriel Kolko, *Confronting the Third World: United States Foreign Policy, 1945-1980* (New York, 1981).

For a look at Eisenhower administration policy regarding the Third World, a good starting place is Stephen Ambrose, *Eisenhower,* Vol. 2, *The President* (New York, 1984). Ambrose's general history of the Eisenhower presidency should be supplemented with works that focus more specifically on foreign policy, such as H. W. Brands, *Cold Warriors: Eisenhower's Generation and American Foreign Policy* (New York, 1988), and Robert A. Divine, *Eisenhower and the Cold War* (New York, 1981). An older but still valuable work with much information on foreign policy is Blanche Wiesen Cook, *The Declassified Eisenhower: A Divided Legacy* (Garden City, NY, 1981). Charles C. Alexander, *Holding the Line: The Eisenhower Era, 1952-1961* (Bloomington, IN, 1975), blends coverage of Eisenhower's foreign and domestic policies into an account that emphasizes the administration's overall moderation. Also valuable is Chester J. Pach and Elmo Richardson, *The Presidency of Dwight D. Eisenhower* (Lawrence, KS, 1991). Several essays in Richard A. Melanson and David Mayers, eds., *Reevaluating Eisenhower: American Foreign Policy in the 1950s* (Urbana, IL, 1987), touch on the Third World. A new account of Eisenhower's foreign policy that is primarily quite positive is Robert R. Bowie and Richard H. Immerman, *Waging Peace: How Eisenhower Shaped an Enduring Cold War Strategy* (New York, 1998). Some of the earlier literature on Eisenhower's handling of Third World problems is discussed in Robert J. McMahon, "Eisenhower and Third World Nationalism: A Critique of the Revisionists," *Political Science Quarterly* 101 (Fall 1986): 453-73. In-depth discussions of various aspects of the Eisenhower administration's foreign policy may be found in Richard H. Immerman, ed., *John Foster Dulles and the Diplomacy of the Cold War* (Princeton, NJ, 1990). Additional foreign policy discussion is contained in Shirley Anne Warshaw, ed., *Reexamining the Eisenhower Presidency* (Westport, CT, 1993), and Joann P. Krieg, ed., *Dwight D. Eisenhower: Soldier, President, and Statesman* (New York, 1987).

Good general accounts of Kennedy administration foreign policy include Herbert Parmet, *J.F.K.: The Presidency of J.F.K.* (New York, 1983); James N. Giglio, *The Presidency of John F. Kennedy* (Lawrence, KS, 1991); and Richard J. Walton, *Cold War and Counterrevolution: The Foreign Policy of John F. Kennedy* (New York, 1972). Specific coverage of Kennedy's foreign policy may be found in two good edited volumes: Thomas G. Paterson, ed., *Kennedy's Quest for Victory: American Foreign Policy, 1961-1963* (New York, 1989), and Diane B. Kunz, ed., *The Diplomacy of the Crucial Decade: American Foreign Relations during the 1960s* (New York, 1994).

Although book-length studies of Lyndon B. Johnson's foreign policy do not abound, a few have appeared in print. A good general study is H. W. Brands, *The Wages of Globalism: Lyndon Johnson and the Limits of American Power* (New York, 1995). Also worth consulting is Philip Geyelin, *Lyndon Johnson and the World* (New York, 1966), which lays out LBJ's worldview. LBJ's foreign policy is also covered in Warren I. Cohen and Nancy Bernkopf Tucker, eds., *Lyndon Johnson Confronts the World: American Foreign Policy, 1963-1968* (New York, 1994), and H. W. Brands, ed., *The Foreign Policies of Lyndon Johnson: Beyond Vietnam* (College Station, TX, 1999).

The literature on U.S. relations with the various regions and nations discussed in this book is extensive. Among the numerous volumes on Vietnam, the best are Robert D. Schulzinger, *A Time for War: The United States and Vietnam, 1941-1975* (New York, 1997), the newest general survey of the war; George C. Herring, *America's Longest War: The United States and Vietnam, 1950-1975*, 3rd ed. (New York, 1994), an excellent overview that maintains a balanced perspective; and Marilyn Young, *The Vietnam Wars, 1945-1990* (New York, 1991), which is especially good on the Vietnam side. Gabriel Kolko, *Anatomy of a War: Vietnam, the United States, and the Modern Historical Experience* (New York, 1985), is highly critical of U.S. policy, as is Frances Fitzgerald, *Fire in the Lake: The Vietnamese and Americans in Vietnam* (Boston, 1972). Two studies that cover the road to the U.S. war in Vietnam are Lloyd C. Gardner, *Approaching Vietnam: From World War II through Dienbienphu, 1945-1954* (New York, 1988), and Andrew J. Rotter, *The Path to Vietnam: Origins of the American Commitment to Southeast Asia* (Ithaca, NY, 1987). Fredrik Logevall, *Choosing War: The Lost Chance for Peace and the Escalation of the Vietnam War* (Berkeley, CA, 1999), concentrates on the process of U.S. escalation. Accounts that focus in detail on various presidents' policies toward Vietnam include, on Eisenhower, David L. Anderson, *Trapped by Success: The Eisenhower Administration and Vietnam, 1953-1961* (New York, 1991), and Melanie Billings-Yun, *Decision against War: Eisenhower and Dien Bien Phu, 1954* (New York, 1988); on Kennedy, Orrin Schwab, *Defending the Free World: John F. Kennedy, Lyndon Johnson, and the Vietnam War, 1961-1965* (Westport, CT, 1998), and John M. Newman, *JFK and Vietnam: Deception, Intrigue, and the Struggle for Power* (New York, 1992); on Johnson, Lloyd C. Gardner, *Pay Any Price: Lyndon Johnson and the Wars for Vietnam* (Chicago, 1995), George C. Herring, *LBJ and Vietnam: A Different Kind of War* (Austin, TX, 1994), Brian VanDeMark, *Into the Quagmire: Lyndon Johnson and the Escalation of the Vietnam War* (New York, 1990), and Larry Berman, *Lyndon Johnson's War: The Road to Stalemate in Vietnam* (New York, 1989); and on Nixon, Jeffrey Kimball, *Nixon's Vietnam War* (Lawrence, KS, 1998). An overview of presidential policy toward Vietnam is David L. Anderson, ed., *Shadow on the White House: Presidents and the Vietnam War, 1945-1975* (Lawrence, KS, 1993). Two good accounts of the antiwar movement are Charles DeBenedetti, with Charles Chatfield, *An American Ordeal: The Antiwar Movement of the Vietnam War* (New York, 1991), and Melvin Small, *Johnson, Nixon, and the Doves* (New Brunswick, NJ, 1986).

For the Middle East in general, see William B. Stivers, *America's Confrontation with Revolutionary Change in the Middle East, 1948-1983* (New York, 1986); Steven L. Spiegel, *The Other Arab-Israeli Conflict: Making America's Middle East Policy from Truman to Reagan* (Chicago, 1985); Seth P. Tillman, *The United States and the Middle*

East: Interests and Obstacles (Bloomington, IN, 1982); and Wilbur C. Eveland, *Ropes of Sand: America's Failure in the Middle East* (New York, 1980), one of the more critical accounts currently available.

For studies specifically focused on Israel, see Abraham Ben-Zvi, *The United States and Israel: The Limits of the Special Relationship* (New York, 1993); Michael J. Cohen, *Truman and Israel* (Berkeley, CA, 1990); Edward Tivnan, *The Lobby: Jewish Political Power and American Foreign Policy* (New York, 1987); David Schoenbaum, *The United States and the State of Israel* (Oxford, UK, 1983); and Isaiah L. Kenen, *Israel's Defense Line: Her Friends and Foes in Washington* (Buffalo, NY, 1981). A novel approach to the subject is taken by Peter Grose, *Israel and the Mind of America* (New York, 1983).

Several excellent overviews of U.S. policy toward Iran are available: James F. Goode, *The United States and Iran: In the Shadow of Mussadiq* (New York, 1997); James A. Bill, *The Eagle and the Lion: The Tragedy of American-Iranian Relations* (New Haven, CT, 1988); Mark Hamilton Lytle, *The Origins of the Iranian-American Alliance, 1941–1953* (New York, 1987); and Barry Rubin, *Paved with Good Intentions: The American Experience and Iran* (New York, 1980). For the Iranian oil crisis itself, see Mary Ann Heiss, *Empire and Nationhood: The United States, Great Britain, and Iranian Oil, 1950–1954* (New York, 1997), and James A. Bill and Wm. Roger Louis, eds., *Iranian Nationalism, Musaddiq, and Oil* (Austin, TX, 1988).

For Lebanon in general, see Kamal Salibi, *A House of Many Mansions: The History of Lebanon Reconsidered* (Berkeley, CA, 1988); Helena Cobban, *The Making of Modern Lebanon* (Boulder, CO, 1985); Michael C. Hudson, *The Precarious Republic: Political Modernization in Lebanon* (New York, 1968); and Leila M. T. Meo, *Lebanon, Improbable Nation: A Study in Political Development* (Bloomington, IL, 1965). Irene Gendzier, *Notes from the Minefield: United States Intervention in Lebanon and the Middle East, 1945–1958* (New York, 1997), and Erika Alin, *The United States and the 1958 Lebanon Crisis: American Intervention in the Middle East* (Lanham, MD, 1994), provide in-depth coverage of U.S. interventionism in Lebanon.

A number of excellent volumes treat U.S. policy toward South Asia, including Robert J. McMahon, *The Cold War on the Periphery: The United States, India, and Pakistan, 1947–1965* (New York, 1994), and William J. Barnds, *India, Pakistan, and the Great Powers* (New York, 1972). For the bilateral U.S.-India relationship, see Kenton J. Clymer, *Quest for Freedom: The United States and India's Independence* (New York, 1995); Dennis Merrill, *Bread and the Ballot: The United States and India's Economic Development, 1945–1963* (Chapel Hill, NC, 1990); H. W. Brands, *India and the United States: The Cold Peace* (Boston, 1990); and Gary R. Hess, *America Encounters India, 1941–1947* (Baltimore, 1971). Richard Cronin, *Imagining India* (New York, 1989), and Ronald Inden, *Imagining India* (Oxford, UK, 1990), take a different tack by focusing on images and perceptions. R. K. Gupta, *The Great Encounter: A Study of Indo-American Literature and Cultural Relations* (New Delhi, 1986), focuses on cultural interactions. U.S.-Pakistani relations are covered in M. S. Venkataramani, *The American Role in Pakistan, 1947–1958* (New Delhi, 1982).

U.S. relations with Latin America are capably covered in Stephen G. Rabe, *Eisenhower and Latin America: The Foreign Policy of Anti-Communism* (Chapel Hill, NC, 1988), a balanced assessment; Edwin McCammon Martin, *Kennedy and Latin America* (Lanham, MD, 1994), and Cole Blasier, *The Hovering Giant: U.S. Responses to Revolutionary Change in Latin America,* rev. ed. (Pittsburgh, PA, 1985), two good introductions to the subject; Stephen G. Rabe, *The Most Dangerous Area in the World: John F. Kennedy Confronts Communist Revolution in Latin America* (Chapel Hill, NC, 1999), a newer and more complete account; and Gaddis Smith, *The Last Years of the Monroe Doctrine, 1945–1993* (New York, 1994), which is highly critical of U.S. policy. An interesting account that emphasizes cultural history is Frederick B. Pike, *The United States and Latin America: Myths and Stereotypes of Civilization and Nature* (Austin, TX, 1992). A highly theoretical work is *Close Encounters of Empire: Writing the Cultural History of U.S.–Latin American Relations,* ed. Gilbert M. Joseph, Catherine C. LeGrand, and Ricardo D. Salvatore (Durham, NC, 1998).

For the Caribbean region in particular, the best place to start is Lester D. Langley, *The United States and the Caribbean in the Twentieth Century,* 4th ed. (Athens, GA, 1988), which provides an excellent introduction to the subject. Also useful are Robert Freeman Smith, *The Caribbean World and the United States: Mixing Rum and Coca-Cola* (New York, 1994), and Charles D. Ameringer, *The Democratic Left in Exile: The Antidictatorial Struggle in the Caribbean, 1945–1959* (Coral Gables, FL, 1974). Studies with shorter chronological sweeps include G. Pope Atkins and Larman C. Wilson, *The Dominican Republic and the United States: From Imperialism to Transnationalism* (Athens, GA, 1998); Abraham Lowenthal, *The Dominican Intervention* (Baltimore, 1995); Bruce Palmer, *Intervention in the Caribbean: The Dominican Crisis of 1965* (Lexington, KY, 1989); and Piero Gleijeses, *The Dominican Crisis: The 1965 Constitutional Revolt and American Intervention* (Baltimore, 1978).

U.S.-Venezuelan relations are treated in Stephen G. Rabe, *The Road to OPEC: United States Relations with Venezuela, 1919–1976* (Austin, TX, 1982), which emphasizes oil; and Robert J. Alexander, *Rómulo Betancourt and the Transformation of Venezuela* (New Brunswick, NJ, 1982). An excellent account of twentieth-century Venezuelan history is Judith Ewell, *Venezuela: A Century of Change* (Stanford, CA, 1984). Also useful are Daniel Hellinger, *Venezuela: Tarnished Democracy* (Boulder, CO, 1991), and Sheldon B. Liss, *Diplomacy and Dependency: Venezuela, the United States, and the Americas* (Salisbury, NC, 1978).

Excellent coverage of events in Taiwan may be found in Nancy Bernkopf Tucker, *Taiwan, Hong Kong, and the United States, 1945–1992: Uncertain Friendships* (New York, 1994). For U.S. policy toward Asia in general, consult Gordon H. Chang, *Friends and Enemies: The United States, China, and the Soviet Union, 1948–1972* (Stanford, CA, 1991), and Michael Schaller, *The United States and China in the Twentieth Century* (New York, 1979). Studies that focus specifically on economic development include Alan P. L. Liu, *Phoenix and the Lame Lion: Modernization in Taiwan and Mainland China, 1960–1980* (Stanford, CA, 1987); David Aikman, *The Pacific Rim: Area of Change, Area of Opportunity* (Boston, 1986); Thomas B. Gold, *State and Society in the Taiwan Miracle* (Armonk, NY, 1986); Ching-yuan Lin, *Industrialization in Taiwan, 1946–1972: Trade and Import Substitution Policies for Developing Nations* (New York, 1973); and Neil H. Jacoby, *U.S. Aid to Taiwan: A Study of Foreign Aid, Self-Help, and Development* (New York, 1966).

Scholarly attention to U.S. relations with Africa is really just beginning. Good places to start for this subject are Peter J. Schraeder, *United States Foreign Policy toward Africa: Incrementalism, Crisis, Change* (New York, 1994); Thomas J. Noer,

Cold War and Black Liberation: The United States and White Rule in Africa, 1948–1968 (Columbia, MO, 1985); and Henry F. Jackson, *From the Congo to Soweto: U.S. Foreign Policy toward Africa since 1960* (New York, 1982). For the Congo in particular, consult David N. Gibbs, *The Political Economy of Third World Intervention: Mines, Money, and U.S. Policy in the Congo Crisis* (Chicago, 1991); Thomas Odom, *Dragon Operations: Hostage Rescues in the Congo, 1964–65* (Fort Leavenworth, KS, 1988); Madeleine Kalb, *The Congo Cables: The Cold War in Africa from Eisenhower to Kennedy* (New York, 1982); Fred E. Wagoner, *Dragon Rouge: The Rescue of Hostages in the Congo* (Washington, DC, 1980); and Stephen R. Weissman, *American Foreign Policy in the Congo, 1960–1964* (Ithaca, NY, 1974).

Good introductions to cultural studies may be found in the work of Edward Said, especially *Culture and Imperialism* (New York, 1993), and *Orientalism* (New York, 1978). See also the valuable, albeit controversial, work of cultural anthropologist Clifford Geertz, especially *The Interpretation of Cultures* (New York, 1973). Also of use are Sander L. Gilman, *Difference and Pathology: Stereotypes of Sexuality, Race, and Madness* (Ithaca, NY, 1985), which explores the connection between mental illness and gender constructions, among other topics; and Laura E. Donaldson, *Decolonizing Feminisms: Race, Gender, and Empire-Building* (Chapel Hill, NC, 1992), which explores representations and images. The essays in Christian G. Appy, ed., *Cold War Constructions: The Political Culture of United States Imperialism, 1945–1966* (Amherst, 2000), are also useful.

General studies of the Peace Corps include P. David Searles, *The Peace Corps Experience: Challenge and Change, 1969–1976* (Lexington, KY, 1997); Milton Viorst, ed., *Making a Difference: The Peace Corps at Twenty-Five* (New York, 1986); Gerard T. Rice, *The Bold Experiment: JFK's Peace Corps* (South Bend, IN, 1985); Kevin Lowther and C. Payne Lucas, *Keeping Kennedy's Promise: The Peace Corps, the Unmet Hope of the New Frontier* (Boulder, CO, 1978); Brent A. Ashabranner, *A Moment in History: The First Ten Years of the Peace Corps* (New York, 1971); David Hapgood and Meridan Bennett, *Agents of Change: A Close Look at the Peace Corps* (Boston, 1968); and Robert B. Trextor, ed., *Cultural Frontiers of the Peace Corps* (Cambridge, MA, 1966). Personal accounts may be found in Karen Schwarz, *What You Can Do for Your Country: An Oral History of the Peace Corps* (New York, 1991). Also of use are Elizabeth Cobbs Hoffman, *All You Need Is Love: The Peace Corps and the Spirit of the 1960s* (Cambridge, MA, 1998), and Lawrence H. Fuchs, *"Those Peculiar Americans": The Peace Corps and American National Character* (New York, 1967).

CONTRIBUTORS

Robert Buzzanco is associate professor of history at the University of Houston. He is author of *Masters of War: Military Dissent and Politics in the Vietnam Era* (1996) and *Vietnam and the Transformation of American Life* (1999). He is working on books on the Cold War and the economic impact of the Vietnam War.

Elizabeth Cobbs Hoffman is Dwight Stanford Professor of American Foreign Relations at San Diego State University. She is the author of *The Rich Neighbor Policy: Rockefeller and Kaiser in Brazil* (1992) and *All You Need Is Love: The Peace Corps and the Spirit of the 1960s* (1998).

Nick Cullather, associate professor of history at Indiana University, is the author of *Illusions of Influence: The Political Economy of United States–Philippines Relations, 1942-1960* (1994) and *Secret History: The Classified Account of the CIA's Operations in Guatemala, 1952–1954* (1999).

Piero Gleijeses is professor of American foreign policy at Johns Hopkins University (School of Advanced International Studies). His most recent book is *Shattered Hope: The Guatemalan Revolution and the United States, 1944–1954* (1991). His essay in this volume is drawn from his forthcoming book on U.S. and Cuban policy in Africa, 1959–76.

Peter L. Hahn is associate professor of history at Ohio State University and associate editor of *Diplomatic History*. He is author of *The United States, Great Britain, and Egypt, 1945–1956: Strategy and Diplomacy in the Early Cold War* (1991) and is completing a book on U.S. policy toward the Arab-Israeli conflict, 1945–61.

Mary Ann Heiss is associate professor of history at Kent State University and associate editor of *Diplomatic History*. She is author of *Empire and Nationhood: The*

United States, Great Britain, and Iranian Oil, 1950–1954 (1997). Her current work focuses on Anglo-American visions of empire between the end of World War II and the Suez Crisis.

Douglas Little is chair and professor of history at Clark University, where he has taught since 1978. He is author of *Malevolent Neutrality: The United States, Great Britain, and the Origins of the Spanish Civil War* (1985) and of a series of articles on U.S. relations with the Middle East in the *Journal of American History*, the *Middle East Journal*, and other scholarly venues. He is completing a book on U.S. policy toward the Middle East since 1945.

Robert J. McMahon is professor of history at the University of Florida. He is author of, among other works, *The Limits of Empire: The United States and Southeast Asia since World War II* (1999) and *The Cold War on the Periphery: The United States, India, and Pakistan* (1994).

Stephen G. Rabe is professor of history at the University of Texas at Dallas. His most recent book is *The Most Dangerous Area in the World: John F. Kennedy Confronts Communist Revolution in Latin America* (1999).

Darlene Rivas earned her doctorate at Vanderbilt University in 1996 and is assistant professor of history at Pepperdine University. A specialist on the role of nongovernmental organizations in U.S. relations with Latin America, she recently completed a book manuscript on Nelson Rockefeller's post–World War II development projects in Venezuela.

Andrew J. Rotter is professor of history at Colgate University. He is author of *The Path to Vietnam: Origins of the American Commitment to Southeast Asia* (1987) and *Comrades at Odds: Culture and Indo-American Relations, 1947–1964* (2000) and is editor of *Light at the End of the Tunnel: A Vietnam War Anthology* (rev. ed., 1999).

INDEX